Disney

& APOLOGETICS

EXPLORING THE MORAL POWER AND THEOLOGICAL SIGNIFICANCE OF DISNEY STORIES

"Enter into a serious examination of the whimsical worlds created by the kingdom of Disney through the eyes of those inhabiting a Kingdom centered in another world—the Kingdom of Christ. [In this two-volume work, *Disney & Apologetics*] you will discover why Disney's moral logic of good and evil, darkness and light, move us toward affirming goodness and justice. Here you will encounter the similarity in moral structures between the kingdoms. Bringing curiosity rather than judgment, the authors delve into the depths of well-crafted stories, visual imagery, and musical delights to capture the treasures. They return from their adventures wiser as they reflect on the joys of this journey, ever mindful of the dangers of taking the comparisons too far."

—**ANNALEE WARD**, Director of the Wendt Center for Character Education and author of *Mouse Morality: the Rhetoric of Disney Animated Films*

"[*Disney as Doorway to Apologetic Dialogue*] is an excellent introduction and guide to the personal background and biblically-shaped vision of Walt Disney and of many of the films he and his company would create. These movies so often depict crucial themes in the biblical metanarrative—the reality of the conflict between good and evil; the need for a champion to step in and overthrow the forces of darkness and reverse the curse; the importance of self-sacrificial love and the value of community; and the good ultimately triumphing over evil. This book serves as a valuable resource to show how Disney films provide not only illuminating insights and inspiration for our children and our congregations; they also serve as bridges for the gospel in a world of people longing to find their true identity and true home and to see fulfilled their deepest desires to 'live happily ever after,' which are ultimately fulfilled in Jesus Christ who is, as C. S. Lewis wrote, 'myth became fact.'"

—**PAUL COPAN**, Pledger Family Chair of Philosophy and Ethics, Palm Beach Atlantic University (Florida), and author of *The Gospel in the Marketplace of Ideas* and *Is God a Vindictive Bully?*

"More sense needs to be made of the relationship between the world making we have all been enchanted by in Disney and the Christian faith. For a century now, Disney has invited us into stories that have shaped our worldviews, our hearts, and our imaginations. Much of what we've come to know of truth, goodness, and beauty, both culturally and personally, we've known through Disney's animated world-making. Yet, it could be argued that Christian believers have not thought deeply enough about Disney's importance in crafting conversations about these virtues. In *Disney as Doorway to Apologetic Dialogue*, Scarbrough and Sawyer have revealed just what depths there are to plunge. Scarbrough and Sawyer do a beautiful job of theologically and apologetically walking us through Disney's spiritually latent worlds, showing us glimpses, in fantastic castles, princesses, and beasts, of a very real Kingdom."

—**COREY LATTA**, Vice President of Academics at Visible Music College and author of numerous articles, poems, and three books, including, "Election and Unity in Paul's Epistle to the Romans," Functioning Fantasies: Theology, Ideology, and Social Conception in the Works of C.S. Lewis and J. R. R. Tolkien," *C. S. Lewis and the Art of Writing*, and *When the Eternal Can Be Met: A Bergsonian Theology of Time in the Works of C. S. Lewis*.

"As a parent of four school-age children who have grown up with Disney, this fascinating book [*Disney as Doorway to Apologetic Dialogue*] helped me more deeply appreciate the themes of virtue, justice, love, and sacrifice that permeate the Disney canon. Good stories move us because they point to a greater story. This volume is an excellent way to start conversations about our longing for a perfect kingdom, for true beauty, and for the ultimate conquest of good over evil."

—**NEIL SHENVI**, Author of *Why Believe? A Reasoned Approach to Christianity*

"*Disney as Doorway to Apologetic Dialogue* is a great example of cultural apologetics done well. We need more deep-dive theological analyses of Hollywood—resources that go beyond superficial readings and model substantive, layered engagement with an eye toward common grace engagement rather than critical dismissal. This scholarly, insightful book is a fantastic resource for both students and creators of pop culture."

— BRETT MCCRACKEN, senior editor, The Gospel Coalition, author of *The Wisdom Pyramid: Feeding Your Soul in a Post-Truth World*

"Disney is obviously a dominant force in mass entertainment and may even be growing in influence. Theological reflections on the arts, however, often steer toward narratives aimed primarily at adults. [*Disney & the Moral Imagination*] helps to examine the universal stories that shape so much of our collective imagination. Here you will find many writers with depth of theological and artistic insight who take time to examine a major player in contemporary culture."

— PHILIP TALLON, Dean of the School of Christian Thought, Houston Christian University, and author of *The Absolute Basics of the Christian Faith* and *The Poetics of Evil*

"Sometimes I'm asked, why did God reveal himself through a long history of interactions with fallen and suffering human beings rather than by simply downloading information about himself directly into our minds? I think this volume of essays points to the answer: A truth embodied in a story affects us more deeply, shapes us more effectively, and reveals its goodness and beauty more robustly than any mere proposition could. *Disney & the Moral Imagination* capitalizes on the power of stories by exploring various aspects of philosophy, theology, and moral formation through our culture's beloved Disney movies. If you're looking for creative ways to discuss the Christian worldview with those who don't yet know our true, good, and beautiful God, this book models a promising approach."

— AMY K. HALL, Christian apologist, Stand to Reason

"This fine collection of essays on Disney's animated features strikes just the right balance between academic and popular, scholarly and accessible. It opens up the films without vivisecting them, drawing out deeper moral and spiritual meanings without bending and contorting them to fit a Christian worldview. [*Disney & the Moral Imagination*] has much of value to say on the nature and power of music, virtue, beauty, imagination, and hope."

— **LOUIS MARKOS**, Professor in English and Scholar in Residence,
Houston Christian University; author of *On the Shoulders of Hobbits* and *The Myth Made Fact*

"*Disney & the Moral Imagination* is a valued contribution to the discussion of ethics education through creativity and story-telling. This collection of essays takes a thoughtful approach to the cultural influence of Disney animation in a time of moral upheaval... [The authors] draw well on the interdisciplinary traditions of Classical Christian Liberal Arts education to enrich the dialogue on issues across ethics, aesthetics, and theology."

— **BRYANT K. OWENS**, Professor of Philosophy and Ethics,
The American Musical and Dramatic Academy

Disney

& APOLOGETICS

EXPLORING THE MORAL POWER AND
THEOLOGICAL SIGNIFICANCE OF DISNEY STORIES

Edited by Jeremy E. Scarbrough

HIGH BRIDGE BOOKS
HOUSTON

Volume I:
Disney as Doorway
TO APOLOGETIC DIALOGUE

Jeremy E. Scarbrough
Pat Sawyer

Volume II:
Disney
& THE MORAL IMAGINATION

Edited by Jeremy E. Scarbrough

To intellectual mentors I've never met, but only read
Yet each of which has taught me well
To love truth and seek wisdom
And to understand the times by considering the history of ideas
"As iron sharpens iron" (Prov. 27:17), so too have I been sharpened

To my children
That you will learn to seek dialogue with charity
over division and disparaging
That you will learn to see how worldviews inform and
influence aesthetics, ethics, and politics
That you will look for meaningful conversations in all
aspects of pop culture and the arts
That you will seek to understand why goodness and
evil are unintelligible apart from God
And that you may learn to walk in friendship
with the God who is there

To the One who grounds logic
To the Archetype of artistry
As J. S. Bach taught me to keep ever before my mind:
Jesu Juva
and
Soli Deo Gloria

Contents

VOLUME I: DISNEY AS DOORWAY TO
APOLOGETIC DIALOGUE _____ 1

Preface _____ 5

Part 1: Prolegomenon _____ 9

1. Faith and Fantasy _____ 11

2. Walt Disney's Moral Influences and the Moral Power of a
Disney Story _____ 29

Part 2: Disney's Moral Meta-narrative and Recurrent
Theological Imagery _____ 39

3. Kingdoms in the Making and Diamonds in the Rough: Disney's
Recurrent Moral Motif _____ 41

4. Kingdom-Oriented Archetypes in Disney's Animated
Moral Canon _____ 53

5. Imagining the Kingdom: Archetypes of Beauty and the Moral
Enchantment of Disney's Aesthetic Allure _____ 65

6. An Archetypal (Christian?) Ethics and the Kingdom-Ever-After _ 81

7. True Love and the Ever-After: The Kingdom Come _____ 91

Part 3: Approaching Disney as Doorway to Dialogue: Mediating
Contemporary Narratives on Justice and Social Goodness ___ 99

8. Injustice: Everywhere but Within _____ 101

9. Delimitations, Definitions, and the Descriptive/Prescriptive
Distinction _____ 107

10. The Materialist Backdrop _____ 117

11. Critical Theory and the Conceptual Foundations of the Critical
Social Justice Movement _____ 127

12. Clarity, Charity, and Disney's Ability to Mediate
the Dialogue _____ 137

13. On Justice: God Help the Outcast _____ 157

14. Goodness Beyond Just-ness _____ 177

15. Liberated to Love Goodness: The Light of Reason and the
Darkness of Depravity _____ 189

Epilogue _____ 201

Disney as Doorway to Apologetic Dialogue **Notes** _____ 205

VOLUME II: DISNEY & THE MORAL IMAGINATION _____ 239

Prologue _____ 243

**Part 1: Imaginative and Aesthetic Apologetics: Exploring
Disney's Moral Magic and Narrative Power** _____ 251

1. Imagination, the Incarnation, and the Moral Power
of Storytelling _____ 253

   Holly Ordway

2. Disney's Live-Action Animated Musical: A "Satisfactual"
Glimpse of Transcendence _____ 263

   Joel W. Paulus

3. Beauty and the Beat _____ 273

   Doug Powell

4. The Moral Magic of a Disney Musical _____ 283

   Jeremy E. Scarbrough and D.J. Culp Jr.

5. Nostalgic Deliberation and the Moral Imagination: Music's
Referential Power _____ 295

   Jeremy E. Scarbrough

Part 2: Exploring Questions of Theology and Moral Formation Within Disney Stories. _____311

6. Marionettes, Moral Excellence, and Characters Worth Imitating _ 313

   Shawn White

7. The Pretty Princess: Disney's Theology of Becoming Beautiful__ 325

   Miguel Benitez Jr.

8. The Lost Princess: The Theological Anthropology of Disney's *Tangled* _____ 337

   Timothy E. G. Bartel

9. I Am Moana: MacIntyre's Virtue Theory and the Reality of Animated Morality _____ 349

   Sean C. Hadley

10. The Bare Necessities of Augustinian Virtue _____ 361

    Eric Williamson and Russell Clayton

11. Sin, Salvation, and the Human Condition in *Pinocchio* _____ 375

    Paul Miles

12. On Becoming a Real Boy: Conscience and the Formation of Character _____ 387

    Mark D. Linville

13. Cosmology and Natural Law in Disney's *Hercules* _____ 397

    John L. Weitzel

14. Have Courage and Be Kind: *Cinderella* and the Problem of Evil _____ 409

    Lori A. Peters

15. A Kierkegaardian Reading of *The Lion King*: Simba Becomes a Person _____ 421

    Josh Herring

16. Christian Hospitality in Disney's *Beauty and the Beast*: Two Perspectives _____ 431

    Zachary D. Schmoll and Neal Foster

17. Faith, Hope, and the Human Condition in *Raya and the Last Dragon* _____ 443

    By Jeremy E. Scarbrough

Epilogue_____ 455

Appendix: Film and Television References _____ 459

Acknowledgments _____ 469

Index _____ 473

About the Authors _____ 495

Illustration by John D. Batten, from "Beauty and the Beast" in
Europa's Fairy Book *(1916) by Joseph Jacobs*

Illustration by H. J. Ford, from "The Sleeping Beauty in the Wood" in
Andrew Lang's The Blue Fairy Book *(1889).*

Illustration by Arthur Rackham, from "Briar Rose" in
Snowdrop & Other Tales *(1920) by the Brothers Grimm*

VOLUME I:

Disney as Doorway
TO APOLOGETIC DIALOGUE

Disney as Doorway
TO APOLOGETIC DIALOGUE

Jeremy E. Scarbrough
Pat Sawyer

HIGH BRIDGE BOOKS
HOUSTON

Preface

There are numerous ways to approach questions of pop culture and apologetics. Some may reject outright that theology has anything to offer, thus rejecting its pop-culture relevance. Others may see religious narratives as manipulative and harmful, thereby exposing to oppose theological transcripts in mainstream culture. Still others see aesthetic experience as inseparable from theology. Some theists assume a position of antithesis, emphasizing God as righteous and rejecting or condemning culture as corrupt, though burning dialogical bridges in the process.[1] Others adopt an approach of synthesis, emphasizing God as love and community as inclusive, though potentially watering down moral and theological truth.[2]

A third paradigm embraces a sort of biased dualism. Living between two worlds, one seeks goodness within the culture, while his or her allegiance is ultimately to God.[3] This position synthesizes where appropriate (but without compromising the seriousness of moral considerations) and becomes antithetical when necessary (though attempting to build rather than burn dialogical bridges). Yet it generally approaches artistic expression within culture as reflecting a deep goodness in creation, or it presses into worldview assumption and a concomitant prescription to foster dialogue. In Acts 17, the apostle Paul used Greek culture—appealing to both religious practices and poetic wisdom—as a doorway to dialogue concerning deeper theological truths. This is the power of cultural apologetics: engaging culture with culture; uncovering worldview narratives through the arts, and teaching deeper truths by reaching longing hearts. In the words of philosopher Paul Gould, "The cultural apologist works to awaken those within culture to their deep-seated longings for goodness, truth, and beauty.... to resurrect relevance by showing that Christianity offers plausible answers to universal human longings... [and] to resurrect hope."[4]

This work explores the power of the arts and pop-culture narratives to speak to moral conviction and imagination. Namely, it argues that notable aspects of Disney lore appeal to a grand moral narrative that aligns strikingly (if not intuitively) with a Christian vision of reality. This thesis has apologetic value not only for the study of moral apologetics, but also for cultural apologetics and moral dialogue. We presume the reader has at least some familiarity with Disney's celebrated animated musical features. This book is designed for the educated lay reader as well as for the scholar whose research interests lie at the intersection of aesthetics, philosophy, theology, apologetics, and pop culture. Our claim is not that Disney is necessarily unique in its storytelling. Many good stories function in a manner similar to that of Disney. Disney *is*, however, a deeply rooted, century-old cultural artifact and juggernaut of societal influence and shaping. Our claim is that Disney *exemplifies and embodies* the power of pop-culture narratives to engage aesthetically our moral imagination—especially ideals of goodness and justice.

Disney presents us with a canon of nonsectarian narratives that resonate with certain basic convictions concerning universal, objective moral truth. Many of the recurrent moral motifs we see in Disney align strikingly with the moral metanarrative we see in the biblical story of reality, that is, classical, orthodox Christianity—especially as it relates to an interest in Kingdom theology and a complementary virtue ethics (a perspective which emphasizes virtue but is inclusive of some of the concerns of ego-based, duty-based, and utility-based ethical theories). The term "kingdom theology" can be confusing for some, and so it requires some caution and clarity. We apply it in the broadest and most basic sense of Christian theology, which is essentially this: Evil or darkness has taken hostage and corrupted the beauty of the earthly kingdom. We are called to be citizens of a heavenly kingdom. Upon accepting this invitation, we become foreign ambassadors of the heavenly kingdom while remaining resident aliens in the earthly kingdom. Living in light of the heavenly kingdom, ambassadors struggle to model the character and love of that kingdom; in this sense, the kingdom has already come. Nevertheless, life in the earthly kingdom includes unavoidable encounters with evil and daily struggles with the dissonant desires of flesh and Spirit.[5] Moreover, this dual citizenship welcomes a potential for persecution. Thus, there is an eagerness in awaiting an ultimate justice and the eventual defeat of evil, as the kingdom comes in a future sense. Its citizens dwell thereafter in the very presence of goodness and true love.[6]

According to Jesus, it is the understanding of a teleological way-it-should-be and the aim of a Kingdom-ever-after that must frame morality. We argue that this presupposition frames much of Disney's moral meta-narrative, as well. Disney's interest in virtue and its connection to beauty appeals to our convictions concerning goodness, while its emphasis on a Kingdom-ever-after appeals to our longing for just-ness. That sort of Kingdom is understood to be a place where justice reigns and to which goodness and beauty are directly connected. Thus, Disney stories appeal effectively to both moral conviction and aesthetic desire.

The volume is divided into three parts, progressing from a discussion of goodness exemplified in Disney stories, to beauty inferred, to the consideration of how this points to an expectation of the Kingdom, and finally to a dialogue on the nature of the justice anticipated in light of our longing for such a Kingdom. Part one sets the academic tone and apologetic significance of our approach—though the work proceeds at more of a high popular rather than high academic level of writing, as this book is written as much for the lay reader and student of apologetics as it is for the interdisciplinary scholar and seasoned apologist. Part two explores moral motifs and theologically rich symbolism recurrent in Disney narratives. Here we draw out key strands of Disney's moral metanarrative viewed through the lens of Christian theology. Part three is more philosophical, with Disney films functioning less as the object of study and more as applications of argumentation, as stories are able to awaken, more powerfully than propositions, certain convictions within us.

Part 1

PROLEGOMENON

1

Faith and Fantasy

All cultures share stories, and our stories help us to make sense of who we are. Some stories are more effective than others because they speak to our deepest convictions and resonate with our deepest desires for answers concerning identity, the good life, the cessation of suffering, anxiety, estrangement, community, meaning, and every facet of the human experience. Our stories presume, prescribe, and reify certain values and truth assertions about the world and our place in it. A central question, of course, is whether our stories are robust enough to account for the moral convictions embedded within them, and the desire for significance to which they appeal.

Stories are powerful. They can take us in and influence us with subtle prescriptions for how we should view the world and act within it. Yet the most powerful stories are those which actually wake us up to ponder deeper questions or to question the prescriptions and presuppositions of our own stories—snapshots of our lived experience that we bracket and compartmentalize to frame how we see ourselves in the world. In the words of Scottish author George MacDonald, "The best thing you can do for your fellow, next to rousing his conscience, is — not to give him things to think about, but to wake things up that are in him."[1] What philosopher Louis Pojman once wrote of literature also applies to film:

> [A good story] often highlights moral ideas, focusing on particular people in their dilemmas, awakening our imagination to new possibilities, and enabling us to understand the moral life in fresh and creative ways. [A good story] compels us to rethink and revise our everyday assumptions. It sets before us powerful particularities that serve both as reinforcers and counterexamples

to our sweeping principles.... [Like the parables of the New Testament, good stories] make the abstract concrete, bring it home to the heart, and force us to think with innovative imagination.[2]

Disney similarly offers stories which both rouse the moral conscience and wake our deep convictions to the beauty and goodness associated with a Kingdom-ever-after.

The Walt Disney Company, as a prominent stakeholder of culture, has enshrined itself as an authoritative storyteller in the contemporary world. Disney lore possesses a unique power to captivate audiences of all ages from around the world. As innovative storytelling led to imaginative worlds of theme-park wonder, sitcom socialization, morale-boosting, documentary education, and ultimately a globalized market, Disney firmly established itself as its own culture. Yet, at the heart of everything else that Disney may entail—for better or for worse—lie the narratives that first captivated Disney's audiences and compelled them to want more. Disney effectively capitalized on a deep desire within us, our often unspoken convictions about the way the world is or ought to be, by offering such contemplation through the aesthetic allure of musical animation. We long (consciously or subconsciously) for a "full" life. We want to "truly live." We want to feel the range of emotions of a life filled with rich, robust, textured experiences. Disney provides a window into such a life. An immediate question, however, arises. Can the Disney story hold up, compete well, with the myriad of other cultural voices prescribing for us how we ought to see ourselves, who we ought to become, what we ought to love and value, or how we ought to live?

Though viewers likely take each story on its own terms, and it is often appropriate to do so, it is also worth pondering whether any common threads emerge from the collective tales of a given storyteller. Indeed, this is what we find with a noteworthy number of Disney features. The grand moral meta-narrative running throughout the majority of Disney's canon of animated classics from 1937 to 2021 depicts an arguably theistic world: Good triumphs over evil; an *agape*-like, sacrificial love is the highest virtue; and faith and hope in the Kingdom-ever-after is foreshadowed and built upon the bonds of love and community. Such a perspective offers much fodder for apologetic dialogue and highlights the value of cultural apologetics in particular, as it demonstrates the importance of the arts and the power of storytelling to stir our moral convictions. When we are most morally awakened and morally alive, our moral sensibilities resonate most profoundly with the moral grand narrative of the Bible, and Disney narratives (though presented in a nonsectarian, inclusive manner) have often aligned strikingly with key aspects of Christianity's grand moral narrative.

The topic of narrative as an object of study has attracted many philosophers, including Martin Heidegger, Charles Taylor, Paul Ricouer, and Alasdair MacIntyre. Philosophers have long understood that there is a connection between worldview (metanarrative or grand narrative) and stories because our myths are deeply entwined with our questions about the nature of our world and meaning of our lives.[3] In the words of Rollo May, "A myth is a way of making sense in a senseless world. Myths are narrative patterns that give significance to our existence."[4] As David Naugle observed in his study of the history of worldview as a concept,

> Enlightenment denarrativization came at a high human cost, and nobody has understood that cost better than Friedrich Nietzsche. In *The Birth of Tragedy* he writes, 'But without myth every culture loses the healthy natural power of its creativity: only a horizon defined by myths completes and unifies a whole cultural movement.'[5] Nietzsche knew, however, that the western world had been drifting slowly toward the destruction of its narrative resources... by its intoxication with scientific rationalism. Consequently, modern humanity, 'untutored by myth,' is famished and in search for any narrative morsel on which to feed itself, as the frenzied activities and compulsions of contemporary life indicate.[6]

After recounting Alasdair MacIntyre's argument that our stories are essential in understanding ourselves and others, and that "mythology, in its original sense, is at the heart of things,"[7] Naugle concludes,

> The narrative stories which are lived out in the world of human experience are a product of bedrock, first order myths that essentially constitute a worldview.... Human beings, as semiotic creatures and inherent storytellers, come to grips with themselves and the nature of life in the cosmos through the formation of worldviews *as* [emphasis added] systems of narrative signs that form a basic outlook on life. they provide narrative answers to the fundamental questions about the realm of the divine, the nature of the cosmos, the identity of human beings, the solution to the problems of suffering and pain, and so on.

Even the seemingly nonnarratival aspects of a *Weltaschauung*—
its doctrinal, ethical, or ritual dimensions—can be explained by
a fundamental narrative content.

....Worldview narratives create a particular kind of 'mind,'
and serve in a normative fashion as 'controlling stories.' the
most fundamental stories associated with a *Weltaschauung*—
those closest to its metaphysical, epistemological, and ethical
epicenter—possess a kind of finality as the ultimate interpretation of reality in all its multifaceted aspects. Such stories are
considered sacred, and they provide the adhesive that unites
those who believe in them into a society characterized by
shared perspectives and a common way of life. They also provide a tenacious grid by which competing narratives and alternative claims to truth are judged.[8]

Even Disney's critics would likely agree that Disney has established itself as just such a power of authority and influence over the contemporary
imagination. Disney Culture holds significant potential for influence over social narratives, and Disney animated narratives have great influence on the
moral imagination. Moreover, Disney has become the perennial standard by
which children's animated features are judged.

Disney's widespread reach gives its films an outsized influence on the
contemporary cultural imagination. The central questions its films ask, along
with the underlying assumptions about the world embedded in their narratives, have shaped the intuitions of countless viewers. As Charles Taylor has
explained, it's not so much a matter of belief that needs to be unearthed but
"the way the universe is spontaneously imagined, and therefore experienced."[9] Those worldview assumptions penetrate more deeply and are
sometimes harder to dislodge than propositions that can be challenged
through reason and discourse. Alister McGrath put it this way, in his manifesto for a narrative-based Christian apologetics:

Christians must engage the dominant stories of our culture, either by telling a better story that shows these stories are inade-
quate or incoherent, or through subversive storytelling in
which they enter into a rival cultural narrative and retell its
story in light of the Christian worldview. We are called to out-
narrate the dominant stories that shape our culture, by exposing their weaknesses or showing how they are enfolded by our

own or how they are eclipsed by a more luminous and compelling story."[10]

The latter—the enfolding nature of Christianity—represents the approach of this book, and echoes H. Richard Niebuhr's claim that the Christian story has a revelatory potential for illuminating other aspects of our lives.[11] This would include other *narratives* in our lives.

For as Augustine once advised regarding the age-old question, "What has Athens to do with Jerusalem?": "If those who are called philosophers... have said [anything] that is true and in harmony with our faith, we are not only not to shrink from it, but to claim it for our own use."[12] Similarly, despite any explicit or embedded worldview differences, the stories we tell often resonate with echoes of a deeper truth we intuit. The more effective the storyteller, the more powerful the story; and the more powerful the story, the more potent the impact of this resounding conviction. If the Christian story of reality is true, then it will naturally encompass any shards of truth and gems of wisdom to be found within the other stories human beings tell.

Narratives are imbued with moral philosophy, and theology is inseparable from moral philosophy because philosophy is inseparable from faith (in a broad sense). Faith, whether intentional and apprehended in our consciousness or accidental and embedded, hidden from consciousness, is a worldview wager. We may believe many things about the world, but we do not necessarily act upon all of those beliefs. When we do act according to our convictions—whether poorly or properly justified—we are wagering our view in light of reality. One may personally have nothing invested in the belief that horses can sleep while standing. However, when he stops at a red light, he is fully invested in the belief that his brakes will cause his car to stop rather than accelerate. To coalesce the arguments of seventeenth-century philosopher Blaise Pascal and late-nineteenth-century philosopher William James, when it comes to questions of God and morality, actions are wagers of faith at the end of the day.[13] Acting is inevitable, and often instinctive. We do act; we will act; and actions reveal presumptions as well as bear consequences.

Admittedly, the interest in worldview will likely make some readers uncomfortable. This is understandable. In the modern moment, just what is a "Christian Worldview"? The term is meant to evoke a *classical* Christian understanding, a generalized outlook that is framed according to a unified position on doctrinal essentials, as articulated by early Christian leaders. But that usage is often unable to allow for all the historical nuances in theological and philosophical perspectives which have attached themselves to the identity of "Christian." It is meant to refer to the biblical narrative as the early Christians understood it, yet contemporary perspectives convolute the conversation to such an extent that the term "worldview" now carries a great deal of baggage. Taylor has observed, similarly, the difficulty with describing a "secular worldview" — which is not, simply, a subtraction of belief in God, but rather the product of myriad historical movements, influential ideas, and background presumptions concerning the way in which one has been taught to imagine the world.[14]

As James Sire points out, there is a fluid nature to worldview, as it is constantly under the pressure of further contemplation, new information, and our encounters with evil and suffering. Although he remains convinced that analysis of basic worldview categories is nonetheless helpful in navigating the plurality of perspectives which paint the contemporary context, he acknowledges that "these broad strokes both miss the finer points of our individual worldviews and somewhat misrepresent any one person's worldview."[15] This does not, however, mean that worldview as a concept of study is unimportant. Nor does it mean that a Christian worldview has no consistent form and cannot be meaningfully identified. Rather, it means that scholars and lay people alike should be careful in how they use the term, and they may need to consider seeking alternative descriptions where appropriate. While some contemporary scholars are convinced that worldview studies is an outmoded method of research and investigation, McGrath observes, to the contrary, that

> Difficulties in defining 'religion' — for example, the existence of 'atheist religions' such as Buddhism — have led some scholars to suggest that the notion of a 'worldview' is less problematic and potentially more illuminating.... As psychologist Mark Kolto-Rivera observes, 'A worldview is a way of describing the universe and life within it, both in terms of what is and what ought to be.... Worldviews include assumptions that may be unproven, and even unprovable, but these assumptions are subordinate, in that they provide the epistemic and ontological foundations for other beliefs within a belief system.'"[16]

Indeed, in his work on *Cultural Apologetics*, philosopher Paul Gould argued that "Worldview analysis is necessary but not sufficient for cultural apologetics."[17] We act upon a faith according to the background presumptions of a given imaginary, or reality. This is not to say that we act on preconceived systematic convictions (nor that we do not[18]), but that we do act, and this is according to what seems right, and that step, calculated or impulsive, conscious or subconscious, involves a wager. Our sense of rightness or oughtness is based upon presumptions—whether systematic or a part of what Charles Taylor calls our social imaginary. That is, the background assumptions we have unthinkingly—more precisely, unconsciously—accepted because they are part of our socio-cultural worldview narrative.

The phrase "background assumptions," then, means something akin to "worldview" yet less apparent. We may not all stop and analyze the nature of the world and our beliefs about it, but we do imagine the world to be a certain way. The most popular beliefs and value transcripts of the cultural moment work themselves into the backdrop of a collective imaginary—and, thereby, into various seats of pop-culture power, influencing value hierarchies and presumptions about the nature of human beings and the world, and about the meaning of life. Thus, "social imaginary" refers to the prominent, collective presumptions and prescriptions of a given cultural context. While "worldview" is a satisfactorily comprehensive term, for some it signals a systematic analysis and attention to one's own perspective. The phrases "background assumptions" and "social imaginary," on the other hand, are able to sidestep that concern and press into the idea that, regardless of our own beliefs about our beliefs, we carry with us a sort of perspectival foundation—a default way of imagining our world to be and, in light of this assumption, presupposing what is right and good. It is this background way of seeing (presupposed and unanalyzed) that is so easily and powerfully shaped by pop culture through our stories and via covert transcripts from the marketplace and media.

Whether or not our actions are grounded in theory and propositional logic, they are ultimately influenced by our hierarchies of values. And our values are informed by, or embedded within, our outlook—our perspective on, or presumptions concerning, reality. In other words, our worldview. Based upon the presuppositions of our unexamined, embedded philosophical commitments, we take a chance any time we act in light of an implicit ethical or eternal question. Simply put, faith is conviction wagering action.[19] Thus, all worldviews are faith wagers. Since it is morality that is wagered against eternity, moral philosophy is inescapably tethered to questions of theology (broadly understood even to incorporate atheism).

In our storytelling, we react, again according to what seems right, and while this does not necessarily expose our worldview wagers, it does reveal something about our deepest convictions invested in those wagers to such a degree that if we were to give pause to ponder deeply those convictions, we would be raising some of the very questions at the heart of our worldview wagers. While Socrates believed the unexamined life is not worth living,[20] the unexamined art object, such as a Disney film, may still be worth beholding. For beauty, art, and stories possess arguments all their own—and Disney's canon of celebrated animated narratives from 1937 to 2021 exemplify the power of pop culture to speak to our deepest moral convictions, condition our background assumptions, and influence how we imagine our world.

The Intertwining of Ethics, Aesthetics, Theology, and Pop Culture

Pop culture is often an expression of individual perspectives and a reflection of culturally embedded presumptions, or culturally relevant questions concerning beauty, ethics, God, society, or the human condition. As philosopher William Irwin writes, "Philosophy is the love of wisdom, and it is the philosopher's task to seek wisdom wherever it may be found, even on television."[21] It has already been established that stories possess transformative power. To an extent, we understand ourselves in so far as we see ourselves within historical, cultural, and social narratives. Diogenes Allen and Eric Springsted contend, "To the degree that we share narratives, we share understanding; and to the degree that there is no sharing, there is the same degree of incomprehension.... [We] cast about the narratives that we have in order to make [that which we seek to understand] come into light."[22] Pop culture contains many of the narratives we share, and we naturally use some of those narratives to understand ourselves and our world better. Moreover, we often draw water from the wells of more than one popular cultural influence — each with its own stories and values. This means our identities are intertwined with moral and theological (aware or unaware) narratives, for pop culture is replete with narratives that tell us who we are, what we should love, and how we should act. Stories present or prescribe actions, and behind those actions are particular moral stances—and sometimes such stances either imply particular background assumptions or raise questions concerning theology relative to the human condition, especially as it pertains to significance and meaning. Yet the allure of pop-culture often involves more than just stories.

The stories of pop culture are often written across an array of artistic expression, and the visual and musical arts are often used to enhance the aesthetic impact of the literary arts. All good marketing capitalizes on visual and musical cues which communicate ideas and prescriptions concerning what we ought to value. Artistic expression, however, goes beyond this. It often attempts either to evoke an emotional reaction or experience, or to facilitate some form of meaningful contemplation. Music, moreover, like a good story, offers the added depth of an organic experience through time (of order and chaos, frustration and the fulfillment of expectation) which can influence physiological reaction. Film is an especially potent aesthetic experience precisely because it is a coalescing of the visual and the musical with the power of narrative, presented in such an organic artifact which must be *lived through*. So powerful is the living-through of aesthetic experience that some seek it spiritually.

The insights of Charles Taylor are especially helpful. As a backdrop to his considerations, remember that Taylor has argued there is a discernable historical shift in philosophical presumptions, from a pre-modern world enchanted with notions of a cosmic order and immaterial truths to a modern, disenchanted world, with its cross-pressures of seeking out our own personalized transcendence found within our individualized quests for enchantment and leading to a sense of sacred community within our collective interests.[23] Taylor observed the "haunting" existential anxieties of the contemporary world, and saw our desire for aesthetic experience as a nostalgic longing for a sense of "fullness," which leaves us wanting more.[24] He argued that we are "narrative animals" who form our identities according to stories in which we can see and place ourselves[25] and that, following the Enlightenment, we began to place ourselves within the story of exclusive humanism — the presumption that significance is constructed by human beings, apart from any reference to supposedly outmoded notions of divine truths, transcendence, or teleological order. Curiously, however, our faith in the secular age and our modern "stories" of significance—in science, humanity, in self-assertion—are inescapably religious in nature. Interestingly, he claimed that the role of the arts in the contemporary age, especially as a new means of seeking a sort of transcendence, is deeply intertwined with the reforming of our social imaginary into an exclusive humanism.[26]

In many ways, and to a notable degree, modern, contemporary thought seems to present itself as a sort of pendulum swing between classicism and Romanticism—the back-and-forth of an emphasis upon the nature of objective truth and the significance of the subjective and embodied experience. Taylor referred to this tension as the cross-pressures that arise from living in a disenchanted world (resulting from the pushback against the transcendence and enchantment of the pre-modern world). Significance has been flattened to whatever we can fit into a buffered world (our safe and self-oriented space) wherein the notion of a robust transcendence has been dis-embedded and dislodged from our social imaginary.[27] Just as March Hare corrected Alice, "If you [can't] think, you shouldn't talk,"[28] so too some twentieth-century philosophers suggested that we must remain silent when it comes to ethical and aesthetic meaning because such language does not fit within an "enlightened" frame. Many twenty-first-century thinkers reject this prescription, although they accept the frame of disenchantment. Thus, contemporary thought, according to Taylor,[29] is neither a progressing of the Enlightenment nor a progressing dialectic in reaction to the Enlightenment, for both sides of this pendulum swing are attempts to find meaning within subtraction stories.

The subtraction of religion and premodern ideals of purpose, essence, or a way-it-should-be, liberates us to find significance either within our stories of courage and enlightenment in the name of science, or else our stories of freedom in determining our own purposes. In either case, the enchantment of the possibility of an actual transcendence has been subtracted. Contemporary thought, in many ways, reflects a quest for enchantment that is torn between the flattened ideals of a disenchanted Enlightenment.

If the Enlightenment's subtraction story involved removing the religious and stripping meaning down to the rational and empirical, Taylor argues that Romanticism was, in many ways, an effort to fill that void with significance by locating it within nostalgia (the felt qualities of experience itself) or in the power of artistic minds to bring forth their own worlds of meaning.[30] As James Smith elaborates:

> Conveniently, art is never going to ask of you anything you wouldn't want to do. So we get significance without any ascetic moral burden.... The result is [that many now seek aesthetic experience in itself, for itself, as an attempt] to satisfy a lost longing for transcendence; in short, this creates a 'place to go for modern unbelief'.... And so we get these new sacred places of

modernity: the concert hall as temple; the museum as chapel; tourism as the new pilgrimage.[31]

To this we might add that those who accept a world without meaning yet attempt to assert their own moral truth as meaningful in the face of the void, are likewise seeking a sort of aesthetic experience, by approaching moral meaning as mere art expression in an effort to *create* an aesthetically significant life. Taylor's observation suggests that ideas impact the arts, and those philosophical presumptions which begin to show up in the arts hold great power for shaping culture through a reforming of the social imaginary.

Francis Schaeffer, an influential Christian apologist writing at the popular level, argued that this impact happens in a more linear fashion—from academic influence to the arts, to pop culture. He also suggested that as the new "true" (the new background assumptions) becomes increasingly unquestioned, thereby solidifying certain *unthought* ideals, such presumptions not only work themselves into pop culture but also begin to spread across academic discipline, eventually influencing the discipline of theology.[32] Others may argue that it is pop culture and the arts which first begin to influence new academic perspectives. Perhaps it is best to see this influence as both bidirectional and circular. Academic perspectives on knowledge and reality can affect perspectives on aesthetics, influencing student perspectives on the nature and purpose of the arts (or storytelling).

The next generation of artists (or storytellers) apply these beliefs, while a new generation of educators propagates them. Other students may simply carry these perspectives with them as they assimilate into society. Education concerning what we ought to believe influences the formation of culture(s) while the arts sell us certain cultural values, tethered to ideals of identity and visions of the good life, which may even begin to shape academic presumptions. Scholars are not removed from culture, after all, nor are they immune to its influence and societal pressures. Taylor's insights suggest that the arts possess a unique power to influence as they may even take on the role of religious significance (a background theology), even for the "unbeliever" whose faith is placed in self, science, or community. Wherever they fall in order of influence between pop-culture and academy, the arts are powerful forces in disseminating philosophical claims regarding truth to such a degree they may even, eventually, begin to impact and transform one's perspective on theology or religious experience.

Philosophy and theology, then, seem to relate to pop culture and the arts in at least three ways. First, as explained above in light of Taylor's observations, ideas impact culture and culture impacts worship (broadly construed as that which wields the most power in orchestrating our phenomenological lives). Second, whether seeking expressions or experiences, we often tie meaning to markets (value related to monetized worth, the pressure of neoliberalism) and habit to worship (broadly understood, indicated by repeated, consistent expressions of how we use our time). As James Smith argues, "Because our hearts are oriented primarily by desire, by what we love, and because those desires are shaped and molded by the habit-forming practices in which we participate, it is the rituals and practices of the mall—the liturgies of the mall and market—that shape our imaginations and how we orient ourselves in the world."[33] Education, formal and informal, is central to the formation of not only our understanding but also what we desire and, consequently, value. Value education happens to some degree almost everywhere in culture, but it happens to an astounding degree through the purchase and acquisition of pop culture via the marketplace. Essentially, people buy their values. They buy the things that form and shape their values. While this value formation is rarely noticed or named, it is no less real.

The third way the arts are entangled with theology and philosophy is that arts are often expressions of worldviews (or worldview questions) as they are embodied and lived out. This embodiment and living out is not done in isolation, but in community, because we are instinctively social animals. How could we not be? We were fashioned and created in the context of companionship.[34] As we live in community, in the "plurality of others," as Hannah Arendt's work reminds us,[35] one meaningful expression (or question) often moves others to consider our "meaning making" and ponder it in relationship to themselves. As our reference to the market has already intimated, we are desperate for meaning and consequently rabid consumers of anything and everything we believe can deliver it. As we consume that which provides us meaning (often along the binary of acquiring the "good life") or a cathartic means of voicing our dissatisfaction with the human condition— we accept, often subconsciously, the subtle and, at times, not so subtle worldview prescriptions therein. To take a cue from Taylor, we breathe in the presumptions of a disenchanted social imaginary (socially embedded worldview narratives). At times, this work like a virus, spreading from person to person and compromising our moral imaginations. At other times, it works like "paying it forward," spreading from person to person and bolstering our moral imaginations. Either way, our perspectives on morality and the super-structures of our individual theologies both inform and are informed by the arts manifested and delivered through pop culture.

Two Foundational Presumptions

When we participate in, live through, a Disney story, we are taken to another world wherein we often encounter a sense that something is not as it ought to be. We may even encounter an unmistakable evil or appalling injustice, and we almost always encounter an undeniable optimism that the Good, a right-order or proper relationship, will prevail, that the individual is significant, that there is an ever-after happiness where suffering and injustice is eclipsed by the light of love and kindness, and an awakening conviction that the beautiful soul and virtuous character is directly connected to the Kingdom. Disney stories are quite effective at awakening our desire for Beauty, our hope in Goodness, and our convictions of Justice.

The apologetic value of approaching the works of a culturally authoritative storyteller as a cross-narrative exploration, attempting to draw out the moral metanarrative which comes into view as one surveys common moral motifs presented across a number of celebrated stories, might be better appreciated by emphasizing two points exemplified in the apologetic approach of C. S. Lewis. Lewis regularly relied on two key propositions: (1) the fact that human beings share a universal conviction concerning the *fact* of justice (though they may differ over definitions of the good life, descriptions of right action, and the "just" distribution of "goods"), and (2) the idea that stories and aesthetic experience possess a pronounced power (one that appeals to our desire for a teleological just-ness—our hope for the fulfillment of an ought-to-be, a right purpose of justice) to go deeper than mere propositions, to stir our moral convictions, and to awaken our hope for finding significance and identity. The cultural apologist recognizes that the authority of a storyteller is directly connected to the aesthetic allure of its tales, and that enchantment is attached to a deep desire for moral meaning. Moreover, the fact that we desire it, even expect to find it, is because, deep down, we share a conviction that there is a way-it-should be, a just-ness, and that human significance is somehow tethered to knowing the beauty of such a goodness realized.

The first point, the universal conviction of a just-order, is brought to light in Lewis's *The Abolition of Man*.[36] In this 1943 work, Lewis criticized philosophies of education that were built upon moral subjectivism—the belief that moral truth is relative to the individual. "You have your truth and I have mine" amounts to little more than emotivism, the belief that moral utterances function merely as expressions of our feelings.[37] Lewis presented a case for moral objectivity, defending the fact that all human beings share a deep foundational conviction of universal, objective moral truth. As Michael Ward explains, "[Lewis's] thesis is not that all moralities coincide on every point, only that they all derive from a single source, the universally accessible Tao, and all therefore agree in principle on the objectivity of moral value. The Tao is not something human beings simply make up; it is something they discover."[38]

The sagacity of Lewis's work is made evident when placing his observations next to the ancients who argued for relativism. Herodotus, after studying several contrasting cultures, concluded, "If one were to order all mankind to choose the best set of rules in the world, each group would, after due consideration, choose its own customs; each group regards its own as being by far the best.... I think Pindar was right to have said in his poem that custom is king of all."[39] Whereas Herodotus observed value diversity and concluded that conventionalism must be true (culture is the bedrock of conviction; moral truth is relative to cultural convention), Lewis's work demonstrates the opposite conclusion. In the appendix to *The Abolition of Man*,[40] Lewis included a number of moral testimonies taken from diverse sources and backgrounds (across cultures and throughout history), in order to show that all of them demonstrated a keen sense of justice as objective truth. They differ on the details yet reveal an agreement on the substance—they share a deep conviction that there is such a thing as universal objective moral truth; there is a real and robust, shared sense of justice.

Moral truth, then, is not subjective nor relative to culture all the way down. Rather, differing cultures often reflect a similar awareness of moral conviction. Now this is not perfect, of course. There is not a 1:1 correspondence on all moral perspectives between cultures. Of course not. At times there are notable, drastic differences. But these differences do not reflect a lack of a universal standard. Actually, our differences often come down to non-moral beliefs, on which we differ, which are coupled with moral principles, on which we often agree (such as the conviction that certain things are *due* to certain beings). Our differences also reflect the Fall.[41] The Fall of humankind has marred and skewed our sense of morality and made it susceptible to subjective cultural influence. It is a misstep, however, as Lewis essentially points out, to imagine that our sense of morality is wholly captive to a reigning subjectivity. There is an echo, faint at times, but no less real, of a universal and absolute moral standard tethered to the reality of the *imago Dei*,[42] reverberating through the conscience of every man and woman.

As we will argue, the moral metanarrative observable across Disney films similarly points to the fact of an objective, universal truth. Moreover, even if they often champion a sense of individual empowerment for the protagonist, Disney films often make clear that relativism is not an option or, if it is, that it simply does not work. Elsa's *letting go* is one of her more celebrated moments: "No right, no wrong, no rules for me. I'm free!"[43] Yet, even if it is good for her to let go of the bondage of her self-imposed guilt and the fear that held her back from knowing the goodness and beauty of communion with her sister, the audience sees clearly that her decision to throw moral truth to the wind and live her own truth did not really work out so well. Elsa knows this, and we see it in *Frozen II*, when she is able to see past memories and cringes when she encounters a memory of this existential anthem.

Lewis's second point, concerning the power of aesthetic experience, including the allure of good stories, and its connection to the desire for the right purpose and expression of justice, can be found in Lewis's shift from a propositional style of apologetics to a purposeful use of fiction, and in his concept of *Sehnsucht* (wistful longing). While Lewis was renowned for his propositional defenses of Christianity and moral objectivity, in the latter part of his life he found narrative apologetics—emphasizing symbolism within fiction—to be preferable. In the words of Alister McGrath, "We can rightly see Narnia as the imaginative outworking of the core philosophical and theological ideas Lewis had been developing since the mid-1930s, expressed in narrative rather than a rational manner.... Fiction becomes the means of allowing readers to see—more than that, to *enjoy*—the vision of reality Lewis had already set out in his more apologetic works."[44]

This approach resonates with an observation by Smith, in summary of Taylor's work. "If Taylor is right, it seems to suggest that the Christian response to such converts to unbelief is not to have an argument about the data or 'evidences' but rather to offer an alternative story that offers a more robust, complex understanding of the Christian faith."[45] The Romantic concept of a deep, inexpressible longing for a direct encounter with the Beautiful (*Sehnsucht*) is foundational both to Lewis's spiritual development and to his moral and imaginative apologetics. McGrath explained it as "a deep yearning for seemingly unreachable states of life or poignant desire for something agonizingly elusive."[46] This is why Lewis famously argued, "If I find in myself a desire which no experience in this world can satisfy, the most probable explanation is that I was made for another world."[47] Jack Skellington felt something similar in *The Nightmare Before Christmas* , when he sang, "There's something out there far from my home; a longing that I've never known,"[48] and this led him to look, first, to other worlds, and later to love. As Peter Kreeft put it in the preface to his work, *The Philosophy of Tolkien,* "The deepest healing is the healing of the deepest wound. The deepest wound is the frustration of the deepest need. The deepest need is the need for meaning, purpose, and hope."[49]

For Lewis, human experience testifies to there being another world for which we were made. Thus, a central Narnian theme is the door to another world.[50] McGrath explains:

> For Lewis, the narrative of Narnia has the capacity to re-enchant a disenchanted world. It helps us to imagine our world differently. This is not escapism, but is about discerning deeper levels of meaning and value in what we already know.... [As Lewis explained this 'double seeing,'] 'I believe that the Sun has risen, not only because I see it, but because by it I see everything else.' We can look at the sun itself; or we can look at what it illuminates—thus enlarging our intellectual, moral, and aesthetic visions. We see the true, the good, and the beautiful more clearly by being given a lens that brings them into focus.

Lewis recognized the power of the imagination to apprehend arguments from experience and intuition portrayed within a well-crafted narrative. We are not saying that a propositional argument from intuition rises to the level of a logical defeater. Rather, arguments from intuitive experience can carry an existential and pragmatic force that is difficult to ignore. Again, we live with deep convictions concerning good and justice, evil and injustice. (This is true universally; while we differ on prescription, we are unified in conviction). Sometimes, as Grandmother Willow informed Pocahontas, when we listen with our hearts, we understand the deepest truths to which nature herself testifies.[51] The key point to appreciate in Lewis's work, says McGrath, is that his apologetics "allows the integration of an appeal to human longing."[52] We submit that Disney presses into a particular longing which we all share—a longing for the Kingdom-ever-after, or what Lewis might call the far-off country.

For Lewis, good fiction profoundly appeals to our sense of order, justice, desire, virtue, and the good. Moreover, the acquisition of virtue (especially in contrast to self-indulgence) is both central and indicative to renewal and transformation. Such narratives captivate the heart, stirring within us a desire for order and justice, appealing to our intuitive sense of wisdom, beseeching us, in Platonic fashion, to pursue the Good which lies in a far-off country wherein we find ourselves growing ever more real, and we discover the things of this world to have been something like weak shadows of reality.

In Narnia fashion, Disney narratives offer us a glimpse into another world where we encounter *Sehnsucht* as it awakens our hope for significance and identity. We want to know the restoration of Kumandra is possible (*Raya and the Last Dragon*). Like Mirabel (*Encanto*) we also desire to know that there is something special about *us*, and like Elsa (*Frozen II*), we want to know that our life is meaningful, that we have a purpose. As demonstrated in *The Abolition of Man*, we encounter—we are forced to feel—our convictions of teleological justice. We understand that there is a proper order in *Moana*—a way-things-ought-to-be. Sensing that the ought-to-be for human beings entails more than justice alone, but also a goodness beyond just-ness, we also long to experience the Kingdom-ever-after implied at the end of stories like *The Lion King, Cinderella, Sleeping Beauty, Aladdin, Beauty and the Beast, Tangled,* Frozen, and *Frozen II*. (We may even want to experience a Disney park because it is the closest tangible experience we can get to that kingdom-oriented aim). In a well-told story, as Lewis once wrote in review of Tolkien's *The Lord of the Rings*, "we do not retreat from reality: we rediscover it. As long as the story lingers in our mind, the real things are more themselves... By dipping them in myth we see them more clearly."[53] We contend that Disney lore similarly offers a multi-layered and textured realm of theologically sensitive illumination and moral contemplation designed to draw us in and enrapture us through aesthetically rich encounters with desire, conviction, and the power of imagination.

2

Walt Disney's Moral Influences and the Moral Power of a Disney Story

W alt Disney's imaginative tales have become a formative force in contemporary pop culture. These stories were not created in a vacuum, however. They were the outworking of one man's vivid imagination and artistic originality. These tales not only reflect Walt's aesthetic interests but also his interest in moral education. The latter interest poses problems when trying to communicate something about the universal and objective nature of moral truth across a wide array of audiences with great diversity in perspectives on religion and morality. Nevertheless, there is undeniably something communicated across Disney films, something that resonates with myriad viewers across the globe. It is prudent to begin our exploration of Disney's stories with a brief look at Disney, the man. Since Disney lore—from its characters to its imagery to its philosophy to its moral commitments—is organic to Walt Disney, we must understand him and have a sense of him as a person, at least to some degree, if we are ever to have a right sense of his art and contribution to the world.

As a driven entrepreneur, Walt had an interest in appealing to and capitalizing upon the aesthetic desires of his audience. This already raises questions of significance for aesthetics apologetics—for one interested in arguments from beauty, order. Moreover, some of us believe the moral and aesthetic spheres of experience to be tightly intertwined, especially when it comes to the nature of storytelling. The capitalizing in itself on any avenue of aesthetics such as storytelling, music, visual art, or an art of their synthesis in film, however, does not also require a need to appeal to or underscore moral conviction. Yet Walt clearly had an interest in moral education, and the effectiveness of his nonsectarian approach, especially given the difficulty of establishing a non-sectarian moral education, warrants contemplation. It is therefore worth considering what ideas on morality, both nonsectarian ideas and those influenced by Christianity, Walt brought to the films upon which his legacy was built.

It is also worth considering how Disney's aesthetics were viewed by some of his contemporaries. Given Disney's moral emphasis, especially in so far as it suggests a theological aim or grounding, it would be of particular interest to consider what contemporaries who were also interested in drawing out moral and theological elements in their fiction had to say about Disney films. In fact two of the most popular names in twentieth-century literature relating to a moral and theological interest, J. R. R. Tolkien and C. S. Lewis, had something to say about Disney — one less forgiving, the other more charitable. Given their stature, it is worth hearing their criticisms — especially given the irony that Disney's non-sectarian approach to film actually aligns with Tolkien's perspective on writing in a manner suggestive of, though without naming it, theological symbolism. In addition, Disney stories seem to capitalize on the *Sehnsucht* (yearning for the beauty of a seeming sense of the ought-to-be, a far-off country) in which Lewis was so deeply interested.

Walt Disney

Walter Elias Disney (1901–1966), born in Chicago, IL, did not receive an education comparable to other celebrated figures of grand aesthetic achievement. Although he took a few art classes, he joined the Red Cross during WWI, at age 16, after lying about his age. While serving in Europe, he designed posters and newspaper cartoons. After returning to the U.S. and experimenting with animation in Kansas City, MO, Walt eventually joined his brother Roy in Hollywood, CA, in 1923. There, they formed what would eventually become Walt Disney Studios. After losing several animators and the rights to Oswald the Lucky Rabbit (due to the deception of his distributor), Walt started over in 1926. Shortly thereafter, he would design a new character would change the history of both animation and music.

Today, Mickey Mouse is an icon of icons. But it hasn't always been so. In fact, his first two cartoons (which were silent films) were decidedly unsuccessful. However, for his third outing, Disney altered course and incorporated fully synchronized sound. *Steamboat Willie* debuted in 1928 with immediate success. Mickey Mouse was finally, effectively introduced to the world and established Disney as a revolutionary figure in animation. Disney's entrepreneurial spirit led to success in creating and capitalizing on Disney-themed merchandise. The *Silly Symphonies* were notably popular—debuting "Flowers and Trees" in 1932 as the first full-color cartoon. In 1937, he launched the first animated feature film, *Snow White and the Seven Dwarves*, which, at the time, became the highest grossing film of all time.

Disney expanded his film legacy to include live-action films, live-action animated films, educational films, morale-boosting wartime propaganda, and a significant number of subsequent successful cartoons and animated features. In addition, *The Mickey Mouse Club* began in the 1950s as a sort of moral, music, and cultural education—featuring Mickey cartoons, of course. Disney spent the latter part of his years investing in the development of theme parks. Disneyland opened in 1955, and Walt Disney World opened in 1971 after Walt's death in 1966 from complications related to lung cancer.[1]

Walt's Moral Influences

An interesting and potentially significant observation concerning Disney's history and impact involves his early career in Kansas City. During this time, Walt became a member of the Order of DeMolay—an organization for developing leadership skills in young men, founded in Kansas City the very same year Disney began his career there.[2] The possible significance lies within the organization's essential values: filial love, reverence for sacred things, courtesy, comradeship (encouraging strong ties of membership, loyalty, and trust), fidelity, cleanness (which includes respectful thoughts, actions, and words), and patriotism. Concerning sacred things, the DeMolay website explains; "An individual's religious beliefs are their own. We encourage them to carry out their teachings, while still respecting the view of others."[3] Membership is strongly tied to this tenet. "DeMolay is an inclusive organization that only asks of young men interested to believe in a higher being." In 1963, Disney wrote, "In DeMolay, I learned to believe in the basic principle of the right of man to exercise his faith and thoughts as he chooses. In DeMolay, we believe in a supreme being, in the fellowship of man, and the sanctity of the home. DeMolay stands for all that is good for the family and for our country."[4]

Given DeMolay's influence, it is no surprise that Disney's approach to film was similarly ambiguous when it came to the particulars of religion. Still, he nevertheless emphasized a higher grounding as necessary for objective goodness and morality, and its connection to virtue—as well as the significance of a child-like faith in imagining a better world:

> Deeds rather than words express my concept of the part religion should play in everyday life. I have watched constantly that in our movie work the highest moral and spiritual standards are upheld, whether it deals with fable or with stories of living action. This religious concern for the form and content of our films goes back 40 years to the rugged financial period in Kansas City when I was struggling to establish a film company and produce animated fairy tales.... Both my study of Scripture and my career in entertaining children have taught me to cherish them.... Children are people, and they should have to reach to learn about things, to understand things, just as adults have to reach if they want to grow in mental stature.... The important thing is to teach a child that good can always triumph over evil, and that is what our pictures attempt to do.
>
> The American child is a highly intelligent human being — characteristically sensitive, humorous, open-minded, eager to learn, and has a strong sense of excitement, energy, and healthy curiosity about the world in which he lives. Lucky indeed is the grown-up who manages to carry these same characteristics into adult life. It usually makes for a happy and successful individual. In our full-length cartoon features, as well as in our live action productions, we have tried to convey in story and song those virtues that make both children and adults attractive. Whatever success I have had in bringing clean, informative entertainment to people of all ages, I attribute in great part to my Congregational upbringing and my lifelong habit of prayer. To me... [all prayer] has one thing in common: supplication for strength and inspiration to carry on the best human impulses which should bind us together for a better world. Without such inspiration, we would rapidly deteriorate and finally perish.[5]

Disney's vision of family and fellowship —both in films and in parks— seems to aim for an enchanted meeting ground, where community both bridges and transcends diversity and children and adults alike are enraptured by wonder. Notwithstanding the challenge that potentially harmful cultural or ethnic stereotypes might hinder the actualization of such an ideal of unity, the intent of Disney seems nevertheless to have been one of community.

While some may be unsatisfied with Disney's ambiguity, this approach is nonetheless successful in uniting such a wide array of perspectives (both sacred and secular) in a shared celebration of artistic beauty, moral virtue, family, community, and the significance of faith and trust. While the object of one's faith—whether God, self, or something else (dreams and magic)— remains an important issue, the point is that faith in the triumph of a higher goodness, reflected through beauty, modeled in virtue, and experienced in community, is an essential ingredient in Disney's depiction of the good life— and a powerful starting point in moral apologetics.

B. Edward McClellan surveyed the history of moral education in America and exposed the inability of non-sectarian approaches to ground moral education satisfactorily.[6] Since it is our value hierarchies which ultimately inform our ethics, and since our value hierarchies and subsequent prescriptions ultimately rest upon our worldview narratives, the best a non-sectarian ethics can do is to emphasize general and ambiguous ideals of goodness and fellowship; the less ambiguous and more particular our moral prescriptions become, the more divided (sectarian) our narratives on education will become as well. In this regard, Disney seems to have been quite successful in providing a far-reaching (ambiguous yet universally appealing) moral education. Although Disney lore does not go far enough in explicating foundational justifications, it goes as far as a nonsectarian moral education can go in unifying its audience in an experiential awareness of a deep-seated conviction concerning the fact of a universal, objective goodness. To this end, it might be said that Disney was in line with the approach of J. R. R. Tolkien, who refrained from explicit theological allegory even though theology permeated his writings. On the other hand, Disney stories carry potent moral messages. Disney's theism is present in the background, yet unlike C. S. Lewis, Disney avoided particular religious references and opted instead for a nonsectarian approach. This is part of what made his narratives so widely appealing and approachable.

Aesthetic Criticisms

Disney's aesthetics has not been without its critics. In fact, the comparison of Disney to Tolkien and Lewis may seem odd to some. Lewis and Tolkien were enthralled with Norse mythology whereas Walt was influenced by The Brothers Grimm. Moreover, Tolkien and Lewis were quite critical of Disney's oversimplification and infantilizing of fairy stories (of which they thought so highly). Tolkien apparently found Disney quite repulsive. Across several letters, he expressed his loathing and encouraged vetoing anything Disney. He saw *Snow White* with Lewis, and disliked Disney's treatment of dwarves. Moreover, he evidently found Disney's merchandising tasteless, vulgar, and filthy, and he made explicitly clear that he would never want *The Hobbit* to be made in such a ridiculous manner as that of Disney films. (Disney and Tolkien fans can likely agree that the 1977 Rankin/Bass classic was the more appropriate animation adaptation for the Tolkienian tale).

Tolkien criticized Walt's business practices and stated that he would never give a Disney proposal any serious consideration. Part of his disinterest in Disney seems to have been a general aversion to dramatization. (Tolkien is not alone in such book-to-drama criticism. While people often leave a movie complaining that it was nothing like the book, one should bear in mind that books and movies do not necessarily work in the same way). In one letter, Tolkien stated, "Though in most of the 'pictures' proceeding from his studios, there are admirable/charming passages, the effect of all of them is to me disgusting. Some have given me nausea."[7]

Lewis was also critical, though more forgiving (and more understanding over time). He recorded his initial critique of *Snow White* in a letter, stating that it was both good and bad. The dwarves were drawn poorly, and they had a poor choice of music. But the scary parts were well-done, and the animals were mostly well-drawn. Lewis acknowledged that Disney's use of shadow was genius, yet he criticized Disney's originality and imagination. He lamented, if only Disney had received a proper education, his storytelling might have been better.[8] This is a good example of how difficult it is to please everyone when it comes to aesthetics and aesthetic criticism—especially when evaluating works on a spectrum between what some designate as "high" and "low" culture. Part of the conundrum is that to be original is to ignore literary tradition, yet to stick to literary tradition is to lack originality.

With time, Lewis's view on cinema matured and, revisiting his criticism, he conceded there was value in artistically using a non-traditional form to connect with a popular audience. Disney, he said, had a strange blend of genius and vulgarity:

> There was a bad originality in the bloated, drunken, low comedy farce of the dwarves. [Lewis was particularly fond of dwarves]. Neither the wisdom, the avarice, not the earthliness of true dwarves were there, but an imbecility of arbitrary invention. But in the scene where Snow White wakes in the woods both the right originality and the right unoriginality were used together. The good unoriginality lay in the use of small, delicate animals as comforters.... The good originality lay in letting us first mistake their eyes for the eyes of monsters. The whole art consists not in evoking the unexpected, but in evoking with a perfection and accuracy beyond expectation the very image that has haunted us all our lives.[9]

Lewis was beginning to see a potential value in both cinema and Disney. The early criticism of Lewis and the main criticism of Tolkien appear to have centered around two objections: (1) Disney was not going about storytelling the proper way, and (2) film is a disservice to the imagination. Lewis later concedes that (1) film has its own unique ways of engaging the imagination, and (2) there was both some notable originality and some aspects of classical storytelling present in Disney's film.

Despite Lewis's and Tolkien's criticisms, and notwithstanding differences in style and aesthetic preference, Walt's animated tales, even in their infantilized simplicity, actually seem to bring to life many of Tolkien's arguments about fairy stories while also capitalizing on Lewis's point about our deep desire for the beauty of an ought-to-be. The latter actually completes the former. Tolkien argued for the potency of meaningfulness revealed through fiction—wherein we can rediscover our own world by seeing it through another imagined. One of the greatest functions of the fairy tale is to provide, whether for children or adults, a lifting of the heart towards joy in the wake of an unexpected turning toward the good, even amidst looming tragedy or crippling angst. This joy represents a window into the truth and reality of an ultimate goodness. While Tolkien depicted imagination as uncovering our deeper understanding of the good, Lewis pressed the point that we have been longing for the good all along—in both our recurrent need to encounter the beautiful and our repulsion to injustice.

In this way, Disney tales are not merely entertainment stories. They are perspectives on deeper truths. As Joseph Campbell wrote of myth, "Mythology is the penultimate truth—penultimate because the ultimate cannot be put into words. It is beyond words. Beyond images, beyond that bounding rim of the Buddhist Wheel of Becoming. Mythology pitches the mind beyond that rim, to what can be known but not told."[10] We believe the Disney canon is able to serve similarly as a medium for moral apologetics, as it has a history of effectively engaging the hearts of its viewers often in service to pointing the mind to the reality of an objective, universal truth concerning goodness. Walt Disney pressed intently into our convictions of an idealistic beauty and awareness of a great goodness. In both film and the live, embodied experience of their theme parks, Disney seems to capture the essence of Lewis's concern for a nostalgic longing—for the world to be just-so. Disney uses the art of animation, music, and storytelling to reinforce the conviction of a universal, objective goodness which triumphs over evil and is connected to the fostering of virtue within the individual and beauty within community.

Disney Stories as Doorway to Dialogue

Walt Disney's approach to narrative through an artistic coalescing of animation and music testifies to the power of storytelling and the arts to go where arguments at times cannot—pricking our hearts and exposing convictions which signify a belief in beauty, love, and justice (a way-it-should-be). Disney understood his audiences and context well, and, notwithstanding criticisms from those who take issue with capitalizing on pop culture in general, and children's stories in particular, he was undeniably effective in reaching both children and adults all over the world. Disney stories have enchanted several generations and Disney culture has maintained a thriving global market for decades.

When it comes to apologetics in general, and cultural apologetics in particular, impact is everything. After all, we often approach dialogue like we approach music; we let a small excerpt determine whether we continue to listen. Similarly, we let soundbites and memes influence us, speak for us, or, unfortunately, oversimplify our rejection or acceptance of complex ideas into which we may not have actually looked deeply. Given the significant impact that many Disney films have had upon pop culture since the 1930s, Disney stories hold a special power over the imagination. This can serve as a powerful tool for facilitating moral and theological dialogue. Disney beckons both children and adults to long for and believe in the ultimate reign of a supreme goodness, to embrace the significance of the individual, to affirm the importance of community, and to hope for a happiness-ever-after. This ability to enchant such an expansive audience is an artistic embodiment of the power of *Sehnsucht* to enliven narratives with the joy of truth. We submit that Disney can enable us to defend moral objectivity and explore intuitions which point to theism, and make certain aspects of philosophy and theology more accessible to a wider audience.

Disney films expose our beliefs concerning the existence of beauty and the fact of an objective goodness and way-it-should-be—an absolute justice wherein good conquers evil, hope is enlivened, and love reigns. Walt Disney's animated musical canon underscores common themes of fellowship (in community and family), the significance of the brave individual, even in the face of overwhelming odds, the significant role that even the seemingly incapable or inconsequential character has to play (the child, the mouse, the clown fish, *The Small One*), the consequence of character, the joy of the good turn,[11] the hope of the happily-ever-after; and the classic yet ever-powerful motif of the great journey—transformation over tragedy, triumph over trial, hope and determination over despair, and feat over fear and failure. This book will explore the ability of Disney to evidence the power of narrative, especially through the media of film and the animated musical, to captivate moral intuition to stimulate and facilitate moral deliberation and theological dialogue.

Part 2

DISNEY'S MORAL META-NARRATIVE AND RECURRENT THEOLOGICAL IMAGERY

3

Kingdoms in the Making and Diamonds in the Rough: Disney's Recurrent Moral Motif

hroughout its history, since the 1937 debut of *Snow White and the Seven Dwarves*, Disney animated features have repeatedly shown a particular interest in virtue and character ethics. Some recent films have delved more into the complexities of character formation and analysis. We see this in *Inside Out*'s concern with emotional growth and anxiety, *Wreck-It Ralph*'s question of whether a "bad guy" is always a "bad" guy, and *Frozen*'s true-to-life depiction of the bad guy (Hans) as a seemingly good guy. Still, the primary moral concern of many Disney narratives seems to be, in Walt's own words, "that good can always triumph over evil," that there are certain "virtues that make both children and adults attractive," and—strikingly akin to Walt's philosophy of prayer—that we must find the strength "to carry on the best human impulses which should bind us together for a better world."[1] The triumph of the good is proportional to the character of the characters.

Walt aimed purposefully for a non-sectarian religious ambiguity in order to facilitate more effectively a cross-cultural meeting ground of shared aesthetic and moral interests, accessible to children (and adults) of a variety of perspectives and backgrounds. Although some have criticized Disney for replacing God with magic and self-empowerment, watering down religion to little more than wish fulfillment and a superficial faith in "faith,"[2] this work proposes a different take and consideration. While one interested in moral considerations can agree to an extent with some of the criticisms of

Disney, there is much fruit to be gleaned from the fact that Disney films often present powerful apologetic arguments for the existence of an objective morality and a vision of ethics which often aligns with Christian theology.

First, the fact that we all share basic convictions (not agreement in the details but the fact of) concerning good and evil, justice and injustice, is itself one of the most powerful arguments for theism (broadly understood). This point has been made by many philosophers and theistic apologists, but perhaps most famously, at the popular level, by C. S. Lewis. Lewis contended that a basic, universal, objective sense of morality is apparent, across cultures and throughout history, in the simple fact that all of humanity expresses a deep conviction concerning justice and injustice, a way-things-should-go, or *Tao*.[3]

> This thing which I have called for convenience the *Tao*, and which others may call Natural Law... or the First Principles of Practical Reason... is not one among a series of possible systems of value. It is the sole source of all value judgements. If it is rejected, all value is rejected. If any value is retained, it is retained. The effort to refute it and raise a new system of value in its place is self-contradictory. There has never been, and never will be, a radically new judgement of value in the history of the world. What purport to be new systems or (as they now call them) 'ideologies', all consist of fragments of the *Tao* itself, arbitrarily wrenched from their context in the whole and then swollen to madness in their isolation, yet owing to the *Tao* and to it alone such validity as they possess.... The rebellion of new ideologies against the *Tao* is a rebellion of the branches against the tree.[4]

Lewis famously argued that, just as crookedness makes no sense without some concept of straightness,[5] our deep convictions concerning injustice make no sense without the reality of an objective, universal moral standard concerning justice. Such a standard, a way-things-should-be, implies a Creator or Designer, one who has deemed a way-things-should-go. In addition, Lewis was fascinated by the nature of myths and legends to convey reality (a reflection of things that are true) concerning natural of social phenomena. As Merida's mother insisted, "Legends are lessons; they ring with truth."[6] Similarly, Lewis was convinced that myths and legends often ring with the truth of general revelation (knowledge about God gleaned through observations of the physical world and the application of reason).[7]

Disney's animated canon offers a moral metanarrative that tends to es-chew moral relativism in favor of something more permanent and universal regarding truth. It asserts things are not as they should be, defines and pro-motes a moral goodness determined to overcome evil and injustice, and looks for a better world to come. In this, it finds some notable commonality with the Christian witness and hope.[8] Understood in this way, Disney films lay a foundation for discussion and deliberation that is ultimately theological in nature.

Second, although Disney films are not consistent in how they reference religion, the influence of a Judeo-Christian view of morality is unmistakable. As Tonje Belibi asserts, "Many Disney movies mix Judeo-Christian teaching with other religious elements and spirituality."[9] The biblical narrative em-phasizes a Kingdom-ever-after, the character of Kingdom ambassadors and their role in sharing the good news of the Kingdom-ever-after, and a double-danger of living in light of that Kingdom. Similarly, Disney has continually emphasized an interest in the Kingdom-ever-after, agapism, and the double-danger that arises from living in light of the good, yet central to any discus-sion of Disney's vision of Beauty, Goodness, and the ideal ever-after is an understanding of Disney's interest in virtue ethics.

Normative Ethical Theory: An Introductory Overview

The four basic theories of moral foundations in the traditional approach to the study of normative ethics (the branch of moral philosophy which digs at the theoretical criteria for calling some actions right and other actions wrong) are egoism, utilitarianism, deontology, and virtue ethics. Egoism holds that one ought to do whatever is in his or her own self-interest. The strength of this appeal is psychological; we do seem to act out of self-interest. This is linked to self-preservation. While people certainly act in ways that appear altruistic, and certainly feel so at the point of consciousness, it can be argued that, at bottom, even in these situations people are motivated by self-inter-est—the praise of others, or the feeling acquired when engaged in the act of helping, or a host of other reasons. Egoism insists that one cannot escape self-interest. As Ayn Rand argues, altruism "is more than immoral; it's impossi-ble."[10] Ought Cruella to care for anyone else's feelings or only for her own furs? Why ought Mother Gothel treat Rapunzel as anything more than a means to the end of her own youth and beauty?

Utilitarianism similarly judges goodness and rightness in terms of consequence but prescribes that one ought to do whatever results in the greater good for the greater number.[11] Merida's (*Brave*) arranged marriage is said to be for the good of her clan. It is right for Mulan to deceive others if she is acting for the good of her country and the wellbeing of her father. The strength of utilitarianism is simplicity, or at least it appears to be. It *would* seem that the essence of morality should be easily accessible if it is to be universally applicable, and utilitarianism indeed offers a clear and concise definition of right and wrong. Whatever benefits the majority; do that. The problem with utilitarianism is that under this rubric a majority-appeal always trumps a minority view, and since the "good" is not necessarily a true good and is often understood merely to mean "whatever benefits" the majority, utilitarianism is susceptible to justifying unjust practices.

Whereas egoism and utilitarianism are concerned with *consequence*, deontology and virtue ethics are concerned with *principle*. While deontology and virtue ethics are both concerned with principles, they differ on the nature and purpose of principles. Deontology emphasizes principles of *right action—doing*. There are right and wrong actions, and the essence of morality involves fulfilling one's duty to the moral law.[12] Virtue (moral "excellence"), on the other hand, concerns principles of *good character—being*. Without necessarily denying that there are right or wrong actions, the virtue ethicist is concerned with the character of the individual, and not just the apparent good of the action demonstrated. It is not enough to *do* a good act; it is important to *be* the sort of person who habitually acts in morally excellent ways.[13] Whereas the essence of deontology is conduct, the crux of virtue ethics involves human *telos* (nature and purpose) and character. Why shouldn't Aladdin lie to Jasmine? Deontology stresses one's duty to tell the truth—lying is wrong. Virtue ethics calls one *to be* an honest person—to be one who loves truth because truth is good, one who loves honesty because it is good to be truthful with others.

When we focus on utilitarianism and deontology, the former attempts to grasp the essence of morality as being concerned with the alleviation of suffering and the aim of human flourishing. Yet, it also brings justice into question as it seems to legitimize apparent injustices against minority perspectives. The latter (deontology) recognizes that principles play a significant role in the foundation of justice, nevertheless an emphasis on principles and propositions can be insufficient in speaking thoroughly to the complexities of the practical life, day-to-day "lived experience."[14] Principles of action are important, however, stressing principles without addressing character at times misses the mark. For instance, is it really the case that lying is always wrong if lying might save the life of an innocent human being? Should we not call the one who lies to a Nazi officer while hiding a Jewish family during WWII a "good" person—one worthy of emulation and honor? Even if stealing is wrong, is it permissible for Aladdin to steal in order to eat? What if he ends up giving the food to starving children, instead of eating it himself? There is no disguising the fact that Mulan lied—deceiving even her closest friends. Yet we understand that her deception was actually an honorable act if human life and wellbeing (in this case, that of her father) are more valuable than customary expectations and sociocultural duties. Mufasa confronts Scar for failing to attend the presentation of Simba, as Scar was expected to do.

Suppose, however, that Scar had attended. Would this gesture—doing his duty—have really mattered given the character that we know Scar to be? Is it only when Scar actually kills Mufasa that we can call him morally wrong, or is it the case that there is something morally problematic about his attitude and character long before he acts in any clearly immoral way? The moral rule "do not murder" is an important rule, but such an action is an outworking of an issue within an inner disposition. According to Jesus, whatever is within one's heart has already condemned him even if he has not yet acted on that passion (such as anger or lust).[15] While principles may be important, virtue seems to animate the principles in question. The reasons we ought to do or ought not to do seem to have something to do with the sort of people we ought to be, and not merely with the nature of an act in itself. Questions of moral excellence are therefore inseparable from questions of *telos*.

This needs some unpacking. The term *telos* refers to an ultimate aim, and it is often defined as "end" or goal," and left at that. This unfortunate oversimplification of a complex concept lends itself to much confusion because any action can be directed toward an end goal, and so the robust concept is too often reduced to speak merely of "ends justifying means"—which is why ethicists often present "teleological" theories in contrast to deontological theories (for which a seemingly good end can never serve as justification for an apparently unjust means). Utilitarianism and egoism both, in this narrow sense, qualify as "teleological" ethical theories. The end goal of egoism is self-interest. The end goal of utilitarianism is majority-satisfaction. Alas, these are questionable ends, and the question hangs upon *the way the world is* (the design or end goal for the created order), including the nature and purpose of human beings as moral agents and social creatures. Now *this* is a teleological question, but it is not concerned merely with the end goal of one's desired action or ideology. Rather, it is a question of whether there *is* a created order—a way-things-should-go—and with it, a question of whether human beings have an intrinsic value and purpose. Neither egoism nor utilitarianism is able to answer these teleological questions satisfactorily. Higher ideals of created order, like intrinsic value tethered to human nature and purpose—human rights—find no convincing grounding within the "end goal" of majority-happiness or self-interest. For this reason, it is far more helpful to speak of "consequentialist" theories when referring to theories ultimately concerned with consequences or situational outcomes, and to reserve the term "teleological" purposefully for a deeper moral dialogue, as in whether reality is imbued with a moral order.

One can better appreciate the philosophical weight of this term, and the notion of an end "goal" or "fulfillment," by studying the Aristotelian sense of a final cause. Aristotle famously distinguished between four types of causes, yet when he spoke of an end, a final cause, it was an especially pregnant concept which carried with it everything else—all the other types of causation and the key to understanding the what and, especially, the *why* of a thing.[16] What is a house? 1) A house is something made of bricks, wood, or some other substance. These are the *material causes*; they do "cause" the house to come into being (if they are moved to that end by something else). But this is not a satisfactory answer to the question. 2) A house is an enclosed space, covered with a roof, with partitions separating larger rooms from smaller rooms, doors, areas with plumbing, and the like. This is the *formal cause*—the house comes to be as it adheres to the blueprint; the design "causes" the materials to take a particular form.

This answer is still not enough, however; a house is more than its rooms, and its overall form is inconsequential to "house-ness" if houses can take different forms. 3) A house is that which housebuilders build (the builders are an *efficient cause*, giving motion to the materials and shaping them into their intended form). Of course, while it is true that builders indeed "cause" the house to come to be, this still does not answer the question, what *is* a house. It is only when a house is completed—at the very least, the *idea* of a house, in the mind of an architect—that one can understand the nature and purpose of a house and thereby answer the question: 4) a house is something which, once completed, provides shelter, rest, relief, and privacy. It is only at the *end* of these other processes that we can understand a thing's *purpose*.

What is Pinocchio? Pinocchio is wood. This is true, but the material cause is not enough. Pinocchio is wood that has been carved in a particular way, assembled in a particular way, and painted in a particular way. Pinocchio is a composite of wooden pieces, carved and painted, connected to one another with bolts and hinges, and perhaps glue, held up by strings which have been fastened to yet other pieces of wood. We might even add that Pinocchio is a wooden thing that has been crafted to look like — it has the form of — a boy. This formal cause does not really tell us what Pinocchio *is*. A Pinocchio is a wooden craft, which Geppetto has created. It is the wooden product of a wood-carver's hand. It is the invention of this inventor.

This efficient-cause explanation is not enough either. What *is* Pinocchio — what is the purpose of a Pinocchio? Pinocchio is foremost a puppet. It is meant to function as puppets do. Yet *Pinocchio* is not the tale of a mere puppet. This Puppet was meant to fill a void — to serve as the symbol of the son for which Geppetto longed. Because of the blessing of the Blue Fairy, the puppet was enlivened and thus able to serve a different end, as a son. Moreover, this Pinocchio, though still a puppet, was given a chance to *become* yet something more. The story of *Pinocchio* is a tale of two transformations in the final cause (telos) of one mere puppet. The first transformation requires only a change in the efficient cause (magic, a miracle was needed). The second is a complete transformation in nature. To become a real boy will require additional stuff, and so a moral conscience becomes part of his efficient cause (in addition to the requisite magic) and moral character becomes part of his formal cause. What is a Pinocchio? A Pinocchio is a *real boy* — a moral agent — who was once a mere puppet.

According to Aristotle, knowledge necessarily gets at the "why" question. The former explanations are necessary variables for a complete picture. You cannot have a house without building materials, builders, and a blueprint. Without a final end, however, these explanations are insufficient to answer the question. So too with the question, what is the good? What *is* morality? An assertion or definition of what *seems* good — *a* "good," — is not enough to speak of *the* good. Utilitarianism, for example, offers an assertion of what seems to be a "good" outcome for the majority, yet utilitarianism does not really answer the question of morality; it only raises the grounding problem and questions about the nature and purpose (the final end or *telos*) of moral conviction. (This is why, again, it would be more helpful overall if people would stop thinking of consequentialist theories like utilitarianism as "teleological" theories; the resulting ambiguity potentially hinders the real teleological dialogue which needs to take place).

Telos is bound up with what a thing is *meant to be*. Since a goal (meant-to-be-ness) brings with it the idea of hitting the mark, actions (even goals) carry a potential for missing the mark. A pile of building materials dumped on the ground by builders holding blueprints of a house is not a house. It is a deficient example of a house and the builders have performed poorly. Doing something in the most excellent way (in the case of the builders) or being or becoming what one is meant to be (in the case of the house) is called virtue (excellence). Thus, questions of virtue are inseparable from questions of telos (purpose), which is why Harvard professor and political philosopher Michael Sandel has observed that most political debates are really disagreements over questions of *telos*.[17] Is abortion good or permissible in most cases? Is transgender ideology correct? Is it true that there is no way-it-should-be when it comes to sex, sexuality, or marriage? These examples of political dispute are not really questions of greater happiness or self-interest; they are questions concerning the way the world is and whether there is an intended order (a way the world ought to be), intrinsic human value, a designated human nature and purpose, an archetype for familial institutions, and a higher moral standard of social expectation for human action. There is something that stands out about virtue ethics, and the question of *telos* is key both to virtue ethics and to moral dialogue.

Disney's Virtue Motif

Disney's repertoire is replete with an interest in character development through archetypes of virtue and vice, and, while different narratives spotlight different virtues, vice is commonly depicted as egoism and *hubris*.[18] Utilitarianism is often an implied question as protagonists struggle with culture, tradition, perspective, and practice over the nature of goodness and the question of what is truly in everyone's greater interest. *Pinocchio* struggles with moral duties. Yet, the point and purpose of *Pinocchio* isn't his ability to keep moral commands *per se*, but a celebration of his becoming a *real* boy, cultivating such excellence in character as to transfigure him into a more beautiful and profound being—from a simulation and mere copy to actual flesh and blood.

Beauty and the Beast is the story of a Prince wrestling with his own *hubris* and inability to extend charity. His physical form becomes a direct reflection of his heart. Belle is an archetype of beauty—modeling bravery, justice, fortitude, altruism and sacrifice, though struggling with self-control when it comes to respecting Beast's request and privacy. As Beast begins to grow in light of Belle's influence, she observes, "There must be something there that wasn't there before."[19] She connects goodness with his change of disposition and development of character. At the end of the 2017 live-action adaptation, Beast makes explicit what was implied but unstated in the 1991 animated original. As Gaston pleads, "Don't hurt me beast," the cursed prince responds mercifully, declaring, "I am *not* a beast!"[20] (Actually, it is Gaston who turns out to be the real beast. As Clopin Trouillefou would later riddle concerning Quasimodo and Claude Frollo, "Who is the monster and who is the man?"[21]).

The whole problem in *Moana*, namely Te Kā, results from the fact that Te Fiti's heart is not in its proper place. Moana redeems her antagonist, singing, "This is not who you are! You *know* who you are!"[22] To be who one is meant to be is an issue of *telos* and character. Maui wishes to be whatever will make others love him. Although there are some existential undertones[23] in Moana's self-declaration, "the call isn't out there at all, it's inside me... I am Moana,"[24] she is driven by a sense of identity and meant-to-be-ness. Tamatoa tries to be beautiful by equating identity with an accumulation of goods. Others seek Te Fiti's heart to acquire a sense of identity through power. Yet identity turns out to be teleological; ideally, it involves learning to become the best version of who we are meant to be—knowing our place within a created and meaningful order and seeking excellence in light of it.

The Lion King asks us, what is the nature and character of a good king? Of a good son? Simba is meant to be an heir and ambassador of his father's kingdom. Scar is the epitome of pride and self-assertion through deceit and manipulation, even murder. Here, we gain insight into another aspect of virtue theory. Virtue is realized in victory over one's internal struggle, wherein reason dominates desire and spirit or ego.[25] Mufasa's reign is tempered by wisdom and self-control (in his reason and respect for the Order, the Circle of Life, and in his use of power). Scar, however, is driven by pride—his desire is for mere power. Even Simba, as a cub, exhibits this misunderstanding of what it means to be a king, and he just can't wait for the power to look down on others and become his own moral authority. The real devastation of Scar's reign is seen in the aftermath of the hyenas. When those with insatiable appetites were allowed free expression without self-control and respect for an underlying order, everyone suffered. According to Aristotle, the habituation of the appetite is central to the acquisition of virtue.[26] Every virtue lies at the mean between two extremes—excess and deficiency. We must condition our appetites and desires, developing habits of self-control rather than excess, while also reorienting a deficient understanding of, love for, and will to seek and model the Good. Given the subjective quality of this struggle, however, how can one be sure she has obtained virtue? What does virtue look like? How is it defined? While habits can be conditioned, and principles of virtue taught, the apprehension and grasp of virtue is often best realized from finding and imitating moral exemplars—archetypes of excellence. Simba must learn what courage looks like in the face of fear and guilt. Once a king, he will have to model justice as well. What better model to imitate than Mufasa—a pillar of strength and compassion, power and wisdom?

Disney presents us with numerous archetypes of virtue but refrains from simply giving us fully-formed moral exemplars. Disney stories invite us to *live through* its characters' moral development. We are asked to see their faults or in some cases, the injustices with which they are faced and to feel (as they feel) that there is something morally deficient either within them or surrounding their circumstances. We sense (as they sense) that there is something better, morally superior, to which we are all called, even amidst unfortunate circumstances. And through these stories, we live through their reorientation toward or recovery of the good and recognize beauty in association with their acquisition or demonstrations of moral virtue. We are called to approve of its association with the good life and finally to want something similar for ourselves. Having lived through these characters' stories, Disney presents us with moral models—archetypes—not of moral perfection (more like diamonds in the rough), but nevertheless beautiful characters on the right track, growing toward goodness.

Although *Aladdin*'s impoverished context has reduced him to theft for the sake of survival, he still has a protector's heart for the poor, their dignity and worth, even giving up his stolen meal for the sake of another.[27] In this regard, he represents altruism and justice rather than egoism. Nevertheless, he doubts the beauty and value of a good heart when it is all he has to offer and is tempted to place self-interest over truthfulness. Thus, Genie pleads, "*Be* yourself!"[28] Though he may be rough around the edges, this "diamond in the rough" wins the interest of Jasmine, who cares more for the quality of heart than status and money, which naturally speaks highly of her character. Aladdin's struggle is ultimately one with his own heart.

In *The Little Mermaid*, we do not see a lot of character development in Ariel, whose adolescent impulses lead her to act imprudently in ways that bring harm to others. However, she does display fortitude in her fight for love. Nevertheless, the weight of her wager is not lost on her audience, and the film highlights several virtues and vices in others. Ursula is an egoist, with a gluttonous appetite for power and revenge. We see Triton struggling with charity because of a prejudice he holds against humans. Flounder and Sebastian, refreshing additions to the cast of characters, represent the virtue of loyalty. While we will not go into detail about the two films, loyalty is a central theme in both *The Fox and the Hound* and *Toy Story*.

Cinderella is the poster child for fortitude, hope, and humility. The live-action edition significantly enhanced both the backstory and insight into Ella's character and emphasized "have courage and be kind" as its primary theme.[29] Ella is the sort of person who forgives her wrongdoers. When she finally presents herself unadorned to the prince, she introduces herself as Cinderella, not Ella, for she understood that what she had been through had become a significant part of who she was. *Dumbo* is also a story of perseverance. Specifically, his is a tale of fortitude in seeking dignity amidst diversity.

Snow White's character is more superficial. We do see bravery and kindness, even an intercessory prayer, but we infer her beauty more in contrast to what she is not—an envious egoist driven to murder. The ugly hag represents the queen's true nature; the only fruit that such characters offer others is poisonous. A self-interested butler is willing to kidnap and abandon *The Aristocats* for the sake of fortune. *Robin Hood* targets sociopolitical injustices against the poor, contrasting Prince John's greed and selfishness with Robin's compassion and self-sacrifice.[30] *The Black Cauldron* depicts self-sacrifice as the most potent defeater of the most formidable evil. In *Oliver & Company*, Fagin perseveres to develop the courage to stand up for justice, even when doing so is not in his best interest. Though deceitful, Mulan demonstrates sacrifice on behalf of both her father and country. Hercules learns that it is only in practicing self-sacrificial love that one *becomes* a true hero, worthy of fellowship with the gods.

It seems that only a certain quality of character can retrieve *The Sword in the Stone* and Arthur is the one who fits the bill as he represents courtesy, honesty, loyalty, fortitude, a love for learning, and a desire to do good in service to others. While *The Rescuers* enlivens our concern for justice and charity, we also find Penny modeling both cardinal and theological virtues (courage and fortitude; faith and hope) in the face of kidnapping and child exploitation—while greed and egoism drives Medusa. In *The Hunchback of Notre Dame*, Frollo hides the excesses of his own appetites behind a condemnation of others. We see beauty in a deformed Quasimodo, while we abhor the "Justice" Minister who is so quick to justify genocide and infanticide for his own purposes. *The Emperor's New Groove* demonstrates how egoism can breed bitterness and ultimately backfire. Perhaps self-preoccupation is not really in one's self-interest. *One Hundred and One Dalmatians* sets the altruistic advocate for animals and their worth against the egoistical hedonist—that cruel devil, Cruella de Vil.

Fiercely independent Tiana (The Princess and the Frog) exemplifies fortitude and perseverance in her work ethic and in pursuing her dream, but she finds transformation only after learning to trust others and being willing to give up the very thing she longed for. She learns she cannot just rely on herself and that her personal ambitions are paramount. In so doing, she achieved what she wanted from the start (her restaurant) but with the interdependency of a greater and newfound love. Naveen and Lawrence are both egoists. Charlotte is self-absorbed as well. Yet Charlotte is willing to sacrifice her own dream for Tiana and the maturing Naveen is willing to sacrifice his own happiness for the sake of Tiana's dream. Shadow Man's lust for power consumes him, as do the devils with which he dabbles.

Tangled is a tale of child abduction and deceit, all in the name of self-interest. Flynn began as an egoist, but his journey found transformation within the beauty of Rapunzel's compassionate heart and the refreshing innocence of her perspective. Rapunzel's struggle is more epistemological than moral. The moral concern of the film focuses on Flynn's heart in contrast to Gothel's. *Sleeping Beauty* explores archetypes of valor and vice in Phillip and Maleficent. We are only given a superficial understanding of Aurora's character, but she is understood to be loyal, honest, and respectful of her guardians and their rules. Examples abound, but this overview is sufficient to support the claim that the Disney canon is strongly concerned with virtue ethics.

4

Kingdom-Oriented Archetypes in Disney's Animated Moral Canon

A s we have seen, virtue lies at the heart of Disney's moral canon, yet Disney's moral metanarrative is more complex and robust than virtue ethics alone. Disney's films love to underscore the point that good will triumph, that we have more strength than we realize, and that even *The Small One* has a significant role to play, but also, importantly, that justice and injustice, good and evil, are issues that begin with a question, and reflect the condition, of one's heart. Recurrent themes include Nobility and the Kingdom, hope for the Orphan (even tramps and alley cats), rescue and redemption of the Lost, the Cursed and the Savior; the Beautiful and the Atrocious, and, relatedly, the Virtuous contra the Egoist. Even when the primary theme is not that of hero or heroine contra villain (as in *Frozen*), virtue remains a major motif and egoism still plays a minor role (such as Prince Hans). Those virtues "which should bind us together for a better world"[1] are frequently presented as faith, fortitude, hope, humility, courage, compassion and an altruistic love—many of which require the virtue of temperance.

Disney's emphasis on archetypes of virtue and vice indeed points us toward a virtue-oriented ethics, but this ethics looks toward a particular end, a particular vision of the Good Life, an ever-after happiness—and that ever-after is often, interestingly, depicted as a kingdom. Disney's fascination with the kingdom motif is no secret. Disney parks are built around kingdom-oriented themes and the castle logo has become unmistakably connected to the name Walt Disney. What Disney's parks and kingdom-oriented films seem to share is an attempt to grasp a sense of the Good. In its films, Disney communicates certain things about the Kingdom-ever-after. It is a place where injustices cease and justice reigns—the Good always triumphs—and certain superior moral impulses bind us together. Thus, while Walt Disney features are largely nonsectarian, the overall moral concern of the most celebrated animated features in the canon has often aligned with a classical Christian moral narrative—one that is framed in light of a teleological way-it-should-be and a future-kingdom-oriented eschatology. The theological significance of this kingdom-oriented vision warrants unpacking, but it must be understood that such a kingdom is most clearly realized through its representative inhabitants.

The Power of Archetype and Disney's Kingdom-Oriented Eschatology

Archetypes are essential in moral storytelling. Shades of gray continually complicate contextual considerations, so classical narratives are often idealistic, not realistic. Yet archetypal clarity is an effective tool for navigating situational complexity. Models or representatives are essential in virtue education—indeed, in most education, principles are not enough; examples are needed. Narrative structure itself often relies upon archetypal contrast: context, conflict, resolution; Creation, Fall, Redemption. In moral storytelling, we are often meant to contemplate higher ideals—namely, goodness, *telos* and, relatedly, justice—and we often do so more effectively through archetypal contrast.

Because it plays such an important role in cultural narratives, archetype has become a subject of particular interest to psychologists, and, as it is applicable to theological narratives as well, theology is able to suggest some important implications connected to the role that archetypes can play in orienting our attention toward the consideration of higher ideals and deeper truths. As Alister McGrath explains,

> Carl Jung famously suggested that certain 'universal psychic structures' underlie human experience and behavior—an idea taken up in Joseph Campbell's influential account of the fundamental plotline of stories, such as the 'myth of the hero.' [From this,] Campbell developed the notion of 'monomyth'—the idea that all mythic narratives are basically variations of a single

great story, so that a common pattern can be discerned beneath
the narrative elements of most great myths.[2]

Responding to a question of fascination with the fact that such diverse
cultures can still share an overwhelming amount of similarities when it
comes to myths, Joseph Campbell stated that "one explanation is that the
human psyche is essentially the same all over the world.... Out of this common ground have come what Jung has called archetypes, which are the common ideas of myths."[3] While we certainly do not lean heavily on Jung, we
think in this instance he is onto something. We think Beauty is one of these
archetypes, along with the Kingdom-ever after (which we think is not simply
"the good life," but rather a deep sense of justice, that something wrong has
been set right, and the goodness of the Kingdom-ever-after is reflected in the
renewed hearts and minds of its citizens). In light of this, it is worth pondering Disney's kingdom-oriented interest in archetypes of virtue.

In so far as Disney means to communicate that a certain caliber of character—demonstrated through different archetypes of virtue—is directly associated with the beauty of a goodness-ever-after (especially, since the
archetypes of virtue are often presented as archetypes of nobility), then the
Kingdom is a sort of archetype in itself. This recurrent motif of the beauty
and goodness of the ever-after becomes a sort of model. The Kingdom of
Goodness looks like *that*. Its representative inhabitants—its noble ambassadors—look like *this*. If you wish to aim for such a kingdom, then you ought
to imitate the sort of characters who dwell there; reach for the Kingdom-ever-
after by aiming to become like its model citizens. There is, then, an intwining
relationship between Disney's virtue motif and its interest in beauty and
kingdoms. The Kingdom is unmistakably tied to beauty, as it is meant to
communicate something about an everlasting Beauty. And beauty is implicitly tethered to character, that is to virtue. To speak of Disney's recurrent
Kingdom motif is to call to mind the sort of characters who dwell there.

Thus, many Disney characters—especially Disney nobility—are presented as archetypes of this Kingdom-ever-after, and as we encounter more
of these Kingdom ambassadors, the Kingdom itself begins to come into view.
The Kingdom is *like* that; it involves *that* kind of goodness. Notice that we do
not ever really get to see and experience the Kingdom itself. It is not in the
here-and-now but the there-after—after justice is realized, goodness has
overcome evil, love abounds, and we have grown into a certain sort of character. Experiencing the magic of Disney parks is the closest thing that Disney
can offer to an actual Kingdom-experience, and while it may indeed be the

most magical place on earth, it still leaves us wanting where the kingdom implied at the end of Disney stories, yet never experienced by the audience, communicates a fullness where everything is as it should be, goodness abounds, and joy knows no cessation. Disney parks may help us to forget our anxieties momentarily, but they do not really help us to glimpse the Kingdom. The deep magic which the parks possess is the power of nostalgia — and that capitalizes on an enchantment already within us, a longing for the fulfillment of the Kingdom which was promised in the Disney films most park-goers have already lived through. The closest we can ever really get to glimpsing the Kingdom-ever-after is to see a representative goodness modeled through its ambassadors.

Now, the term archetype can carry a few senses, and so it is worth clarifying the sense in which we are speaking. In the most general sense, an archetype is a representative, especially ideal, example. Cinderella, for instance, exemplifies kindness and fortitude amidst suffering. In another sense, archetype can refer to a perfect original of which all other examples are merely imitations. In this sense, Cinderella is not the archetype; even she is merely reaching for a standard modeled foremost and perfectly, and prescribed, by Jesus Christ. A third sense views archetypes as inherent concepts — certain ideas present in the backdrop of the collective human subconscious. The moral apologist will quickly point out that Beauty, Goodness, and the notion of a Just-Order indeed seem to lie at the foundations of collective human conviction. Thus, whatever one believes about moral truth and the afterlife, it can be argued that the notion of a Kingdom-ever-after qualifies as a candidate for being considered an archetype in this sense, and when we speak of the Kingdom-ever-after we are speaking in terms of an appeal to a deep conviction within each of us — an ardent longing for the Just-Order and the Good life, and a belief that it entails beauty and goodness (and even, that love in some sense may be entwined with these concepts). When we speak of archetypes of nobility or virtue or Beauty (the beautiful soul), however, we are speaking in the first and more general sense, of examples, depictions of the sort of person meant to be associated in some way with the Kingdom-ever-after.

Although many approach ethics and aesthetic as different realms of investigation, many philosophers — from the ancient Greek philosophers Plato and Aristotle to eighteenth-century English philosopher Anthony Ashley Cooper and contemporary Swedish philosopher Elisabeth Schellekens have suspected, and rightly so, that the aesthetic and the ethical are actually two sides of the same coin. They are two modes of investigating the same realm of experience, namely, value conviction. Moreover, some philosophers have insightfully realized that beauty and goodness work together to point to something else—a right order. Thomas Aquinas understood that beauty describes our delight in right order, due proportion, while goodness refers to our desire to know the right order realized and experienced.[4] Justice entails a right-order. Because we *long* for such a state of just-ness (a world free of injustice, suffering, and evil), we associate goodness with the fulfillment of that desire. (There are other theological factors to be considered in relation to our desire for the Kingdom, but we are speaking here primarily of Disney's kingdom-oriented vision and the fact that Goodness and Beauty are related to a sense of and longing for justice realized in the Kingdom). Because we sense that the Kingdom is *like that*—that there is a right-order implied— we associate beauty with the idea of the Kingdom..

Kingdom Theology and Disney's Store of Theological Symbols

Because archetypes—representative examples—are so effective in contrasting good with evil and that which is beautiful with that which is undesirable, Disney speaks most powerfully and broadly about goodness and beauty when it narrates through Kingdom-oriented archetypal ideals—of virtue, of beauty, of nobility. Yet Disney also likes to present us with representatives of ourselves, of our own struggles and often seems to suggest that the human condition is not beyond hope of experiencing the goodness of the Kingdom or acquiring the virtues representative of its citizens. There is much to unpack here. Let us first (in this chapter) consider the potential theological symbolism to be drawn from certain specific archetypes and motifs—less generalizable though more obvious—which resonate with certain themes in Christian theology, before moving on to consider how the more generalizable archetypes of character and Disney's kingdom-oriented ethics are similarly enfolded by the Christian vision of the Kingdom-ever-after.

Layered as they are, Disney archetypes and motifs naturally become more robust when viewed through a theological lens. The following deliberation is not meant to assert exclusivist prescriptions for interpreting Disney films, but simply to suggest potentially powerful analogies for drawing interdisciplinary connections between Disney films and Christian theology. Disney films lend themselves easily (and interestingly) to theological interpretations built around the symbolism of kingdom theology, which emphasizes both spiritual warfare in the present age and the eventual triumph of good over evil in the age to come. The conviction "that good can always triumph over evil"[5] was, by Walt's own admission, the central tenet of Disney's moral concern. The Christian story can be summarized in the word "kingdom" and expressed through five central points:[6] God (King and Judge); mankind (human condition or the curse); Jesus (the redeemer and archetype of virtue and true love); Cross (death to the curse, the single act of redemption and a daily struggle and self-sacrifice); and Resurrection (restoration of all things, final justice, the coming of the kingdom-ever-after). Disney presses similarly into themes of the curse, virtue, true-love, an inner-struggle with self-sacrifice, and a final justice in the Kingdom-ever-after— and occasionally into the nature of the good king.

Two key themes in Christian theology are the inner struggle between self-assertion and self-control,[7] and spiritual warfare (a war over ideas and impulses[8]) with Satan and principalities and powers.[9] Satan, importantly, is also known as the serpent, the father of lies,[10] the epitome of *hubris*.[11] The Christian journey involves dying to one's natural disposition—*hubris*—and growing into the image of Christ—truthfulness, temperance, and Love and Charity (*agape and caritas*).[12] *Aladdin* portrays this symbolism potently. Struggling with both truth, identity, and self-interest, in certain ways, Aladdin can be seen as an archetype of Humanity (the Human Condition) while Jafar, driven by *hubris*, reveals his serpentine nature—playing well the archetype of the Devil. Like Satan, Jafar's pride is his fall.

We are often devils unto ourselves, as there seems to be a war raging within. For the unbeliever, this war is with the conscience (until it is muted or seared) and the flesh (though always ultimately unsuccessful in fighting it). For the believer, it is a war between flesh and the reborn spirit, with the aid of the Spirit. It is important to note that these dynamics are no respecter of persons. We can easily find the Humanity archetype not only among paupers (Aladdin), but also among princes; Beast (*Beauty and the Beast*) and Naveen (*The Princess and the Frog*) are royals wrestling with rotten dispositions. Interestingly, Flynn Rider's (*Tangled*) real name means "well born." He holds a name of nobility, yet hedonism grips his heart.[13] After finding transformation of disposition and committing to love, Eugene (alias Flynn Rider, *Tangled*) embraces the name he was meant to carry. Even princess Merida (*Brave*) must learn that the greatest variable shaping her fate is pride.

In *The Lion King* , we see Scar as the tempter and accuser, a stalking lion,[14] envious of the king. He seems to occupy the Devil archetype. Simba, on the other hand, reflects the Christian calling to inherit the kingdom after Mufasa's sacrifice, in his struggle with the guilt of his past, and in acquiring identity in Mufasa's indwelling spirit. Annalee Ward noted that *The Lion King* actually encompasses the biblical stories "of paradise, the fall, desert wandering, the reign of Satan, the need for a savior, and the cataclysmic destruction of the earth, followed by the return of the savior who restores peace and the beginning of his full reign as rightful king."[15] She urges her reader to compare the elephant graveyard with the state of the earth in the last days before the return of Christ.[16] The early films are especially rich with the restoration motif.

The Great Theo-Drama: A Princess, a Curse, a Prince, and a Dragon

Though its central theme is kingdom, the majority of the biblical narrative is framed between the onset of a curse,[17] which inhibits the original goodness, and its restoration in the coming of God's kingdom, which entails the fullness of justice and the cessation of the curse.[18] Likewise, Disney has revealed a fascination with curses and deep magic (which seems to serve as the nonsectarian symbol of spirituality).[19] In *Moana*, the curse correlates to a profaning of an original order. In *Beauty and the Beast,* the curse correlates to an inability to love and a preoccupation with shallow conceptions of beauty. We note it was only the truest beauty and love that could liberate the captives and lift the curse.[20] In *Brave*, curses are connected to mishandled magic and pride, while reconciliation is required for breaking the curse. Elsa's magic (*Frozen*) is a gift, but also a potential for great harm if misused. In *Frozen II*, injustice has profaned an original beauty, and nature has retaliated. Tiana (*The Princess and the Frog*) is indirectly cursed because Shadow Man dabbles with demons, and we lament Ariel's (*The Little Mermaid*) desperation to deal with dark forces, wagering her future and freedom on an optimistic impulse.

One of the most fascinating and theologically rich depictions of human-condition-as-curse comes from *Raya and the Last Dragon*, as the *Druun* represents a sickness in the world which (1) came from human hearts, (2) turns human hearts to stone, and (3) both dissolves human communities and increases human antipathies. *Encanto*, highly celebrated for its depiction of diversities and its attention to culturally significant details, continues the fascination with curses, yet does so from a different angle. Instead of beginning with the move from a state of perfection which progressed to a cursed condition, the backstory of *Encanto* begins with the human condition (misfortune, the problem of pain, and perseverance amidst persecution) and then transitions to a state of *blessing*. The curse which arises is presented as a potential impending *loss* of blessing resulting from pride and an inability to understand the true nature of family and community — the *sharing* of blessing and burden. This may not depict the human-condition-proper, but it effectively communicates some aspects of the human condition at the level of family and village. It also allows for degrees of *hubris*. Rather than seeing pride as only a willful opposition to authority, *Encanto* suggests that perhaps pride can also arise from a combination of fear, pain, pressure, and perspective. However it arises, it always carries a potential for discord. It seems undeniable that there has been a clear interest in the motif of the curse, from Disney's first animated feature film, in 1937, to its more recent features in 2021. (We have only explored films between 1937 and 2021) .

Apart from theology, *Snow White* may present one of the most superficial takes on the prince-princess motif. Through the lens of kingdom theology, however, "Someday my prince will come"[21] is saturated with eschatological significance, notwithstanding those who see it only as patronizing sexism. Mark Pinsky suggests Snow White is a portrait of sin and salvation — the profaning of Eden with an apple and a curse.[22] He even observes the seemingly divine intervention when justice is served to the evil queen. Equally symbolic, hope lies in a future king. Returning on a white horse, he resurrects the beautiful from a deathlike sleep, breaking the curse. Something is missing, however, from Disney's debut; there is no sacrifice with Snow White's prince as there is with Phillip (*Sleeping Beauty*) and later with Anna (*Frozen, Frozen II*). Just as folklore is often expressed through a number of variations, *Cinderella* is a recast of *Snow White*.[23] Yet it comes not in the form of curse, salvation, and resurrection, but rather in the form of tragedy, transformation, and restoration. Thrown into the problem of evil, like Job, Ella endures much suffering with a potent and inspiring faith in goodness, and eventually her tragedy is transformed into triumph over her circumstantial misfortunes.

Here, Prince Charming is not Christ-as-savior, but acting Christ-like, he sets his love upon Ella, pursues her relentlessly, and rejoices over her.[24] While Ella is not forced to marry Charming against her will (free will is not wholly absent), she is invited to do so. Here we run into a point of theological dispute over the nature of free will, but some perspectives may find significance in the point that Charming's pursuit of Ella is not contingent upon whether she will accept the invitation; he pursues her because of *his* love for her. Moreover, he does not pursue her because she is royalty. He pursues her because he sees something appropriate about her heart. Again, we run up against theological points of tension here because, from an orthodox (small o) perspective, it must be stressed that God does not pursue us because *we* are worthy (as it can be argued that, given her virtue, Ella is worthy of a royal's pursuit), but rather because *He* deems it good to bring us into His presence and Kingdom. And yet, part of the point of Cinderella's tale is to emphasize the almost unbelievable notion that royalty would pursue a seemingly insignificant "nobody," and this *is* what is presented in the biblical account of a perfect God pursuing mankind.[25] Thus, Ella may or may not serve as an apt symbol of humanity when it comes to questions of free will in the acquisition of virtue and in relation to God's pursuit of the human being.

Yet Ella does serve well as an archetype of the human condition regarding the problem of evil and suffering. Regardless of one's perspective on issues of dogmatic theology, in so far as one is comfortable with the analogy of God relentlessly pursuing the individual who is fighting to know and demonstrate virtue amidst a context of depravity, suffering, and injustice, Ella's tale of the pursuing prince is not unlike that of the Good Shepherd.[26] And in many ways, Ella demonstrates the faith, fortitude amidst persecution, and lovingkindness to which the Christian is called.

At this point, as we step in and out of Christian symbolism, a point of delimitation might be helpful. Some who approach Disney films through a Christian lens expect a Disney film to "give the gospel," that is, to present a coherent portrayal of salvation. If not, and especially if the characters' transformation comes from within the character and without an apparent external agent, a mediator, some Christian readers may be tempted to reject the film as offering anything of theological substance. Our readers should understand that we do not approach this book with that presuppositional lens. We take the characters as they are and the story on its own terms, and we ponder how the film, as it is presented, may yet be enfolded by any aspect of Christian theology. In some cases, this may be a portrait of salvation, or an aspect of salvation, but in many cases it maybe a portrait of some other aspect of the human condition, if not a portrait of spiritual struggle and growth.

In a historical context saturated with Christian teaching about the self-centered nature of the heart, the transformative nature of love and a profound goodness in subverting one's own interests on behalf of another's goodness, it is possible that some aspects of salvation (namely the struggle with moral depravity and the transformation of character in association with a sacrificial love) might have been assumed into the background moral imaginary. Even if the particulars of the experience which led to the change of heart—which is important dialogue to have—are stripped from the narrative, and whether or not this is due to the presuppositions of a theistic or humanist lens; whatever its terms, a story may still be enfolded by some aspect of the biblical drama. The Christian story is a story of reality and of humanity—as it was intended to be, as it is, and as it is called to become—and other stories may press into any point of conviction along these lines.

Perhaps *Sleeping Beauty* provides the most potent Christian symbolism in all of Disney lore—even if it is a recapitulation, in many ways, of Snow White. Though previously blessed to experience a life of beauty, Aurora's curse is inescapable. Although it cannot be undone, it can be softened by hope. Consequence is inevitable, yet salvation remains possible, but only if kissed by true love; and this requires war with the Dragon holding power over the cursed. Bearing spiritually symbolic armor[27]—a shield of virtue (faith?) and the sword of truth[28]—Phillip, an effective Christ archetype is willing to fight the serpent to save the cursed. Note that Aurora does not need saving because she is a woman; she needs saving because she is cursed. Nor is Phillip required to save her; he saves her because he loves her. Just as Jesus is the original Archetype of true and sacrificial love incarnate, the prince to rule as king in the ever-after, so too this imperfect yet admirable prince serves as archetype of the Christ. The princess is rescued from the curse and restored to know the riches of life and love in the Kingdom-ever-after.

The film is framed in terms of the curse and an eschatological showdown, consequently there is only marginal attention given to the loss of the good life and the subsequent identity crisis. Yet, the woods—the context between the onset and cessation of the curse—is *our* setting. C. A. McIntosh offers compelling and intriguing questions pertaining to Aurora's knowledge while dreaming.[29] Does she even know she is cursed? Her question is ours as well. In the depths of depravity, do we really understand our moral brokenness? Most do not. Whatever Aurora's level of awareness, a battle was raging over her. Pinsky insisted that this was the last time the resurrection motif was used.[30] To the contrary, however, the resurrection motif continued to show up, albeit in new ways. Consider the resurrection of the

Beast (*Beauty and the Beast*) and Flynn Rider (*Tangled*), or the unfreezing of Princess Anna (in *Frozen*) and Elsa (in *Frozen II*). Furthermore, the broader theme of redemption has remained prominent throughout the history of Disney films.

Disney stories no doubt carry great potential for drawing out some of the more obvious themes in Christian theology, and this may be useful in so far as one wishes to use Disney stories to help communicate certain truths about Christianity—about curses and the human condition, about spiritual battles between good and evil, and about the problem of pride, an ongoing, internal battle between conscience and desire. Still, the critic might challenge that, while it is possible to draw out such themes from Disney stories in order to consider how they might symbolize aspects of systematic theology, this does not mean that Disney narratives in themselves align with the Christian story of reality—that Christianity *enfolds* Disney tales. This is a fair challenge, at this point, and demonstrates the need to look more closely at Disney's more generalizable archetypes of beauty and nobility, the seemingly Christian nature of Disney's kingdom-oriented ethics, and the significant role that a self-less love plays in the Kingdom-ever-after. The next three chapters take up these themes respectively.

5

Imagining the Kingdom: Archetypes of Beauty and the Moral Enchantment of Disney's Aesthetic Allure

The moral power of Disney's animated features finds its source in the significance of mimetic idealism and archetypal contrast. Disney's appreciation for symbolism is extensive—observable even in character names[1]—but the attention given to archetypal and motivic symbolism is particularly powerful. It is precisely this appreciation for symbolism (along with the well-composed music, of course) that makes Disney lore so accessible. The significance of archetypal symbolism in storytelling is akin to the importance of balance between familiarity and repetition and unfamiliarity and change in music. Psychologically, lackluster repetition tends to bore listeners, while excess complexity and unfamiliarity can lead to frustration and disconnection, thereby hindering appreciation. We desire both fulfillment of and challenges to expectation.[2]

With narrative, while we do expect new challenges, as contexts vary, we also long for a sense of accessibility in order to live vicariously through them. As Monique Wonderly has argued, it is character accessibility through which children's films are able to expand moral reasoning by drawing children into pondering the human condition.[3] While Disney animation indeed plays a role in character accessibility, more interestingly, Disney's depiction of beauty also seems to play a role in communicating something about the virtuous soul, the Kingdom ambassador—thereby communicating something about the Kingdom-ever-after itself.

As an aside, but related, there is a problem with any attempt at universal, public moral education. As B. Edward McClellan has shown, in his historical survey of *Moral Education in America*, secular attempts at moral education have continually failed for lack of grounding, and non-sectarian approaches have proven difficult because morality is so tightly tethered to worldview presumptions and deeply informed by the value hierarchies that follow. Moreover, moral definitions and public education itself are both susceptible to politicization. Thus, no moral education can really be inclusive of all worldview narratives.[4] The question of morality, however, is not what best accommodates the majority of beliefs, but what is right—and this, of course, means that some views are wrong. Although a satisfactorily robust moral education is not possible in a secularized and non-sectarian, universal education system, Disney has shown us how an artistic approach to non-sectarian ambiguity and an archetypal appeal to an objective morality can allow the arts to speak as broadly as possible from a non-sectarian starting point achieving an ability to educate about morality, where traditional institutions of education and schooling have found it more difficult.

There is another, related difficulty, however. One can come to different conclusions depending on one's method of analysis. From a strictly psychological perspective, some Disney characters are not good role models as they are. From Virtue theory, however, we look beyond to who they are meant to be or who they are becoming. From a socio-cultural approach, or from the lens of critical social theory, one may find problematic cultural representations (and this is complicated by the fact that Disney lore spans several cultural contexts). As Annalee Ward observed, "The stories children are exposed to will form the standards for testing the truth of other stories later in life. Consequently, charges of racism, sexism, misrepresentation of history, and so on, particularly in children's films, are not something to be taken lightly. If children believe that what they see represents a true picture of life, then the potential for cultural change and growth is diminished."[5] In our own context, amidst culture-wars surrounding questions of the nature of identity, gender, sexuality, family structures, uses of technology, and institutional power, this rings especially true.

As Mark Pinsky explains, in the aftermath of Disney's 1937 debut, "a social contract was born. Parents could put their faith in Walt Disney, and he would not disappoint them or betray their values. The founder kept that pledge as long as he lived. In the decades that followed his death, the studio has tried to uphold that contract—with uneven results."[6] Regarding this social contract, it seems that Disney is able to speak most powerfully when it speaks through archetype and aesthetic idealism rather than trying to appeal to any particular narratives in pop culture. It could be argued, there is a greater narrative power in the "once upon a time," as opposed to "in our own time." As it relates to methods of moral analysis, approaching Disney films through the lens of mimetic idealism provides a more fruitful method of investigation.

Beholding the Beautiful

As we've established, concurrent with Disney's emphasis on good and evil is an interest in the Kingdom-ever-after, and tethered to Disney's depiction of the Kingdom is an interest in capturing the beautiful within its ambassadors. In drawing this out, Disney animated classics seem to have revealed an interest in mimetic symbolism—a shared interest of theology. *Mimesis* is an aesthetic theory that stresses artistic value within *imitation*. This complex concept, used by different philosophers in different senses, can refer to *realistic* imitations wherein artists depict things as they are or as they seem to be, in our experience, or *idealistic* imitations in which art imitates things as they *really* are (beyond sense experience) or *ought* to be concerning our situation. The latter carries a teleological concern. Art calls our attention to things-as-they-ought-to-be-seen. We submit that Disney often aims for *mimetic idealism*—the teleological concern which permeates virtue theory.

We want to be careful here that our intent is not misinterpreted. When we speak of beauty in an *ideal* sense, we are not referring to body type. The bodies of many Disney characters are clearly unrealistic and nonrepresentative. Nor are we attempting to speak authoritatively about Walt's perspective on physical beauty. We are interested in the classic fairytale fascination with beauty. We are interested in Walt's seeming interest in linking beauty to virtuous characters, and we suggest there may be an artistic virtue apologetic at play within Disney animation.

This does not mean that the art has no connection to some sense of physical beauty whatsoever. There *is* an objective quality to beauty, at some level; beauty is not merely subjective. From a Christian lens, the Fall introduced a literal ugliness into the picture, and there are aspects of our experiences— from aging to health-related issues—which can actually uglify the body in some sense. It would likely not be the case that a well-drawn 95-year-old virtuous man, for example, is "beautiful." Therefore, our experiences of beauty cannot be entirely stripped of all their empirically situated aesthetic features. There is a clear aesthetic difference in the attractiveness of Cinderella when compared to her Fairy Godmother. If the Fairy Godmother is good, why is she not drawn more like Cinderella—unless the animation is serving multiple purposes in the visual storytelling, and not solely telling us about virtue.

Disney animators are clearly attempting to offer a take on physical beauty—especially as it involves facial attractiveness—to some extent and for some purpose. For reasons to be considered below, there must be some level of appeal, and clearly the need even to have this conversation arises from the fact that Disney princesses are often taken, by many viewers, to be, actually, beautiful—what fantastic hair Moana has! Our suggestion is that, while Disney may appeal to some general sense or degree of beauty, it does so for purposes other than merely drawing attention to a sexualized form. We suggest Disney is trying to use visual metaphor to communicate something about its characters, and this often includes something about virtue.

If we are right, then the visual art is intimately involved in the storytelling, albeit in an unspoken way, as it attempts to communicate, through metaphor and contrast, what is left unsaid by the script. This streamlines the film by communicating visually what could take some time to establish through context, interaction, and dialogue. In other words, there is something striking about this character, something good about his or her character. We are meant to pay close attention to this character, and goodness will somehow be learned or experienced through her actions or character development. Such visual streamlining avoids irritating the audience by explaining too much and leaves some aspects of deliberation up to the imagination—which Elisabeth Schellekens has argued is an important aspect of connecting the ethical and aesthetic realms of deliberation.[7]

Notwithstanding criticisms, it may not actually be the case that Disney films are purposefully trying to propagate idealist prescriptions concerning *physical* beauty, although we understand the concern that children—who learn largely through imitation—might internalize culturally relevant implications and thereby seek to imitate physical qualities, adornments, and mannerisms rather than the character of a character. Amanda Rutherford and Sarah Baker, for instance, lecturers in language and culture and communication studies at Auckland University of Technology in New Zealand, have taken issue with Disney's "princess bubble." While some of their interpretations are questionable, they understandably challenge that

> The impression often cast on audiences by Disney princesses emphasizes that beauty = worth.... These princesses are flawlessly beautiful, capable of winning the heart of the prince by triumphing over their less attractive rivals.... This creates the illusion among young audiences that physical attractiveness is enough to achieve success, and emphasises beauty as the priority above all else....
>
> The slim bodies of these princesses are disproportionate, and include long necks, demure shoulders, medium- to large-sized perky breasts, with tiny waists, wrists, ankles and feet.... The importance of the physical form is so valued that the first blessing given by the fairies to Aurora from *Sleeping Beauty* is the gift of physical beauty.... If women do not conform to the standards of representation [as in Cinderella] , they are presented as outcasts, and happiness eludes them [see Anastasia and Drizella].[8]

So, we want to be careful here to distinguish the idealism to which we are referring from the culturally dictated and prescribed ideals of "Beauty Culture." The former is concerned with an artistic, metaphorical reference to immaterial qualities in themselves and without reference back to the physical form, whereas the latter is concerned with prescriptions or implications concerning physical qualities primarily. We are aware that some historical perspectives have suggested that an inner excellence works itself out to reflect an outer beauty; that an inner virtue is to be suggested by one's excellent habits in being attentive to cultivating an appearance in keeping with cultural norms concerning the ideals of feminine and masculine physical features.

Such cultural narrative can be manipulated by those who hold hegemonic power to perpetuate the notion—or even create a market, selling individuals a normative identity based upon a prescriptive presumption—that one has a social duty to present oneself in a given way. On this line of thought, if one can cultivate within one's own body a physical ideal of health and beauty, then it might be posited that one's external habits of physical appearance (dieting, exercise, attention to detail concerning appearances) reflect an inner sense of excellence in habituation concerning a tempering of one's spirit and passions within the reigns of reason. To say it another way, this perspective (which we challenge) might suggest that hard work, self-control, and attention to detail and upkeep concerning the body *automatically* reflects a similar inner life of hard work, self-control, and attention to detail in the upkeep of a virtuous soul.

This perspective we might call a *naturalistic* idealist realism—meaning that, it is supposed there is an ideal of *natural* beauty which is believed to be actually achievable (a "beautiful" body) which, once attained, is believed to be axiomatically correspondent to a "beautiful" soul, and therefore connected with a good (virtuous) and happy life. We view this perspective as problematic and potentially harmful, and we believe Walt would concur. While Disney is clearly attempting to draw characters in an attractive manner, and while we do believe this may serve a virtue-related purpose in Disney's visual storytelling, this does *not* mean that Disney is suggesting a character is virtuous simply *because* she is physically attractive. We believe Walt, as an artist, was interested in manipulating the visual to tell us stories, without words, about character types—not body types—and the beautiful soul—not the beautiful body. Contrast is a powerful and purposeful tool of the arts. While there is a place for emphasizing the natural, the realities of our circumstances, we submit that myths and fairy stories are often concerned more with the symbolic, that is, with emphasizing a metaphysical realism, rather than the physical realities of our experiences.

Disney princesses seem to be drawn in such a way as to pull the viewer's eye to her face. And this seems to happen in two predominant ways—one perhaps more significant than the other. First, many princesses have a tiny waist that is hardly there. After Snow White, whose 1937 proportions might have been more believable though, of course, unable to stand in as representative of all female body types, princess waist sizes seem to have only gotten smaller. Aurora's waist is not much wider than her neck, and this trend continues with "Disney Renaissance" princesses, like Ariel (*The Little Mermaid*), Jasmine (*Aladdin*), and Pocahontas. While not a "Disney princess," this is true of Megara (*Hercules*) as well—whose elongated torso at times appears to be the *same* size as her neck. (It is worth noting that our suggestions below, about Disney's virtue-oriented visual storytelling, may also apply to non-princess characters including Esmeralda (*The Hunchback of Notre Dame*), who does not hesitate to stand against unjust treatment of society's marginalized persons, and Megara, who is struggling with her own character development throughout the film).

The trend of petite proportions continues with twenty-first-century princesses, like Tiana (*The Princess and the* Frog) and Rapunzel (*Tangled*). Though still petite, it could be argued that *Moana* finally returns to a more believable proportion (her waistline more in alignment with her armpits), and this visual rendering is carried forward with the protagonist Mirabel (*Encanto*), although Mirabel is not a princess. *Encanto* actually seems to explore and celebrate diversity in body type, and even Isabela, who is presented as being privileged to an atypical beauty, has a waist in line with her shoulders. What is going on, then, with Disney's historical caricatures of the body between 1937 (*Snow White*) and 2016 (*Moana*), as Disney is working out its approach to visual storytelling?

Rather than presume it to be Disney's definitive statement on natural beauty, is it not possible that such artistic rendering naturally results in the eyes being drawn toward the head? In princesses like Aurora (who has smaller eyes comparatively), the voluminous hair helps to accentuate the face. Perhaps Disney was not necessarily trying to emphasize a particular statement on the beauty of a physical body. Is it not possible that Disney artists were attempting to de-emphasize the body in order to accentuate the face? Perhaps the de-emphasis of body is because we are not meant to think of the protagonist as a sexually mature being, since there is often a sense of innocence assumed to accompany sexual inexperience. Admittedly, it could be challenged that Disney female protagonists are nevertheless drawn in an effort to appeal to the "male gaze" in so far as Disney often attempts to present us with a "beautiful face." However, since the ultimate concern of "male-gaze" criticism is to take issue with the representation of women as sexual objects, and since drawing the eye toward the face rather than the hips and chest (if that is what Disney is attempting to do) is arguably effective at de-emphasizing a sexual-centric, body-focused "gaze," it is possible that Disney *is* concerned with speaking to the viewer's sense of beauty in regard to the face, for some purposeful reason, without attempting to present the female body as an object of sexual desire.

As a side note, Megara is clearly more sexualized than, for example, Mulan, but this too seems purposeful since Megara, prior to a change of heart, is actually trying to play the role of temptress, while Mulan is attempting to deceive others into believing that hers is a male body. The point is that even though Megara's physique is emphasized as it relates, possibly, to our association with the "male gaze" of Hercules, the use of physical beauty as a means of deception is not lost on the viewer—and this is worth noting.

Similarly, in *The Hunchback of Notre Dame*, Esmeralda's being subject to the "male gaze" of Claude Frollo is part of the plot. Thus, when the sexualization of the female body *is* presented in Disney's animated stories, it seems reasonable to conclude that the audience is meant to understand this and to connect it in some way with vice.

What is certain is that Disney animators had a particular interest in drawing attention to the eyes. In the words of former Disney animators Frank Thomas and Ollie Johnston, "The eyes are the most important part of an expression and must be drawn with extreme care. Any jitter or false move on an inbetween [*sic*.] destroys both communication and believability."[9] It is also apparent that they were aware of the fine line, mentioned above, between aesthetic accessibility or allure and disinterestedness or repulsion. They further state, "A more difficult challenge arises when the villainous character is somehow visually disturbing. In addition to the normal problems of making him or her convincing and theatrically sound, there is the increased burden of designing the appearance in a way not only acceptable but appealing. Without appeal, no one will respond enough to become involved with either the character or the story."[10] From this we can conclude that, whatever its purpose, those with whom we are meant to associate beauty, as well as those with whom we were meant to associate evil, were drawn purposefully, and this purpose involved communication, character accessibility, and audience acceptance.

Thomas and Johnston further explained that Disney wanted to captivate audiences with a sense of the real, exaggerated for the sake of an appeal to immerse viewers in the drama:

> Instead of thinking of cartoon material as being "entertaining," one might find a better concept in the word "captivating." Audiences have to be impressed, absorbed, involved, taken out of themselves, made to forget their own worlds and lose themselves in ours for cartoons to succeed. Walt had to find actions that were funny in themselves yet easily recognized as something familiar, gags that were plausible even though very imaginative, situations that were based on everyone's experience, and characters that had interesting personalities. These were the things that could hold an audience, and to Walt they added up to one simple approach—a caricature of realism.[11]

While Disney *was* interested in artistic realism when it came to things like timing and extent of natural motion, or accuracy in detail concerning the depiction of animals and nature, when it came to visual storytelling, there was clearly an interest in caricature as well.

The second way in which Disney princesses are drawn in an effort to highlight the face involves an accentuation of the eyes. With "Disney Renaissance" princesses, like Ariel and Jasmine, we begin to see much larger eyes. We see the same thing with Tiana. When it comes to computer-animated characters such as Merida (*Brave*), Rapunzel, Elsa, and Anna (*Frozen*), the eyes get even bigger. This is interesting in light of a 2008 study, where psychology professors Leslie Zebrowitz and Joann Montepare outlined an ecological approach to face perception, "emphasizing that face perception guides behavior, expanding the domain of face perception to include perceived traits and social interaction opportunities."[12] They further state that "people with attractive faces are judged more positively," and, "the fact that people from diverse cultures as well as infants and young children all show similar reactions to faces that vary in attractiveness suggests that these impressions reflect some universal mechanism rather than arbitrary cultural influences."[13] In addition, psychologists have linked the facial qualities that influence attractiveness to fitness. These qualities include symmetry, youthfulness, and sexual dimorphism (non-reproductive differences in males and females, for example, a larger physical size in males or high cheekbones in women).

Zebrowitz and Montepare also found that "babyfaceness" is perceived as being associated with naiveté, warmth, and honesty. The features of a "babyface" include large eyes, a small nose, a round face, higher eyebrows, thicker lips, a lower placement of features, and thus a smaller chin with a higher forehead. Because adults with one or more of these features are perceived as honest and warm, they are more likely to be seen as innocent, and more often cleared of criminal charges.[14] Baby faces are also seen as weaker. This may tie into some animated storytellers' interest in depicting the protagonist as an underdog or celebrating a child's strength of heart to overcome adversity, or even to the above suggestion concerning the de-emphasis of sexual maturity in association with the suggestion of naiveté. There is a connection between the immediate impression of a character as lovable and our perception of them as non-threatening.

The authors also considered the perception of facial expression and explained that we make predetermined judgments about one's behavioral tendencies based upon the expression of emotion displayed upon one's face.[15] The default expression suggested by one's seemingly fixed facial structure can therefore influence us to a significant degree. We recognize a lot of what we have just reviewed is intuitive, nevertheless it is important to understand some of the research being done in these areas that may influence how Disney animators are approaching more recent films, or explain why animators may have, intuitively, drawn their characters in particular ways through the years.

A final and fascinating observation—one which corroborates some of the points made above about music and storytelling—involves the issue of familiarity. As with music, and storytelling, familiarity can influence reaction. The faces of strangers from other racial groups with which one is less familiar tend to be seen more negatively than the more familiar faces of one's own group. The authors suggest that this contributes to culturally informed racial stereotypes. While Disney eventually made a more purposeful effort to expand its cultural representation, as it expanded its cultural reach, perhaps this offers insight both into why such cultural (and non-controversial) representations may have taken so long to reveal themselves in the Disney canon.

What is clear from Zebrowitz's and Montepare's study is that appearance does matter to some extent. Cross-culturally, we seem to associate certain qualities of symmetry, health, and fitness with beauty, and certain characteristics with biological ideals of masculine and feminine beauty. We see babyfaceness as more trustworthy, less threatening, and more likely innocent. Conversely, the greater the degree of perceived unfamiliarity the more likely we will be to perceive a character negatively, and thus the less likely we will be to connect with a character. Such data might explain why so many Disney princesses seem to share similar features. Since Disney began, it seems that most Disney princesses' eyes seem unusually large, and they have only gotten bigger over the last 20 years. The facial features of a Disney princess are no doubt intentional, but to what end? While challenges to Disney's apparent reification of hegemonic beauty standards are well known, perhaps Disney has had more noble intentions than some suspect. It is clear that Disney's emphasis on the eyes bring attention away from the body (which Disney often draws as noticeably small). One could argue that Disney is trying to honor women by drawing attention to the face and away from the body, in effect attempting to reverse societal trends that want to oversexualize women.

Might Disney's animation, then, in some cases—although quite interested in realism when it comes to motion and certain aspects of appearance—be non-realist when it comes to certain aspects of the male and female body, in order to draw our attention elsewhere, namely, to the face? Perhaps Disney princess animation represents an effort to speak to a better *sense* of beauty. One that draws us in to an emotionally-engaged anticipatory investment—a contemplation of character, a sense of trust, and an investment of faith in a goodness we believe to be reflected from the heart, through the eyes.

Some narratives do have an interest in realism. Bambi's mother dies. Child abduction is a reality (*The Rescuers*). It was regrettable, though necessary, for Travis to shoot his beloved *Old Yeller*. Walt expressed disbelief in "playing down to children" as though they are "fragile flowers." Real life contains light and shadows, and "you are not doing a child a favor by trying to shield him/[her] from reality."[16] Nevertheless, Disney animated narratives are more often idealistic than realistic, and thus more accessible to children.[17] Mimetic realism can be found in Disney's use of live models, rendering of nature, and concern for authentic motion[18]—even in its animated adaptation of Notre-Dame.[19] Mimetic naturalism does play an important role in the history of Disney animation—such as in *Bambi*. Still, in many cases (especially within what we might call the kingdom canon of princess tales), the artists do not usually seem to emphasize the real, but rather they often seem to suggest something about immaterial qualities (such as Rapunzel's and Anna's innocence or the appalling nature and extent of Jafar's and Cruella's disregard for others) and ideals (such as the goodness of Cinderella's courage and kindness or the devoted nature of Tiana's heart). This, we believe, is key to understanding archetypes of nobility, beauty, true love, and the Kingdom-ever-after.

Archetypes of Nobility

The archetype of nobility and its connection to beauty is a complex topic, as the prince-princess motif has drawn much criticism over the years. Behind a qualified Kingdom-oriented theological lens, however, it holds much power. We understand, and think valid, the concern for the negative impact of stereotyping ideals of physical beauty and defining cultural prescriptions of feminine perfection. But again, we do not think Disney's visual intent involves mimetic naturalism, which is crucial. While our intent is not to defend

Disney wholesale,[20] it seems that Disney princesses are purposefully ideal.[21] We are supposed to be stricken with an awareness of their beauty; something inside of them comes through visually and strikes us immediately. There is little time to get to know them, so the artist concerned about inner beauty may choose to attempt to reflect that inner beauty in outward ways, in judicious aspects of their physical embodiment.[22] Similarly, while we can understand the contemporary concern with depicting princesses as damsels in distress, we are not convinced that the concern is always warranted or that one sex being rescued more often by the other sex is somehow devaluing or degrading.

As we have alluded, we understand and acknowledge socio-cultural concerns over questions of hegemonic power with respect to beauty.[23] However, this is precisely why archetype is important. In any cultural context, there is a place where the natural and the ideal meet. If Disney is to communicate effectively visual beauty as metaphor for character, it must attempt to do so in a manner palatable to the cultural context. It will be difficult to communicate beauty as metaphor for higher truth and virtue if Disney is unable to present a character that society and the broader culture generally and immediately understands as beautiful. That is to say, the artist makes a princess or prince strikingly beautiful at *some* level, according to *some* objective sense of beauty—lest he or she seem unappealing, and thus the symbolism is lost. Yet, this is done in a way that signals a pushback from hegemonic devaluing by not oversexualizing the beauty. However, this should not be taken as a defense for a particular conception of naturalistic beauty rather than a mode of idealistic communication. Consequently, there is a chasm in communication here, not unlike the historical divide between sacred and secular and "fact" and value.

To the extent that it has merit, Disney has purposefully addressed this challenge by offering strong, independent female leads. Still, there is something not to be missed in the classic Princess narrative. The ideal is a key feature in classical storytelling, and the Disney princess is an archetype of Beauty. What makes her beautiful? Her strength of heart and character; her virtue. Beauty is not her virtue; her *virtues* are beautiful. The visual artist is able to use a general sense of what a culture understands to be beautiful on the outside in order to convey, through symbolism and contrast, an unspoken quality about the character of the one we are meant to understand as being a beautiful person. In order to understand this perspective on how and why Disney may have purposefully animated its princesses as archetypes of virtue, one has to understand Disney's apparent concern for and emphasis upon virtue ethics. Consequently, the Disney princess is drawn in such a way as to convey an outward depiction of an inner disposition. In *The Little Mermaid*, we are not meant to mistake Ursula with the beautiful, and so it is intentional that she is both literally and symbolically obese. Her physicality is meant to represent the gluttonous, envious ugliness deep within her. In contrast, Ariel's physicality is meant to represent something beautiful about Ariel's heart and something attractive about her perspective. We don't believe this is an attempt to body shame by Disney or to unbreakably attach deviance to ugliness. We personally reject such actions as well. We know this because Disney at times ties profound virtue to the aesthetically unappealing (Quasimodo, *The Hunchback of Notre Dame*). Rather, we think for Disney it is an issue of artistic symbolism and contrasting metaphors.

Love and Virtue

There is some validity to skepticism concerning an unrealistic depiction of the *process* of love—for example, Aurora and Phillip are supposedly in "love" by the end of their dance. It is dangerous to equate such a flippant, adolescent emotional experience with true and lasting love. If we take narrative-time literally, how could "love" happen this quickly? What could he possibly see in her at this point, beyond external beauty? However, while such concerns have merit within a literal interpretation, it seems that these stories, although situated within a specific context for the sake of accessibility, are presented as generalization, even idealization. Such narratives rarely afford the time necessary to address any number of concerns. If the point is to stress ideal character or to streamline the plot—where love is just part of the story—then we can overlook some of the less-than-ideal oversimplifications. From Disney's standpoint, if this is correct, we are not meant to nitpick the literal; we are meant to understand the general, in order to ponder the ideal. So, we get it: (1) something about them is beautiful; (2) they fall in love.

What about the prince? Who is worthy of a princess's heart? He too must be a model of virtue—respectful, admirable, courageous, compassionate, and one who values her so highly (for who she is) that he is willing to obtain any other excellence necessary to demonstrate his love for her. Love is demonstration—action, not merely expression. Generally speaking, the knight-in-shining-armor motif conveys an ideal of possessing praise-worthy valor, with such respect for love and the beautiful soul that one is ready to fight any foe or face any fear, should the need arise. This doesn't mean the princess can't protect herself (though she may not be able to), nor does it imply that she needs her knight in an ultimate sense (although true love requires real vulnerability, which does imply a relative need, and need is not in opposition to true power). Disney offers us an ideal depiction of a prince, a standard to strive for, one of valor and chivalry. Ultimately, virtue, beauty, and excellence in character is the standard (in different ways) demanded of all princes and princesses.

We should note that Mother Gothel (*Tangled*) and Snow White's queen both pursue natural beauty, and prince Hans selfishly uses a princess as a means to the apparent good life. Yet, in each of these cases we understand that their pursuit is wrong-focused. To use Platonic language, they chase distant imitations of beauty rather than The Beautiful. As it has been alluded, Disney occasionally explores non-idealistic depictions of natural beauty in order to communicate that the most ideal, or truest sense of beauty is non-physical. In *The Hunchback of Notre Dame*, Quasimodo is the ideal beautiful soul, while Esmerelda's natural beauty is a burden. In *The Little Mermaid*, even as Eric is deceived by Ursula's physical façade, we know there is little admirable about her. Disney nobility, however, usually seem to serve as archetypes of beauty; and such archetypal contrast is critical to virtue ethics.

Despite misguided presumptions about beauty in the eye of the beholder, humanity has always held deep convictions concerning beauty and excellence. As Abraham Kuyper observed, "No matter how superficial.... a certain appreciation for beauty is still a shared feature of our human nature."[24] One of Kuyper's most insightful points involves a rupture caused by the Fall. Beauty was abundant in the original state of creation, but the curse of the Fall greatly diminished the beauty of the whole created order. The profundity of Kuyper's observation targets archetypal contrast.

> The curse is observable everywhere, but was restrained.... This world can still display to us so much beauty. Nevertheless, beauty no longer adorns the whole earth. On the contrary, we discover alongside each other the beautiful, the ordinary, and the ugly. A lion is beautiful; a calf is ordinary; a rat is ugly.... The cedar enthralls us with beauty, the willow strikes us as ordinary, and the thistle turns us off...
>
> Repeatedly God shows you and gives you a sense of what your lot on earth would be, and how ugly the world would be, if the curse had been carried out to its ultimate conclusion. And

then God lets you behold an exhilarating natural phenomenon that makes you homesick for paradise. Then you sink again back into the ordinary where nothing excites you or repulses you, but instead where everything around you lacks any vitality and chills your enthusiasm.[25]

While God's grace has preserved a sense of beauty throughout nature, archetypal contrast is pivotal to seeing it. Eyes that stare at brilliant light become blinded, says Kuyper, and eyes that dwell in darkness become damaged, "but when our eyes enjoy alternating views.... those contrasts provide exercise needed for clarity of vision."[26] It is precisely because grays abound that archetypes are so powerful. In the words of Maeve Louise Heaney, "just as evil helps us to know the good so too the ugly helps us to understand the beautiful.[27] Disney often depicts its archetypes of virtue as representatives of the kingdom—nobility—and draws these noble characters in such a way as to signal that there is something beautiful about their hearts. Even if they are diamonds in the rough, there is an inner beauty revealed through their journey and associated with an acquisition of moral understanding, a reorientation of conscience, or a demonstration of moral excellence. In drawing them in such a way as to draw us in to see them metaphorically as ambassadors of Beauty, Disney is communicating something about the Kingdom-ever-after. It looks *like that*—it is inhabited by beautiful souls who love truth and live in light of the Good; and a kingdom made of such citizens is directly connected to a just order.

6

An Archetypal (Christian?) Ethics and the Kingdom-Ever-After

D isney is concerned with a Kingdom motif and its connection to both the beauty of a virtuous heart and a conquering goodness. But why think Disney's vision of the Kingdom is really enfolded by the Christian story of reality? The answer lies in a closer look at its Kingdom ambassadors as archetypes of moral excellence—namely, the standard for which they reach. While Disney is primarily concerned with virtue in principle, what do we see communicated in practice?

After arguing that virtue lies at the heart of Disney's moral canon, we also contended that Disney's moral metanarrative is more complex and robust than virtue ethics alone. As we distinguished between ethical theories, we observed that principles of moral duty are weakened without virtues, yet virtues are essentially blind without principles to guide them. Furthermore, while the consequentialist theories are lacking, they still bring something to the table. After all, if the Kingdom-ever-after is the end for which our ethics aims, is it not in some sense consequential if we believe that choosing to love the good, to live in light of moral excellence, will result in our one-day becoming a Kingdom citizen? Although the selfishness and *hubris* which might flow from a foundation of egoism stands in clear opposition to a kingdom-oriented virtue, is it not in one's self-interest to seek such a just society as that which the Kingdom-ever-after promises to be? Thus, while virtue ethics stands out among the other normative theories, it would seem the most satisfactory ethical theory must be a complementary one—able to encompass the strengths of each contending paradigm, while also allowing a degree of flexibility in order to navigate the criticisms and questions of contextual complexity.

Secular ethics, however, can offer little satisfactory compromise because of a difficulty in grounding human worth and equality. Moreover, if virtues and principles reduce to mere human constructions, it becomes all the more difficult to ground justice. If a satisfactorily robust complementarity perspective is possible, then, it must come from a non-naturalist grounding. We must remember that virtue theory requires moral exemplars worth imitating, and many are quick to acknowledge Jesus as an archetype of moral excellence. Actually, he is the original Archetype of a particular kind of ethics. Jesus's teaching exemplifies the complementary ethics for which philosophers are searching, and we submit that Disney's moral concern in notable respects aligns closely with distinctive aspects of Jesus's moral theology.

What do we mean? Jesus's teaching demonstrates moral complementarity while accentuating character ethics, and this perspective is irremovably tethered to the Bible's primary theme of God's Kingdom.[1] Jesus stressed love and unity, yet did so in light of exclusivist, absolute moral truths. In many ways, so did Walt's animated features. Without sanctifying Disney, we submit that his nonsectarian approach to creating an easily accessible and inviting narrative realm (wherein he pressed into our convictions of a teleological way-it-should-be and evangelized the good news that good will conquer evil) follows this model to some degree. In *Frozen II*, Anna and Elsa are not driven by a desire to assert their own personal, "my truths" onto the world, but rather by a sense of ultimate purpose and a search for *the* truth. For, as Pabbie warned, there is no future without the truth. While acknowledging an inner struggle over interests, Jesus encouraged a proper ultimate form of self-interestedness.[2] While condemning pride (self*fish*ness), Jesus nevertheless beseeched listeners to reorient their values in light of what was ultimately, even paradoxically, in their best interest.[3] So too, Disney films have a place for self-interest and self-realization, but places the greater weight on a readiness for self-sacrifice.

Jesus emphasized an ultimate duty (due reverence) to God and secondary duty to others. The entire Moral Law hangs upon these duties.[4] Still, the root of our soul sickness and the beginning of its cure involves something deeper and more important than duty.[5] For God delights not merely or principally in sacrifice, but in a changed heart.[6] Similarly, Pinocchio needs principles to guide him and a conscience to remind him of these principles (indeed there are consequences for ignoring them), but what he really needs is transfiguration—his becoming something more and other than his wooden nature.

The overarching theme of the Bible prioritizes God's nature and Kingdom. Kingdom-ethics involves a qualified utilitarian concern. There *is* concern for the greater good now, seeking the best in our city and relationships with a view towards righteousness, but ultimately—as it relates to the *greatest* good in the Kingdom-ever-after—the cessation of evil and injustice and the eternal reign of holiness and love. There is similarly a qualified utilitarian concern in Disney lore. Take *Frozen II*, for example. While her grandfather was willing to murder in the name of Arendelle's "greater good," Anna is willing to flood her beloved city and pillar of stability (which is not in the greater interest of its inhabitants) in the name of an even greater good (reversing the treachery of the dam's construction). Anna understands that the greater good in this instance cannot be merely equated with the immediate interests of the immediate many. What is ultimately good and right, in the correction of injustice that had disenfranchised a great number, a people (the Northuldra), had to prevail. When truth is found and justice reigns, it is in the greatest interest of everyone in the Kingdom-ever-after.

In Christ's teaching, there is content related to self-interest, duty, and utility. However, it is the character of the human being, in right relationship to the Creator, thus in right relationship to creation, that brings about right actions which work toward the greatest Good. And although the greatest good may not entail the greatest number of human beings, it will entail the full number of kingdom citizens—those who love the Good. A number no man can number.[7] Sin is an issue of *kardia* (the locus of our understanding). The Scriptures teach that those who receive Christ, the King of Kings,[8] are given the right to become children of God.[9] The heart of stone is removed and replaced by a new heart of flesh,[10] a virtuous heart that desires what the King desires and loves what the King loves.[11] Under this economy, law is not necessary[12] as the kingdom-people truly love the king and his domain, including its inhabitants.[13] Nevertheless, such love comes only with a certain disposition—a transformation—of character.[14]

It is therefore, according to Jesus, a teleological way-it-should-be (the order of creation) and the Kingdom-ever after which frames morality and grounds moral complementarity—in other words, a complementary ethics which is able to account for the nuances of situational complexities and the strengths of each of the contending theories of action. Disney is similarly enthralled with the notion of *telos* and kingdom as key to the good. (The parks themselves might be seen as an effort to imagine the joy of a Kingdom-ever-after). There is, for example, a rich symbolism of the relationship between kingdom and character in *The Lion King*. Everything the light touches defines the kingdom. This has an unmistakable Neoplatonist ring; goodness within the kingdom is an emanation from the Sun and, in the earthly kingdom (to use Augustinian language), this light is directly proportional to the character of the king. In the Shadowlands, there is a privation of both light and life. When Scar becomes king, this privation extends into the pride lands. Therefore, the life and light of the kingdom is a direct reflection of the character of the king himself. Kingdom, here, is an analogical archetype of the heavenly and earthly cities, as well as a metaphor concerning the heart and character required of an heir to the true kingdom.

In addition to this interest in a complementarity virtue ethics and the fascination with a Kingdom-ever-after, Disney often stresses theological virtues consistent with the Christian heritage. While Plato's and Aristotle's virtue ethics have notable compatibility with Christian ethics,[15] the legacy of the latter significantly transformed the altruism of the former. Aristotelian virtue ethics was an ethics of self-realization. The notion of loving others for their own sakes—the background assumption of contemporary ideals of love and care, which Charles Taylor referred to as the *agape*-analogue which has embedded itself within the modern social imaginary—is very much the product of a Christian heritage.[16] Augustine most famously expounded on the theme of kingdom theology in light of a tension between heavenly and earthly cities. This tension is built around a disordered appetite, which favors self-interest over charity.[17] While Disney often spotlights cardinal virtues (prudence, temperance, fortitude, and justice) through self-perception and self-realization—as portrayed well by Merida (*Brave*), Mulan, and Moana—there is also a common emphasis on the theological virtues of faith in the Good (conviction that good will defeat evil), hope in the Kingdom-ever-after, and charity. Disney, through films like *Frozen*, suggests the greatest of these is *agape*. We concur!

In ancient Greek ethics, there is room for altruism, but it is usually grounded in self-realization by being excellent in friendship, loyalty, or courage. Yet, as Kant sharply criticized, even villains can be virtuous in the sense of demonstrating excellence in ability[18] (courage, fortitude, calm deliberation, among other traits). From a Christian standpoint, however, since God *is* love, we are most like God and expressive of our love for God (in so far as love is not placed in opposition to truth, lest it not be actual love[19]) when we love others as valuable in themselves, without condition.[20] The focus of the former is on the self, in light of human nature and potential, and the benefits of a flourishing community that might follow; the emphasis of the latter is on the Kingdom, and the character expected of those called to be ambassadors of that Kingdom.[21] It is a kingdom of true love, goodness, and joy-ever-after, where one forgives their enemies and lays their life down for their friends.[22] Cinderella, in forgiveness, and Anna, in self-sacrificial love, point to this kingdom.

The concern for *telos* finds greater depth of significance in light of the Judeo-Christian worldview. The very fact of our moral convictions powerfully points to the fact that there is a way-it-should-be. Aristotelian virtue ethics involves seeking excellence according to one's nature, but Christianity involves seeking an excellence beyond one's nature. Aristotelian excellence involves a challenge to become the best version of what the rational human being can be, while Christianity involves an expectation to be who we were *meant* to be (image-bearers of goodness), and moreover, a call to become more, to become new creations[23] and heirs of the Kingdom.[24] We can be "good" at being a human being (doing what human beings by nature do, in exemplary fashion) without really being a "good" human being. Further, according to Jesus, we can do good and recognize goodness, yet fail to *be* good, and thus fail to know the goodness-ever-after.[25] Note that Moana does not remind Te Kā, "This is not who you *could* be; you are not living up to the full potential of your nature." Instead, she pleads, "This is not who you *are*." Elsa proclaims, "I've never felt so certain... I'm here for a reason!"[26]

Here we might make a helpful distinction. Disney's *Soul*[27] does not really seem to target the question of virtue, but rather a readiness and openness to live and a sense of thankfulness which allows one to find a greater sense of happiness in the now, despite fears and frustrations. Moreover, it can be argued that the film is non-essentialist in some ways—as it presents a subtle polemic against the idea that one has some special pre-determined destiny or purpose that one is meant to find or fulfill. However, a closer analysis shows that souls in *Soul* are being prepared in a clearly pre-determined way—with certain teleological essences. Next, it can be argued that we do indeed see virtue in the film. For instance, gratitude is deeply entwined with the theological virtue of faith, making possible the ability to live one's life giving thanks in all circumstances, a critical element in God's will for His people.[28] Finally, and most importantly, when we reference teleology here, we are not referring to one's *individual* purpose (although this is what Elsa is referencing in the quote above, which is significant, because in her case it actually refers to a greater teleological order); we are speaking, secondarily, to a broad sense of purpose for humanity as a whole, and, primarily, of the teleological order that is necessary to ground such a reference. From a Christian theological perspective, we were created morally perfect (but not immutable) and then we experienced our Fall.[29] We became less, radically less, than what was intended. In God's perfect wisdom, He used the Fall as a pathway to justification, redemption, and glorification, a perfect reflection of His love in us.

Beast is expected to be *more*, but he is not punished for failing to be the most excellent version of a human being, or a prince — unless we presuppose that human excellence entails a moral obligation to show kindness and extend hospitality. What does he really *owe* to the beggar? Why do we expect him to act as though compassion is really *due* her? Yet we do seem to expect that the most excellent human being will demonstrate lovingkindness toward his or her fellow human being. (Why do we expect this?) It is because he knew not love that Beast was transformed into the unlovely, and only when he learns what love is — if he can learn it in time — will he be able to recover the humanity he was meant to know. Moreover, paradoxically, he will only be able to learn to love through the experience of *being loved* while he was yet seemingly unlovable. We sense that Beast's conscience was as absent as Pinocchio's, and like Pinocchio Beast's journey will require a complete transformation of disposition. He is punished precisely because, like Te Kā, whose heart is literally not in the right place, Beast's heart is corrupted.

We do not simply wish for Simba to be a good lion; we want him to be who he was *meant to be* — he is called to be an heir of the kingdom. While Aladdin is struggling with issues of self-realization, this comes at the heart level. Plato and Aristotle would agree that it is better to be just, though poor, than to acquire riches by an unjust means, yet Aladdin's moral struggle is not over wealth but identity. Is he the sort of person that should sacrifice his own happiness for the sake of Genie's freedom? If he was given three wishes, then they are now his property. Would it be wrong for him to do whatever he wishes with what is his? We could question whether Genie was really Aladdin's property simply because a contract of servitude — imposed upon Genie by another power — declared it to be so. However, it could also be argued that, *if* the power of the lamp is indeed Aladdin's *property*, then it would not be unjust for Aladdin to acquire a kingdom and wealth at the expense of

Genie's freedom. This, of course, would hinge on a particular conception of property rights, an area where competing perspectives abound.

Yet Disney encourages us to desire more for Aladdin than this; we long for him to be the sort of person who chooses charity and compassion over self-absorbed self-realization. While it can be somewhat elusive to grasp, we understand there exists a better identity beyond mere fulfillment of one's own potential, along a vector assumed to be most ideal—one that often bends towards self-centrism. We have capacities for potentials that involve other-centeredness, the sharing of oneself with another, that may (and likely) offer greater ultimate fulfillment than pathways of optimum potential that are self-centric. We also want Genie to be free because we sense something deeply special about *persons*. That is, Disney presses effectively into a moral conviction held by many of its viewers in a post-abolitionist context; the enslaved *other* is still an intrinsically valuable person. Thus, Genie's longing for freedom appeals to our sense of justice and right-order.

As argued above, themes of charity, self-sacrifice, and a grand sense of telos (not fullness of potential, but a sense of meant-to-be-ness or ought-to-be-ness) abound in Disney lore. The Rescuers fly into the face of danger in order to rescue the captive (Penny in *The Rescuers*; Cody in *Rescuers Down Under*) from injustice. Robin Hood's bravery carries with it the risk of imprisonment, even death. Indeed, Friar Tuck shows us that courage is costly, as his willingness to stand up for the poor and protest their exploitation leads to his arrest and an order of execution. Hercules relentlessly pursued divinity through self-realization but discovered his true heroism within sacrifice instead. We want Rapunzel to discover who she really is (meant to be), as opposed to the false identity she has been taught to embrace through Gothel's manipulative storytelling, and we are moved when Triton sacrifices his own freedom on behalf of Ariel's. Consequently, it seems Disney's emphasis on virtue may be more Christian than Aristotelian.

The moral life is not like a simple recipe, easy to follow, but is a continual practice of habituating the orientations of our desires. It is a daily struggle, even for Christians who have the Spirit of God,[30] requiring a constant aim for excellence[31] and wisdom for discernment. We submit that Jesus's moral teaching and depiction of the kingdom of God represents a crucial part of the vision Disney has had for many of its archetypes of virtue that permeate its canon. Alas, a life in light of the Kingdom-ever-after is no easy journey.

Double-Danger

The path of the kingdom-minded (the lover of goodness) is a daily struggle in itself because of the conflicting tensions within the soul, but there is another danger looming. The combination of these two is what Søren Kierkegaard called the Double Danger of the Christian life. The first danger is the path of egoism—to give into impulse—which can be stoked as one commits to the narrow path of Jesus (committing to grow into the image of the archetype of moral excellence which threatens sin's previous hold). The second danger arises from the commitment to the narrow path as it prompts persecution from travelers of the broad path. Interestingly, some Disney characters model this second danger as well.[32] For instance, Beast sacrifices his own desire, sending Belle away to care for her father. Yet, it is because of her return, as the villagers learn the truth of the beast, that a mob ensues to kill him. Choosing charity over egoism was good in so far as it concerned the condition of his heart. Yet, doing so brought persecution right to his door. It was good to extend mercy to Gaston, although grace came at a great price. The very moment in which Raya (*Raya and the Last Dragon*) and her friends take a step of faith, they expose themselves to the Druun. Their demonstration of love, an invitation of redemption and a potential restoration of community extended to Namaari was not without risk. At times, the very act that demonstrates a love of the good invites jeopardy and peril.

Simba must face a similar decision. To assert his identity as heir to the kingdom is to welcome the opportunity for Scar to use his past against him, and for others to resent him. Love itself is dangerous; although it overcomes egoism, it brings with it vulnerability and the potential for pain. This (vulnerability and potential for pain) is precisely the danger that Elsa wishes to avoid by isolating herself, and Mother Gothel uses to cast doubt into Rapunzel's heart. It was acting in the name of justice on behalf of Quasimodo that brought Esmeralda into conflict with Frollo. To live in light of the heavenly kingdom is to welcome antipathy in the earthly kingdom.

The Archetypal Inspiration in Disney's Background Moral Imaginary

Disney reminds us that self-realization is important, yet egoism is problematic. It reminds us there is a greater good for which we ought to strive, but also that what might be in the interest of tradition or social expectations may not actually be in the interest of goodness. Disney reminds us that greatness and goodness can become slippery terms when wedded to utilitarian ideologies; that duties are important but sometimes become a chain of legalism. While the concept of legalism or moral traditionalism can be applied easily to films like *Mulan*, it is demonstrated perhaps most powerfully in *Frozen*. For Elsa, the burden of a deontological imperative was more than she believed she could bear: "conceal." Do *not* let your powers go, which became, for her, synonymous with "don't feel." From this perspective, she only saw her magic as a curse and herself as a liability to others. Yet, upon "letting it go" and declaring her own truth, she learned that egoism did not work out for her either. She ended up becoming a liability to others. When she discovered freedom in a *teleological imperative*,[33] however—a proper end and expression of her powers—she understood her magic as a gift and love (which requires relationship, not isolation) as the key to using her powers in the most *excellent* way.

Disney films offer powerful, though mostly implicit, apologetic arguments for both a theistic worldview and a virtue-oriented ethics. At times they go beyond general theism and align strikingly with a Judeo-Christian moral philosophy, enabling them to offer rich insight into a kingdom-oriented theology. Historically, Disney animated classics have regularly gripped our convictions and reminded us of what we already know (whether we can always name it or not). There is moral truth of an absolute nature. There is a way-it-should-be. Goodness will ultimately defeat evil. And individual (and often very minor) characters have a significant part to play in realizing the goodness-ever-after and bringing about the kingdom come. While a kingdom-oriented ethics offers a more robust, complementary ethical perspective, it also stresses that it is ultimately the *character* of a character that makes all the moral difference. It seems Disney's moral archetypes are actually imitations of an original Archetype—the moral teaching of Jesus.

7

True Love and the Ever-After: The Kingdom Come

A final kingdom-oriented idealization which must be addressed, because it both permeates Disney's canon of animated features and expands our case that Disney's moral metanarrative seems to model itself after the Christian story of reality, is the belief that true love is somehow, in some way, directly connected to the happy-ever-after. According to Giselle (*Enchanted*), two things are certain: "Everybody wants to live happily ever after," and "everybody wants to know their true love is true."[1] This concept may seem unrealistic in reality, as it concerns the now—like trying to find a predestined "The One" who will perfectly fulfill all requirements for the good life and magically cause all of life's other anxieties to cease.

In so far as "happily ever after" refers to the remainder of a character's life (and not to eternal life), how could this be taken literally? However, need "happily-ever-after," as it relates to the now, literally and necessarily imply "sorrow-never-after"? Growth and pain go hand in hand, after all. And love is sometimes a lot of work, a series of tests concerning one's character. Perhaps the "happily ever after" implied at the end of most celebrated children's stories is more a sentiment of gratitude and faithfulness. Whatever life throws at them, their thankfulness for one another and the love they share strengthens them to hold onto a faith in one another, to work toward an ideal end. Falling in love is not the good life, but only a step along the path to learning more about the truth of love and the beauty and goodness for which one's life ought to aim. The fairytale, then, does not end with the actualized ever-after, but only an aim and, with it, a teleological question.

From a theistic lens, however, that aim is ultimately a question of eternity, and a longing for the perfection of a rightly-aligned created order. Yet, while aiming for the Kingdom-ever-after, our journey takes place in *this* kingdom, the kingdom where we find ourselves. Thus, there is a Kingdom-ever-after and a kingdom-of-the-now, and fairytales end in the kingdom-of-the-now, yet with an ever-after aim. *Our* story takes place between the actual and the ideal, and our stories often remind us that there is something ultimately unsatisfying about the actual as it is now, though we can find reflections of goodness. To paraphrase C. S. Lewis, there is something that is not here for which we desperately long, and the Kingdom wherein that Goodness reigns is one we deeply sense we were made to know.[2]

For this reason, it is interesting to ponder the Kingdom-ever-after of the Disney story through an Augustinian lens. Augustine argued that sin has disordered our loves, yet the good life and virtue require rightly ordered love (Charity). He distinguished between two kingdoms. The earthly city in which we all dwell is always a mixture of virtue and vice. The "saved," who seek God to re-orient their loves, while doing what they can to habituate their own impulses, are also members of the heavenly city.[3] Christians, then, live as both resident aliens within the earthly city and ambassadors of the heavenly Kingdom.[4]

As God is the source of all truth and love, this Kingdom is the domain of true love. Thus, true love cannot be fully known in the earthly kingdom, though we may catch glimpses, which enrapture our desire. Consequently, the greatest happiness is not actually in the everyday of the earthly kingdom. Our happiness, our joy, is at its highest when we set our minds on things above,[5] looking to the Kingdom-ever-after, where we will experience God's presence in the now, where there is fullness of joy and pleasures forever-more.[6] Trusting in their convictions concerning the nature of true love, the prince or princess (of the heavenly Kingdom) has assurance concerning the hope[7] that follows from their commitment to true love—that they eventually will grow evermore into the likeness of true-lovers. They are not perfect, nor will their life be, but they have faith in the ever-after in which, with time, the truth of love becomes more fully known. Moreover, they commit themselves to an archetype of true love aiming to grow into its likeness in order to love one another more fully. Faith, hope, and love are intertwined with ever-after happiness, but the greatest variable in the Kingdom is love.[8] Only true love can thaw our frozen hearts, after all.

Frozen is a film pregnant with symbolism, as love is continually questioned therein. It is not so shallow as to be known at first sight, nor must it always involve marriage. Love, it turns out, is complex. What makes the *Frozen* films so special is precisely the fact that Disney has tackled complex questions involving true love. Yet shades of gray do not overshadow archetype.

In *Frozen*, Elsa struggles with the emotional temperance and courage expected of a leader—seeking the mean between fear and recklessness. In *Frozen II*, it is Anna who faces fear, seeking courage to "do the next right thing"—a quality fitting for a future queen. Both films explore fear and the connection between *agape* love and the acquisition of inner-strength. In the first film, the fear is difference; in the second, it is change. (*Frozen II* also connects fear to enmity, exposing egoism within utilitarian logic). In these films, Disney strays from the classical emphasis on contrasting virtue and vice to remind us that there are different types of love, that *agape* is stronger than *eros*, and that, in reality, devils often present themselves as desirable[9]—as does Hans.

At the end of *Frozen*, as the ice in Anna's heart finally seems to overtake her life, Elsa is moved with an outpouring of expressive love. This climactic moment is resolved as we find Anna's heart thawing; she has finally found true love. It is understandable, although mistaken, to interpret this as meaning Elsa is the truelove—moreover that Elsa's expression of love thawed Anna's heart. Her heart was frozen from within, however, and the warmth of love resulting in its thawing likewise originated from within. While Anna truly loves Elsa, "only an *act* of true love," according to Grand Pabbie, "can thaw a frozen heart." It was Anna's self-sacrifice—even at the moment when the curse overcame her—that began the freeing of her heart from the curse.

While the Christian understands that this is not an accurate picture of salvation in the sense of *justification*—we cannot save ourselves, but need the mediating sacrifice of a savior—perhaps it can serve as an effective portrait of Christ's *sanctifying* work in the Christian's heart, in the sense that a transformation concerning Anna's understanding of love has a power not only to reorient the outworking of her actions (to offer her own life in the name of *love* rather than to become someone else's object of love), but also to reverse the reach and severity of the curse, and even to redeem relationships and restore communion. Bearing in mind we make no claim that Disney ever attempts to "give the gospel," but rather that certain aspects of the gospel enfold Disney's nonsectarian moral messages, *Frozen* presents a curse—not

Elsa's *gift* but the misuse of a gift, which results in Anna's *condition*—and the curse promises death.

While the process of salvation is a critical question that needs unpacking, what seems apparent in many Disney films is that Disney wants us to draw the conclusion that the key to the curse—to the human condition?—involves a sacrificial love. Anna's sacrifice resonates with the moral convictions of many western viewers, influenced by a Judeo-Christian sentiment that the greatest love is tethered to self-sacrifice on the behalf of another. Consider Baloo's self-sacrifice when defending Mowgli, and Bagheera's eulogy when he believed Baloo to be dead. This is one of the few times Disney offers an explicit reference to the Bible. "Greater love hath no one than he who lays down his life for his friend." [10] Whatever initiates the salvific transaction (the "marvelous exchange" of salvation), the *process* of salvation (sanctification) working itself out in the life of the believer requires God regenerating the heart of the believer, and it is in this sense that goodness and the Kingdom-ever-after is tethered to a reorientation of the heart—from self-centeredness toward a concern for others, and even a willingness to sacrifice self-interest in service to the good of another.

Beauty and the Beast suggests that even a love without clear sacrifice can still play a redeeming role. In this case, it was Beast who laid down his life in the name of love. Alas, it seems Beast's good deed was not enough to save himself. We are left with the impression that it is precisely because Belle *chooses* to love the prince, even after he had given up hope—"for who could ever love a beast?"—that her love had salvific impact. Yet the film raises an interesting question about the extent to which the salvific processes taking place within one's heart are actually observable to one another (and, thus, to the viewer). If we do not even understand our own hearts,[11] why think we can accurately evaluate all that is taking place within the heart of another?

Of course we recognize that Matt 7:16 indicates we will know people by their fruit. But our point, our main concern, given that the two events coincide (Beast's sacrifice and Belle's confession of love), is that it is possible Beast's transformation actually involved something which had already begun to take place within *his* heart, rather than with Belle's confession *per se*. After all, Belle had already begun to see "something there that wasn't there before." From one perspective, where Belle plays the role of salvific mediator, we can get a portrait of justification. From another angle which refrains from looking for an actual depiction of the Savior archetype, supposing, for example, that God may already be at work in the hearts of these characters (looking for the fruit rather than the source of salvation, in other words), we might see with Beast, as with Anna, that a reorientation of understanding within the heart was working itself out (sanctification) in acts of sacrificial love to such a degree that it began to have a redeeming impact on the observable effects of the curse.

Frozen is among the most popular and highest grossing of Disney animated features. Perhaps these sisters resonate so profoundly with us because they are symbolic of two sides of ourselves. Anna is naive with a passion for adventure and a longing for community, while Elsa is so aware of the weight of responsibility on her that her fear of failure has created a legalistic guilt that separates her from others. Psychologically, when fear is exposed, it often responds with anger and aggression. Upon an existential awakening, Elsa rightfully *let's go* of her legalistic chains of self-imposed guilt, but then moves to the other end of the spectrum—asserting a sense of individualistic freedom, which ironically has no more room for communion than her guilt and legalism. It is only after witnessing the excellence (virtue) of Anna's self-sacrifice that Elsa understands true love as the only magic strong enough to cover guilt and fear.[12]

Both girls longed for love (in different ways). While both misunderstood love, love was exactly what they needed. Anna was not in need of a prince, nor did she need Elsa's love *per se*; what she needed was an ability to know, within her heart, the sort of love that causes one to lay down their life for another. Elsa needed to see that she was truly loved as she was, not as she could have been—love is not an affirmation of lifestyle, but a declaration of value.

From a Molinist standpoint there is even more to unpack in this film. Molinism has a long history in the Christian tradition,[13] although it is not a perspective that we both hold. Sixteenth-century Jesuit Luis de Molina developed the idea in an attempt to reconcile human agency with God's providence. By drawing on the notion of God's *middle knowledge*, Molinism retains conviction in a radical depravity and traditional view of the Fall, but also reasons that the biblical account of human agency while interpreting scripture[14] as affirming a greater degree of libertarian free will than other theological perspectives. On Molinism, true love redeems, but it respects free will.[15] (This is why, as Aladdin learned, genies have no power over love). In this regard, it could be argued that Anna gives us a unique portrait of God's love—demonstrating patience and persistence in pursuing us, but also a respect for free will. From this perspective, the saddest line of the entire movie, following Elsa's command to go away, is Anna's acceptance of Elsa's rejection. "Okay. Bye."[16] Of course, her willingness to leave did not diminish her eagerness to die for Elsa. In the Christian narrative, from this perspective, humanity struggles, like Elsa, with a gift (free will). Though it may allow a potential for all kinds of trouble, it is necessary for obtaining any real and robust understanding of love at all.

Regardless of one's particular theological perspective, from any perspective that acknowledges the Fall, *Frozen* reminds us of the human condition. We have pricked our own hearts with a frigid curse that threatens both to overtake us (as with Anna) and to overwhelm us (as with Elsa) to such an extent that it drives us, inevitably, to a self-imposed seclusion from one another, and from even being capable of knowing true love. For true love requires demonstration and is not possible in isolation. It is only through the sacrifice of true love by which our hearts are cured—liberated to love. *Frozen* also demonstrates well a conviction which pervades the Disney canon—that what we ultimately long for is the ever-lasting goodness of a right-order, the beauty of a Kingdom-ever-after, and this Kingdom is one in which Love reigns.

Goodness beyond Justice

Disney has purposefully used idealistic archetypes to personify beauty, virtue, and the good life. Because of this, Disney films are not only able to speak to our deep sense of moral conviction, but they are also able to offer powerful depictions of, or perspectives on, Christian theology and the Kingdom-ever-after. As Francis Schaeffer once wrote, while we may assert disbelief in God or differing ideas concerning God, we still live in the world of the God who is there.[17] Despite our assertions concerning the narrative in which we find ourselves, if there is an author then the story is the author's—and the plot, unclear as it may be at times, is framed in terms of the story's genesis and eschatology. If indeed we were made to know beauty, true love, and the Kingdom-ever-after, then it is little surprise, despite its non-sectarian ambiguity, Disney's archetypal emphasis speaks so plainly to our moral convictions. All truth is God's truth; and truth, like light in the darkness, has a way of piercing the heart of our narratives, even, and especially, our personal narratives. Disney lore, in many respects, beseeches us, like the apostle Paul, to contemplate deeply the goodness, truth, and beauty of a Kingdom-ever-after, and to find archetypes of moral excellence worth imitating.[18]

Both the Judeo-Christian story of reality and Disney's Kingdom-oriented moral metanarrative emphasize that the Kingdom is one in which justice is realized—good triumphs over evil—but also that injustice and moral depravity are ultimately issues of character, requiring a reorientation of the heart for those who choose to seek the Kingdom and to live in light of the goodness expected from those who wish to become a citizen. Moreover, the just Kingdom, while one of freedom because love must be freely offered, is one in which its inhabitants *choose* to live in light of a sacrificial and supererogatory love. Now this is an extremely important point, as it opens the door to moral dialogue significantly. For the suggestion that our Kingdom-oriented aim involves a goodness which transcends justice—which goes beyond just-ness—allows us to explore to a deeper degree the complexities of justice in society. For when we speak of justice, we do so in light of our Kingdom-oriented convictions, we desire to see more than actual just-ness; we long for, even expect to find, a tangible sense of goodness which goes beyond the limits of justice in order to bring about a more beautiful ideal. It is to precisely such a complex topic that we now turn.

Part 3

APPROACHING DISNEY AS DOORWAY TO DIALOGUE:

Mediating Contemporary Narratives on Justice and Social Goodness

8

Injustice: Everywhere but Within

I n Walt's view, "Deeds rather than words... [represent] the part religion should play in everyday life."[1] Indeed, while systematic theology may help us better to grasp the concept of God's Kingdom, it is *practical* theology by which the Kingdom is largely expressed. Recall that, according to Walt, "the important thing is to teach a child that good can always triumph over evil, and that is what our pictures attempt to do.[2] To rephrase this in light of our discussion of the goodness and beauty of the Kingdom-ever-after—which, as we have seen, entails both a foundational sense of justice but also a goodness that goes beyond duty—*justice will prevail* (the Good will stand in victory over evil). He continues, "In our full-length cartoon features, as well as in our live action productions, we have tried to convey in story and song those virtues that make both children and adults attractive."[3] That is, *there is something beautiful about virtuous souls....* But to what end?

Addressing the nature of prayer, Walt stressed our need "for strength and inspiration to carry on the best human impulses [as we have seen, *habits of virtue and* love] which should bind us together for a better world [*a Kingdom-end?*]. Without such inspiration," he adds, "we would rapidly deteriorate and finally perish." (Recall that the crux of virtue ethics involves a conditioning of our impulses, a reorientation of our habits). It is the goodness produced by our best collective *impulses*[4] to live in light of love and virtue which Disney envisions as bringing us into moral unity even amidst cultural diversity.

Yet it is crucial to see that when we envision the Kingdom, an everlasting just-ness where love reigns, we long not merely for *justice* (whether we are cognizant of this or not), but for a *goodness* which goes beyond and perpetuates just-ness. Justice is not the end, then, of goodness. That which is good in so far as it involves a right order we call justice, and there is a sense in which we would call this beautiful in so far as we delight in the idea of justice—of things as they ought to be. However, it seems it is this goodness beyond justice to which we really refer when referencing the ultimate ideal, the Beauty, of the Kingdom-ever-after. This needs careful unpacking, and before we can speak of what justice is, we will have to consider what it is not.

Not only has Disney consistently (at least largely) appealed to the over-all, everlasting goodness of a Kingdom-ever-after, a way it should be, many Disney tales have also purposefully pointed out that things as we find them are *not* as we expect them to be. That is, Disney often brings us face to face with cases of undeniable injustices. While Disney seeks to awaken within us a desire for the Kingdom, and calls us to model our own moral lives after its representative citizens, it also reminds us that our current context is *not* that Kingdom, that there is still work to be done both in our own souls and in our communities before that Kingdom comes.

While it is true that Disney wants us to focus on the inside, Disney also calls us to consider something bigger than character development, namely, the very real impact of injustices which flow from corrupted characters. In some films, Disney uses archetype to embody the concept of a great evil. Consider Maleficent and the Evil Queen in *Snow White,* or even Hades and the Horned King. Such clear examples of evil are helpful in the sense of distinguishing the good from the bad in order to underscore that good will triumph over evil. Yet, still somewhat abstracted as they are—"evil" because they are supposed to be the "bad guy" or villain in a dualistic depiction—they remain somewhat foreign to our personal experiences. Other tales make us live through unfortunate events, unfair situations due to ignorance, arrogance, or prejudice, and sometimes very real, even scary, injustices.

Aladdin prompts us to *experience* frustration with a caste system. One who is born a "street rat"—even with a beautiful heart—"will die a street rat," while one as sinister as Jafar is privileged enough to become a royal advisor. It is Aladdin's lot in life to remain impoverished simply because he was born into poverty. Is that fair? In order to bring honor to her family, Mulan is told that she must present herself as favorable to men, according to the cultural standards of beauty determined by the men in her culture. She will need to be beautiful enough to inspire men to go to war, which includes having a tiny waist, and she must be an obedient and fast-paced worker. To honor her father by protecting him, to defend her country, to master admirable feats as a soldier is all counted as dishonor simply because she is a woman. Does that seem right? We *know* that the citizens are being mistreated in Nottingham. We are appalled by Penny's situation in *The Rescuers*, and we are outraged by the poacher's disregard for both human and animal life in *The Rescuers Down Under*. Dumbo is mistreated simply because he is not "normal," and we see that this is not right.

The Incan emperor Kuzco (*The Emperor's New Groove*) has no concern for the struggles and livelihood of the peasants far removed from his palace, as he intends to demolish an entire village simply to build his summer getaway. He cares not what happens to others and makes clear that he has the power to do whatever he wants. We feel injustice both concerning the abuse of his power and the taking of the villagers' property. There is no mistaking that Scar's seizure of power in *The Lion King* wreaks havoc on the circle of life. We feel, with Pocahontas, a great frustration at the unnecessary violence and injustice which flows from ignorance and prejudice. We suffer with Cinderella through the abuse of her "family." Mother Gothel's willingness to abduct the baby Rapunzel, her self-absorbed, insincere, and manipulative stories of looking out for her "flower," and her willingness even to kill Rapunzel's love in order to keep Rapunzel's power for herself—fill us with a fury to see justice served. Although it is somewhat atypical in representing the films in Disney's animated canon—focused as it is on institutional abuses, theological issues involving the sin of lust and a related sense of guilt, and exploring beauty in a slightly different manner than that observable in the princess tales—*The Hunchback of Notre Dame* may represent one of Disney's richest takes on the issue of injustice and the question of grounding justice.

In this film, Frollo—the Minister of "Justice" who "longed to purge the world of vice and sin"[5]— views all Gypsies as vermin and thieves. He kills a Gypsy woman while snatching an allegedly stolen item. Discovering it is a deformed Gypsy child, he intends to kill *it* also, until a priest intervenes. We sense injustice here, but what is it? Is it an issue of power structures *per se,* or of corruption within persons? Is it the religious narrative Frollo supposedly serves, or something in *him* which perverts that narrative? If the former, why was it the priest who rebuked him? Is it an inequality in opportunity for achievement—the fact that Gypsy culture was not highly valued —or is it the fact that some members of the human species were excluded from human community —deemed less valuable than others, or denied acknowledgement of due dignity? Disney presses the point that Frollo justified genocide and infanticide, because he "saw corruption everywhere except within."

In the world of live-action non-fiction, injustice is not always easy to identify with unanimity. This may be due to ignorance, poor reasoning, or even disagreement over core values. In contemporary dialogue, it is also due to the fact that, while injustice remains a universal conviction, "social justice" has become a confused and confusing claim to moral truth. It is a complex topic involving a complicated intersection of ethical and political issues, but it ultimately speaks (or attempts to speak) to questions of basic rights and due privileges.

The grounding for human dignity is difficult enough, though foundational to any sense of justice able to transcend perspective. The question of justice as distribution is more complex, involving debate over just how far entitlements extend beyond basic rights (assuming one can establish we have them). As philosopher Wyndy Corbin-Reuschling observes, "Concepts such as freedom, rights, fairness, and equal opportunity are bundled into conversations about justice as if those terms are synonymous."[6] Does one have a right to one's property or inheritance (including inherited privileges) or a responsibility to share everything with everyone else? Do some have unquestionable "rights" necessarily to the same power, property, and privileges which others enjoy? Is anyone *due* validation that their feelings or lifestyle are worth celebrating? Have we a moral duty to affirm all moral views as equally worth valuing? While ideals come easy, such appeals often involve a convoluted interweaving of questions concerning nature, ethics, and goodness. Thus, the appeal to justice as equal distribution (of power, property, privilege, or affirmation) is *more* difficult to ground than the appeal to intrinsic human value (as matter of fact).

Historically, with the rise in popularity of materialism (the view that there exists nothing beyond the material world), even the latter (the appeal to intrinsic human value) has been questioned by staunch empiricists. If there is no immaterial grounding for human value, morality reduces to perspective. If it is presupposed that morality is *defined* by social contract—there is no moral meaning beyond culture—then neither due-dignity nor due-distribution are easily grounded. There is no *real* injustice, only inconvenience—the social oppression of some individuals or groups according to the power, purposes, and prejudices of other oppressing groups. Some may deny materialism—*believing* in immaterial things like rights, human value, or a self-identity that is different from one's body—yet attempt nevertheless to define morality as socially constructed through discourses of hegemonic power via norms, customs, traditions, and various institutions, like media and the academy, and persuasive ideologies, such as neoliberalism and progressivism, among other examples. Unfortunately, this again relegates value claims to perspective. Though problematic, this view is nonetheless influential.

Since oppression comes in the form of one group's power-narrative (truth and value claims and moral prescriptions) denying freedoms or privileges to others by condemning such freedoms as wrong, some believe that "justice" involves liberating those marginalized perspectives from the moral censorship of the oppressor group's "truth" or value-narrative. This is the core claim of "Critical Social Justice" (hereafter CSJ)—a soft syncretism of historic Critical Theory (CT) and contemporary critical social theory (CST). Alas, even if an advocate of CSJ believes in immaterial truths or ideals, their definition of morality, and therein its prescription for justice, faces the same grounding problem as materialism. Even if they deny materialism in theory, they advance its prescriptive presuppositions in practice.

The main problem, then, is the grounding problem—first, for morality; second, for human dignity. For instance, the claim that an LGBTQ+ *person* is valuable, and it is unjust to harm them, is an appeal to human dignity, whereas the general claim that one's gender is not the same as one's biological sex, or that certain sexual practices are permissible and others are not, is a question of right-knowledge and moral truth. Pro-life arguments and pro-choice arguments both appeal to a sense of human dignity but differ concerning its epistemic grounding; the former appeals to an absolute sense of dignity due *all* human beings, while the latter appeals to a relative sense of dignity due to more fully-formed and cognizant beings over lesser-developed beings. Yet whether rights are *given* or simply appear wherever we deem "personhood" to begin is a question of right-knowledge and truth. One's morals and beliefs do not determine his or her (or another's) value, yet *only if* human beings are *intrinsically* valuable is it unjust either to harm them or to deny one's freedom to choose to harm another. Since both sides of the debate assert antithetical claims on human dignity, it is precisely the grounding for human dignity that is central to the debate. As John Warwick Montgomery argued, "The quest to define rights cannot be separated from the need to justify them."[7] Thus, the cornerstone of any satisfactory universal claim concerning human justice is the grounding for human dignity.

Using Disney as doorway to dialogue, the remainder of this work digs at the grounding for justice. We argue that CSJ offers insufficient grounding for a forceful appeal to justice, though it raises valid concerns for perspective and the alienation or mistreatment of human beings. Theism provides the only substantive basis for Justice, and the Jewish and Christian perspectives offer the most robust grounding for intrinsic human dignity and vision for human community. We submit that Disney attempts to mediate (not necessarily knowingly or always successfully) between these perspectives—advocating for consideration of perspective and care for the alienated, while also appealing to objective truth and right-order. Herein lies the apologetic power of approaching pop culture in general and Disney in particular as a doorway to moral dialogue and theological inquiry. Disney lore includes a canon of stories—widely accessible given its nonsectarian nature—which, taken together, present a grand moral narrative that, at times (perhaps surprisingly), aligns strikingly with the biblical narrative and reflects a Christian vision of reality. We focus not on questions of distribution, but the question of human value as grounded beyond individuals or groups, and justice as tethered to that grounding. Disney lore has regularly envisioned justice *not* as liberation in itself, but as an appeal to a grand-moral-narrative, and a goodness *beyond* justice.

9

Delimitations, Definitions, and the Descriptive/Prescriptive Distinction

Merlin wants Wart (*The Sword in the Stone*) to learn more about his world by becoming a fish, a squirrel, and a bird. As a fish, Wart learns that the world functions around concepts of contrast and an ability to navigate a natural sense of give and take: to and fro, high and low, stop and go. Within this lesson, he also learns that there is also a relationship between strong and weak, yet strength need not be determined by size and power alone. In song, Merlin explains a troubling but true aspect of human life: "The strong will try to conquer you, and that is what you must expect unless you use your intellect."[1] To a notable degree, we habitually identify things in terms of what they are not. Yet often, in education, a student must first learn to identify what something is — to understand the definition, for example — before moving on to compare and contrast similar and dissimilar things. In the same way, amidst dialogue, it is important to listen well, to understand, before engaging with conflicting commentaries.

Likewise, at this point, while it would be ideal in a work like this to saturate each chapter and "pepper" each page with Disney references, this is a deep topic which warrants a different approach. *Pocahontas* demonstrates well how ignorance can be just as dangerous as villainy, as both can lead to harms and hinderances, and both can foster division over dialogue. In fact, it was ignorance coupled with a zeal to react against apparent injustices which caused the settlers and the Powhatan people to view each other as villains. It was Mor'du's (*Brave*) ignorance (of what determines real strength, character) coupled with his arrogance that shaped his identity towards the villainy for which he was known.

It is important to attempt to see clearly the position with which one takes issue. Otherwise, one's ignorance risks either moving one to act too hastily in villainizing all aspects of "the other" perspective or causing one's own perspective to come off as slanderous and in bad faith because it is associated with defamation versus dialogue. The point is we must be careful in how we approach and "deal with" a theory as problematic—especially when it is one so entangled in popular parlance and contemporary culture wars. There is much debate in our cultural moment over questions of "social justice" and much talk concerning the claims of various social theories within the critical tradition. Advocates of CSJ may understand what they believe justice to look like, while many who oppose "critical theory" may understand what they think they are resisting. Yet while we will argue that CSJ *by itself* is not positioned to know justice, and so it is unable to speak of justice as fully as it believes, it is also possible (and potentially damaging if it fosters division over dialogue) that the one who disagrees with CSJ does not fully understand it or understand it at all.

We believe it will ultimately be more helpful, at this point, if we limit the Disney references while we attempt to make clear the claims with which we take issue. Too many references for the sake of engaging interest (though they are relevant to the book's overall thesis), at this point, risks convoluting our argument as it concerns what is at stake in the debate in defining justice. Before the reader fully understands what CSJ is and what it is not (with focus on the particular prescriptive aspect with which we take issue and the descriptive methodology with which we do not), we need to unpack several delimitations, make clear our definitions, draw out some historically relevant details, and then give at least an abbreviated form to the ideology of Critical Theory in general, and specify some of the unique claims of Critical Social Justice in particular. This will require more than one chapter. Given the complexity of the issue, then, the reader should understand there is much ground to cover, and while covering this ground it may not always be advantageous to engage Disney directly. Therefore, the reader should expect little to no references in the remainder of this chapter, and also in chapter 11, which draws out the influence of Critical Theory and identifies those aspects of CSJ which are particularly problematic. We should note that we feel this approach is appropriate at this moment and is even allowed relative to the needed cohesion of the work because of the multitude of references to Disney that pervade much of the overall text and analysis.

Aesthetic Appreciation and Cultural Critique: Two Paradigms of Pop-Culture Evaluation

Readers who are concerned about "social justice" might expect to see our analysis exclusively dedicated to issues pertaining to misrepresentation, co-optation, misappropriation, marginalization, and so forth. While this is not our primary approach, we recognize its value when rightly done and applied. Our emphasis is to get underneath things a bit more. "Social justice" is a popular phrase in our day, and while we all want justice (at least for ourselves), we differ on what justice looks like. We differ because we have different value hierarchies, which are informed by different background assumptions and presuppositions.

A prevailing justice ideology of our cultural moment exists under the banners of Critical Social Justice (CSJ) and Antiracism (most popularized by Robin DiAngelo and Ibram X. Kendi respectively). While the two ideologies are not identical, they are notably similar. Our primary concern involves the problematically ambiguous nature of the term "social justice" (or even, simply, "justice") when advanced from a progressive lens influenced by certain presumptions and freighted with certain presumptions that have arisen within contemporary social theories influenced by the historical and philosophical traditions of Critical Theory. And so, while cultural movements like CSJ, Antiracism, and others may overlap in some places, and while our argument may therefore be applicable to a number of particular critical social theories, we will be focusing our critique on the prescriptive banner of "CSJ" because it is specifically contemporary pop culture definitions of "social justice" downstream from the Critical-Theory tradition with which we take issue.

We acknowledge we have approached Disney from a predominantly positive standpoint, one of aesthetic appreciation, and not from a posture of the critical, from any number of critical social theories or critical approaches in media and cultural studies that are apt to problematize cultural artifacts and hegemonic institutions, such as Disney. It's not that we don't see the value in some of these approaches. We agree with Douglas Kellner that "media culture teaches individuals how to fit into the dominant system of norms, values, practices, and institutions" and that "critical media literacy can empower individuals to critically engage the images, stories, spectacles, and media that constitute culture..." and "thus help empower one in relation to dominant forms of media and culture."[2] While some of this perspective certainly influences our analysis, our enterprise is not principally concerned with identifying every ostensible power imbalance resident within Disney with a view to challenge and rectify how its expression is being reified in society.

We mostly affirm the position, as outlined in Robert T. Craig and Heidi Muller's work on *Theorizing Communication*, that "critical theory's exclusive focus on power relations and ideological critique ignores the numerous ways that communicative practices make universalistic claims on us quite apart from their role in any particular social order."[3] Additionally, while it is true that society to a certain extent is established and re-established by powerful cultural stakeholders and the art and products they produce (such as Disney), it doesn't follow that a specter of suspicion, and a need to deconstruct and then challenge, necessarily hovers over every entertainment moment. We assert that the joy, sadness, fear, elation, jeopardy, hope, and triumph, indeed the full complement of human emotions, generated by art that captivates our reason and rivets our consciousness has a power to unite us across difference, from diverse ethnicities, class locations, gender, and sexual orientation.

Given this assumption, it is with a lens of aesthetic appreciation that we have approached Disney because our intent is to focus (although not exclusively) on the phenomenological and even moral implications that unite us, versus those which divide us. Yet, before we offer any critique of CSJ, we want to stress that we understand that some readers may take issue with Disney's cultural depictions and caricatures. As noted in a previous chapter, we agree with Annalee Ward's statement that, "the stories children are exposed to will form the standards for testing the truth of other stories later in life. Consequently, charges of racism, sexism, misrepresentation of history, and so on, particularly in children's films, are not something to be taken lightly."[4]

Delimitations

Several delimitations are needed. It is not our goal to deal extensively with materialism, but to provide a primer on why materialism is unsatisfactory as moral grounding, and how even non-materialists often accept its presuppositions in contemporary moral dialogue. Nor is it our aim to deal extensively with all the complexities of historic Critical Theory (CT), Critical Social Theory (CST), and Critical Social Justice (CSJ), but to provide a succinct summary of some of CSJ's popular claims and, while acknowledging some of its strengths, expose its inability to speak thoroughly and fully concerning the justice to which it appeals. Further delimitation is necessary here. It should not be assumed that we are speaking to every area of interest or inquiry that would fall under this large and multifaceted knowledge area. As we write, Critical *Race* Theory in particular is a hot topic. It should not be assumed that we are reacting to nor specifically addressing CRT (which has had a significant evolution since its formation in the 1980s). We are specifically addressing particular aspects of historic CT and contemporary CST and some of its *prescriptive ideology*, known at the popular level as Critical Social Justice (CSJ).

We should note that historic Critical Theory, contemporary critical social theory (encompassing a number of critical social theories, such as critical race theory, critical pedagogy, queer theory, and postcolonial theory), antiracism, and critical social justice are not identical areas of knowledge, and it is incorrect to make or imply a 1:1 correspondence between them. Nevertheless, there is notable overlap among them and they at times inform one another. Notwithstanding the popularity of critical race theory and antiracism, we believe critical social justice (given its big-tent, broad range of ideas, and the massive popularity of Robin DiAngelo at the time of this writing, who has promoted CSJ) best captures the *manifold* ways this overarching ideology and knowledge area is impacting society, particularly at the popular level.

Consequently, while our analysis may involve related strands from the other areas mentioned, for economy of terms and thought we will primarily make reference to critical social justice (CSJ). We also note, our concern does not question that there exist systemic prejudices within any society, at any point in history, but that certain specific, popular presumptions (outlined below), commonly and historically associated with contemporary expressions of critical theory, are problematic once advanced as epistemic creed and moral mantra rather than inquiring and descriptive methodology.

In an effort to extend charity to multiple perspectives on critical theories, we want the reader to understand that people employ a critical methodology to approach a wide array of ideas. They come from a variety of worldviews and concerns and vary (at least to some degree) in intent and definitions of truth and justice. Journalists, for instance, often apply a critical methodology in order to scrutinize popular presumptions, investigate un-asked or unanswered questions, and potentially expose ignorance or abuses (to which no tradition, institution, organization or representative position of power is immune). Yet journalism is simply the business of exposing infor-mation. The *condemnation* of ignorance or abuse as bad or wrong is not an appeal to journalism *per se*, but to a moral conviction beyond it.

Many people do use a critical methodology as a means to a prescriptive end—a call to action—but, assuming that they can ground their calls to jus-tice, they may envision that "just" end differently. One might seek a social, political, or economic equality of opportunity, based on merit, while another might seek an equal distribution of representations in lieu of merit alone. Some might advocate for a general sense of safety in society, wherein one is free to choose one's own cultural preferences without fear of harm. Others are passionate to ensure that our social structures do not deny a basic affir-mation of special dignity due all human beings, despite their lifestyle prefer-ences or belief systems, or differences in race or gender. And some who employ a critical methodology specifically seek cultural and sociopolitical affirmation—even celebration—*not* of basic due-dignity, but of all moral val-ues. Obviously, some of these concerns are more controversial than others.

As a further point of delimitation, we are not addressing individual crit-ical theories. Our pointed concern involves an exploration of certain pre-scriptive presumptions that have historically accompanied the longstanding critical tradition in general, and often reveal themselves in popular contem-porary claims on social justice—prescriptions which, once asserted, raise some significant questions concerning foundations of justice. While most critical traditions question presumptions concerning truth and justice within established systemic foundations, we argue there is a need to question pre-sumptions concerning truth and justice within *CSJ's* moral foundations (or at least presuppositions), lest any systemic revolutions only perpetuate in-justices within newly formed or reinvented institutions.

In challenging materialism and relativism, we are not calling all advo-cates within various critical traditions materialists or relativists. We *are* sug-gesting that, despite one's beliefs about objective moral truth, it is possible for one's applications—however well intended—to misalign with one's foundations. (This happens all the time in politics when viewers are moved more by a candidate's stories than the strength of his or her arguments them-selves). We are primarily interrogating the insufficiency of *materialism* to back the particular prescriptions outlined below, but we also suggest that theists will likewise be unable to back such claims. This does *not* mean that theists who employ critical social theory *always would*, but, *in the event that they do* assert that the prescriptions below necessarily flow from their theistic narrative, we insist that he or she will be unable to ground such claims.

We do not address theistic narratives which some advocates may claim can ground the CSJ *prescriptive ideology*—we leave it to them to bear the burden of proof for such claims—but we do build a case for the sort of theism, rooted in biblical orthodoxy, that is robust enough (required) to ground substantive appeals to justice, and we explore what does and does not follow from that grounding. (An important distinction between social "justice" and social "goodness" is offered). We do understand the critical theorist's concern for personal applicability, rather than cold logic *per se*—that there is a problem if abstract propositions are too far removed to compel one to act (that justice understood means little if not applied). We do believe that both action and understanding are important, but also that an understanding of justice precedes the application of justice—lest we act in ignorance that may institutionalize new injustices.

The next delimitation is one of language. It is important to separate CSJ as descriptive (as methodology) from CSJ as prescriptive (as ideology). CSJ as a descriptive discipline is admirably interested in pointing to social and political institutions, cultural presumptions and practices, and even artistic expressions concerning these things, in order to describe a situation, to ponder potentially underrepresented perspectives, and to prompt inquiry about the nature of justice and injustice. This necessarily includes dialogue over the moral permissibility of actions, beliefs, and lifestyles that would understandably be prohibited if there is good reason to believe they are immoral, or at least censored so long as their moral rightness remains discordantly in question. Deliberation is a laudable aim. We note that when we say "CSJ" it should be understood that we mean, specifically, "CSJ *as a prescriptive ideology, removed from a well-grounded moral authority, that asserts particular claims concerning injustice and imposes particular definitions on justice.*"

CSJ *as prescriptive* should be understood as the problematic move beyond description and inquiry, *yet without an adjoining, satisfactorily grounded, moral authority*, wherein it is presumed that: (1) the marginalization of any perspective or practice (such as those which the status quo may consider immoral) is unquestionably oppressive and therefore necessarily wrong;[5] (2) the more intersectional[6] one's perspective, the more qualified that perspective is to speak on moral truths and values related to justice concerns; (3)

"justice" is to be defined unquestionably as the "liberation" of any such marginalized perspective; and (4) liberation is to be achieved by securing "tolerance," which is understood as affirmation, acceptance, or encouragement of the marginalized perspective and practice. Alas, this prescriptive approach encourages *intolerance* (of the mainstream) over *inquiry*, and shame and silence over truth-seeking.

Because this topic has such breadth and depth, further qualification is needed. The critical tradition at times seems to want action over analytical argument. The CSJ advocate reading this may already take issue with the notion that he or she should remain within a descriptive place, without offering anything prescriptive to drive the action forward. Yet this is not what we are saying. We are saying that the CSJ advocate, in theory, cannot make this move. She can attempt, obviously, and will, because of the phenomenological realities of disparities and injustices one believes one is seeing, but these realities in and of themselves, without a moral grounding determining the objective, immoral wrongness of the disparities and (supposed) injustices witnessed, are insufficient to legitimize the loud, yet epistemologically hollow, protestations.

CSJ's narrative of morality is borrowed. It is the nature of what is borrowed that concerns us. Both the materialist approach of historic CT and the postmodern synthesis and assembly of critical social theories that inform CSJ have problems in that—whether or not the advocate ostensibly believes in objective truth—certain claims upon justice actually bring into question one's understanding of or ability to ground justice objectively. If one cannot ground justice, one is left only with warring perspectives—or a perspectival relativism.

We agree that if we fail to evaluate critically the powers of influence within a society, or potential abuses of that power or harmful prejudices behind those powers, then, if the injustices occurring within those systems are caused or reinforced by the systems themselves, we risk allowing those abuses of power and influence to reproduce themselves. Critical social theories are concerned about this reification and thus can play a role in the overall dialogue regarding justice and injustice. Whether something *is* in fact "unjust" or whether a proposed solution to systemic prejudices *is* "just," however, will depend on the strength of the moral narrative accompanying the critical methodology. One's *application* of "justice"—even if there is "goodness" reflected within the application—will only be as strong as one's *understanding* of justice. A majority in a society, sector, or institution may *define x* to be "just" and publicly support x because doing so *seems* appropriate, yet if it turns out to be the case that x is wrong, then the majority has simply encouraged and facilitated a new systemic injustice. We agree wholeheartedly that critiquing influential ideologies that are present within societal institutions and systems is both good and necessary to right understandings and applications of justice. (That is actually what we are doing here relative to Disney). What we question is the nature of the accompanying narrative that is necessary for grounding justice, and we take issue with some particular presumptions that can and do arise when one advances CSJ as the grounding narrative—as prescriptive ideology rather than accompanying methodology—in lieu of an accompanying narrative substantive enough to ground justice.

The reader should also understand that the emphasis of skepticism is upon perspective, not person. What is in question here is the *grounding* for value, virtue, and moral truth and rightness. To marginalize a perspective as incorrect and immoral is not the same as marginalizing the human being who holds that perspective. The issue of CSJ's prescription specifically involves whether it is necessarily oppressive to assert that a given perspective on value is incorrect and immoral. (This, after all, is what CSJ does in condemning mainstream narratives). Equal human value is not in question, although its grounding *is*. Entitlement is not the concern, but whether the CSJ *prescriptive ideology* (removed from an adjoining moral authority robust enough to ground a substantive claim on justice) can ground the moral foundations from which it prescribes social justice as equal-entitlement-to-an-equal-affirmation-of-all-moral-perspectives.

As a final point of delimitation, the scope of this work does not include a deep dive into the Moral Argument, nor into the claim that theism in general (the classical Jewish and Christian narratives in particular) provides the most satisfactory grounding for human value. These points will only be referenced with a degree of explanation. As we consider the weaknesses of materialism and CSJ and the strength of theism to ground an authoritative appeal to justice, we will use Disney stories as an exploratory lens for contemplating the nature of justice and a goodness that goes beyond it. While there is overlap with CSJ's concern for perspective and community, theism in general is *necessary* for grounding justice, while the Jewish and Christian traditions provide the stronger foundation for one's convictions of human value and community. We submit that it is the former to which Disney appeals concerning justice; the latter which it envisions concerning goodness.

10

The Materialist Backdrop

Justice asserts the conviction that there is a way things *ought to be*, thereby pointing to an ideal social order and a perpetuating principle-oriented end. A Kingdom-ever-after bespeaks the idea of the Good Life in its fullest sense, which entails an order wherein justice reigns and injustice is not allowed to be. But what does justice require? Moreover, what can motivate us to bring about that end? Why believe such an ideal to be achievable?

"All you need is faith and trust,"[1] right? Actually, that still is not enough, according to Peter Pan. You also need something else, something more than belief itself. In the Darling children's case, "Pixie Dust" was required. In *Raya and the Last Dragon*, the characters needed to place faith in one another, yet in itself this was not enough either; the restoration of Kumandra was not possible without a mediating magic. Pinocchio's transfiguration was not possible from moral obedience alone; the intervention of a supra-natural agent was requisite, along with an ensuing miracle (or what some might call "magic" from the perspective of the natural realm). Justice and hope for Cinderella rests similarly upon the need of a mediating magic. So too, the salvation of Alma Madrigal and her children (*Encanto*), as they flee an armed conflict, and the Madrigal family's subsequent gifts come not from any assertion of a will to life or power or identity, but from the enchanted blessing of a mediating magic. The object of their faith takes the form of an enchanted candle, but the magic is not the candle; the magic is embodied in the candle, which enlivens the house. While Mirabel expresses faith in her casita, Alma places her faith in the candle, and the other family members exercise faith in their powers, all of them have faith, ultimately, in a mediating magic.

Beast's enchanted punishment contains a moral condition, and any hope for restoration is dependent upon fulfilling this condition before the last petal of the enchanted rose falls. His faith expressed in pursuing love is not a belief for the sake of belief, but a trust placed in the power of a mediating magic and the supranatural promise represented in the enchanted rose. As he begins to experience love, he also begins to place his faith in love as well—to such a degree that he is even willing to sacrifice his hope on behalf of Belle's happiness. He begins to understand that love is key to this mediating magic, but also, perhaps more importantly, that the transformative beauty of love involves his growing into a goodness which transcends his need merely to meet a moral condition.

Why do Disney films seem to work so hard to get us to believe in magic, in the power to achieve and overcome, in a mediating hope for restoration, reconciliation, or transformation—in anything, really? One of the challenges from conservatives[2] is that Disney attempted to replace God with magic. While that seems inconsistent in many ways with the moral metanarrative we have considered in this work, there may be a degree of truth in it. What Walt did seem to have a problem with (because of personal experiences largely centered around the character and actions of his father) was religion in some of its institutionalized forms. Yet he nevertheless professed to believe in God and he placed great emphasis upon the importance and power of prayer. Mark Pinsky explains that all authoritative biographies of Walt's religious life begin with Elias Disney:

> The father of Walt and Roy was a man greatly conflicted about faith.... [As a child, Elias was taught to adhere] to an austere form of methodism.... In Canada, the family was so strongly opposed to music and dancing that Elias had to head for the backwoods to play his fiddle, and on one occasion his mother discovered him performing at a dance and smashed the instrument on Elias's head. 'The devil was in the fiddle, to their notion,' Roy recalled. 'Dancing was just evil.' ...[Later] the young father became quite religious and joined a Congregational church.[3]

Pinsky continues to explain the impact of Elias's character upon Walt's perspective:

> Most historians agree that Elias's authoritarian and sometimes cruel nature—and his propensity for whipping and even beating his sons—played a role in turning Walt and Roy against the

church. The brothers' ambivalent relationship with organized religion is well documented, as is their strong personal faith in God... As an adult, Walt did not start attending church until he was forty.... [Quoting Disney biographer Marc Elliot,] 'Walt considered himself religious yet he never went to church. The heavy dose of religiosity in his childhood discouraged him; he especially disliked sanctimonious preachers. But he admired and respected every religion, and his belief in God never wavered.'"[4]

Walt also understood, as we have seen, that, in public education and the entertainment industry, the emphasis on moral objectivity, virtue, and the beauty of a Kingdom-ever-after have a wider reach when (at least, at first) presented in a non-sectarian manner.[5] The reason is because these things—the fact of moral objectivity, the goodness of virtue, the desire for justice, and even the praise of a goodness which transcends just-ness—resonate with our deepest moral convictions. In this sense, even without naming the Maker, Disney stories call us to ponder the Maker's Grand Narrative. This approach was encouraged by renowned popular-level Christian philosopher and theologian Francis Schaeffer, when he wrote, "We must never forget that the first part of the gospel is not "Accept Christ as Savior," but "God is there." Only then is one ready to hear God's solution for man's moral dilemma."[6]

It is no surprise that early Disney films seemed, to some, to call us to believe in anything, as long as we see the need to believe. Belief for the sake of belief in itself, even belief in oneself, cannot, of course, be the end of significance, or Camus was correct in suggesting that the meaning of life is whatever keeps you from killing yourself.[7] Yet this is still a productive place to start in an age of non-believing. Since the modern age, many philosophers have concluded that life is one of meaninglessness and insignificance.[8] Because this thrownness into absurdity and anxiety is an unbearable experience to live out, many postmodern thinkers continued to push back against premodern notions of higher truths and grand narratives but also began to emphasize a leap of faith into belief for the sake of belief. Without a higher narrative to ground meaning, however, the leap is ultimately one of futility. Disney films were born during an age in which many people in the world were struggling with the pressures of materialism, and Disney films were so well received that they continued on into the postmodern age.

What many moderns and postmoderns share, ultimately, is a non-belief in higher truth—a truth beyond humanity and the physical world. For the one, the world is all fact and no magic. For the other, magic is a personalized or communal experience. *Experience* is the only thing which gives life meaning.[9] Both views, then, are impacted by materialism (the rejection of higher truths and a moral metanarrative), and Disney films can foster dialogue in both directions. For the one, Disney films call us to believe in, to acknowledge that there is, that we need to experience, something beyond ourselves. Chief Tui rejects Moana's perspective because of a seeming disbelief in a mediating magic. There is no Heart of Te Fiti—Moana's rock is just a rock—and Tui's mother, the one who loves to talk about supernatural things, is seen as the village crazy lady. Yet Disney asks us to reconsider. For the other, Disney begins with the belief that something is there—that we *ought* (we are meant) to experience and be a part of something significant—and then presses more sharply into that conviction (pointing us to the hope of a Kingdom-ever-after). In *Frozen*, Elsa's self-imposed seclusion from her sister strikes us as not right—and Disney presses into this—while Elsa's pull, in *Frozen II*, to discover her purpose, a meaning to her powers, resonates with us as good—and Disney presses into this as well.

When approaching a conversation on CSJ, it is appropriate to discuss materialism for two reasons. First, historic Critical Theory (CT) grew out of Marxism (and into Neo-Marxism). Karl Marx began as a philosophical idealist, a Hegelian believing that reality ultimately reduces to a single Absolute Spirit, and history amounts to the process of its ideas (our experiences) working themselves out through *dialectic*—the procedure of one idea coming into prominence, then being challenged by a contrary perspective, until finally achieving synthesis, thereby welcoming a new era.[10] Marx converted to materialism under the influence of Ludwig Feuerbach. Feuerbach agreed with Hegel in that history amounts to a dialectical process, but he challenged that it is the *material conditions* of any given age that influenced the ideas and developments of the times.[11] Claude-Henri de Rouvroy, Comte de Saint-Simon related this historical change and ideological power more specifically to class conflict.[12]

Synthesizing these influences, the worldview that came to be associated with Karl Marx and Friedrich Engels (who coauthored *The Communist Manifesto* in 1848) is known as Dialectical Materialism—the view that because there is no higher truth beyond the material world, history simply amounts to a series of class struggles between oppressor and oppressed, as determined by the material conditions of the age. As economic structures changed, ideologies, values, and powers changed, but social stratifications remained, and oppression remained tethered to such class division. In the modern age, with its emphasis upon individualism and the advent of capitalism, this division and oppression has manifested itself into two large classes—the "haves" (the economically oppressive class who owns the means of production and has greater access to property) and the "have-nots" (the economically oppressed working class whose livelihood is bound to producing capital for the owning class).[13] Although Marx's primary interest was in *economic* materialism, his worldview foundation of *philosophical* materialism—the belief that all that really exists is matter in motion; there is *no* immaterial aspect to reality—presents a significant obstacle to a full-orbed sense of justice.

The shift toward Neo-Marxism is associated with the influence of Max Horkheimer. Neo-Marxism expanded Marxist ideology in an interdisciplinary manner, so as to include an investigation into the broader aspects of social and historical contexts, and the potential systems of oppression within. Thus, oppression comes not only from economic hardship, but also from social norms, customs, or any manifestation of hegemonic status quo.[14] Although CT's origins trace themselves to the Marxist/Neo-Marxist tradition of social theory heralded by the Frankfurt School, the central ideas concerning an emphasis on class struggle, oppression, and liberation branched out into other schools of thought, which may or may not identify themselves as "Marxist." The spirit of dialectical materialism permeates CSJ, nevertheless.

This brings us to the second reason. As syncretistic as postmodernists can be, CSJ advocates may identify as materialists or non-materialists. As noted above, however, contemporary ideologies have advanced several materialist presuppositions to the point that pop culture has breathed them in like a virus. Many non-materialists have no idea their belief system has been compromised.

When we accept to the point of compliance the prescription that we ought not to bring moral and religiously informed convictions into politics and the public square, we have implicitly affirmed materialism's presumption that such beliefs are only privatized personal opinions, having no *real* reference to any clearly objective truth about reality. Thus, as Marx claimed, immaterial ideals, like the truth-claims of religion, function more like an opiate—a drug we take to make ourselves feel better about the fact of our misery—while the only "facts" that we can discuss in the public square and political arena are empirical claims about the material world and socioeconomic claims about the power structures which surround material goods.

Disney actually took a jab at Marxism in *Fun and Fancy Free* (1947), wherein Jiminy is befuddled by the book, *Misery for the Masses*. (U.S. citizens at that time were well aware of the early twentieth-century atrocities of regimes associated with the ideological impact of Marx).

Some believe that intrinsic value and objective, universal moral responsibilities simply do not exist; morality is relative to cultural or individual perspective. Others believe that a secular case for moral objectivity can be built upon an appeal to our rational nature. If materialism is true, however, then a survival-of-the-fittest explanation provides the best explanation of what we should expect concerning social interaction. Thomas Hobbes understood this well when he wrote of a natural state wherein "every man has a right to everything, even to one another's body."[15] On such grounding, "right" is only a product of might; inequality is a fact of nature. Nothing is *really* "unjust" on any system in which justice is defined *solely* in terms of a social contract.

Some appeal to a sociobiological empathy, but this is a leap of faith in itself. Sociobiologist E. O. Wilson theorized that moral sentiment is the product of evolution. From value learned via reward and punishment, we find reward amidst role fulfillment and meeting the expectations of others. We then construct a system of values based upon conformity to shared standards.[16] Philosopher Michael Ruse has similarly advanced the idea of cooperation as a biological strategy. Although "there is no foundation for [morality] 'out there,' beyond human nature,"[17] and while nature has made us self-centered, self-preservation sometimes warrants cooperation. Thus, we evolved a moral mechanism to help to that end.[18] So, morality is based on feelings; inherited impulses move us to adopt a sort of golden rule.[19] "We need to believe in morality, and so, thanks to our biology, we do."[20]

Norman Geisler and Frank Turek have pointedly challenged this approach. And many other philosophers have likewise found it to be a problematic leap with an unsatisfactory grounding. First, ideals like love are nonmaterial. Second, when we witness someone being mugged, our natural instinct for safety and survival is in competition with any desire to help. Third, the notion that morality is an evolved sense of cooperation for the sake of survival presupposes an evolutionary end—survival—yet Darwinian evolution "by definition, has no end because it is a nonintelligent process.... [Nor can it] explain why people knowingly engage in self-destructive behavior... [or] subvert their own survival instincts to help others."[21] Fourth, it is assumed that survival is "good," but good is undefined; there is no standard to judge between the definitions of Hitler vs Mother Theresa. Fifth, Geisler and Turek continue, sociobiologists confuse the fact of morality with stories about how we might have come to know morality.

> Even if we come to know some of our 'moral sentiments' because of genetic and/or environmental factors that doesn't mean there is no objective Moral Law outside ourselves.... [As William Lane Craig observed] 'at best that would show how moral values are discovered, but it would not show that those values are invented.' Indeed, I may inherit a capacity for math and learn the multiplication tables from my mother, but the laws of mathematics exist regardless of how I come to learn them. Likewise, morality exists independently of how we come to know it.[22]

Finally, a biologically derived 'moral sentiment' poses problems. "Why shouldn't people murder, rape, and steal to get what they want if there is nothing beyond this world? Why should the powerful 'cooperate' with the weaker when the powerful can survive longer by exploiting the weaker?"[23]

Disney's *Zootopia* raises several fascinating questions here. In this film, there is a functioning social order inclusive of all types of animals—including those traditionally identified as predators and prey. Yet within this zoological utopia, there is an underlying sense of fear and microaggression toward the "predator" types. A young fox who is excited to join the Junior Rangers is beaten and muzzled just for being a predator-type. This fear even reveals itself between partners (fox and rabbit). As the story advances, we see many predator-type animals mysteriously turning "savage." Judy's (the rabbit's) press-conference faux pas is to note that this was only happening to predator types and then to suggest that perhaps this behavior is connected to their "predatory biology." As it turns out, the assistant mayor (a sheep) is behind the plot to frame the mayor (a lion) and create these "savages." Stressing that "fear always works," she admits that she is willing to turn every predator in the city into a savage if they stand in her way. For there is no stopping a social force even of "prey-types" when "ninety percent of the population [is] united against a common enemy."[24] As long as prey-types fear the predators—as long as the mayor propagates the narrative that predators cannot help but revert, inevitably, to a savage nature—she will be able to remain in power. This is an inverted Hobbesian state, where a social order has somehow occurred, yet, if it is truly a state of nature, it cannot help but fall back into fear and hostility. In a state of nature, why should we expect the predators to treat prey-types with equal respect? This film asks just the opposite question, but from the perspective of the prey. In a Hobbesian state, "right" is simply the product of might, yet "might" may come in the form of intelligence rather than physical power. In a true state of nature, if some members of the prey-type group are intelligent enough to orchestrate a permanent disempowerment of predator-types, why should they not do exactly this? Though the sentiment of an evolutionary biological development of moral sentiment sounds good, the sentiment of moral sentiment is, ultimately, morally impotent if materialism forms the foundation.

While some argue from evolutionary biology, others attempt to argue, more specifically, from human autonomy. According to James Rachels, although humans have no basis for special dignity and treatment simply due to their biology, it is still somehow a given that we should respect their autonomy.[25] In this case, it seems that, although moral obligations are not really real, we objectify morality because our own biographical life compels us to identify with other rational, sentient beings.[26] But why? To emote, "*I* wouldn't want anyone to do that to *me*," offers no reason as to why they *shouldn't*—especially if there is no reason as to why they *couldn't!* Scott Smith has thoughtfully criticized the naturalist attempt to ground morality in the autonomy of reason. Such appeals are "doomed to failure because they trade on naturalism... [yet the] evidence for our self-reflection and forming reasons for action actually serve as evidence that naturalism is not true."[27]

Grounding morality in the natural world, or a shared rational nature, does not provide the obligatory force that many believe. There is no real reason to expect, for instance, that survival of the species must include the entire species. Why think that any given creature ought to be concerned with all like creatures simply because it can? At best, we can appeal to a set of basic moral principles that serve human needs, but even here there is no reason that we (or anyone) ought to go along with your contract—especially when it is not in our best interest, or you are not watching. As Elliot Sober summarizes; "Evolutionary theory cannot, all by itself, tell us whether there are any ethical facts. Nor, if ethical facts exist, can evolutionary theory tell us... what some of those facts are."[28] While some place significance upon human autonomy, others, like Bertrand Russell, have attributed our autonomy to the realization that we are merely helpless atoms in a world not really made for us.[29] While we might believe there to be some sort of significance in our ability to assert our own meaning in the face of a nihilistic void, obligations would be absurd facts in such a world. [30] Thus, materialism succumbs to moral relativism the moment an autonomous will asserts itself over another; there is no grand perspective to judge between them, only contending perspectives and the bullying of the more powerful over the weaker.

Disney's *Raya and the Last Dragon*—a creative depiction of the human condition—presents a world in which Kumandra (the ideal of human unity and community) has become fragmented by distrust and self-preservation. We sense that this *ought not* to be—that this division *ought* to be fixed and that reconciliation plays a key role in restoration. Yet, what may be lost on many viewers—masked by the deeper conviction of the ought-to-be—is that, if this *is* in any way comparable to the human condition, and if there is no higher truth, no all-encompassing moral narrative, then not only would we *not* expect reconciliation, but we should never have expected Kumandra to exist in the first place. But we *do* expect Kumandra to be achievable, and Disney presses into that moral expectation.

Materialism—a reality with no higher truth and moral metanarrative—succumbs to power-play. Moral prescriptions then fall to contradiction because the ideal of moral obligation carries no real substantive force. Consider the American Anthropological Association's 1947 declaration. Because "standards and values are relative to the culture from which they are derived,"[31] they concluded it would be wrong for one culture to dominate another. Because individual perspectives develop via individual cultures, we owe it to individuals to preserve their freedoms—by championing individual rights and contesting the domination of one culture by another. In particular, Western values ought not be imposed upon other cultures. Respect ought to be due cultures. This comes via respect of individuals. Therefore, respect ought to be due individuals.

Yet why think cultures and individuals are really equal? Why value equality if value is relative? Furthermore, how is the AAA able to impose a universal mandate that no one should assert universal mandates? Such is the illusion of tolerance without a grand narrative—a dominant perspective to ground an appeal to justice. Moral relativism commonly trades upon presumption and equivocation (see brackets):

1. [Belief about] Right/wrong varies from culture to culture.

2. So, what is right/wrong depends upon the prescriptions of one's culture. [Morality is determined by culture].

3. Therefore, there are no objective, universal moral truths. [Morality is determined by culture].

As you can see, ambiguity is deceptive. The conclusion is often asserted as a premise.[32]

If morality is relative to culture, perhaps we can form a cultural pact wherein we pledge to work together, but upon what grounds can materialism stand to decry as "unjust" the imposition of one culture's values upon another, and since any mainstream culture includes subcultures and countercultures, what grounding can judge between them when values clash? Further, even if we do not believe in materialism personally, if appeals to higher truth *ought* to be kept out of the public square (see the contradiction?), what hope is there for grounding inalienable, non-arbitrary rights? Whether we identify as materialist, relativist, or neither, we must take caution in relativizing moral truth to perspective, or we will have questionable grounds for asserting claims of justice or injustice. More directly, even if we deny relativism in theory our worldview may nevertheless reduce to relativism in application.

11

Critical Theory and the Conceptual Foundations of the Critical Social Justice Movement

Recalling the reasoning from chapter nine, it was explained that a chapter like this one requires careful articulation on our part and careful consideration on the part of the reader. While examples are helpful, they can also become distracting when lines of reasoning warrant close attention because they are spread across several ideas. The reader should therefore understand that we will refrain from using Disney references in this chapter. It is essential to understand fully the position with which we take issue, with minimal distraction.

Critical Theory formally began with the establishment of the Frankfurt School in Frankfurt, Germany in 1923. The Frankfurt School was an institute of social theory and critical philosophy whose epistemological origins were initially rooted in orthodox Marxism and focused on two primary concerns: 1) the analysis of power and domination in society derived and reified from the labor process, the 'means of production', and manifested in class struggle and division, with a view of empowerment and emancipation for those outside mainstream society and 2) a rejection and refutation of traditional theory and its adherence to positivism, quantitative methods, and maintenance and reinforcement of the status quo. Prominent figures of the Frankfurt School were Max Horkheimer (whose directorship in 1930 galvanized the institute), Theodor Adorno, Walter Benjamin, Erich Fromm, Herbert Marcuse, and later, Jurgen Habermas, among others.

In time the Frankfurt school moved from Marxism to Neo-Marxism (an amendment and expansion of Marxism) and expanded its analysis of power to all areas of society including the understanding, articulation, and use of 'reason' and the prevailing hegemonic norms, customs, and traditions undergirding society's cultural superstructure. Today Critical Theory's influence is most clearly seen in contemporary expressions of critical social theory, encompassing a number of critical theories (small c, small t, plural) including critical race theory, critical pedagogy, postcolonial theory, feminist theory, gender studies, and queer theory, among others.[1] In summation, when we think about critical theory, past or present, we must keep squarely in view that "since its inception, critical theory has been primarily concerned with the elimination of oppression and the promotion of justice. Liberation is a theme that runs through critical theory; liberation from objective oppressors such as colonizers and exploitive employers, and liberation from subjective forces such as mass culture and ideology."[2]

Hence, as William Gorton observes, all critical theories advance "liberation ideologies" which critique "economic, social and political structures, institutions or ideologies that are held to oppress people. The aim of critical theory is human emancipation, and this is accomplished in part by laying bare structural impediments to genuine freedom, contradictions and incoherencies in people's beliefs and values, and hidden ideologies that mask domination. Liberation thus comes through enlightenment,"[3] and oppression is believed to reveal itself within any "normal"/other, us/them dynamic that may manifest in society—such as in an abled/disabled dichotomy.

The ideological influences of CSJ run deep—including Herbert Marcuse's critique of oppression in industrialized society, Paulo Freire's philosophy of education and oppression and his pioneering of critical pedagogy, a preoccupation with intersectionality, introduced by Kimberlé Crenshaw, and an oppressor/oppressed template as a way to view and understand society, as popularized by Özlem Sensoy and Robin DiAngelo, among others.[4] Critical social theories and aspects of postmodernism (particularly poststructuralism) share a concern for exposing potential ways in which oppression is reinforced through the domination of values, beliefs, and practices often associated with grand metanarratives. There is a shared Marxian interest in cultural struggle, often through a Foucauldian lens. Michel Foucault replaced the idea of struggle over class-power with power over language and claims to knowledge. Truth-claims do not reflect a way-it-ought-to-be; they reveal facts about power relations within a given context. Morality simply amounts to power-play, and power is asserted through (embedded within) claims of knowledge.[5] Foucault states,

> "We should admit...that power produces knowledge (and not simply by encouraging it because it serves power or by applying it because it is useful); that power and knowledge directly imply one another; that there is no power relation without the correlative constitution of a field of knowledge, nor any knowledge that does not presuppose and constitute at the same time power relations."[6]

The call to liberation from grand metanarratives and associative grand moral narratives also finds roots in the philosophy of Nietzsche, who understood that without a grand, enslaving narrative (as he believed Christianity to be), we are free to assert ourselves as masters of our own fate.[7] Here we find another Hegelian influence (though Nietzsche was an atheist). Hegel's dialectic understood the thesis-antithesis-struggle toward synthesis (new knowledge) in terms of a master-slave tension, wherein each perspective sees itself as authority on knowledge and therefore attempts to dominate the other in order to assert its own consciousness as truth. The winner, the master or dominant-view, ironically becomes limited in its ability to acquire meaning beyond its assertion of power, while the slave-perspective is expanded by the realization that the master actually needs the slave for affirmation of the master's power. Thus, the slave perspective acquires greater understanding of both slave and master, while the master cannot see beyond its own power. As the slave's perspective is enlightened to understand itself as equal to the master and the master as dependent upon it, it rises to demand affirmation from the master as well; hence, the new perspectival unity is reached.[8]

Nietzsche inverted this dynamic, praising the oppressed as the true masters. Moral narratives include a herd-mentality that believes in higher value-truths (for lack of boldness or creativity to face a meaningless world) and asserts prescriptive power over those who do not buy into the herd-morality. In flipping traditional morality on its head, the idea is this: as the oppressed masters-of-their-own-truth and fate are able to liberate themselves, they consequently may liberate the real "slaves" from the real oppression of the grand moral narrative.[9] This idea was echoed by Freire: "It is only the oppressed who, by freeing themselves, can free their oppressors. The latter, as an oppressive class, can free neither others nor themselves."[10] And why is this the case? Because, as Kate Lockwood Harris explains, the so-called lived experience of oppressor groups leads to pronounced societal blindness, "a less complete view of the world," and, alternatively, the lived experience of oppressed groups leads to pronounced societal understanding as they "not only understand their own experience, but also the experiences and knowledge of groups with more power."[11]

Marx, Nietzsche, and Foucault all challenged traditional ideas, but Nietzsche (and postmodernists thereafter) challenged more than this. As David Naugle explains, Nietzsche's philosophy is one of perspectivism.

> In *The Genealogy of Morals* Nietzsche states, 'There is only a seeing from a perspective, only a "knowing" from a perspective, and the more emotions we express over a thing, the more eyes, different eyes, we train on the same thing, the more complete will be our "idea" of that thing, our "objectivity."' Thoroughgoing perspectivism thus renders genuine objectivity farcical. There is only perspectival seeing and knowing implies that 'there are no facts, only interpretations.'[12]

Similarly, standpoint theory, initially domiciled to feminist theory but now expanded to other critical social theories, holds that knowledge and truth are socially situated and as such, as Marcel Stoetzler and Nira Yuval-Davis explain, "it is vital to account for the social positioning of the social agent."[13] Standpoint theory believes itself to escape perspective-relativism because, it is believed, continual self-critique and reflection can provide a stronger sense of objectivity than the traditional appeal to absolutes.[14]

There is also a *tension* between the modernist roots and postmodern shoots of the critical tradition. Whereas modernist materialism *reduces* to relativism, postmodernism openly *embraces* a form of it. There is no one truth, only multiple ways of knowing—and sees human nature as socially constructed (here, there is also brief overlap with existentialism).[15] Some critical theorists seem to crown the social scientists (and qualified academic peers) as the esteemed experts on knowledge. Gorton expounds, "The truth—provided by the expert—enlightens the subjects of inquiry and, it is hoped, thereby sets them free. They trade in their distorted ideological understanding for the clear-eyed perspective provided by critical theory."[16]

Postmodernists are skeptical of this point, however. Alas, many critical theorists *claim to be* postmodernists, and critical social theory *borrows from* postmodernism. The question, then, is whether the critical theorist is advancing a grand narrative of enlightenment or simply, descriptively, uncovering multiple perspectives. "Critical theorists maintain that ultimately an objective picture of society can be rendered" and believe "that there is an identifiable universal human nature in need of liberation."[17] Postmodernists beyond the critical tradition, however, see this as yet another form of imperialism. Despite this tension, because of the syncretistic influence of postmodernism, it can be difficult to identify whether an advocate of CSJ is advancing relativism or CSJ-as-privileged-authority-on-objective-truth. (Likely both, inconsistently).

Critical Social Justice

Let us turn to CSJ more specifically. The term *critical social justice* and the ideas that animate the term have been used by a number of academics and scholars from diverse fields writing in the area of critical scholarship.[18] Given the popularity of Robin DiAngelo's work at the popular level and her book, *Is Everyone Really Equal*, with Özlem Sensoy, at the academic level, our analysis will focus on content from *Is Everyone Really Equal*.

When it comes to defining CSJ, Sensoy and DiAngelo state, "To clarify our definition, let's start with the concept *social justice*. While some scholars and activists prefer to use the term *social justice* in order to reclaim its true commitments, in this book we prefer the term *critical social justice*. We do so in order to distinguish our standpoint on social justice from mainstream standpoints."[19] A key element of CSJ is that it is social justice that is informed by Critical Theory. Sensoy and DiAngelo state, "Our analysis of social justice is based on a school of thought known as Critical Theory."[20] Taking its cues from both the analysis of hegemony and the emancipatory concern of Critical Theory, CSJ "recognizes inequality as deeply embedded in the fabric of society (as structural), and actively seeks to change this."[21] Sensoy and DiAngelo acknowledge several core principles of CSJ, including: individual identity is entwined with group identity; society is divided along social group lines which are valued unequally; more highly valued groups have greater access to resources; and social justice involves requires an ongoing, lifelong commitment to correct inequality.[22] While their intentions may be well-placed, ambiguities abound.

For instance, does the fact that groups are valued unequally mean that human beings within groups are deemed invaluable, or that some groups' ideologies are deemed incorrect—not worth affirming? This is a big difference. If the latter, does justice involve seeking dialogue over why a given perspective or practice has been marginalized as immoral or unworthy of affirmation, or are we simply to assume that all marginalization is an issue of arrogance, ignorance, or prejudice?

It is similarly important to distinguish *action* from *being*. Even if it can be shown that we ought to value a being, this does not necessarily mean that we have any moral obligation to value their doing. People can agree that all persons are valuable while also disagreeing that all practices are morally right and permissible or good and appropriate. If people disagree on the latter, they will necessarily disagree on sociopolitical obligations concerning that practice.

Some issues overlap with questions involving the *telos* of family and morality of child-rearing. Advocates of CSJ have a valid concern for the imposition of *problematic* norms, but some go beyond this to imply that essentially *any* traditional norm that determines some views as morally questionable and others as morally virtuous is unjust. Yet norms are unavoidable; mainstreams by nature marginalize ideologies that are not valued. If there *is* a way-it-should-be, however, there is reason to give pause; for what CSJ gets right is that whatever we institutionalize as morally right becomes a placement of "truth" or knowledge for the next generation — teaching children that *x* is right because it is "normal."

As presented by Sensoy and DiAngelo, while there are a variety of means by which we come to hold our beliefs, the most authoritative claims on knowledge include not only peer-reviewed academic scholarship but also insight from the lived experience of marginalized group members, given the unique perspective of their "insider standing".[23] Sensoy and DiAngelo appropriately distinguish between knowledge gleaned through individual and pragmatic experiences, via interactions with culture, and popular knowledge as institutionalized by culture,[24] yet they go beyond this, questioning the very idea "that objectivity is desirable or even possible.... Knowledge is socially constructed.... Knowledge is reflective of the values and interests of those who produce it.... All knowledge and all means of knowing are connected to a social context."[25]

Again, there is a potential ambiguity here, in that knowledge does not necessarily equate to truth. In a sense, they are correct in stating that our perspective depends upon where we stand (our "positionality"[26]). However, the authors' emphasis upon all knowledge would include knowledge about true knowledge. Thus, we have fallen to relativism. Yet, recalling the postmodernists' challenge, the social scientist (and social justice education advocates) has somehow secured a privileged access to speak of objective knowledge to the rest—the "ignorant" folk, the proletariat. This smacks of colonialism,[27] if there is no higher truth above socially constructed knowledge. They are correct in observing the importance of critical thinking's connection to "an informed perspective after engaging with new evidence and accounting for multiple layers of complexity."[28] This does not, however, mean that a less informed perspective cannot have access to truth.

At the heart of CSJ lies a concern for normative power-plays institutionalized through a dominant sociocultural ideology (a grand narrative), and the fact that "media consolidation necessarily limits the range of perspectives available to us."[29] Of course, the fair question remains as to why we should think anyone owes it to us to value or represent all perspectives. One can rebuke a perspective as wrong or not worth regarding in high esteem without rejecting the perspective-holder as worthless. Because knowledge is determined by perspective, they insist, "the dynamics of intersectionality are deeply significant and it is impossible to develop critical social justice literacy without an ability to grapple with their complexities."[30] Still, CSJ does not actually seem to define justice as "grappling with the complexities of various perspectives," but rather as yielding claims on value and truth to the perspective and authority of CSJ. While higher education values intellectual diversity (or should!) and the synthesis of perspectives, a plethora of perspectives and ensembles of experience do not necessarily make one more qualified to speak. Moreover, there is a difference between "grasping with" multiple perspectives and asserting what amounts to an intersectional framework as a template for determining what "truths" are authoritative.

From the standpoint of CSJ, all social groups are organized into binary, either-or constructs, and "all forms of oppression.... exist on binary terms."[31] Thus, learning to adopt the perspective of the oppressed is the only way to acquire right knowledge (knowledge of the way things really are), and thus the only way to understand the issue of justice (the way things should be). Again, problems abound. First, social-identification binaries and value binaries are not the same and truth or moral-value discernment is impossible without asserting a binary. Consider, for example, the proposition that a racist/not-racist binary is a false division because prejudice is systemic.[32] This statement has truth value, and consequently *is* a true/false binary. The embedded prescription that you should believe it asserts a right/wrong binary. While some us-normal/them-other social-identification binaries may be inappropriate, this does not mean that some us-right/them-wrong binaries should not exist. The astute skeptic will catch the irony; CSJ's *own* narrative exists on binary terms—oppressor/oppressed; priviledged-ignorant-exclusive/intersectional-enlightened-inclusive. While the critical theorist might believe they are simply *describing what is*, they are in fact *asserting* an us-right-and-good/them-wrong-and-bad binary.

Another problematic concept worth noting as it allows CSJ a strategic power-play is the idea of asserted and internalized oppression. Since ideology is key to oppression, hegemony (cultural control of ideology) happens tacitly via sociocultural institutionalizations and media propagandizing. Thus, one is oppressed by consent or manipulation and not by force.[33] When a majority-narrative tells a minority perspective it is wrong, this is an assertion of oppression. When a minority accepts this narrative, defends this narrative, or criticizes its own minority-narrative, he or she has internalized the oppression. This allows CSJ to silence its opposition; either your perspective has been liberated to see things via the CSJ lens, or else you are attempting to assert your own dominance as oppressor, or you have developed a sort of Stockholm syndrome. The dialogue is silenced; the only "objective" perspective allowed to speak as authority is the "liberated" lens of CSJ. Indeed, there *is* a power-play at hand! Yet the real question is not about power, but truth.

In expecting naysayers, Sensoy and DiAngelo prepare for the challenge that oppression is human nature. To this they counter with deflection, by asking, "Whom does it serve to say that oppressing others is natural?"[34] Still, it is a fair question to ask why one should think oppression is not an issue of human nature. The authors are simply evading their critics if they think they are satisfactorily refuting the challenge merely by hiding behind the optimism of a secular humanist view of human nature. From a lens of philosophical materialism, what if oppression *is* natural to the survival-of-the-fittest narrative? Why believe it to be otherwise? They deflect, "A more constructive and ethical use of a human nature argument is to notice that, throughout history, humans have strived to overcome oppression and make society more just."[35] Alas, they miss the point; what humans *do* says nothing of what they *ought* to do! In addition, "more just" is meaningless without a broader narrative to ground it. It might as well mean "more convenient"—yet this easily succumbs to power-play. Moreover, many humans have done just the opposite; they have tried to oppress others and been fine with making society less just.

There is no justice if there is no ought, and there is no ought binding on humanity if there is no value *intrinsic* to humanity. From the CSJ lens, there is no universal essence to humanity. "We are all human, of course.... [but] our group is the standard for what it means to be normal or 'just human.'"[36] Such a conclusion cannot satisfactorily ground an appeal to justice that is binding on *all* human groups and autonomous individuals within them..

At best, the social scientist (and the critical theorist) could point and make assertions about what *seems* to be, but without a grand narrative beyond social science, there is nothing to ground any claim as to what *ought* to be. Science (including social science) is tethered to the realm of description, whereas morality occupies a prescriptive space. Something—another narrative—must adjoin the scientific observation in order to make the prescriptive move. It seems that CSJ (as prescriptive) faces a dilemma: *Either* it concedes (and provides!) a grand narrative in which it can ground its special claim to privileged knowledge, proper discernment, and human rights, *or* it is merely the assertion of a new dominant perspective (and if we take its advice seriously, as mainstream cultures become more influenced by the CSJ narrative—especially through any manipulation of media or propagandizing through education—then we should reject rather than internalize its potential "oppression").

As philosopher and atheist A. J. Ayer asked, without the help of a grand narrative, "Can life be seen as having any meaning? It can have just as much meaning as one is able to put into it. There is, indeed, no ground for thinking that human life in general serves any ulterior purpose but this is no bar to man's finding satisfaction in many of the activities which make up his life."[37] Without a grand narrative, one can assert personal meaning, but not universal normative force; morality can amount to peer-pressure, cultural norms, or power-play, yet oppression cannot be decried as "unjust," but only inconvenient. As R. Scott Smith argues, if nothing is given and all is interpretation—if universals and essences do not exist—then "everything is interpretation all the way down."[38]

There is some truth to the notion of ideology as key to marginalization, but why think the ideology of CSJ is conveniently immune? For it assumes a privileged position on truth in opposition to grand narratives, and in prescribing truth to others, it establishes a new grand narrative. It is naïve to think that institutionalized manipulations of power would cease, or that "justice" is actually achievable, simply by de-marginalizing marginal perspectives and suppressing mainstream perspectives, without reference to an overarching, grounding narrative. One perspective will inevitably lord itself over others.

CSJ seems to take injustice for granted. One can assert whatever she likes—"*I'm* special! *My* rights!"—but one does not have value or rights simply because one says so. Why think that anyone has any real worth? Why think that anyone has a basic right to anything? Why think anyone owes any respect to anyone else? Without appeal to a grand, grounding narrative, the embedded claims within these questions lose rational force. The fact that they maintain emotional and existential force should tell us something. Alas, such narratives necessarily discriminate against lifestyles, actions, or character-flaws identified as improper or immoral. While contextual complexities may involve shades of gray, morality asserts the law of non-contradiction and is therefore, ultimately, a binary. Consider how even the phrases, "There are no moral binaries" or "Moral truth is *not* either-or, but both-and," still assert a truth binary concerning morality. These statements are either true or false.

Creating an environment in which all perspectives have a voice, and one in which all perspectives are affirmed are not the same thing. Let us *explore* underrepresented perspectives. If *x* is believed to be wrong, let us *dialogue*, with charity and respect, as to why one should think it wrong. If *x is* wrong, and there are reasons to believe it is wrong, then it is *not* unjust to hinder that perspective or forbid that action (although a malicious will toward a person of contrasting perspective is another issue altogether.)

Here is a major concern of the virtue ethicist. Children *do* learn by imitation; they *do* assume that what they see as institutionalized *must be* good, right, true, or at least permissible. If then, we affirm a morally questionable perspective as good, true, right, or at least determine it to be morally permissible, and if we are in fact wrong, then future generations are raised with a natural bent toward the affirmation, approval, and tolerance of what is in fact immoral. Is *this* not an injustice against *them*?

12

Clarity, Charity, and Disney's Ability to Mediate the Dialogue

While we take issue with the prescriptive narrative that can accompany CSJ, we *do* see some value in the methodology, and because of this we understand the general concern of the CSJ advocate. We want to make sure our readers understand this, and this is one of the places where Disney is able to mediate the dialogue. CSJ advocates are concerned with oppression, with the imposition of power by way of manipulating mainstream narratives, with *seeing* "the other," and with the importance of being able to consider another's perspective or standpoint. While Disney films call us to hope in a mediating moral magic — the conviction that Good *will* overcome evil — and to look toward a goodness ever-after, they also ask us to *live through* many of the anxieties and injustices of their characters. Moreover, there are many times in which these anxieties and injustices rub up against these concerns of the CSJ advocate.

In *Coco*, Miguel discovers that both the legacy of his musical idol and the history and identity of his father rests upon a false narrative, concealing an injustice. In *Wreck-It Ralph*, while Ralph struggles to be *seen* as more than a "bad" guy, Glitch is oppressed by a false-narrative when her arcade game *Sugar Rush* is taken over by the real glitch in the system. The racer from another game, Turbo, has hacked *Sugar Rush* so that everyone believes him to be the benevolent King Candy, while the true royal of *Sugar Rush*, Princess Vanellope von Schweetz, is outcast as a mere glitch in the system. Whether it is fair to call it a true "oppression," it could be argued that Moana seems to *feel* oppressed by traditionalism and its seeming resistance to any dialogue concerning change — a tradition for the sake of tradition, which actually suppresses the truth of her people's identity. Chief Tui is even willing to burn the boats—the evidence—to suppress the truth that they were really voyagers, not islanders.

While the injustice against Miguel's father, the imposition of King Candy's power narrative, and the empty traditionalism of Chief Tui's narrative strike us as clearly problematic, in other Disney films, we are also exposed to subtler notions of oppression. For one way that the oppression of a false-narrative can be powerfully felt is through the injustice of false-accusation and false-representation. Even a child understands and recognizes the injustice of false-accusation and the feeling that you have no voice. Thus, the child viewer sees clearly it is not right for Lady (*Lady and the Tramp* \ f "2") to be blamed and muzzled for the mischief of the Siamese cats—for this defender of fish and baby to be framed as a troublemaker and threat to infants.

The Madrigals (*Encanto*) accuse their own devoted Mirabel to be the reason the family's magic is feeling the pull of a palpable pressure. Bruno Madrigal is also treated unjustly simply because his gift is inconvenient and unwelcome. Alice (*Alice in Wonderland*) asks us to consider a trial in which the institution has framed the outcome from the beginning. "Sentence first! Verdict afterward," declares the Queen of Hearts.[1] It was the less-empowered king who beseeches his wife for a trial. Since the evidence did not really matter to the queen anyway, however, we see, instead of a fair trial, only a parade of foolishness which ends with yet another false-accusation. In *Incredibles 2*, over the course of the film, we move from one form of unfair-depiction (superheroes are reckless and so it ought to be illegal for "Supers" to use their powers in public) to an even worse form of false-accusation (by way of manipulating the free will of the Supers), as the antagonist's intention was to make the public image of the Supers irreparably negative—Supers are dangerous, believe themselves to be superior, and *will* abuse their powers. Because Cinderella's mice companions had labored to create a ball dress from scraps around the house, she is humiliated as she takes the blame for stealing those items from her sister. Even the child is able to *feel* the sense of powerlessness that one experiences when someone else's narrative about key aspects of one's own identity is used to oppress him or her directly, or else to create an air of moral criticism in the eyes of others (as with the cases of Wreck-It-Ralph and Glitch).

This sense of injustice is connected to the desire to be *seen*, and this is also not lost on the child viewer. Disney presses into this desire frequently, as the protagonists are often depicted as underdogs. Cinderella longs to be seen by one who would love her as an end in herself and not as a means to an end, nor as one possessing no or little value. It is Anna's desperation to be seen, in *Frozen*, which causes her to fall so quickly and foolishly for Hans. Sometimes we long to be seen for more than a particular feature, or even at all. Ralph wants to be seen as a person, as an important part of the game, and not just as the "bad guy." We see (and Disney wants us to see) Dory (*Finding Dory*) for more than her disability—it is her *personality* that defines her. Similarly, in *The Incredibles*, the villain, Syndrome, was driven by a need to be seen—first by his hero and later by others *as* a "hero." Both animated films like *The Lion King II: Simba's Pride* and live-action films like *Descendants* are based around the sort of being seen that is needed in order to see one for more than the abuses of those who went before them. Mal struggles to be seen as more than just "the daughter of Maleficent" while Kovu desires to gain Simba's favor in order to be seen as more than merely "Scar's son." As Simba hastily passes Kovu's judgment of exile, we hear the chorus, "He is not born of us. He will never be one of us."[2] In *A Goofy Movie*, Max must learn to *see* his dad, and Goofy must learn to *see* Max. It is no mistake the lead song from the film stresses the need for finding those places in the dialogue where we are seeing eye-to-eye. "If we listen to each other's heart, we'll find we're never too far apart."[3]

The Value of Gaining Perspective and the Point of Pondering Standpoint

What is it *like to be* Dori? What is it like to be the bad guy in a popular video game? What is it like to be a fawn whose mother is killed by a hunter? Disney wants us to understand the desire to be seen and calls us to consider how things seem to the "other." This generally happens in one of two ways. In one sense, the emphasis is on perspective—understanding another's point of view. In another sense, the concern involves standpoint—understanding another's *experience*. The latter, especially, reflects some of the concerns of CSJ, yet without taking intersectionality as far as some try to take it. In its *descriptive* role, the concern for gaining multiple perspectives and considering multiple standpoints is quite beneficial to moral dialogue, and these concerns are all over Disney films.

In *Incredibles 2*, the problem driving the plot comes down to one of perspective. Whereas Winston Deavor sees the re-establishment of hero culture as the key to problems with crime, his sister, Evelyn turns out to be the antagonist working to destroy the public image of heroes indefinitely. Their parents once had a close connection to Supers, but, when their home was burglarized, their parents died because their father was trying to reach heroes who never came (because of the ban on Supers) instead of getting his wife to the safe room. One child saw this as proof of the need for heroes to be legally able to intervene, while the other saw this as proof that it is foolish to place one's hope in such false idols. One child placed hope in the ideal of justice. The other lost hope because of an instance of injustice. In *Meet the Robinsons*, similarly, the antagonist's motivation is revealed to stem from resentment at the fact that Lewis's scientific success came at the expense of young Michael's ability to sleep. Michael (who grew up to become "Bowler Hat Guy") failed to make the important catch at his Little League Baseball game because he was exhausted, due to Lewis's late-night experiments, and blamed his inability to get adopted (due to related anger issues) on Lewis.

Sometimes learning to see as others see is presented not around a sense of injustice, but rather around an ability to move forward, to grow in a healthier way, or to help others. Tarzan and Mowgli must learn to *see* in the way of other human beings in order to become more fully what they are. In *Lilo & Stitch*, the Galactic Federation must learn to see Stitch as more than just "Experiment 626," while Stitch learns to see Lilo and Nani as *'ohana* ("family"). In *Brother Bear*, Kenai, who despised bears, must learn to *see as* a bear. Once transformed into a bear, and after befriending the young cub Koda, Kenai sees the tragedy of the orphaned Koda's situation and then learns that he (Kenai) was the one who killed Koda's mother. This prompts him to remain a bear, instead of seizing an opportunity to become human again, in order that he might watch over Koda as a Brother Bear, given Koda's situation and Kenai's hand in bringing it about. Although Kenai's choice belittles the intrinsic value of the human being, the point is that Disney's emphasis on the need to take better care of nature, to consider the impact human actions may have on wildlife, is communicated through the standpoint of an orphaned bear cub. In *Brave*, Disney wants us, first, to see what it is like to be Merida, a spirited princess with talent and ambition, who is told when and who to marry, and is expected to become... well, her mother. Yet, Disney ultimately wants us to see the harms and hinderances of pride on both sides. Merida and Elinor both needed to see one another in order to grow together in a healthier way.

There might even be a Marxian concern for standpoint in *The Emperor's New Groove*. Kuzco, empowered by wealth, uses his power to oppress the masses, the have-nots, the peasants. One of Marx's concerns was that we define ourselves, we find our identity, in what we make. Yet when the factory workers simply reproduce the products of the owning class, they never have the opportunity to create anything of their own, and so they are not really able to know themselves. They can only know themselves as the instrument of another's identity. In the case of the Disney film, there is no industrialized society, but there is a similar question of identity and ownership. The villagers' identity, and even their family history, is tied up with their property — that which they have built up for themselves and where their family has lived for generations. Kuzco comes along with all his wealth and decides that their village will be the prime location for his getaway mansion. As Kuzco declares to Pacha his intention to demolish their village and kick them off of their land, Pacha experiences the anxiety of losing everything. He will still have his family, so what is his real loss? It is the identity that was intertwined with that which ought to be his, that which is going to be taken from him. The change of Kuzco's heart comes about only from a change in his standpoint (as he was turned into a llama). Only *then* does he understand what it *feels like* to be powerless, as that which was once his is seized, and he too loses not only his property but also his identity.

At its core, Standpoint Theory is concerned not with the rationalistic and often scientistic nature of analytic thought, but rather the subject-centered *being-in-the-world*. And yet, when one moves beyond mere methodology and begins to assert things about what can be known, what is true about social justice, and who has the right to speak on moral issues because of their perspective(s), he or she has moved beyond an observation of the subjective self and onward to an assertion of certain objective truth claims about reality. At that point, the analytic methodology has a role to play in evaluating the logic of such claims, whereas logical analysis cannot really dissect the nature of one's experience in the same way that it can the nature of an argument, or even certain aspects of physical nature itself.

Consider a situation in which someone is watching the classic live-action Disney film, *Old Yeller*. At the end of the film, Old Yeller has acquired rabies while protecting his family. Travis faces the most difficult action he's ever had to take. It is for the good of the dog and the safety of his family that Travis must shoot his beloved canine companion. Anyone who has ever loved a companion can identify *to an extent* with the potential pain of potential loss — anyone who has ever loved and lost even more so. Yet not just anyone can *really know* what Travis is experiencing. For many viewers, all they can say is, "That must be so painful" or "I cannot imagine how hard that was." Still, some viewers *do* know. Some viewers have shared the standpoint of having to watch their K-9 family member be euthanized. They've had to make that difficult decision, struggling with the desire to have their companion a little longer, yet knowing that the more reasonable thing to do is to prevent unnecessary and prolonged suffering. But that reasoning—no matter how right it is—does not make the existential living-through any easier. To wait with one's companion, to see them release their anxiety and then cease to be; and to know that the main variable in whether they continued to live or not, at least a little while longer, was *you*, the one who made the ultimate decision resulting in the act which would end their life—this is an experience of grief that only some can truly understand, while others must wait a little longer before becoming fully able to understand. The viewer who has *lived through* Travis's pain can say, "That *was* so hard" or "There is nothing so painful as the loss of a companion." There is a deeper sense of knowing, a depth of understanding when one has access to the standpoint of another.

Amidst the existential, the *rational* logic does not always carry as much personal force as the *meaningful* option. What good is theodicy (abstract arguments in defense of God's goodness, omniscience, and power, against the problem of evil) for Cinderella as she suffers abuse and loneliness? Such arguments may be powerful as far as having hope in the long-term goes, but there are moments—seasons, even—when what one is desperate to hear is not the abstract argument, but the practical application.

The issue of standpoint is also a theologically relevant one to ponder. Paul Gould draws out the significance that character can play in one's perceiving, by referencing C. S. Lewis's tale *The Magician's Nephew*.[4] In this prequel to *The Lion, the Witch, and the Wardrobe*, two children, Digory and Polly, along with two adults presented as lesser desirable characters, Uncle Andrew and the wicked queen Jadis (later known as the White Witch) happen to stumble into Narnia at the very beginning of its creation. They get to witness Aslan, the Great Lion, Narnia's creator, *sing* the world into existence. They get to see it swell and live and grow and transform. Yet whereas the children witness this with awe and appreciation. Jadis and Andrew are horrified and appalled. Lewis writes, "For what you see and hear depends a good deal on where you are standing: it also depends on what sort of person you are."[5] Whereas the children expected to find *wonder* in the world, Andrew who had reduced magic to a science, saw no good potential in a world that has nothing to be scientifically dominated for the sake of prestige, and

Jadis, who could not bear the thought of something more important than *her*, saw something in this world she despised — one who is able to create worlds, one who is more important than her, namely, Aslan.

Fairy tales can help us to explore perspectives and to contrast standpoints. Works like Lewis's fiction have the power both to show us why it is important to see different standpoints, and also to challenge that, while the standpoint can help us to see the perspective, this does not necessarily mean that the perspective is a good one. That is, while the truth-as-defined-by-one's-perspective is important in understanding different *claims* on Truth, this does not mean that *Truth* is reduced to or isolated within perspective — for the very reason we need multiple perspectives is *to ponder Truth* more thoughtfully. While there is a historical tension between the two schools of analytic and continental philosophy, *both* have something to offer. In fact, they need each other, lest the rational mind become fragmented while truth and knowledge become deconstructed in one way or another. The strongest method and most effective approach to critical thinking will learn to temper the concerns of both camps in order to seek wisdom. Standpoint, alone, however plays a *descriptive* role in moral dialogue. No number of intersecting perspectives alone can give it the obligatory force of moral prescription. Moral obligation must come from beyond the perspective *per se*, and Disney films (at least, those released up until 2021) seem to have understood and underscored this as well.

Was it gaining a new standpoint as a beast or love which reoriented Beast's understanding? Certainly the standpoint plays a role in helping Beast to see love clearly — "for who could ever love a beast?"[6] Yet it is exposure to Belle's character (experiencing her lovingkindness), and not the standpoint of a beast *per se*, that is ultimately able to magnetize his moral compass. Gaston gains perspective when he *experiences* the mercy and humanity of Beast, yet he chooses to continue to see the beast as a "beast." Does Beast understand marginalization? Yes. And it is precisely because he has gained an additional standpoint that he is better able to understand marginalization, this is true. It could be argued that Belle understood Beast precisely because she too was a bit of a social outcast. Of course, Belle did have to learn to *see him*. This, however, does not mean that it is the intersection of perspectives which determines moral truth. Quite the opposite. Belle saw the "beast" not as he was, but as he ought to be — how he was meant to be seen. Belle did not have to see the Beast *as a beast* in order to love him, she had to learn to see him as a human being. In the same way, we can (and should) learn to *see* one another as human beings—loved by the maker and made in His image. Ultimately, it was truth (through love) which transformed the beast, and not perspective *per se*. He had to learn to *see himself* as the sort of person he ought to become.

Gaining perspective can allow the opportunity for deepened understanding. But standpoint *alone* cannot guarantee knowledge because standpoint does not guarantee truth. The need for moral deliberation to consider multiple perspectives testifies to this. Truth is ultimately correspondence and understanding is deepened by perspective *when* allowed to see *more clearly*. Here, it might be helpful to address a point of historical tension concerning objective knowledge and universal truth in light of a contemporary issue of ethical controversy (abortion).

Throughout history, there has been a struggle over the nature of objective knowledge and universal truth. Philosophy has, time and again, ebbed and flowed between an emphasis upon the analytical and the practical, or to put it another way, the abstract and the personal. This tension can be seen within the Classicist/Romantic divide of the eighteenth and nineteenth centuries and the analytic/continental divide of the twentieth.[7] The analytic approach, to oversimplify, has tended to scrutinize language and stress rational or empirical logic and *abstract argumentation*. It stresses the necessity for some sense of (and grounding for) objectivity in order to make any appeal to authority (and presses the point that all claims on morality are necessarily appeals to authority). On the other hand, the continental approach has tended to emphasize the significance of the subjective, *lived experience* (as we struggle with anxiety in the face of our seemingly absurd circumstances and the quest for meaning and significance); historical developments in perspective; ideological power struggles relating to socio-political structures, and ideologies ingrained within cultures through institutionalized norms and systems (and related to the latter, "social justice"). It is more comfortable with the notion of truth as something that works itself out, over time, through a continuing dialogue of multiple perspectives.

A key point to understand as it relates to the emphasis on social justice, is that the continental school has almost always had a concern for the individual who is alienated by systemic structures. This is why Marx was so concerned about the working class being alienated by the nature of the owning class, a social structure which he considered to be the resulting evil of a capitalist system. So too, the CSJ movement, is concerned for the individual whose values are marginalized (ergo oppressed) by social systems tethered to mainstream ideologies.

We can understand the tension and disagreement between the analytic and continental perspectives using the example of abortion. Although analytic defenses have been given in favor of abortion, the more popular appeals tend to stress the *experience* of the one who must make the choice, rather than rational arguments *per se*. Defenders of pro-life stress the analytical point that it is wrong to kill an innocent human being; human unborn babies are innocent human beings; so, it is wrong to kill human unborn babies for the reasons typically given in justification of abortion on demand. Although this is a noteworthy argument, it does not mean much to the advocate of abortion whose best friend or family member conceived a child after being raped. The concern of the former perspective is on what is right and what is wrong — and this is a terribly important point, if any human social system is ever to be freed of injustice. But the concern of the latter is on the significance of the embodied, individual subject dealing with the absurdity and brutality of the experience which has thrown her into a tragic dilemma. Thus, the existential choice (though morally incorrect) carries a greater weight, *from this perspective,* than rational propositions. This is likely why continental thought has become so prominent, even in pop culture (the simplified ideas are more applicable to the individual struggling for identity within culture, and the applied seems more immediately meaningful than the abstract), while analytic philosophy has continued to seem, for many, abstract, removed, and even esoteric.

Here, we want to underscore that, when it comes to the question of injustice within systems, *the theistic question is analytically essential to the question of justice.* Continuing with the abortion example: If there is a God, if human beings really are special in God's eyes, and if God considers it an affront to his design for any human being to destroy any other human being, at any level of development (for the reasons typically given in justification of abortion on demand, save a genuine threat to the life of the mother), then institutions which support abortion are unjust institutions. Some argue that any system that makes abortion on demand illegal is unjust. Others argue that any institution that can legalize the killing of unborn human beings is unjust. We might identify with the logic and the appeal to human experience on both sides.

However, our definition of "just" and "unjust" will depend upon the narrative which accompanies our claims, and *real justice* will ultimately depend upon *the way the world is meant to be* (a grounding concept that can only be established in a grand moral narrative). This is why it is such a big deal.

If we institutionalize an injustice because it fits *our* narrative, then we incur guilt and inflict injury. Both sides should be able to come together on this point; the advocate of CSJ is challenging certain established norms as unjust; the critic of CSJ is challenging certain ideals of "justice," which might be prescribed to follow from critical observations, as incorrect and therefore, *if institutionalized* with a view to become an established norm, unjust. Thus, it all comes back to the strength of the moral foundations which accompany one's critical narrative.

Points of Agreement

While the prescriptive foundations of CSJ are unsatisfactory, there *are* some points where CSJ's and theism's (especially Christianity's) view of reality overlap. Oppression *is* unjust *if* oppression and justice are correctly defined. Power *can* corrupt and often imposes devastating harms and hindrances when wielded by morally depraved hearts.

Christianity is also sympathetic to critical theorists' sensitivity to potential hate crimes[8] that can foment and flow from fear, ignorance, or a projection of one's own anger—something we see in Frollo (*The Hunchback of Notre Dame*).[9] Whereas CSJ emphasizes injustice as systemic, Christianity, while not denying that injustice is at times systemic, emphasizes that injustice is located in human nature, at the level of the individual. The impact of *things-which-ought-not-to-be* in the world—upon persons, within persons, between persons—warrants lament.

Lastly, hegemonic power is real. Sociocultural institutions hold the power to shape cultural practices and worldview assumptions. When wielded in a particularly unjust and manipulative way, this is problematic, even egregious. Whoever controls the narrative wields a significant amount of power. Yet this is precisely what is so alarming about the presumptions foundational to the CSJ movement: If a traditional *value-narrative* (not political or capitalistic powers *per se*) is *correct*, then replacing it with an incorrect, marginalized value-prescription—expecting others, in the name of "justice," to affirm and enforce that value-prescription as equally morally good or permissible—is, by definition, wrong. The imposition of this previously marginalized, questionable worldview (through the power acquired from seizing the narrative) may be as problematic in its oppressiveness (or more so) as the traditional value-narrative which was overthrown.

Perspectival Dialectics

Where does Disney fit into this analysis? Some challenge that Disney is itself a force of capitalism using a tactful nostalgia for traditional values as a form of value oppression.[10] It *is* among the few corporations controlling a majority of media pathways. While this may be a fair challenge, in truth, it is irrelevant. CSJ in itself is unable to *ground* any claim to injustice or rights (assertions are not arguments), less so the notion that society should be free of capitalistic power structures or systemic impositions of traditional perspectives. Consequently, it is quite the philosophical and epistemological leap to demand that Disney owes anything to anyone. Notwithstanding, we contend that Disney lore mediates between the interests of both CSJ's advocate and its theistic critic. Disney narratives want us to question perspective, while pointing to a higher grounding for truth. They entreat us to identify with and care for hurting and alienated individuals, but also to look to a higher *goodness-beyond-just-ness*. We address the former in this chapter; the latter will be addressed in subsequent chapters.

We recognize that Disney is not immune to the type of criticisms CSJ offers. In addition, questions over animated insensitivities are legitimate and a good dialogue to have. In fact, in light of criticism over the years, Disney has expanded its own perspective on perspective, while maintaining its longstanding appeal to a grand moral narrative. *The Little Mermaid*'s and *Zootopia*'s challenge to a superior/inferior species prejudice serves as potent metaphor for racism. Consider also Disney's interest in exploring multicultural perspectives and the strengths of female protagonists which began in the 1990s.

The Little Mermaid further explores the knowledge-as-ignorance concern. Scuttle "knows" the appropriate normative value concerning "dinglehoppers" and "snarfblatts." Perspective as key to understanding and compassion is a central theme in both *Brother Bear* and *Brave*. *Tangled* similarly presses the question of perspective-as-knowledge. Here, Mother Gothel might stand as metaphor for the institutional oppression to which CSJ is sensitive. As long as a *false* narrative is lorded over Rapunzel, she is a captive; her liberation indeed stems from the emancipation of her perspective. Nevertheless, there *is* a correct understanding; the narrator has access to the truth-value of contending perspectives[11] and appeals to a right order, without which injustice is imperceptible. *The Princess and the Frog* takes us on a great journey toward the enlightenment of several perspectives—and Tiana was for many the celebration of an underrepresented color and culture.

The Powhatan perspective is contrasted with that of the English settlers in *Pocahontas*, as a particular interest of the film was the question of what defines a "savage." Here, CSJ's sensitivity to colonialism is appropriate, yet this does not mean that the overall moral narrative with which the settlers identify is necessarily wrong. *Tu quoque* is a fallacious appeal; how one *acts* (even if hypocritical) is a question of *applied* ethics, whether one is *acting* appropriately. What one *claims* to be correct about ethics (whether or not one exemplifies it) is a question of moral *truth*. Despite the fact that both sides had particular perspectives, and both perspectives had unjust biases clouding their understanding of justice, it was only through an ultimate sense of rightness known to both sides—an intuition of a greater good—that dialogue over difference (community over diversity) was achievable. The potential injustice between perspectives was mediated only by an appeal to an overarching way-it-should-be! For this to be possible, truth cannot be reducible solely to perspective. At least one perspective must be false (and it is even possible that both contending perspectives are mistaken).

Disney narratives abound with concern for perspective. *Bambi* questions whether humanity is more harm than help to nature's beauty. CSJ is right to challenge Disney's poor-form depiction of crows in *Dumbo*, yet *Dumbo* was onto something in calling us to identify with the bullied—even the helpless parent of bullied victims. *Up* explores the us/them dynamic and coping struggles of older persons, while *The Small One* explores how an old donkey, no longer useful from most perspectives, finds redeeming significance from the perspective of Jesus's expecting parents. *The Emperor's New Groove* explores several perspectives—overlord, underclass, villain, and anti-villain— and the entire plot has to do with Kuzco's enlightenment through the acquisition of a new perspective. In *The Sword in the Stone*, Wart is the underdog. We want more for him than the circumstances which have befallen him, and we champion Merlin's desire to provide greater access to education[12]—an expanded perspective. It is also possible we subconsciously suspect that Wart will come to appreciate the honor of being a divinely appointed king, and ideally be a good king, precisely because he understood what it was like to be an orphaned "nobody." *The Reluctant Dragon* challenges stereotypes that might perpetuate hate and hinder community, while *Mary Poppins* saves a papa from the blinders of his own industrious neglect—liberating him to see what really matters.

Though it may raise questions of determinism, *Inside Out* opened the dialogue to consider the extent to which behavior may relate to emotional and mental experiences on a spectrum. We see Nemo (*Finding Nemo*) for more than just his physical difference, and we also gain a perspective of struggle and adaptation in the absence of accommodation. *Moana* challenges a tradition on knowledge, and *Frozen II* challenges a grand (false) narrative on history and "justice," yet there is an underlying concern for the meant-to-be and ought-to-be. Another powerful example of learning to see one another comes from *Encanto*.

While there is no injustice between sisters Mirabel and Isabela, there *is* a palpable tension, a sense of distaste. From Mirabel's perspective, Isabela is the beautiful one who has everything she could ever want. In beauty, powers, and popularity, she is privileged to such a degree it seems unfair. Mirabel wears her disgust plainly in the song "We don't talk about Bruno," as Isabela descends daintily—carried by nature (a swing made of vines) and displayed angelically in the spotlight while rose petals flutter around her, and the arms of others in the room are outreached toward her. As everyone sings about their woes, of how Bruno's prophecies came true and resulted in their unfortunate circumstances, Isabela sings of how Bruno claimed she would have the life of her dreams. What nerve! Or so it would seem.

It is not until later in the film that Mirabel learns the truth, and this comes about through dialogue, as Isabela helps Mirabel to see things from Isabela's perspective. In fact, she had been quite unhappy with her life, unable to realize, until that point, her own dreams because she was always trying to be perfect according to the expectations of others. "I'm so sick of pretty; I just want something true."[13] Now it begins to make sense why Isabela was contributing to the song about Bruno, a song of people's disappointments in relation to things Bruno had claimed. Bruno's prophecy concerning Isabela was disappointing to Isabela precisely because it had *not* come true. Amidst Isabela's song of discovery, there is an artistic, subtle, return of Isabela's musical motif from the song about Bruno. Now that Mirabel *sees* Isabela, she sings, "It just seemed like your life's been a dream since the moment you opened your eyes." Then she adds, "All I know are the blossoms you grow." Here we understand, the seeing happens two ways. Mirabel needed to see Isabela before she could really pass judgment on Isabela's motives and decisions. So too, Isabela needed to see how she is seen—to consider how she had been presenting herself to Mirabel. If she expects Mirabel to understand her as being more than a perfect child with a perfect life, she will have to reveal more of those "imperfections," the hopes and anxieties which make her human.

CSJ's concern for perspective is a valid concern. Intellectual diversity is a central aim of higher education (or at least it should be). Nevertheless, intersectional understanding is not prerequisite for knowledge of a given truth. Disney films remind us that considering multiple perspectives is an important part of moral dialogue, but also that moral truth is ultimately larger than individual perspectives. Disney also calls us to care for the alienated, the abused, those who are overlooked, and those who are suffering. Yet Disney films also seem to understand that injustice is not simply a matter of one perspective oppressing another. Rather, it involves any perspective, whether determined by individual or group, which stands in antithesis to The Truth of a grand moral order.

The Power and Problem of Perspective

It is true that much knowledge is acquired through critical dialogue, as one perspective is able to expand another. Iron sharpens iron, as the proverb states.[14] This, however, does not mean knowledge is *determined by* individual perspective, nor that the grounding for truth amounts to whatever works for, or is acceptable to, a given community — whether majority or minority. Nor is the academic peer community the first or final say on moral truth. (Recall that Sensoy and DiAngelo place a high value on academic peer review, in addition to positionality and "insider standing," since, they think, knowledge is constructed and the idea of objectivity is questionable. Yet justice, if it means anything of substance, is an appeal to our moral intuitions, not the agreed upon knowledge claims of any group of academic specialists. Moreover, to call anything "injustice" as a matter of fact is an appeal to objectivity). Philosopher Peter Boghossian, though a controversial figure to some, has challenged the contemporary emphasis on critical social theory, insisting that even some avenues of peer-reviewed scholarship and higher education have become more concerned with social grievances than with objective truth.[15] As a professed, even evangelistic atheist, Boghossian's critique of the popular trend of championing positionality and the censorship of opposition over dialogue and logical argumentation concerning the objective nature of reality is worth considering because, in an article for *The American Mind*, he wrote of how strange it might seem for Christians and atheists to align in defense of truth and reason:

> Those people who accept the correspondence theory of truth[16] ...agree on the traditional rules of engagement (discourse, debate, dialogue) and do not view intersectionality as a necessary model for getting to the truth.... [These] include many liberal atheists *and* conservative Christians. Those on the other side... do *not* subscribe to the correspondence theory of truth, believe speech should be shut down if it's hurtful or potentially harmful, and think intersectional, transformative approaches are necessary to refashion systems. These people are also predominantly atheists *and* Christians: *intersectional* "woke" atheists and *intersectional* "woke" Christians.... I am a non-intersectional, liberal atheist. If a conservative Christian believes Jesus walked on water—and believes this either is or is not true for everyone regardless of race or gender—and if she values discourse and adheres to basic rules of engagement, then *she is closer to my worldview* than an atheist who believes race and gender play a role in determining objective truth and that her opponents should not be allowed to air what she considers harmful views.[17]

Neopragmatist Richard Rorty was incorrect in asserting that truth is whatever your peers "let you get away with."[18] If that statement were true, it must be true even if his peers disagreed. Yet Rorty was correct in that some academics do try to get away with ungrounded assertions, and Boghossians is not alone in his observation that contemporary pop culture seems to encourage the idea that one should not voice or stand up for one's convictions if doing so hurts another person's feelings and suggests one's personal truth is incorrect or one's actions are wrong.

In short, from the perspective of CSJ, "justice" amounts to the liberation of any oppressed perspective (as CSJ understands and articulates oppression) and the undermining of mainstream systemic power structures, which impose and perpetuate a particular narrative—often, a traditional western, Judeo-Christian perspective on truth. Note, however, the contradiction and perpetual problem that arises from CSJ's understanding of social justice; since there is no real, objective grounding for justice, we are left with only shifting, clashing perspectives and perpetual power-plays between the "haves" and "have-nots;" between the mainstream and marginalized. The contradiction lies in the fact that, true materialism champions fitness; thus, the mainstream-cultures win. Yet CSJ champions the marginal, the non-affirmed. While *non*-materialists *may* have a satisfactory grounding for *morality*, they still bear the burden to show that CSJ satisfactorily grounds the claim to egalitarian *justice*.

Given that justice is defined[19] as taking from the "haves" and giving to the "have-nots," as marginalizing the mainstream in order to champion the marginalized, CSJ faces two problems. First, it seeks to accomplish its goal by way of systematically seizing and asserting power over mainstream culture and the "haves" (though, in the name of challenging systemic power) in order to force (through its seized systemic power) its own vision of truth and morality. Second, the creed of CSJ is to refute the status quo and seek a sort of salvation for the marginalized, but upon achieving its goal, it has created a new status quo and a new marginalized. Thus, if it is to remain consistent, upon achieving its goal it ought to then begin working to undermine that very goal, to turn the tables once again. CSJ, in and of itself, grounds neither truth nor justice. Nevertheless, it remains undaunted and speaks authoritatively of both.

Truth does not reduce to perspective, nor does it depend on one's standpoint. It is possible for a single, even limited, perspective to see something clearly. Consider the story of the Blind Men and the Elephant. A ruler looks out and sees several blind men grasping different parts of an elephant and arguing over what they've got. This story is often meant to imply that the elephant is religious truth and the blind men represent different religions — that they are all really just digging at the same thing; that no one perspective has a rightful claim to truth. We are expected to conclude there is no religious truth, only multiple perspectives grasping at the same truth. However, as with *Tangled*, there *is* a right truth-perspective — the narrator's. The ruler who looks out sees clearly. No number of multiple perspectives can change the fact that, in this case, there is a single perspective which can see clearly, even without consulting the other perspectives which argue over the elephant. Still, there are plenty of times in which we may not see clearly, and this is why dialogue itself is a doorway to understanding. Truth does not depend on perspective, yet the more we see the more clearly we will be able to understand, if not discern, truth. Seeing one another is an important part of humanity. Learning to see where the other is coming from is an essential part of dialogue.

Why We Don't Talk About Bruno

CSJ sees morality as *defined* by cultural power structures yet appeals to the *ideal* of moral objectivity in order to decry moral impositions. Social stratification may be a legitimate concern, but it is fallacious to look solely at what empirically is (the fact of social stratification) and from this derive an ought-to-be (that social stratification is bad). The appeal to an ought-to-be must come from elsewhere. While liberation from oppression and the cessation of injustice is an admirable aim, the lines between need and want, right and privilege, discrimination-as-hate and discrimination-as-discernment, injustice and inconvenience are often skewed.[20]

If justice is understood only in terms of liberation, and not in terms of a grand narrative order, nothing remains to ground any appeal to justice. To be the ones with the power and pens to decree that moral truth is nothing more than a decree by those with power and pens is self-defeating, a contradiction. To decree further that the truth about justice entails liberation from any imposed oppression stemming from such moral decrees, is a second contradiction. A higher ideal (such as an absolute equality, free of any sense of oppression, because it is free from the influence of social structures and cultural narratives) might be an admirable aim, but it cannot serve as the grounding. If CSJ is meant to provide the scaffolding which helps to erect walls that will support the ideals for which it aims, then those ideals are like a roof. Yet, a roof is not a floor; social ideals cannot serve as moral foundations; it is the moral foundations which must be strong enough to support the ideals.

The reason "we don't talk about Bruno"[21] in *Encanto* is because Bruno Madrigal speaks of truths which not everyone wants to hear. The song reveals multiple perspectives which convey how his gift of prophecy was unsettling because his claims often conflicted with characters' desires. As it turns out, Bruno was blamed for the unhappiness of others, villainized, and estranged from community. Only Mirabel was concerned enough with seeking truth to see Bruno as having a valid concern for the wellbeing of the community, and not merely as a hindrance to the happiness of the community. So too, in our context, it has become popular to ostracize those who appeal to a grand moral narrative if that narrative does not support some of the things individuals want to assert for themselves, or society wants to affirm and celebrate. Of course, there is an important difference between Bruno-claims and moral claims in that Bruno only *described* the future; Bruno never *prescribes* how one ought to act in light of his prophesies. (And the comedic irony is the fact that they really don't mind talking *about* Bruno. They just don't want to hear what he has to say because "your fate is sealed when your prophecy is read"). But the question raised in the film is nonetheless applicable to moral (prescriptive) dialogue. Is the removal of a moral perspective from the dialogue—we don't talk about *that*—wise, just because it makes some people uncomfortable? If it is a claim on truth, is it not worth discussion?

In *The Sword in the Stone*, Madam Mim decides to devour Wart because he does not value her perspective. Wart shows respect to Mim as a *person* even while refusing to endorse her worldview as right or good. Yet justice, to Mim, entails either the affirmation of *her* perspective or the removal of anyone unwilling to affirm it. It is permissible to harm another person if that person's values "oppress" (meaning do not validate) her *perspective*. Are we any better? *If* human beings are special, then injustice follows where *any* narrative (marginal or mainstream) devalues human beings, and *if* there is a grand narrative, then wherever mainstream powers impose *false* narratives there *is* unjust oppression. In so far as CSJ advocates criticize mainstream censorship of morally questionable lifestyles, only to shame and silence those of the mainstream—hypocrisy and contradiction abound, particularly in light of zero moral grounding for such actions.

If there is no higher grounding for moral truth, then *neither* perspective is any better than Frollo (*The Hunchback of Notre Dame*), for they both believe themselves correct and admirable in their longing "to purge the world of vice and sin." It seems both sides are guilty of seeing "corruption everywhere except within." Why think we have human rights in the first place? Just because we say so does not make it so. If there can be no moral truths which apply to all, how can there be a standard of tolerance that applies to all? For:

> If God is dead, as Nietzsche said, then we are truly free.
> But if He's there, we'd best beware to tread more carefully.
> In non-theism, we are freed from guilt and moral obligation.
> Yet severed too from claims of true justice, rights, and indignation.[22]

So far, we have argued that CSJ is insufficient in grounding its appeal to justice and human rights, while validating its concern for perspective and affirming its concern for the mistreatment of human beings. In the following chapters, the case is made that theism is required for grounding justice, and the Jewish and Christian narratives provide the most robust depiction of human rights and meaningful community.

13

On Justice: God Help the Outcast

In Disney's *Bedknobs and Broomsticks*, Miss Price sings of finding hope amidst an age of skepticism. "You must face the age of not believing, doubting everything you ever knew, until at last you start believing there's something wonderful in you."[1] There is an optimism here that reflects contemporary secular discourse, but just because we start believing does not mean we have reason to believe. As Modernity reached similarly an age of non-believing, it unfortunately jettisoned its grounding for belief in the justice it envisioned. Yet, Miss Price was correct; there is a specialness in us, and we've reason to believe in this truth to which we continually appeal.

In the previous chapters, we examined Critical Social Justice (CSJ), a contemporary syncretism of historic Critical Theory (CT) and contemporary critical social theory (CST)—specifically, the popular *prescriptive ideology*, typically removed from a satisfactorily grounded, authoritative grand narrative. we argued that CSJ, in itself, provides insufficient grounds for establishing the rights for which it advocates and the injustice it condemns, although it does raise some valid concerns. We surveyed problems with materialism and pressed the point that, regardless of one's worldview, when we accept the narrative that claims on value and morality and appeals to higher truths are only personal or privatized opinions and have no place in public and political discourse, we have assumed materialism in practice. Similarly, when we accept CSJ's ungrounded prescriptions (self-refuting, if ungrounded) that we ought not impose one moral perspective above another, we have merely internalized CSJ's own oppressive narrative.

We clarified that the problem lies not with the *descriptive* approach to uncovering lesser-understood and underrepresented perspectives, to understand them better and include them in dialogue concerning the nature of a just society. This is an admirable aim because each perspective is held by valuable human beings—their dignity is not derived from their perspective; their perspective is an individual expression of a universal dignity. It is appropriate, for example, to consider whether *Song of the South* is offensive. It is worth considering whether recurrent damsel-in-distress and true-love-as-the-one motifs are harmful to young girls' understanding of femininity and love, or whether princess shape and attire affects girls' body image. The problem involves the *prescriptive* move which teaches (via the objective claims of social science) that there are no objective claims on moral truth because value is relative to perspective. There is a difference between a morally concerned methodology and a morally prescriptive narrative; the latter has no grounding in social science.

This chapter and the next will argue that theism is required for grounding justice, and that the Jewish and Christian narratives offer the most substantive depiction of human value and community. We further submit that Disney films presuppose the necessity of a grand theistic narrative for establishing justice and also align well with the Christian vision of a social *goodness* that goes beyond "justice"—the *shalom* of a Kingdom-ever-after.

Grounding Justice

In *The Hunchback of Notre Dame*, there is a clear abuse of institutional power, and, in this case, justice does have to do with liberation of the oppressed. Additionally, it is true that Esmeralda's perspective is more intersectional than Frollo's. However, Esmeralda understands that justice involves more than mere marginalization of institutional narratives and affirmation of marginal perspectives. She sees that the injustice is an issue of either the oppressor's heart or his understanding of the narrative or nature of the institution, and liberation is not about perspective *per se*, but human dignity. So, she beseeches God to help her oppressed and outcast people. Marx would see this as a means of coping. CSJ might claim she has internalized her oppressor's narrative, but Esmeralda is onto something. Her hesitance to approach God—uncertain that God would listen to a prayer like hers—suggests it is not (has not been) her worldview (at least, in practice), but it is one with which she is familiar, perhaps because it is a dominant one. The outcasts, she says—unworthy to approach God, she believes—look to him nonetheless, desperate for a mercy not found on earth. She does not blame the theistic narrative to which Frollo appeals simply because of Frollo's heinous actions. Rather, she sees no other hope for knowing real justice *than* within a theistic narrative. This appeal presses into the Moral Argument, and relatedly Natural Law Theory.

Natural Moral Law

Why think it wrong to make fun of Dumbo? What would make it wrong? If the principle of utility is correct, and we ought always to act according to the greater happiness of the greater number, then if Dumbo and Mrs. Jumbo are the only ones unhappy while multitudes find great pleasure in seeing Dumbo humiliated, would this not, in fact, be "right," since it is what the majority wants? Does Dumbo *deserve* to be treated differently? Does justice involve an ought-not when it comes to harassment? If so, from where does this oughtness come? Why shouldn't the butler abandon the Aristocats if doing so is in his best interest? Why should Kuzco care what happens to peasants? Scar asserted his individual truth, defining his own purpose, meaning, and identity. If living his own truth can make him king, why *shouldn't* he kill Mufasa and seize the kingdom? What *obligates* him to care about some ideal order and greater good? In *Frozen II*, Anna and Elsa must right the wrong committed by their grandfather, but what makes his actions unjust? What make something an "injustice" rather than simply an inconvenience or unfortunate situation?

Injustice makes little sense from a "down-stairs" narrative which rejects higher truths. William Lane Craig has appropriately asked, "If theism is false, why think that human beings have objective value? ...Atheist philosophers who are humanists do not seem to have faced squarely the consequences of their naturalism.... To think that human beings are special [on the naturalistic view] is to be guilty of species-ism, an unjustified bias toward one's own species."[2] This echoes the conclusion of moral philosopher Richard Taylor, in his observation that moral obligation is an unintelligible concept apart from the idea of God. "The words remain, but their meaning is gone."[3] Or as popular Christian apologist and radio personality Greg Koukl has put it, "Given a Godless, physical universe, the idea that things are not as they should be makes little sense. How can something go wrong when there was no right way for it to be in the first place?"[4] Yet we *know* something is wrong. The Moral Argument is one that presses into our deep awareness of higher truth. Even if we attempt to dismiss it rationally, we cannot help but live out our convictions; the moment we call something unjust or react as if "injustice" means anything more than inconvenience, we have presupposed a way-it-ought-to-be. The most powerful form of the Moral Argument presses into an acknowledgement of this absence:

1. If there is no God (Moral Law Giver; MLG), there is no Moral Law (ML).

2. Evil/injustice exists (we recognize an absence of justice — a disrespected ML).

3. Therefore, God exists. (*modus tollens*)

Traditionally, it is phrased:

1. If there is an ML, there must be an MLG.

2. There *is* an ML.

3. There must be an MLG. (*modus ponens*)

Some are not comfortable with framing the argument in this way because you can also argue:

1. If there is an ML, there must be an MLG.

2. There is no MLG.

3. There is no ML. (*modus tollens*)

The discomfort involves framing the argument in such a way that morality rises or falls with the existence of God. However, despite one's feelings about it, that is exactly what seems to be the case; God and morality do indeed rise and fall together.

If theism is false, why think all human beings have any real worth at all? Why think they are equal? And why *ought* you to act on behalf of others when it is not in your best interest? Angus Menuge has elaborated on the tension concerning unquestionably basic rights:

> In the West, the demand to recognize almost every strong preference as legally protected has led to contradictory rights claims. The right to life appears to be the most fundamental

right of all, since, without it, no other right can be exercised. Yet abortion, euthanasia and even infanticide are also claimed as human rights....

All this disagreement should make us ponder whether our zeal for proclaiming human rights is matched by a clear understanding of what they are. It is one thing to assert that the exercise of a particular interest is a human right. It is quite another thing to *justify* that assumption ontologically, epistemologically, and pragmatically.[5]

After critiquing a plethora of egalitarian arguments, philosopher Louis Pojman contended, "In their present form none of the arguments given for the doctrine of equal human worth are sound.... The doctrine of equal human worth has its home in a deeper metaphysical system than secular egalitarians are able to embrace."[6]

He noted that, apart from a theistic grounding, *inequality* actually seems more sensible.[7] Moreover, "Given a naturalistic account of the origins of homo sapiens, it is hard to see that humans have intrinsic value at all. If we are simply physicalist constructions, where does intrinsic value emerge?"[8] He concluded:

> There are only two choices.... either secular inegalitarian moral/political systems or religious (or comparable metaphysical) systems.... Secular egalitarians have inherited a notion of inviolability or intrinsic human worth from a religious tradition which they no longer espouse. The question is whether the kind of democratic ideals that egalitarians espouse can do without a religious tradition. If it cannot, then egalitarians may be living off the borrowed interest of a religious metaphysic, which (in their eyes) has gone bankrupt. The question is: Where's the capital?[9]

If moral objectivity rises and falls with theism, then justice as anything robust enough to speak of actual human value is tethered to a creation narrative.

It is here worth mentioning, however, that theism in itself does not necessarily guarantee equal worth. As Pojman sharply deduced, "God could have created people unequal."[10] So, both in grounding and prescription, justice involving human dignity is a theological issue. As Pojman quipped, "We can't burn bridges and still drive Mack trucks over them."[11]

The fact that human rights require theism still leaves many questions unanswered, but it also narrows the field considerably. This God must be involved not solely at the moment of creation but also as a judge and administer of justice, otherwise morality becomes trivial. That is, this is the personal God of classical theism and monotheistic traditions. The moral intuition of natural law—the existential conviction that there is a way-it-should-be, the abductive reasoning of a universal pragmatic inference that justice involves a sense of due-ness—is significantly strengthened by the realization that a substantive morality requires monotheism as its grounding. If there is a creator, then there is a proper order.

In one sense, it is God's due justice to have all things as God wishes and designed them to be. In this sense, God is free to command whatever God wishes as it relates to telos, and any created thing is good in so far as it remains according to that design. Moreover, if God is good, then naturally what God designs reflects this goodness in some capacity. Note that injustice does not even come into the equation of creation until one has freely stepped beyond the just-order and attempted to usurp that order or in some way ignore or pervert that design. From that point forward, injustice become identifiable qualities describing that-which-ought-not-to-be. This "not-as-it-should-be-ness" is an absence of goodness and right-order—a misalignment from teleological goodness. Yet ought implies can. If something is impossible, it cannot be morally obligatory. If knowledge of something is impossible, then moral expectation which requires that knowledge cannot be obligatory. Thus, if a Creator is to hold creation morally accountable, knowledge of that for which they are to account for must be readily available.

This is where philosophers and theologians have pressed into Natural Law Theory. If we were created to live and flourish, then it is wrong to murder. If we were created to be free persons with free will, then it is wrong to forcibly enslave or traffic others or to deny them freedom of conscience. If we were created to reproduce, reproduction is good; intentionally killing our offspring is not. The list of basic rights is not exhaustive, but it is enough to ground justice and to serve as foundation for government. Just how far rights extend beyond this foundation has remained a point of dispute. Through general revelation, we may intuit the fact of moral truth concerning a basic sense of rights or due dignity, but any rights beyond basic rights are extremely difficult to ground as fact. Such assertions would require special or divine revelation.

Along this line of thought, John Locke—the seventeenth-century philosopher who influenced the US Declaration of Independence—argued that we are born with basic natural rights to life, liberty, and property (acquired via labor).[12] Jefferson changed "property" to "pursuit of happiness," which becomes ambiguous and confused with the right to an *actualization* of one's envisioned happiness or an unquestionable right to pursue one's vision, even via a questionable means. Locke insisted that we are free to exercise these rights as long as we do not interfere with the natural rights of others. Since our rights include the right to protect these rights, we are justified in forming our governing institutions in order to transfer certain powers to that institution for the purpose of protecting our rights as a whole and investing minimally in our collective well-being. However, importantly, we cannot transfer powers that are not rightfully ours. (If I have no right to take and redistribute your wealth without your consent then neither can I empower the government to do so).

While our focus involves the question of justice as grounded, not the complexities of justice applied, it is worth addressing the common and understandable, though mistaken, assumption that a collectivist distribution of wealth is the focus of justice in Disney's *Robin Hood*. "Stealing from the rich to give to the poor" certainly has a utilitarian ring. To the contrary, however, the story actually appeals to our intuitions concerning Natural Law and property. Prince John was an unjust and oppressive power, but he was not the rightful king. (Already there is a perversion of right order). To the point, Robin's interest was not in redistributing *John's* wealth to the have-nots; his concern involved giving back to the people the property (with interest, perhaps) that was stolen from *them* by a corrupted power. That is, he is defending basic rights and dignity, as established in Natural Law. This also aligns with Locke's thought. Since the sole purpose of government is to protect our basic rights, Locke encouraged revolution whenever government laws detoured from Natural Law. We are given *no* impression that Robin ought to have continued to redistribute wealth once Richard returned. When the king returns, the story ends and we are left with the impression that all is well, that justice and goodness have regained rule.

Recall Pojman's point above, however. The fact of creation alone does not necessarily ground human value as unique among created things. Theism unspecified establishes only that justice—which we might call *just-is(-as-*

was-meant-to-be) — is tethered to *telos*. In so far as the created order functions as it was created to — which, in theory, could include a might-makes-right Darwinian system — there is justice (just-*is*). Something more is needed to establish reason for believing in a particular hierarchy within the created order. Our natural intuitions bespeak the moral order, yet we also need the narrative that we were created to live free and meaningful lives, that we do hold a privileged place in creation, in order to ground the conclusions detailed above.

Contrary to the human-centered optimism of the Enlightenment, as philosophers began to reject teleology and assert individual autonomy as moral authority, in actuality, without a teleological grounding, all that remains as moral foundation is an imperfect and questionable human nature. This leads to a plethora of groundless ideologies warring hopelessly with one another, as they all claim to be the more rational perspective. As philosopher Alasdair MacIntyre powerfully argued, modern "enlightened" moral philosophers — whether Kantian or Utilitarian — deceive themselves into thinking that their moral utterances are meaningful, when in actuality they only assert fragmented remnants of moral meaning, which they have inherited from a great catastrophe, occurring long before them, which stripped moral terms of substance and context. They struggle to assemble these remnants into cogent theses, yet their contemporary moral prescriptions have been stripped of obligatory force and reduced to subjective appeals to intuitions and merely emotive prescriptions. While contemporary moral debate entails a clash between Kantians appeals and Utilitarian ideals, both camps of modernity embody "a matching pair of incommensurable fictions."[13] This is because both speak of "rights," yet, once moral language is removed from a teleological meta-narrative, it does not follow that natural or human rights exist. "For the truth is plain: there are no such rights, and belief in them is one with belief in witches and in unicorns."[14]

The first point raised by MacIntyre's argument is that a teleological meta-narrative is necessary for any talk of rights. Still, a second question arises even so. For he points out that natural rights language often makes a logical error in mistaking "right" with need or desire.[15] We actually see a MacIntyrean picture paint itself quite well in an episode of Disney's *Dug Days*, a mini-series of animated shorts, in follow-up to the celebrated film *Up*.[16] After Russell gives Dug a sandwich, a bird and a squirrel begin to quarrel with Dug over who actually deserves the sandwich. Whereas, they argue, the dog is simply privileged to the sandwich because he happens to be a household pet, the bird actually *needs* food for her babies while the squirrel argues that he will not survive the winter unless he is able to fatten up before it arrives. Dug ends up giving the sandwich away because he is able to empathize with their struggles and recognize that he is not actually in need of the food (for his will always be provided). Still, notice that the appeals to rights, in this case, were never really grounded; they were simply assertions of needs and desires, and efforts to shame another simply for being one who so happened to have been given something which the others did not possess.

Indeed, even in light of a teleological grand narrative, MacIntyre's point may follow. Consider the following: The theist may say, "If I was created, by God, to exist, then I have a right to exist—thus, I have a right to life, and you assault *my right* in attempting to deny what is due to me." First, it might be argued that, even if it is clear that God exists, it might not be so clear that we amount to anything more than mere divine artistic expressions; we might need an *additional* narrative (say, scriptural enlightenment) in order to make that move. Yet it might also be said, second, that even with an additional narrative—with full understanding that we were made special, and that God has a particular interest in us—we still may not have an actual "right" to our own lives. That is to say, some might argue that the most robust theistic perspective sees all teleological due-ness as pointing back to God. (All created things are God's property; any offense to God's order is an offense against God; thus, the only real "right" is the Creator's right to have the sort of world which the Creator intended *to be*, and with it the social and moral order, God may have intended for free agents therein to embrace freely.) In this case, God may have created us, intending for us to live, and not be killed by one another, and yet it may not be the case that *we* actually have a "right" to our life, but rather that *God* holds the right to any life. That is, if God created us to live and not to be killed, then the assault upon us is really, ultimately, an assault upon God's teleological order.

So, perhaps MacIntyre is onto something here. What this suggests is that (1) no rights exist without a teleological frame; (2) even within a teleological frame, it may still be doubtful whether any natural rights exist, unless such a claim is grounded within a particular and explicit metanarrative (and within a teleological frame, accompanied by a moral meta-narrative able to ground a claim to individual rights, since a right cannot be derived from a need or desire, any universally applicable rights to be claimed therein will likely (3) be minimal and (4) apply in a negative sense).[17]

Contemporary ideals concerning basic rights and equal worth actually grew out of the ancient Jewish and classical Christian heritage.[18] As Paul Copan writes, in his 2022 analysis of difficult passages in the Old Testament, "The fact is that [in contrast to ancient Israel] other ancient Near Eastern nations simply didn't believe that all humans are created equal."[19] No rights existed for slaves or war captives, for example, such as those implied in the biblical law.[20] Stanley Benn traced formalized notions of "natural rights" to the ideological developments of the seventeenth and eighteenth centuries — after which, such became common assumption, and the law was expected to protect said rights.[21] Yet the conviction of natural law and the idea of inalienable human rights originated not in the Enlightenment, but in classical[22] thought and medieval[23] theology concerning the *imago Dei*—"image of God." As Copan elaborates, "In the ancient Near East, the earthly *king* was associated with a god's "image" — an honor that didn't extend to ordinary human beings. By contrast, God created humans in his image as corulers with God (*kings*) and worshipers of God (*priests*). These priest-kings were made to care for creation alongside God (Gen. 1:26-28; cf. Ps. 8)"[24] Pojman stressed the necessity of the western theistic heritage in grounding intrinsic human rights:

> The doctrine that all people are of equal worth, and thus endowed with inalienable rights, is rooted in our religious heritage. The language of human dignity and worth implies a great family in which a benevolent and sovereign Father binds together all his children in love and justice. The originators of rights language presupposed a theistic worldview, and secular advocates of equal rights are, to cite Tolstoy, like children who see beautiful flowers, grab them, break their stems, and try to transplant them without their roots.[25]

The Christian emphasis on love was inspiring. In 362, the Roman emperor Julian wrote, "It is disgraceful that, when no Jew ever has to beg, and the impious Galileans [Christians] support not only their own poor but ours as well, all men see that our people lack aid from us."[26] Yet it was the emphasis on human dignity that completely reformed the moral imagination of the western world. Philosopher Luc Ferry has noted this impact of theism upon the modern moral imaginary. "Christianity was to introduce the notion that humanity was fundamentally identical, that men were equal in dignity.... Christianity revolutionized the history of thought. For the first time in human history, liberty rather than nature had become the foundation for morality."[27] Theism is necessary for grounding any appeal to right-order (justice), but it seems as though the ancient Jewish and classical Christian perspectives, in particular, are the source of contemporary presumptions concerning basic rights—and they are best equipped to ground this conviction.

The Imago

According to Locke, whenever there is disagreement between the government and its people, there is no higher appeal except to God.[28] Esmeralda's plea actually presses deeper than the fact of creation, appealing to the special nature of human beings. She cries, "I thought we all were children of God."[29] There *is* proper order within creation, and justice is tethered to order, but raising human beings requires a special level of interest, investment, and patience. Are human beings really special—warranting, by God's design, his special interest?

According to the Christian narrative, to which Esmeralda specifically appeals, human beings do bear a special mark. They are made in the image of God. As Koukl eloquently stated:

> No rules that man invents by himself can ever be binding in any final or universal sense, since the person who makes the rules can simply change them whenever it suits his fancy or whenever the old rules get bothersome. But if there are obligations based on something changeless—for example, man's built-in value—then our obligations toward man cannot change either.... Man's special value is the only reason we have unalienable human rights. Unalienable rights are those that can never be taken away since the reason for our rights.... is always a part of each one of us.... If man's special value falls, then unalienable human rights fall, too. If man is not special, if he is not deeply different from any other thing, then there is no good reason not to treat him just like any other thing when it's convenient for us to do so. If man is just 'the result of a purposeless and natural process that did not have him in mind, as matter-ism dictates, if he is just a gear in the machine, or if he is only an illusion of the universal Mind ['mind-ism'], then there is no good reason for unique and unalienable human rights.....

According to the Christian story of reality, humans *are* special. "God created only one creature who was, in a unique and important and almost indescribable way, like himself, bearing his own likeness, having a soul imprinted with his very image....The Story says you are a creature, but you are not just a creature. You are not a little god, but you are not nothing. You are made like God in a magnificent way that can never be taken from you. No matter how young or old or small or disfigured or destitute or dependent, you are still a beautiful creature. You bear the mark of God. He has made you like himself, and that changes everything."[30]

No matter a person's color, gender, age, level of development, ability or disability, struggles concerning sexual desires, socioeconomic status, individual perspective, or cultural belief, human value lies within the very fact of this specialness.

We intuitively understand that there is something unique about persons (and Disney presses into this understanding, even as it uses personified animal characters like Dumbo and the Aristocats). It is because we see a *person* — the personified character — that we sense injustice when Dumbo is harassed for the amusement of others, humiliated just because he looks different. Even without seeing all the villagers, we *see* the peasants that Kuzco cannot, and we understand that they deserve to be treated better. This is also why we long to see Aladdin set Genie free. Even if it can be argued that genies are not rights-bearing beings, that Genie is the property of the lamp, and the lamp is the property of Aladdin, and even if Aladdin is not wrong for using the three wishes given to him in any way he desires — that he bears no moral obligation to use a wish on Genie's freedom — we nevertheless sense Genie's personhood. We see him as a valuable person and therefore understand that it is not right for valuable persons to be treated as property, as the mere means to the ends of other people's happiness. We sense that Genie *deserves* freedom because he is an intrinsically valuable person.

Even non-theists often appeal to human specialness as derived from the fact that the rational human mind is unlike anything else in nature. Without a higher grounding, however, this is only speciesism. It may accurately describe a Darwinian advantage, but it could not actually speak to an objective, universal truth concerning intrinsic human value. The Jewish and Christian explanation of human specialness significantly strengthens the basic rights to be inferred from Natural Law. The interests of the collective do not *de facto* override the value of the individual, for each one is an image-bearer. All human beings deserve recognition of a basic due dignity because all human lives are sacred—"set apart." (And if this is the case, we must also ponder whether potentially designated functions of humanity, like sexuality, and institutions which reflect this nature, like marriage, are likewise sacred).

Justice as Telos

The entire plot of *Moana* is based around an original order and a teleological injustice. Not only was the injustice a direct assault against the goddess Te Fiti; it was an injustice against the natural order—the way things were supposed to be. That injustice had consequences which were felt throughout creation, and nature itself began to groan with rebellion. A resulting disease and decay even reached Moana's island and began to threaten the livelihood of her people.

On the theistic narrative in general, there is a way-it-should-be (teleological order). On the Jewish and Christian narratives specifically, we are intrinsically valuable. We are also broken, and we know it. (*Raya and the Last Dragon* does a beautiful job of pressing into this conviction). We have a desire for meaningfulness and can sense that something about the world is not as it should be—we call this injustice. Despite claims that there are no universal, objective moral values, there *is* at least one universal to which we cannot help but continually appeal—namely, justice; even if we differ on what justice looks like in practice, we all believe that something is in some way due to someone.

Referencing a tribe that throws deformed children into the river because it is believed that "such infants belong to the hippopotamus, the god of the river," Pojman pointed out that while we may differ about *non-moral* beliefs—such as whether hippopotami are gods; whether deformed children are their property—we actually agree on basic moral principles.[31] The tribe values justice as do we, and shares a universal definition of justice: "give to each one his or her due." Note that the primary moral belief upon which their non-moral beliefs and immoral practice are built is an appeal to property. We agree that if x belongs to person P, then x is owed to P. Where we disagree is whether x in fact belongs to P.

Moral intuition, then, is a reflection of our teleological intuitions—our right-order convictions drawing us back to the very work and nature of the God from whom we have separated ourselves or somehow become removed in some degree. The created being has a strong intuition that he or she is somehow, for some reason, alienated from goodness, and also to an extent from other human beings; that there is an enmity between human beings that ought not be there; that human beings are, in some sense, part of the problem. Nevertheless, we know there is something special about human beings—even if there is an ugliness within humanity as well.

Herein lies the reason theism in general may, and biblical theism in particular does, escape the Euthyphro dilemma—the claim that either "good" really only means "that which God commands" (thus, moral law seems capricious) or else goodness must exist independently of God (thus, God is not necessary); there is a difference between being "commanded by God" and being "teleologically proper." At this point, it might be helpful to think not of "Moral Law," but "Teleological Goodness." On biblical theism, it seems that our strong intuitions concerning the rightness of love are references of an objective goodness internal to God's nature, while our intuitions concerning justice reflect the rightness of a created order—the fact that an ultimate respect is due the Creator, and a consequent respect is due to that which the Creator loves (supposing we have reason to think that God loves certain creatures uniquely). So, here it is better to think of justice in terms of *telos* rather than moral law and God's command.

Moreover, as David Baggett and Jerry Walls have observed, there is a need to be "a little more rigorous in distinguishing between the moral good and the moral right."

> Issues of the moral good are axiological matters, whereas issues of moral rightness are deontic matters. Not everything that is morally good is also morally right, in the sense of being morally obligatory. Giving half of your income to the poor might be morally good, but it is likely not your moral obligation.... One of the great challenges of ethics is to determine which, among many good actions, are morally obligatory. On our view, it's God's commands or will... that best *enable us to determine* [emphasis added] which actions among those that are good are also morally obligatory. God's commands determine what's morally obligatory but not what's morally good. So our view will embrace a non-voluntarist account of the good and a voluntarist account of the right.[32]

Drawing out the two aforementioned points, it is more helpful to think of justice in terms of a teleological goodness or properness (the perfect and proper functioning of the created order), rather than "Moral Law," because we naturally associate "law" with commandments. Moreover, as suggested by Baggett and Walls, rather than thinking of God's commands or will as the foundation of moral rightness, it is more accurate to understand a command as revelation, *enabling us to determine* what is right (what is requisite of a properly functioning Order) while also discerning a goodness beyond rightness. While there *are* times in which we speak of the "Moral Law" and likely have some sort of deontic rule or commandment in mind—such as, "Do not harm innocent human beings for the fun of it"—when we speak of the "Moral Law" within the Moral Argument, we do not really speak of commandments. Rather, we seem to have in mind an intuition concerning a more perfect sense of Moral Order. (Perhaps the argument would be more precise if reformulated, If there is a Moral Order, then there is a Moral Order-er).

The Moral Order is not a series of commands, but a designation of how things ought to be. The obligation to work according to one's created function is not grounded in a command to do so, but within the goodness of the order itself (and the goodness of the order itself is reflective of a goodness intrinsic to the Order-er). Thus, there is a sense of teleological rightness with which we associate the oughtness of the Moral Order that is not the same as the sense of right-action with which we associate deontic commands. So, even when we distinguish "good" from "right," we must take care *not* to limit the idea of "*the* Moral Law" to the realm of deontic commands. Because *the* Moral Order is not grounded within moral commandments, the obligatory nature of moral commandments is not rooted within the commandments *per se*, but within the teleological properness of the Moral Order.

If love is part of God's very nature—a maximal love if we are speaking of a being-than-which-nothing-greater-can-be-conceived—then God will naturally command that which is in accord with his nature; thus, if God is loving, he will command what is good, and if God knows that something is good for us, then God (like any loving parent) may "command" it (unless there is some loving reason for withholding said command). Still, on biblical theism, the "Moral Law" is more of a teleological given, rather than a command *per se*. Respect the One who made you, to paraphrase Jesus[33]—and this includes respecting what God loves and designs.

So, God, in his very nature, is the source of all goodness and determinant for all teleological justice—the only source in which morality is sensible and meaningful. On this view, that which we understand goodness to be is a quality or expression of God's very essence. Evil is a negation, some sort of separation from God or fragmentation of created order. Injustice has to do with some sense of disrespect for the goodness of God's created order. This *justice-as-telos* fits all forms of classical monotheism, but the emphasis on God's love rather than God's command (*justice-as-telos-tethered-to-God-as-love*) points toward the ancient Jewish and classical Christian conception. Allah's love seems to be determined according to whether one is repentant of sin,[34] while YHWH was continually longsuffering, and Jesus died for sinners.[35]

Jesus came seeking a radical reconciliation of both wayward children and *the others*. The "odd," forgotten, and outcast; the weak and poor; aliens and strangers: all are sought for the purpose of adoption into his family. And he promised to come again to end all injustice permanently. If God loves all human beings—deeming them worthy of investing in as potential children, and not merely as art-object expressions of his creativity—then you can be sure that they are all valuable. The possibility of justice is a universal conviction, and the case for *justice-as-telos* is easily established via numerous arguments for theism.[36] The appeal to intrinsic human dignity and unalienable, basic rights, however, requires a more specific grand narrative. Esmeralda approaches God with a sense of unworthiness, but also connectedness. For she considers that God is no stranger to rejection and alienation.[37] Moreover, his people have known oppression and persecution. Jewish believers have known mistreatment in both ancient and contemporary contexts, and Christ warned that the world would hate his followers because he had called them to be different from the world.[38] Early Christians also understood marginalization and martyrdom well. Yet even amidst alienation, early Christians practiced a charity (agapism) that was strikingly counter-cultural.

On the classical Christian view, the ideal of the greater community involves spiritually and practically (where possible) serving one another—the sharing of blessings and burdens is both an appropriate out-working of an appreciation for Christ's sacrifice and a potent portrayal of God's kingdom come.[39] Yet this goes beyond Moral Law;[40] for grace is beyond "justice," and love cannot be forced.[41] The sacrifice of Bing Bong (*Inside Out*) is touching. It was not right for him to die. We sense that loss. Yet we also understand that it was nevertheless and undeniably *good* for him to die on Riley's behalf. This was not justice. In fact, the unnecessary loss of a dear friend feels unjust. Something is not right about the world when good friends must die unnecessarily. Within Riley's mind, however, things are not as they ought to be; there is an observable absence of just-ness. So, Bing Bong understands that his sacrifice actually *is* necessary if there is to be any restoration of Riley's emotional stability. Note, however, that it was—it had to be—*Bing Bong's* choice to lay down his life for his friend. If Joy had kicked him off of the wagon, forcing him to cease existing in the Memory Dump, this would have been an injustice. Yet, when he chooses to jump off the wagon in order to lighten the load and get Joy out of there, we see this as good. So, we do understand that there is a distinction to be made, at times, between justice and a goodness which goes beyond.

On the biblical model, in light of one's respect for God, "justice" involves a basic respect for human life, free will, and (Locke was correct) property (although all property ultimately belongs to God),[42] while we are nevertheless called (not forced) to go beyond justice and seek goodness—to live and love in light of God's kingdom. The kingdom of shared burdens and blessings—in which there is no need, as modeled in Acts 2:42-47—is in the interest of everyone, but this is because it is freely embraced by everyone, according to ability or unique shape and gifts. For one human being to force another to serve, share, or love against his or her free will *would* create an injustice.

This struggle is easily observable in contemporary political tensions between an emphasis on individual autonomy and ideals of the greater good for the greater community. To sacrifice community for self is not good. Yet, while it may be the case that *willingly* subverting self in service to community *is* good, to *force* the sacrifice of individuals (against their will) for community is *wrong*. Only when individuals *freely* choose to serve one another have we glimpsed the social *goodness* of heaven on earth. On the Biblical model there is an equal acknowledgment of dignity due all people, but also a call to practical (moral) discrimination; God's people are not to endorse some of the things that others celebrate. The Bible balances the goodness of individual freedom with the goodness of communal service, in light of the rightness of a respect due the Creator and his creation.

Monotheism in general grounds justice in a created order—a respect due the Creator—but this alone provides no real reason to expect the Creator to love justice between or care uniquely about human beings. Biblical theism in particular situates a more robust understanding of goodness within God's character (rather than primarily emphasizing morality as respect due *to* the

Creator, although that is also a key variable) and speaks more potently to the conviction that human beings bear a special dignity.

Injustice Lies Within

Raya and the Last Dragon provides one of the richest takes on the human condition. Kumandra—the ideal, the meant-to-be, of human community—becomes fragmented and a consuming sickness begins to turn people to stone. The film presses into the fact that human division may involve group tensions and power struggles, but it ultimately stems from and comes down to an issue within individual hearts. For, as James (Jesus's half-brother) observed, "where jealousy and selfish ambition exist, there will be disorder and every vile practice."[43]

To cry "injustice" is to point to the way things are and imply that they are not as they ought to be. If there is a way-it-*should*-be, but human beings disregard that natural moral order—thus "injustice" means perverting the moral order, and disregarding respect due one another—then there is something within human beings that wars against intuition, reorienting our desire to participate appropriately within this natural moral order. Just as cancers cause abnormalities in healthy immune systems, compromising natural functions of one's body, so too, if there is a way-it-should-be, our tendency toward division over reconciliation and the ease with which we justify using others as a means to our own happiness suggests a sort of cancer within human conscience.

If this is the case, then the only way to secure justice is to address the sickness. Simply changing power structures—placing a different set of sick folks in charge of a culture's narrative—will accomplish nothing in the name of true justice, unless the narrative speaks to the sickness. Only theology is able to speak to such a sickness, and only a virtue or character-oriented ethical systems address the hearts of individuals. Yet virtue education necessarily involves a narrative that prescribes the sort of people we ought to become and related principles concerning how we ought to live our lives. Alas, for many CSJ advocates, such language would be oppressive, hateful, and therefore unjust (unless, of course, it prescribes the virtues of CSJ—CSJ is, after all, ironically, propagating its own virtue theory). So, the real question is whether true justice within society is, fundamentally, an issue of its power structures or the hearts of its people. As Aleksandr Solzhenitsyn understood, the former conclusion is naïve although the latter is burdensome.

"If only it were all so simple! If only there were evil people somewhere insidiously committing evil deeds, and it were necessary only to separate them from the rest of us and destroy them. But the line dividing good and evil cuts through the heart of every human being. And who is willing to destroy a piece of his own heart?"[44] If we really possess a deep goodness reflecting an established and right order, then injustice in some way reveals a sickness, brokenness, and deficiency within our humanity.[45]

Esmeralda wisely turned to God because she understood that only God can provide the justice for which her people so desperately longed. She realized that a worldview that sees difference as indicative of human value—or dignity as defined rather than given—cannot ground any real sense of justice; and a perspective that relegates morality to perspective is no authority on justice. So, rather than pleading that all perspectives are *de facto* equal, she appeals to God as the only hope for justice when persecuted by people with a broken understanding of reality. Egalitarian justice is only grounded in a theism that includes the specialness of human beings within the created order, and the issue of injustice, while a problem for humanity as a whole, is an issue of individual hearts. Returning to the issue of CSJ, the critical theorist must understand that the problem lies *within* (all of humanity) and that individuals, not groups, are ultimately responsible for their moral standing in light of the just order; and the theist can agree that understanding justice indeed involves an analysis of multiple perspectives, and the applications of justice in society involves an ongoing evaluation of our institutionalized narratives, organized systems of power, and empowered avenues of information.

14

Goodness Beyond Just-ness

Justice carries a sense of something set right. It entails an ought-to-be, while injustice involves a sense of negation—something is no longer as it ought to be. Because something ought to be, and yet it is not, there arises a sense of due-ness. Something is owed. Something must be returned. Te Fiti's heart must be returned (*Moana*). The injustice against the Northuldra must be corrected (*Frozen II*). Kumandra must be restored (*Raya and the Last Dragon*). The Lost Princess (*Tangled*) must be returned. The victim of abuse and misfortune (*Cinderella*) ought to be removed from her situation. The kidnapped child (*The Rescuers*) ought to be rescued. Since justice involves the setting right of all wrongs, it may also include the unjust person getting what [punishment] they deserve. The Evil Queen and Mother Gothel both face poetic justice.

As we have established throughout this work, Disney films continuously press into this sense of just-ness. Yet sometimes Disney's emphasis goes beyond this restoration motif; sometimes the emphasis is on the Kingdom-ever-after, and that entails a goodness which goes beyond just-ness *per se*. Cinderella exchanges kindness for abuse. Is this "just"? Her abusers do not deserve Ella's kindness. In fact, they *deserve* far worse than what they get. Instead of emphasizing justice in its fullest sense, here Disney emphasizes an undeserved grace, a goodness which is able to transcend justice. Do we not expect the same from Beast? *Ought* he to be merciful when he catches Maurice trespassing and (in the live-action film) stealing a rose from Beast's garden? We expect him to and we see his treatment of Maurice as evidence of his beastly disposition. What obligates the Rescuers to endanger themselves seeking to save a kidnapped and mistreated orphan child? Nothing. Yet the goodness of doing so is unmistakable.

Why should the children of villains like Maleficent, Jafar, Cruella, and the Evil Queen (*Descendants*) be treated any different than their parents? Ought we not to assume the apples will fall near to the trees? What warrants grace and second chances to *the others*? It may not be warranted—it may not be what justice requires—but we understand that grace and forgiveness are good. Namaari did not *deserve* Raya's trust, but we understand there was something good about Raya's step of faith. The restoration of Kumandra required not only a mediating magic to right the wrong--to extinguish the sickness—but also a perpetuating sense of good faith in one another and good will toward one another. Both the ideal of human community and the idea of a Kingdom-ever-after suggest a deep yearning for a goodness that goes beyond justice per se.

The Social Impact of Sin and the Call of the Kingdom-Ever-After

CSJ is not entirely wrong, but neither are many of its popular prescriptive presuppositions necessarily correct. There is a difference between defending and affirming dignity due all persons and defending an affirmation of what they claim to be their rights and liberties. In so far as CSJ remains a *descriptive* approach to philosophical inquiry—drawing attention to underrepresented perspectives and raising questions of injustice, it is an admirable endeavor that does as an academic discipline what the arts have done for centuries.[1] When it moves beyond this to make assertions on rights, removed from a *justice-as-telos-tethered-to-God-as-love* narrative, it lacks satisfactory foundation (even if its vision of the good life includes some admirable aims).

We are social creatures, and our lives are entwined with those around us—even if they are "different" than us and value different things. CSJ is correct in pressing into our conviction that there is a goodness intrinsic to human community—unity over division—and that we ought to have a heart for healing hurts, sharing burdens, encouraging unique expressions of human beauty, and opposing (true) oppression. This is the call of Christian applied living as well: to love the lost; defend the defenseless; provide for the poor; help the homeless; seek healing for the hurting and hopeless; encourage the orphan; fellowship with the outcast; oppose true injustice; love justice (rightly understood); and, where possible (to paraphrase the popular quote[2]) to seek unity in the essentials, celebrate diversity in non-essentials, and practice charity in all things.

While Jesus called his followers to a narrow path in moral under-standing—an exclusivist understanding of truth, re-orientation of desire, and continual tempering of ethical impulse—he also called them to love lib-erally—to live as ambassadors of the kingdom of God. In the biblical story of reality, we see that true justice served is a matter of desert. That is the bad news. It does not matter whether people can do good things if the overall *telos* of humanity as a whole has been compromised or perverted, and a cor-ruption within each individual heart bears witness to this.[3] God does not owe anything to anyone. A Creator who establishes a right-order, but chooses (in love) to entrust some created beings with free will and conscience is justified in destroying creation if those beings freely choose to reject him, disrespect the order, and assert themselves over one another.

What CSJ gets right is that individual identity *is*, in some sense, inter-twined with group identity (yet group identity does not supersede individ-ual accountability). Individuals can bring honor to entire groups—just as Mulan brought honor to China—or cause group suffering—just as Wreck-It Ralph's actions threatened the happiness of everyone within his own game, and the safety of other games in the arcade. If King Runeard declares war on Northuldra (and its spirits), then all of Arendelle is at war with them as well. This is the same idea as that of Original Sin, an original offense by repre-sentative human beings unfortunately welcomed an injustice-virus which in-fected all of humanity and negatively impacted other aspects of creation.[4] Moreover, like an autoimmune disease, sin attacks human community, as it breeds antipathy and hostility within individual hearts. In the words of Har-old Willmington, "Good has only one enemy, the evil; but evil has two ene-mies, the good and another conflicting evil."[5] Or as C. S. Lewis put it, "The more pride one had, the more one disliked pride in others.... Pride gets no pleasure out of having something, only in having more of it than the next man."[6]

Thus, it is *sin* which is systemic, because sin is endemic to every human heart—and from a corrupted heart flows all sorts of injustices. Polity and policy cannot remedy injustices that stem from disposition. Sin is oppression to all of creation. The bad news of the biblical narrative is that we do not deserve God's favor and cannot earn our moral right-standing. Each of us stands condemned according to the moral law of teleological perfection and right-order.[7] The good news we find in the New Testament, however (com-plementary to the narrative of the Old Testament), is that God's favor is nev-ertheless offered, his lovingkindness is longsuffering, and love is willing to go *beyond* (yet without compromising) just-desert—as Jesus's sacrifice depicts justice served (upon a willing and qualified scapegoat) on behalf of humanity, but also grace extended to humanity. According to this story, evil will never be extinguished until the King returns, yet the sword of justice will then swing more swiftly and cut more deeply than many realize. In the Kingdom-ever-after, justice is served in light of the Kingdom order, yet Love also reigns in light of the King's character.

It is essential here to understand the distinction between justice and goodness. In the Words of William Lane Craig, "There is a conceptual difference between something's being good (or bad) and something's being right (or wrong). The former has to do with something's worth, while the latter concerns something's obligatoriness."[8] To love and respect God and the basic rights of others (declared special by God) *is* justice. To love beyond this is not "justice"; it is *goodness* extended—going beyond the just-order and growing, in practice, more fully into the likeness of a goodness that transcends and makes intelligible the right-order.[9] On the Christian narrative, those who accept the invitation to be reconciled to the *telos* of God's kingdom, adopted into the King's family—in addition to being pardoned from the just-deserts of due justice—are then called to become ambassadors of that kingdom. There is a problem, however. Many Christians in western first-world countries seem to rest within the security of Christ's substitutionary righteousness and ignore his call to grow into the likeness of his sacrificial goodness, and some who claim to profess the Christian narrative—like Frollo—actually reflect a contra-Christian message in practice.

The 1995 DC Talk song "What If I Stumble?" begins with a powerful challenge to Christians: "The greatest single cause of atheism in the world today is Christians, who acknowledge Jesus with their lips, and walk out the door, and deny him by their lifestyle. *That* is what an unbelieving world simply finds unbelievable."[10] The quote is attributed to Brennan Manning, who emphasized grace-in-practice over moralistic religiosity. "The American church," on the other hand, "today accepts grace in theory but denies it in practice."[11] This reflects a valid concern of the critical theorist. Has the Christian narrative become so institutionalized that many who identify themselves by that tradition carry so little conviction to embody its calling? If our ability to serve horizontally (as spiritual ambassadors) is affected by our ability to grow vertically (spiritually), has the institutionalization of Christianity, though enhancing its exponential outreach, actually weakened its pragmatic impact? (Without discrediting or belittling the good that can come from organized ministries and organizational networks; is this why Christianity seems to grow so quickly in those regions of the world wherein it is forced to thrive as an underground movement—because the Church exists foremost as a *community* which finds solidarity in the pain of a shared struggle and the power of a transformative hope?)

While the Bible offers a definitive answer to the rational problem of evil, the impact of evil, the problem of pain and suffering, remains an existential concern, it must be lived through. Christians indeed offer a disservice to their neighbors when their lifestyles miscommunicate the hope of liberation (from sin, guilt, and the chains of a meaningless existential angst); the hope for strength to endure the existential problem of sin and suffering (by trivializing the problem or emphasizing "gospels" of health, wealth, and a name-it-claim-it happiness); and the hope for transformation (of both individual and community) found in the gospel. They offer a disservice when they downplay the point that God calls his people to seek the good of their city[12] and serve others as ambassadors of Love's kingdom.[13] Since God created all human beings in his image, it is no surprise that we find non-theists who do good things and serve their community in loving ways.[14] Yet what a shame it is for those who reject God and the kingdom (valuable image-bearers, nonetheless) to do a better job of sharing glimpses of that kingdom, than those who identify themselves as its ambassadors!

So, if the CSJ challenge is that some who advance grand-moral-narratives, such as Christians, are wrong for ignoring (even causing) some injustices, this is a fair challenge *even* if we disagree on the nature of justice. As the biblical narrative presents it, God's will involves our transformation through the renewing of our minds into the (sacrificial) likeness of Christ (God-as-love-incarnate);[15] having a heart of respect and thankfulness in all circumstances,[16] and letting the goodness of our actions silence ignorant accusations raised against the kingdom of God.[17] Yet this is not justice; this involves the power of the cross—where justice and grace collide, and Goodness both satisfies and transcends the perfect demands of justice.[18]

To recapitulate, when we speak of social "justice," we must understand our terms and we should be clear on what follows. First, nothing is due us unless it is first due a Creator to have things to go according to a grand order. Second, we only share an egalitarian sense of basic human rights if that Creator loves us equally. In that case, we are indeed reaching for justice in so far as we are defending human dignity in light of a respect for God's having imbued human beings with a specialness worthy of honor. However, third, given that we find our world in such a state of enmity, there is no reason to expect an ultimate sense of justice unless and until God sets right our bent natures and extinguishes the sickness parasitic to every human heart. Happiness is not guaranteed in the now, and suffering may even bring about a series of events that works for one's own eternal good. Of course, it is still good to seek justice!

Fourth, it is just to defend God's order, but not all alleged freedoms and liberties are reflected in or follow from that order. To affirm that which lies contrary would actually be to prolong injustice. To denounce affronts to human dignity is just. To defend all human beings as equally valuable persons is just. Yet to declare individual choice as morally superior to a just order; to assert that justice entails a liberation and affirmation of all marginalized value prescriptions; to aver that there is no universal telos or essence concerning human nature and that it is necessarily unjust discrimination-as-hate or oppression to reject this existentialist ideology: such claims on truth, knowledge, and morality appear to lie in clear tension with the teleological order which best grounds egalitarian justice. Thus, it is essential that moral deliberation continues.

Finally, to aim for the best possible conditions for desperate and heartbroken human beings in the now — while an admirable and worthy aim — is not actually "justice," because it is not due anyone to have their best life now, in a fallen world. What *is* still due human beings, according to the Christian story of reality — what remains fundamentally each one's "property" (or God's property, entrusted to each one) — is a due respect (whether to human or to God) regarding human life; a due respect (whether to human or to God) concerning liberty (refraining from treating anyone as a mere means to anyone else's ends — respecting each as an end in him or herself); and freedom of conscience. Freedom of conscience is not an affirmation of perspective, but quite the opposite. It is the right (by which is really meant a due respect, whether to human or to God) concerning one's choice *to refrain* from affirming that which is in discord with the convictions of one's perspective. If God created each one to be a morally free agent, choosing for him or herself whether to respect God's order or to reject God and assert his or her own will over God's design, then to coerce one to profess what is contrary to one's moral conscience would be an overstep. This, of course, does not mean that each has an equal right to live according to whatever actions seem right in his or her own eyes, but it is especially clear that one has no grounded moral force to oblige anyone else to support his or her own moral perspective and definitions of the good life. Freedom of conscience, then, is a right of refrain. (Note, as mentioned above, how this takes a negative form; it is not a *right to* something, but a *right-not;* what is meant is an affirmation that *other persons have no right-to* in regard to one's own conscience).

Whenever we move beyond a defense of basic human rights in order to advocate for convenience (as basic quality of life), this is not the same as seeking social "justice." It is seeking social *goodness*—although, importantly, we seek goodness in light of the dignity established by God's just order. Then, when we advocate for conveniences which lie yet a degree further removed from basic human rights, we move a degree further from "justice." As this happens, "goodness" becomes less clear and more questionable. When we assert that all moral perspectives or value prescriptions ought to be equally, publicly, and institutionally affirmed, we are no longer advocating for justice, nor even goodness *per se*, but instead for ideals and value structures built upon presupposed definitions of reality, telos, and goodness. To secure satisfactorily the moral foundations of justice, we cannot equivocate the issue of human dignity grounded in theism with ideals of moral freedom founded upon human autonomy.

What does God ask of humanity? "To do justice, to love kindness, and to walk humbly with your God."[19] What does justice require (*justice-as-telos-tethered-to-God-as-love*)? It involves respect for the King, respect for his domain, and respect for the special inhabitants for whom he cares. Justice, in itself, is not a supplemental string of legalistic to-dos and social ideals which some might wish to add. Nevertheless, Jesus calls us to go beyond justice, to grow into his likeness through grace in practice (like all virtues, practice is key). Just as Christ was the incarnation of God's love, so too the Christian is called to live as an incarnation of the good news. Theism makes the best sense of a moral system that carries any real force. It is an opiate of a secular world oppressed by an internalized materialistic narrative with its ungrounded optimism. An egalitarian justice is unlikely apart from the moral foundations of ancient Jewish and classical Christian theology. Moreover, social goodness is a step beyond egalitarian justice—and goodness is a controversial term because its intelligibility is tethered to worldview. The question is: what worldview secures the strongest grounding for a goodness robust enough to transcend justice and transform society?

Shalom

The sense of wholeness which fills the Kingdom-ever-after so ubiquitous in Disney culture includes much more than justice alone. According to Jesus, the Kingdom is one in which its inhabitants are not coerced but *care* to look out for one another. To serve the King is to love his citizens; to love one another is to love the King.[20] The peace which pervades the Kingdom is one of an inner wholeness matched by outward expressions of warmheartedness toward one another, grounded in respect and thanksgiving toward the King and the Right-Order (just-ness), and resulting in an ultimate sense of communion and flourishing. As Cornelius Plantinga Jr. explains, the biblical portrait of the final (teleological) end of human flourishing — the moral ought-to-be of human community — is a coalescing of an outward peace, an inner fulness, a respect for the just order, and even a delight in the experience of these things coming together:

> The webbing together of God, humans, and all creation in justice, fulfillment, and delight is what the Hebrew prophets call shalom. We call it peace but it means far more than mere peace of mind or a cease-fire between enemies. In the Bible, shalom means universal flourishing, wholeness and delight – a rich state of affairs in which natural needs are satisfied and natural gifts fruitfully employed, a state of affairs that inspires joyful wonder as its Creator and Savior opens doors and welcomes the creatures in whom he delights. Shalom, in other words, is the way things ought to be.[21]

This sense of an ought-to-be, however, goes beyond the mere fact of a right-order, suggesting something more, something greater, something organic. A right-order just *is*. It is a static concept, though it speaks of a dynamic system of interactions. But goodness is dynamic; it can grow and swell and emanate from being to being. This sense of ought implies a *proper-end*.

The fullness of shalom, then, involves not only the ought-to-be of the teleological order, but also the *meant-to-be* of human excellence. Just as injustice begins with individual hearts, this long-lasting wholeness and loving-kindness — the perpetual *shalom* of the Kingdom-ever-after — involves a Kingdom-oriented *disposition* which emanates from within each character within the community... And so we are back to the issue of virtue ethics. Such a Kingdom does not suddenly arrive in a vacuum. It must begin now. Those who choose to dwell there must begin to prepare their hearts now—or else their hearts must be purged and transformed by some mediating magic ... or both. For, as Isaiah once proclaimed to Israel, so it seems to speak for humanity as a whole:

> The way of peace they do not know
> And there is no justice in their paths....
> Justice is far from us,
> and righteousness does not overtake us;
> we hope for light, and behold, darkness,
> and for brightness, but we walk in gloom....
> Justice is turned back,
> and righteousness stands far away;
> *for truth has stumbled in the public squares,*
> *and uprightness cannot enter* [emphasis added].[22]

The apostle Paul also writes of a struggle to know goodness. Despite good intensions, we find that we are at war within ourselves—often doing what we desire not to do and failing to do the good we desire to do.[23] This is why we need a mediator. Yet *we* also have a part to play in the process. For character is formed over time, as each choice carves out a habit, and each habit cuts away at a disposition. Excellence is a long and demanding road, and the virtue (moral *excellence*) necessary for achieving the shalom of the Kingdom will require a forward investment. In short, we must find the strength to push ourselves to start loving our neighbors *today*, if we are going to be able to love others instinctively in the Kingdom-ever-after.

According to Jesus, the Kingdom of heaven has already come near.[24] He came to serve as the only mediating magic potent enough to liberate hearts from the oppression of sin and its suppression of truth. The gospel's emancipation from *spiritual* oppression liberates us to discern truth, to desire true goodness, and, consequently, to love others better, to begin seeking a social goodness which goes beyond justice, and to bring the Kingdom come.

Disney Lore: A Door to Deliberation

In the previous chapters, we suggested that Disney animated films can mediate between CSJ's concern for perspective and the theistic grounding necessary for any appeal to real justice. We further submit that Disney's depiction of the good life can mediate between CSJ's concern for the alienated and Christ's call to serve others with a goodness that goes beyond justice. Disney wants us to identify with and care for the poor (Aladdin), the alienated and lonely (Mr. Fredricksen, Cinderella, Anna, Quasimodo), and the oppressed and the outcast (Esmeralda and the Gypsies, the citizens of Nottingham), but while looking nevertheless to a higher grounding for truth and hope. It is not just a pointless wish upon impotent stars. There is reason to believe in a truth, goodness, and beauty in which it is worth placing expectant hope.

Rescue, Redemption, and Restoration: Dignity of Persons and Beauty in Community

Moral themes abound in Disney films, but especially a concern for alienated persons. While *Bambi* and other nature-oriented films may call us to question our responsibility to care for nature, Disney's repertoire is replete with care for *persons*—abandoned, orphaned, homeless, poor, and outcast. *Pete's Dragon, Oliver, The Rescuers, Bedknobs and Broomsticks, The Aristocats, Lady and the Tramp,* and *101 Dalmatians* are all centered on orphaned or homeless characters and press into the goodness of adoption. (*The Rescuers* even presses into issues of trafficking; adoption, liberation, and justice are all symbolically connected for Penny).

Disney lore presses the point that we are not only alienated, harmed, or hindered by circumstance, tragedy, and villainy, but also by the ignorance and prejudices of one another. Mulan's anxiety and internalized alienation concerning her individual identity[25] (as with many teenaged and adult individuals) is directly related to the external pressures and hindrances of socio-cultural expectations, which are often (not always) unnecessarily embedded within foundations of preference, habit, or ignorance. Disney also wants us to see the connection between Quasimodo's yearning for community and Esmeralda's plea on behalf of her people; both the deformed and the defamed were alienated by superficial social ideals concerning human value. And Pocahontas was perceptive in her observation that we often act as though the only people who are really "people" are those who share our identities and perspectives.[26] (This rings true on both sides of any polarized issue).

Given the historical influence of animated features, we think Disney's gift for not only animating animals, but the personification of animal characters speaks deeply to our convictions about the significance of personhood.

It is not just that animals ought to be cared for rather than abused, neglected, or used for excessive décor—and the point here is not to equate animal sentience with human personhood—but that, with each narrative, we intuit that every soul is special. We want to see the other 84 dalmatians, the aristocats, the tramp, and Oliver all adopted and loved, just as we want to see Penny rescued and adopted to find her value affirmed through a loving family. This is because Disney has personified these moving pictures in order to appeal to our sense of value due all persons, and so we hurt for the homeless, helpless, and outcast. While we have grown attached to their personified animal friends, we also long for Tarzan and Mowgli, self-sufficient as they may be, to know the goodness of human community. There is something special about human persons and there is something especially good about seeing them in community with one another. (*Tarzan* and the live-action *Jungle Book* (2016) also press into the uniqueness of the human mind among all other creatures, and the latter even mentions a deep law within the jungle which goes beyond survival).

Although Disney continually presses into our thirst for retributive justice, and so we want those especially heinous villains to "get what they deserve," Disney also reminds us that life is complex, and it might even be a good thing to extend a little grace to some "bad guys;" or we may grieve at lost opportunities for repentance and reconciliation. It is because we know human beings are special, and forgiveness is not just, but good, that we feel bad for Gaston's unfortunate, avoidable death, and we feel compassion for anti-villains or anti-heroes misunderstood (like Wreck-it Ralph). This is also why we know it is good to give *Descendants* a chance at redemption—it is *who they are* and not where they come from that defines them—and it is commendable for Raya to extend kindness through an undeserved trust in Namaari.

Stories are powerful, and Disney understands this. This is why *Up* chooses to *begin* with a story, and it is actually the most moving part of the film—so powerful in fact that this tale of Carl and Ellie ultimately provides the thrust to drive Mr. Fredricksen's story forward when Ellie is no longer there to journey with him. Recall George MacDonald's claim that "the best thing you can do for your fellow, next to rousing his conscience, is—not to give him things to think about, but to wake things up that are in him."[27] We know there is something special about human persons and also that they belong in fellowship with one another. Disney presses this point, and even its non-human characters often stand in as personifications of humanity in order to appeal to that sensitivity. Moreover, the Kingdom for which we long and the community we desire — Kumandra — is a place where goodness goes beyond justice. Disney seems to get this as well, as Disney stories often attempt to appeal to that sentiment and rouse a desire for that Kingdom-end.

In *The Gospel According to Disney*, Mark Pinsky wrote, "There is relatively little explicit Judeo-Christian symbolism or substance in seventy years of Disney's animated features, despite the frequent, almost pervasive use of a theological vocabulary... The Disney empire, by its founder's design, is a kingdom of magic, almost totally without reference to any kingdom of heaven."[28] While Pinsky may be right concerning the former statement, that latter clause requires qualification. While Disney may never have referenced heaven or an explicitly theological aspect of the good life and the ever-after — except perhaps when Bagheera (*The Jungle Book*) quotes John 15:13 directly — we have shown throughout this work that Disney's interest in the Kingdom-end, especially in so far as it entails a goodness beyond justice and a loving-kindness which emanates from the virtuous hearts of its characters, aligns strikingly with Jesus's moral teaching. Disney may not call it by a theological name, but Disney stories certainly seem to aim for a theological end. Moreover, Disney tales understand that virtue ethics plays a significant role in preparing the hearts of Kingdom citizens.

15

Liberated to Love Goodness: The Light of Reason and the Darkness of Depravity

I n *The Lion King*, Scar and the hyenas overthrow the institutionalized narrative. The previously marginalized were now liberated, but the land knew no justice. When the king returned, the traditional power structure was re-established, yet goodness and justice reigned because there was a proper order. This is because injustice was not an issue of the power structure *per se*. It certainly became an issue of power structures once Scar seized the throne, and it was certainly through seizure of hegemonic power—purposeful manipulation of the historical and moral narrative—by which Scar's new order came to be. The problem, however, was not the traditional system or narrative; injustice came from the hearts of the morally corrupted individuals who seized control of the power structures and the narrative. Compare this to Turbo's seizure of power in *Wreck-It Ralph*; the marginalizing of a traditional (in this case, true) narrative concerning the reality of *Sugar Rush* and the rise to prominence of the new King-Candy narrative was *not* justice, but an institutionalization of *injustice*. The mere act, in itself, of marginalizing mainstream *moral* narratives and asserting or advocating for marginalized *moral* narratives *cannot* suffice as an adequate definition of justice.

It might be worth noting that Simba—who once boasted in his ignorance and from his privilege, "I'm brushing up on looking down"[1]—required an expansion of perspective in order to acquire the sort of wisdom fit for a king. (Some might argue that Simba's journey to understanding involved the acquisition of an additional, intersecting perspective—an experience of the alienation of "otherness"). Nevertheless, we should not miss that, when the virtuous heart heeded its call to fight for a proper order (way-it-should-be) and not merely for a restructuring of power, the traditional perspective re-established a righteous rule. It was right to challenge Scar's reign as unjust, and seek liberation from his oppression, but it would not necessarily have been right to seek thereafter to dethrone Simba—equating justice with liber-ation per se and defining liberation exclusively as the overthrow of any dom-inant narrative, yet missing the fact that justice requires right-order and rule.

People cannot do whatever they want in a kingdom. If it is the king's domain, then its inhabitants must live in light of the king's rule. This is why the question of God is so important. Despite our preferences concerning re-ality, truth, and morality, if there is a God, then we live in God's world. It is God's reality, God's domain, and God's narrative to establish as God sees fit. We have some value, in so far as any created thing has value in light of the Creator's intentions, but if we have any special value over any other created thing, it can only be because God has deemed it so, or we somehow bear likeness to God. Only if there is a created order can there be justice—a way-it-should-be. Only if the Creator cares about humans and justice have we any hope for God's ending injustice and establishing an everlasting justice. Only if God is good, and his commands are not arbitrary, can we establish such hope. This is the God presented in the biblical story of reality.

The irony lies in the fact that, according to this story, we are continually at war with the father of lies,[2] thus spiritual warfare is ultimately a war of ideas—continual battles over the truthfulness of God's grand narrative.[3] CSJ is right in that truth is liberating, and it is good to liberate those oppressed by false narratives or unfortunate circumstances. (The gospel of Christ is lib-eration from the oppression of sin and false narratives concerning our iden-tity, value, and purpose). The solution to securing justice in society, however, is not to attack the very idea of an objective narrative just because it margin-alizes some moral prescriptions—especially a narrative which satisfactorily grounds justice—but to secure precisely such a foundation in order to decry coherently those crimes that contradict this grounding for human dignity, and to encourage those virtues which bespeak the beauty of human commu-nity.

Separating the Demands of Social "Justice" from the Ideals of Social Gospel

We have primarily been challenging *materialist* presuppositions of CSJ, but what of CSJ movements within the theistic tradition—such as liberation theology (LT)? Here the grounding for justice may be strong, and some pastoral applications may be good, yet the guiding prescriptions can still be confused if foundational definitions of "justice" and "gospel" are incomplete. Consider, for example, James Cone's *God of the Oppressed*. Cone writes that the basic question of theology is, "What has the gospel to do with the oppressed of the land and their struggle for liberation? Any theologian who fails to place that question at the center of his or her work has ignored the essence of the gospel"[4] In fact, it is impossible to understand Jesus and the biblical scriptures "unless the interpretation is done in the light of the consciousness of the oppressed in their struggle for liberation."[5] For proper interpretation understands "God in Christ as the Liberator of the oppressed from social oppression and to political struggle, wherein the poor recognize that their fight against poverty and injustice is not only consistent with the gospel but *is* the gospel of Jesus Christ [emphases added]."[6]

There is clearly similarity between LT and CSJ as it relates to the definition of justice as socio-political liberation. There is also similarity in the epistemic appeal to one's positionality within an oppressed community as involving a privileged access to knowledge—in this case, the truth of God's word—as well as the notion of internalizing the oppressor's narrative.[7] Yet Cone does not embrace the materialism commonly presupposed in many contemporary claims of Critical Social Justice. So, what ought we to make of this?

We want to be careful here to stay on track, and we acknowledge that while devoting much space to addressing CSJ in general, we are offering only a succinct analysis of LT in particular. Nevertheless, without speaking to the social application of Cone's theology, we must consider such an epistemic claim on justice. In 2008, he was interviewed by NPR,[8] and asked to clarify the meaning of Black Liberation Theology. He defined it as "a theology that sees God primarily as concerned with the poor and the weak in society." He added,

> It is concern about the gospel for *everybody*, and if one is for the
> *gospel*... then they are for the poor and the weak. And if you are

for the poor and the weak, you're also concerned about the liberation of black people too... [It] sees justice for the poor as the very heart of what the Christian gospel is about.... God is taking sides with those who are voiceless and weak, and he is empowering them to know that they were not made for slavery, not made for exploitation, but were made for freedom, like everybody else in the world.[9]

In so far as Cone is appealing to the fact that all human beings are special, intrinsically valuable, sacred persons, created to be loved immeasurably by their Creator, he is well in line with the points we have already established here. He also explains, "In a society ... where black has been defined as evil ... we have to turn that understanding of black on its head and see ourselves as loving ourselves.... Before you can love anybody, you have to love yourself... [So, Black Theology teaches us] how to be both unapologetically black and Christian at the same time."[10] Here there is not only an appeal to the fact of human dignity, established in Christian theism, but there is also a unique avenue for pastoral applications of the gospel and healing within the black community. Esmeralda similarly struggles with the notion that a Gypsy is loveable in the eyes of God, yet it is the narrative that God is love and that we are all called to be his children which gives her the boldness to hope for his help. A Gypsy Theology, then, might similarly need to start with the individual's worth in light of God's love, before moving on to the heavier issue of our estrangement from God and its relation to guilt. A theology targeting the privileged and powerful, like Frollo, on the other hand, would need to start with the problem of pride, the fact that *none* is righteous, that *all* are guilty, and that the fear of the Lord is the beginning of wisdom. This is why any theology that starts with Jesus is profound; it is a double-edged sword that both pricks the heart of the prideful and breaks the chains of guilt and false identity which imprison the weak and ashamed.

As with CSJ, it should be observed that "liberation" and "oppression" have taken on different interpretations and connotations across time—even "poor" carries multiple senses—and the initial intent and prescriptions for LT in its origins may not necessarily align with contemporary ideals. Historically, there seems to have been a foundational concern for human dignity and dehumanization, yet there also seems to be an interwoven potential for asserting particular socio-economic ideals (which may become controversial depending on claim and context, and sometimes trades on equivocation of terminology). Add to this the problem that in contemporary pop-parlance "oppression" (as "intolerance") often includes the notion of having the free-dom of conscience and speech to claim that another moral perspective is wrong; if LT is interpreted through the lens of such contemporary confusion, then contemporary LT (like CSJ) has a widened margin for error when it comes to grounding claims to justice. (Here the accompanying grand narra-tive is able to ground claims to human dignity, yet the appeal to a gospel-narrative-as-socio-political-liberation is unable to ground many particular claims on justice as applied—even if the goodness of the gospel wholly ap-plied would improve many systemic injustices).

Thus, as with CSJ, it should be understood that there are both powerful and problematic points within the liberation theology tradition. The concern for human dignity and dehumanization is on point. YHWH is a God who sees.[11] Immanuel is God with us.[12] And the ministry and gospel of Christ is God's affirmation of human worth. The life, ministry, and legacy of Jesus brings an affirmation of dignity to *all* human beings which culminates in the cross (justice) and resurrection to a new, better way of life, to the lost, lame, loathed, and lonely; the forgotten, desperate, ashamed, voiceless and ex-ploited; the faithful along with the failures, the foreign along with the famil-iar; shepherds, fishermen, kings, soldiers, rich and poor, male and female, Jew and to all others. LT's concern for human exploitation and dignity is commendable. The insistence that the liberation of the gospel necessarily in-dicates certain socio-political ideals or contemporary definitions of justice— extending beyond basic rights—is a more controversial point.

Christopher Wright has insightfully situated the gospel of Christ in light of the Old Testament, the liberation of the exodus in light of the Abrahamic covenant, and the biblical narrative of history in light of Genesis's framing of humanity's problem. "Genesis 1-11 is entirely occupied with humanity as a whole, the world of all nations, and with the apparently insoluble problem of their corporate evil. So the story of Israel which begins after chapter 12 is actually God's answer to the problem of humanity."[13] Concerning the exo-dus, he writes:

> [Christ's] coming in no way alters or removes the truth of the
> Old Testament story in itself and in its meaning for Israel—
> namely that God is concerned for the poor and suffering and
> desires justice for the exploited. On the contrary, it underlines
> and endorses it. Looking back on the event, however, in the
> light of the fullness of God's redemptive achievement in Jesus
> Christ, we can see that the original exodus was not merely

concerned with the political, economic and social aspects of Israel's predicament. There was also a level of spiritual oppression in Israel's subjection to the gods of Egypt. 'Let my people go that they may worship slash serve me' was God's demand on Pharoah. And the explicit purpose of the deliverance was that they would *know* Yahweh in the grace of redemption and covenant relationship So the exodus, for all the comprehensiveness of what it achieved for Israel, points beyond itself to a greater need for deliverance from the totality of evil and restoration to relationship with God then it achieved by itself.

.... The New Testament affirms that the gospel of the cross and the resurrection of Christ is God's complete answer to the totality of evil and all its effects within his creation. But it is the Old Testament which shows us the nature and extent of sin and evil—primarily in the narratives of genesis 4-11, but thereafter also in the history of Israel and the nations, such as the oppression of the first chapters of exodus. It shows us that while evil has its origins outside the human race, human beings are morally accountable to God for our own sin. It shows us that sin and evil have a corporate as well as an individual dimension, that is, they affect and shape the patterns of social life within which we live, as well as the personal lives we lead.... In short, the Old Testament portrays to us a very big problem to which there needs to be a very big answer, if there is one at all.[14]

Wright further observes a significant connection between the expressions "the way of the LORD" and "righteousness and justice." Moreover, the ethical nature of God's covenant with Abraham was to stand in noticeable contrast with the ethical nature of the surrounding cultures. "In the midst of a world going *the way of Sodom*, God wants a community characterized by *the way of the Lord*."[15]

The original concern of Gustavo Gutiérrez (credited with coining the term "liberation theology"), in regard to dehumanizing exploitations of the struggling poor and outcast peoples in Peru, seems to have been upon the need for orthodoxy to work itself out in orthopraxy.

If theological reflection does not vitalize the action of the Christian community in the world by making its commitment to charity fuller and more radical.... then this theological reflection will have been of little value.... To paraphrase a well-known text of Pascal, we can say that all the political theologies, the theologies of hope, or revolution, and of liberation, are not worth one act of genuine solidarity with exploited social classes. They are not worth one act of faith, love, and hope, committed--in one way or another—in active participation to liberate humankind from everything *that dehumanizes it and prevents it from living according to the will of the Father* [emphasis added].[16]

Theologian Millard Erickson offers a charitable analysis here:

It must be conceded that, of [Gutiérrez's] three levels of liberation, Gutiérrez identifies as the most basic the level of Christ's granting us freedom from sin. In practice, however, the emphasis seems to be placed on the economic and political aspects. There is no question, of course, that God is concerned about these aspects of life, as a reading of the Minor Prophets (e.g. Amos) will indicate. It must be seriously questioned, however, whether these aspects are as significant as the liberation theologians have made them. Rather, the crucial issue in Scripture is our bondage in sin, and the separation and estrangement from God that sin has produced. Even the Exodus, the deliverance of the people of Israel from the Egyptians, was not primarily a political event.... The shortcoming of liberation theology is not in what it says, but in what it does not say. Not nearly enough is said about what the New Testament clearly indicates to be the primary dimension of salvation.[17]

Erickson also noted a scriptural tension concerning LT's advocacy for potential violence,[18] and he expressed concern for minimizing individual sin in order to focus primarily on its social and economic dimensions. "Redistribution of power and wealth does not eliminate 'sin.'"[19] The significance of love as an appropriate outworking of salvation also aligns with many points detailed above—so long as the demand of teleological justice, depending on the issue at hand, is not confused with Christ's call to a representative goodness (as explained above).

The perspective of the oppressed, the overlooked and outcast, is one that certainly belongs in the theological dialogue. While Jesus came to address the spiritual oppression of all, he seemed to suggest that the circumstantially oppressed and broken in spirit were much closer to finding the Kingdom than those blinded by prestige, privilege, and power. It must be remembered, however, that Jesus nevertheless raised the standard for moral perfection[20] in order to point out that none of us actually passes the test of moral perfection and that a horrific justice must be served concerning the guilt of humanity—though he was willing to take that settlement upon himself. So, it is true, in some senses, that the poor (in spirit) and oppressed are close to the gospel, for God welcomes a humbled perspective.[21] He is near to the brokenhearted,[22] and Jesus tells his followers to be willing to take up a cross if they are ready to identify as his disciples.[23]

Yet there seems to be a tempering of love and law—grace and justice—throughout the biblical narrative. God is merciful and patient in waiting for the fullest number to have an opportunity to turn to him—though, admittedly, God's forbearance and delay in serving justice can be difficult, even painful, for those who cry out, "How long O Lord?"[24] Still, the Bible makes clear that, even as God holds open a door for the victimizer, he concurrently fights for the victim. "By no means will he leave the guilty unpunished."[25] Justice *will* be served. God is for the orphan, the widowed, and the alien,[26] and he is concerned for the poor.[27] He encourages his people to allow their abundance to become a blessing to the poor, and he stresses that his people are not to oppress one another. Still, the greatest emphasis concerning justice in society seems to be not upon the alleviation of poverty, but upon right understanding and right judgment—showing partiality neither to the poor nor to the rich.[28] The latter raises a potential point of tension for some of LT's claims.

The suggestion that a social goodness reflecting the Kingdom of God would seem to call one to stand in solidarity with the poor and oppressed against dehumanizing exploitations; that the problem of suffering is one of the hardest to face and ought not to be faced alone; and that there is no us and them in the community of love, but only God and us—these are not at all radical reinterpretations of the gospel. Neither is the notion that the twenty-first century Church should look more like the first-century Church. While community was essential in classical Christianity, and while orthopraxy might have worked itself out in different ways within different communities, it is important to note, however, that orthodoxy (which informs orthopraxy) was never determined by community need nor circumstantial struggle, but by an appeal to God's grand narrative and the authority of those who had directly encountered the risen Christ. It is true that the hope of Christ should so fill our hearts that they overflow with God's love (and that this love should flow so freely that it touches every heart around us), but without the cross there is no gospel, and without the authority of the resurrection there is no hope,[29] and so we must take care that our theology of goodness does not remove the cornerstone of justice.

The assertion that the gospel is one of socio-economic liberation is confused. The main emphasis of the Bible is not us, but God—not as liberator, but king. Of course, he is, importantly, a loving king. This is captured eloquently in the famous Narnian exchange wherein Susan first learns of Aslan, the great Lion. When she asks whether Aslan is safe, Mr. Beaver, exclaims, "Course he isn't safe. But he's good. He's the King, I tell you."[30] In the very symbol of God's demonstrative love—the cross—we see also the culminating wrath of justice. The Old Testament makes clear that God is concerned for the oppressed and estranged, yet it continually reiterates the point that human beings have a bad habit of exchanging the love of God for whatever seems good in their own eyes (and this is reflected in their institutions). It is sin that oppresses, estranges, and creates within us this proclivity to injustice. Moreover, the injustice is foremost against the King, and the disparagement of his kingdom and its inhabitants is derivative of this disdain. C. S. Lewis was onto something profound when he observed:

> We can all understand how a man forgives offenses against himself. You tread on my toes and I forgive you; you steal my money and I forgive you. But what should we make of a man, himself unrobbed and untrodden on, who announced that he forgave you for treading on other men's toes and stealing other men's money? Asinine fatuity is the kindest description we should give of his conduct. Yet this is what Jesus did. He told people that their sins were forgiven, and never waited to consult all the other people whom their sins had undoubtedly injured. He unhesitatingly behaved as if He was the party chiefly concerned, the person chiefly offended in all offenses.[31]

This is why Jesus declared that the love of God and one another (respect for the King and Kingdom) reflect a right understanding which transcends the need for law.[32]

Cone expressed dissatisfaction with his experience of white churches failing to see the gospel as standing in opposition to slavery, segregation, and lynching. This is a poignant point. Similarly, in *The Hunchback of Notre Dame*, it is the dehumanization of the Gypsy people (and of Quasimodo) which makes us indignant. We are not satisfied simply to identify with their suffering; we need to see justice — we need to know that injustice will end. The very fact that the Minister of "Justice" cannot see the injustice is terribly alarming! Though it is not a parallel analogy — ignoring injustice is not the same as inflicting injustice — the fact, as observed by Martin Luther King Jr.[33] and others, that ignoring an injustice can nevertheless play a role in perpetuating (and institutionalizing) subsequent injustices is an alarming observation. To the extent that any theist, claiming a narrative that grounds justice and calls us to embody love, ignores such dehumanizing injustice, this is a call for lamentation and correction. (We applaud the priest's bravery in rebuking Frollo because we know it is good to stand up and not remain silent when human beings are degraded and abused). So, on this issue, Cone's point is powerful.

However, Cone also expressed discontent concerning black churches who viewed the gospel as primarily eternity-focused, when in fact, he says, "the gospel is what happens to you now — in this world." Alas, this is a false dichotomy. God is concerned with both your eternity and your maturity — which he often seems to develop through circumstantial struggles now — in this world. Moreover, if one takes priority, it is eternity.[34] Prosperity and the good life in the now is nowhere promised in the Bible. Jesus claims just the opposite — that trouble is inevitable[35] and that the world will hate his followers.[36] Yet it is promised that God works all things for the (eternal) good of his people,[37] and despite worldly woes, Christians *are* called to show compassion to their neighbors[38] and to love their brothers and sisters not in word or theory alone, but in practice,[39] just as the exiled Israelites were called to seek the good of their Babylonian cities.[40]

So, as with CSJ, Liberation Theology champions some admirable concerns, but its definitions are confused. Justice and goodness are not the same. Justice is not reflected in goodness; goodness is reflected in justice. Goodness transcends justice, and we do not call it just, but beautiful. Goodness, then, has two descriptive daughters — justice and beauty. As established in this and the last chapter, justice involves a basic respect concerning right-order (God's kingship and one another's due dignity in light of the Creator's order). Morality entails restraint in light of this respect. Beauty bespeaks the ineffable goodness beyond order, often experienced wherever free expression is able to transcend — yet without disregarding — the confinements (as in music) or the requirements (as in law) of order. Accordingly, the gospel ("good news") involves understanding a grace extended beyond justice. Social goodness is not "justice" in society; it is a manifestation of a beauty which bespeaks the Kingdom of God—goodness beyond just-ness.

Liberation as Reorientation of Conscience: Reclaiming the Grand Narrative

In *Tinkerbell and the Legend of the NeverBeast*, after Nyx (a scout fairy) prevents the NeverBeast from achieving his goal, she and Fawn (an animal fairy) clash over their perspectives on justice:

> FAWN. What are you *doing*?!
> NYX. Saving Pixie Hollow!
> FAWN. No; *He* was saving Pixie Hollow!

As the ensuing destruction becomes apparent, Nyx realizes that her zeal for justice was misguided.[41] It seems we were created to crave justice. Yet our understanding of justice is darkened, and no matter of intersectionalities will ever be enough to perceive it fully until we can see things from the perspective of the One who grounds its very intelligibility. It is true that we often find ourselves amidst a battle of cultural narratives, yet it can only ever be "wrong" for one narrative to lord itself over others *if* there *is* a "right" narrative—a way-it-should-be—*and* if it is a false-narrative which is lorded over the true-narrative (and a right-narrative, by definition, will necessarily entail a marginalizing of wrong-narratives). If there really is such thing as justice, then it can only be grounded in a particular kind of narrative. Plot and resolution only make sense in light of the entire script. It is essential, then, to ensure that we have the right script. For, as C. S. Lewis observed, "When the author walks on to the stage the play is over."[42]

While Miss Price was correct (we *are* special), the fact that we "*start believing* there's something wonderful in [us]" does not make it so. A grounding narrative is necessary. Issues of social justice are complex because they involve not only the what-is-good question, but also the why-should. Disney offers us glimpses of the what-is-good while pointing to, though without naming, the reality of a grand narrative that pricks our conscience to know existentially the why-should. This volume began by pondering the power of storytelling in appealing to our moral convictions; it is only fitting that it ends similarly by pointing out the power of cultural narratives to play a role in spiritual warfare. The real oppression is an oppression of conscience which malforms understanding. The truest liberation—the one which does not undermine justice—involves being set free to choose goodness because of a *right* perspective.[43] Thus, true liberation involves a calibration, even re-orientation, of conscience (not just the expansion of perspective), and true justice requires the reclaiming of a grand, grounding narrative.

We have attempted to critique the grounding for CSJ as a prescriptive authority, in itself, on a robust and forceful sense of social justice, and we have argued that only a theistic narrative can ground any substantive appeal to justice. We have further insisted that it is the Jewish and Christian narratives in particular that offer a satisfactory foundation for our convictions of intrinsic human dignity and basic human rights. We have clarified a distinction between "justice" as grounding what is morally obligatory and *goodness* as moving (freely) beyond obligation in the name of love and community. We have insisted that this goodness finds its most convincing grounding within the classical Christian narrative. Finally, we suggested that Disney can help to mediate the dialogue between CSJ and theism, especially Christianity. Disney narratives continually draw our attention to the moral significance of perspective, calling us to care for the outcast and alienated, while also reminding us, time and again, that there *is* real goodness that can overcome evil and—as exemplified in the new testament—a substantive, *true* love that can transcend justice and transform community.

Epilogue

As we bring this volume to a close, we hope you have enjoyed our investigation of Disney in light of its moral metanarrative. Disney has offered us a growing canon of stories that do much more than entertain. They speak to our consciences about what is right and wrong. They awaken our convictions about right action. They inspire us to embrace courage in the face of things not being the way-it-should-be by offering us a view and hope of a better and brighter Kingdom-ever after. It is our strong desire that you are leaving this work more strengthened and encouraged than when you found it.

We want to end our time by suggesting other ways Disney could be approached that might yield interesting and insightful analysis. We recognize we have taken a sympathetic look at Disney. While this has been our decided intention, it is largely earned. In a certain sense, how could it not be? Themes of charity, self-sacrifice and a grand sense of telos are pervasive throughout Disney's body of work. As we have demonstrated, Disney films are replete with *virtue*. This is not only seen in how plots are structured and unfold but also in how characters are embodied. Many of which, both plots (stories) and characters, have become iconic. When we think of Disney films *as a whole* and the longstanding (almost a century) impact Disney has had as a meaningful and noteworthy stakeholder in society and in our communities, there is much to applaud. It has been our hope to draw attention to these realities.

Nevertheless, genuine challenges can be made regarding Disney's overall contribution, both to art narrowly and to society broadly. First, we recognize that Disney as an art form can be considered low culture. While we might problematize such an assertion, we take the point and understand how some may take issue with Disney in this regard. Second, we understand that some of Disney's body of work (and the themes heralded) undermines and even contradicts other aspects of Disney's body of work. This is partly rooted in Disney's aggressive expansion and its willingness to buy T.V. and film products they did not originally produce. As their tent has grown, their apparent commitment to certain perspectives has loosened. We see this, for instance, in some of Disney's more current products that challenge heteronormativity, a once firm commitment and assumption in Disney narratives.

We note here that Disney's current leadership, those in power to make narrative decisions, seems to have abandoned Walt's social contract with his audience. How ironic, given they only have their power because they build on Walt's foundation and his indelible and iconic brand, one that was established through the very moral and cultural commitments they seem to question and reject. It is our hope that any concerning departure from Walt's original vision represents an aberration, one where Disney's audience will compel a correction, and not a permanent erosion and alteration of Disney's enduring moral metanarrative. We have considered the significance of a non-sectarian moral education when attempting to communicate across diverse cultural backgrounds and belief systems. The more particularized a moral teaching becomes, the more divisive it becomes. Walt's vision was to stress unity and connection through artfully employed metaphor (such as magic) and archetype in storytelling. Today, however, some consumers want particularized cultural artifacts which speak explicitly to particular identities. While understandable (if not altogether healthy), this creates a point of tension.

As we write, there is pressure in the larger culture upon mediated products and expressions to exhibit sexuality in ways inclusive, even celebratory, of the LGBTQ+ community. This has become a litmus test for being an authentic believer in diversity. Disney is by no means immune to this pressure. In fact, some would argue that Disney itself is in the vanguard of putting this kind of pressure on the larger culture and not the other way around. That their vision now includes the championing of the LGBTQ+ agenda. It is our belief that if Disney takes up the mantle of producing art that seems more in line with identity politics than it does with its original vision (one that stresses a tactful use of archetype and non-sectarian ambiguity) it will undermine its pronounced—in certain ways, unparalleled—power to bring people together. More specifically, if Disney's new leadership chooses to stray from Walt's original vision, championing a more controversial, particular, and discordant approach, the laudable and cathartic unity they have fostered in society for the last eight decades may be replaced by a toxic and deleterious disunity. May it never be.

Third, we also acknowledge that depending on one's presuppositions and precommitments, one's norms and values, ergo, one's worldview, certain themes that permeate the Disney canon may have a disparate impact on its viewers. This dynamic paves the way for certain challenges by some. Take a relatively benign theme that we did not give a lot of attention: *individualism*. Depending on one's point of view, individualism can be either good or bad. Consequently, we recognize that one could approach Disney unsympathetically, with an arsenal of complaints and concerns worthy of analysis and discussion. While that has not been our intent, we respect it, and encourage our readers to consider such viewpoints. Relatedly, we know there are themes that could be bracketed and drawn out from Disney's work that we merely touched on that are worthy of fuller treatment. Themes such as *masculinity and femininity* or *patriarchy and matriarchy*. And many others. While such studies may not have the same metaphysical implications of our approach, or track along the same vector of inquiry, we nevertheless encourage such inquiries.

Another approach to Disney that could be taken would be to consider the difference (if there is any) of the influence Disney has on children versus the impact it has on adults. Walt famously said, "Adults are only kids grown up." These types of studies could be particularly illuminating. It also may uncover things that might qualify as strange, or even disturbing. Perhaps not of course. Nevertheless, tracking Disney's goals for their target audience may yield unexpected results relative to Disney's audience.

Next, we suggest a contemplation of Disney's brand power relative to the ever-present influence of neoliberalism (money as final determinant) in relationship to Disney's mission and core-values would be compelling. While we did not give it attention, an investigation of the power of neoliberalism to set the pace (or not) for the sum and substance of Disney's moral metanarrative, both as *originally conceived by Walt* and *currently expressed by those in power* (against the mounting pressure of cancel culture) would be intriguing.

While much more could be suggested, a final way Disney could be analyzed is strictly from the standpoint of what they are trying to accomplish in their theme parks. While we barely referenced Disney's theme parks, there is obviously much to consider there. A sub-category of such an approach would be to give attention to the type of employee Disney is looking to hire for their theme parks. From custodial and customer service staff to retailers and directors, choreographers, and performers. This data alone would say much as to what impact they are trying to make in the communities they serve and in larger society.

In closing, Disney is a fascinating example of both a cultural artifact and a producer of cultural artifacts. What "was all started by a mouse" has blossomed into a century old world-wide phenomenon. Disney now serves in many ways as both a creator and mirror of society. One worthy of our sustained attention. As you continue to enjoy the art Disney produces, may you do so with its larger metanarrative in view. We are confident your experience will be richer and fuller for the effort. As we come to the very end we leave you with these words from Walt, may you ever "First, think. Second, believe. Third, dream. And finally, dare.

Disney as Doorway
to Apologetic Dialogue

Notes

Preface

[1] This would include Richard Niebuhr's "Christ Against Culture" paradigm and those whom Brian Godawa identifies as "cultural anorexics." H. Richard Niebuhr, *Christ and Culture* (New York: HarperCollins Publishers, Inc., 2001); Brian Godawa, *Hollywood Worldviews: Watching Films with Wisdom and Discernment* (Downers Grove: Intervarsity Press, 2009), 19.

[2] Progressive Christianity would fall into this camp, as it tends to stress care, compassion, and inclusivity, but it is criticized for deemphasizing essential aspects of Christian theology.

[3] This perspective would include Niebuhr's "Christ and Culture in Paradox" and "Christ the Transformer of Culture" paradigms. Godawa advocates avoiding the extremes of both cultural gluttony and cultural anorexia, and instead approaching culture through the lens of redemption—seeing movies, e.g., as all attempting to speak to a sense of loss and recovery.

[4] Paul M. Gould, *Cultural Apologetics: Renewing the Christian Voice, Conscience, and Imagination in a Disenchanted World* (Grand Rapids: Zondervan, 2019), 24.

[5] Rom. 7:19; Gal 5:17.

[6] For more on this, see G. E. Ladd, "Kingdom of Christ, God, Heaven," in *Evangelical Dictionary of Theology*, 2nd ed., ed. Walter A. Elwell (Grand Rapids: Baker Academic, 2001), 657-60.

Part I

Chapter 1

[1] George MacDonald, "The Fantastic Imagination," in *The Light Princess, and Other Fairy Tales* (Digireads.com Publishing, 2009), 7.

[2] Louis P. Pojman, ed. "Preface" in *The Moral Life: An Introductory Reader in Ethics and Literature*, 2nd ed. (Oxford: Oxford University Press, 2004), xiii.

[3] See Plato, *Republic*, books 2, 3, and 10; Aristotle, *Poetics*; Bruno Bettelheim, *The Uses of Enchantment: The Meaning and Importance of Fairy Tales* (New York: Vintage Books, 1976), 35-47. We owe credit to David Naugle's analysis for drawing our attention to many of these sources addressing the intersection of worldview and narrative; David K. Naugle, *Worldview: The History of a Concept* (Grand Rapids: Wm. B. Eerdmans, 2002), 297-303.

[4] Rollo May, *The Cry for Myth* (New York: Bantam Doubleday Dell, Delta, 1991), 15.

[5] Friedrich Nietzsche, *The Birth of Tragedy and the Case of Wagner*, trans. Walter Kaufmann (New York: Vintage Books, 1967), 135.

[6] Naugle, 299-300.

[7] Alasdair MacIntyre, *After Virtue: A Study in Moral Theory*, 2nd ed. (University of Notre Dame Press, 1984), 211.

[8] Naugle, 301-02.

[9] Charles Taylor, *A Secular Age* (Cambridge: Harvard University Press, Belknap Press, 2007), 325.

[10] Alister McGrath, *Narrative Apologetics: Sharing the Relevance, Joy, and Wonder of the Christian Faith* (Grand Rapids: Baker Books, 2019), 97.

[11] H. Richard Niebuhr, *The Meaning of Revelation* (New York: Macmillan, 1960), 109.

[12] Augustine, *On Christian Doctrine* 2.40.60.

[13] Pascal argues that you *must* wager on the question of God's existence and our moral responsibility to God; it is not an option. Blaise Pascal, *Pensées* 3.233; James insists that, while some judgments are avoidable, certain judgments about God and morality are not; they force themselves upon us. Further, while some beliefs are trivial, beliefs about God are momentous. Thus, we cannot escape into skepticism, for skepticism is not an avoidance of options, but a particular option with particular

risks involved. Moreover, in some cases, certain truths *only* reveal themselves fully *through* our actions, in which case there existed a preliminary faith built upon a certain desire which served as foundation to the hope for which we wagered. William James, *The Will to Believe* (New York: Longmans, Green, and Co., 1912).

[14] See Taylor, *A Secular Age.*

[15] James W. Sire, *Naming the Elephant: Worldview as a Concept* (Downers Grove: Inter-Varsity Press, 2004), 153.

[16] McGrath, 121-22.

[17] Paul M. Gould, *Cultural Apologetics: Renewing the Christian Voice, Conscience, and Imagination in a Disenchanted World* (Grand Rapids: Zondervan, 2019), 24.

[18] Some critics may accuse us of cheapening the concept of faith as presented in Heb. 11, but it is just the opposite. Heb. 11 speaks to a propositional faith, a faith of confession (which is specific), and it is this conception to which the non-believer may draw lines between the "faithful" and "nonfaithful"—between faith and unbelief. But that is a false distinction; for our point is that *all* systems of beliefs—even atheistic and agnostic—involve faith, even, perhaps, propositional faith. Yet our ultimate argument is that, for most people, many of our faith-commitments may be acquired through enculturation rather than through propositional forethought and calculation or confession.

[19] Thanks to philosopher Tim McGrew (Western Michigan University) for this insightful clarity in articulation. See: "Peter Boghossian vs. Tim McGrew – A Manual for Creating Atheists," podcast, *Unbelievable?* Retrieved on September 19, 2014 from: https://unbelievable.podbean.com/e/peter-boghossian-vs-tim-mcgrew-a-manual-for-creating-atheists/.

[20] Plato, *Apology*, 38.

[21] William Irwin, "Philosophy Engages Popular Culture: An Introduction," in *Philosophy and the Intersection of Pop Culture*, ed. William Irwin and Jorge J. E. Gracia (New York: Rowman & Littlefield Publishers, Inc., 2007), 3.

[22] Diogenes Allen and Eric O. Springsted, *Philosophy for Understanding Theology*, 2nd ed. (Louisville: Westminster John Knox Press, 2007), 235.

[23] See Taylor, *A Secular Age.*

[24] Ibid., 596-606.

[25] Ibid., 28.

[26] Ibid., 352-67.

[27] Ibid., 307-10.

[28] *Alice in Wonderland,* dir. Clyde Geronimi, Wilfred Jackson, and Hamilton Luske (Burbank: Walt Disney Studios, 1951).

[29] See Part 3 of Taylor's tome.

[30] Taylor, 353-54.

[31] James K. A. Smith, *How (Not) to Be Secular: Reading Charles Taylor* (Grand Rapids: Eerdmans, 2014), 74-6.

[32] Francis A. Schaeffer, *The God Who is There,* in *Francis A. Schaeffer Trilogy* (Wheaton: Crossway Books, 1990), 8-9.

[33] James K. Smith, Desiring the Kingdom: Worship, Worldview, and Cultural Formation (Grand Rapids: Baker Academic, 2009), 24.

[34] Gen. 2:18.

[35] Elisabeth Young-Bruehl and Jerome Kohn, "What and how we learned from Hannah Arendt: An exchange of letters," in *Hannah Arendt and Education*, ed. Mordechai Gordon (Boulder, CO: Westview Press, 2001), 225-256.

[36] C. S. Lewis, *The Abolition of Man* (New York, NY: HarperOne, 1974).

[37] For a brief overview of this work, see Michael Ward, *After Humanity: A Guide to C. S. Lewis's The Abolition of Man* (Park Ridge: Word on Fire Academic, 2021), 11-18. For more on emotivism, see A. J. Ayer, *Language, Truth, Logic* (New York: Dover, 1936), 35, 108.

[38] Ward, *After Humanity*, 15.

[39] Herodotus, *The Histories* 3.38, trans. Robin Waterfield (Oxford: Oxford University Press, 1998), 185-86.

[40] Scarbrough commenting: While this work is somewhat difficult for many students, I discovered, in my own moral philosophy classes, that Lewis's appendix is quite helpful in guiding students through the mires of moral relativism. Students are often overwhelmed with the descriptive appeals to all the ways in which our moral narratives differ. Yet, in Lewis's appendix they can see more easily the very thing that Lewis did not want us to miss! (Lewis, *The Abolition*, 16-18). In many ways, I approach this work like that appendix. I am not trying to present deep and descriptive analyses of various narratives in particular; I am trying to offer glimpses into a plethora of narratives to show the reader how Disney films from 1937 to 2021 seem to convey a moral metanarrative, which may be informed by (as it seems to

align so strikingly with) a theistic metanarrative in general, and the biblical grand narrative in particular.

[41] Gen. 3:6.

[42] Gen. 1:27.

[43] Kristen Anderson-Lopez and Robert Lopez, "Let it Go," in *Frozen*, dir. Chris Buck and Jennifer Lee (Burbank, CA: Walt Disney Studios, 2013).

[44] Alister McGrath, *C. S. Lewis: A Life* (Carol Stream: Tyndale House Publishers, Inc., 2013), 260.

[45] Smith, *How (Not) to Be Secular*, 77.

[46] Alister McGrath, *The Intellectual World of C. S. Lewis* (Oxford: Wiley-Blackwell, 2014), 106.

[47] C. S. Lewis, *Mere Christianity* (San Francisco: HarperCollins, 2001), 136-7.

[48] *The Nightmare Before Christmas*, dir. Henry Selick (Burbank, CA: Walt Disney Studios, 1993).

[49] Peter Kreeft, *The Philosophy of Tolkien* (San Francisco: Ignatius Press, 2005), 17.

[50] McGrath, *C. S. Lewis*, 269.

[51] *Pocahontas*, dir. Mike Gabriel and Eric Goldberg (Burbank: Walt Disney Studios, 1995).

[52] McGrath, *The Intellectual World of C. S. Lewis*, 137.

[53] C. S. Lewis, "Tolkien's *Lord of the Rings*," in *On Stories: And Other Essays on Literature*, ed. Walter Hooper (New York: HarperOne, 1982), 138-39.

Chapter 2

[1] Louise Krasniewicz, *Walt Disney: A Biography* (Santa Barbara: Greenwood, 2010).

[2] See "The Most Famous DeMolay of All: Walt Disney," DeMolay International, accessed May 12, 2020, https://demolay.org/the-most-famous-demolay-of-all-walt-disney/; and "Walt Disney," Historic Missourians, accessed May 12, 2020, https://historicmissourians.shsmo.org/historicmissourians/name/d/disney/.

[3] "Our Mission," DeMolay International, accessed May 12, 2020, https://demolay.org/our-mission/.

[4] Roland Gammon, *Faith is a Star* (New York: Dutton, 1963), 8.

[5] Ibid.

[6] B. Edward McClellan, *Moral Education in America: Schools and the Shaping of Character from Colonial Times to the Present* (New York: Teachers College Press, 1999).

[7] Christina Scull and Wayne G. Hammond, *The J. R. R Tolkien Companion and Guide*, vol. 1, *Chronology* (New York: Houghton Mifflin, 2006), 196, 224, 465, 539, and 619.

[8] Bruce L. Edwards, "C. S. Lewis contra Cinema," in *Light Shining in a Dark Place: Discovering Theology through Film*, ed. Jeff Sellars (Eugene: Pickwick Publications, 2012), 165-8.

[9] Ibid., 167.

[10] Joseph Campbell with Bill Moyers, *The Power of Myth*, ed. Betty Sue Flowers (New York: Anchor Books, 1991), 206.

[11] Tolkien was concerned with a happy turn of events so beautiful amidst the terrible that it moves one to tears of gratefulness. While it might be argued that many Disney films miss this mark of great fairy stories — and Tolkien stressed this was difficult for drama — some Disney films have been arguably successful. Regardless of Disney's success in reaching Tolkien's standard concerning the happy turn, Disney nevertheless stressed as significant the great triumph of the good (the happy-ever-after).

Part II

Chapter 3

[1] Roland Gammon, *Faith is a Star* (New York: Dutton, 1963), 8.

[2] Mark Pinsky, *The Gospel According to Disney* (Louisville: Westminster John Knox Press, 2004), 1-12.

[3] C. S. Lewis, *The Abolition of Man* (New York: HarperOne, 1974), 16-18; and Appendix.

[4] Ibid., 43-44.

[5] See C. S. Lewis, *Mere Christianity* (San Francisco: HarperCollins, 2001), 38.

[6] *Brave*, dir. Mark Andrews and Brenda Chapman (Burbank: Walt Disney Studios, 2012).

[7] Lewis understood myth as mediator between conviction and experience. "What flows into you from the myth is not truth but reality (truth is always *about* something, but reality is that *about which* truth is), and, therefore, every myth becomes the father of innumerable truths down here in the valley... [Myth] is not, like truth,

abstract; nor is it, like direct experience, bound to the particular." C. S. Lewis, *God in the Dock* (Grand Rapids: Eerdmans, 1970), 66.

[8] Rom. 8:18-21; 12:21; Rev. 21:1.

[9] Tonje Belibi, "Spirituality and Values in the Disney Universe: Teaching Discernment to Christian Youth," *Lausanne Global Analysis* 9, no. 1 (2020), retrieved on July 2, 2022 from: https://lausanne.org/content/lga/2020-01/spirituality-values-disney-universe.

[10] Ayn Rand, Interview with Mike Wallace, *The Mike Wallace Interview*, NTA Film Network, February 25, 1959. For more on Rand's defense of egoism, see Ayn Rand, *Atlas Shrugged* (New York: Random House, 1959).

[11] For more on this, see Jeremy Bentham, *Introduction to the Principles of Morals and Legislation*, ed. W. Harrison (Oxford: Oxford University Press, 1948); and John Stuart Mill, *Utilitarianism* (Indianapolis: Bobbs-Merril, 1957).

[12] For more on this, see Immanuel Kant, *Groundwork of the Metaphysics of Morals*, eds. Mary Gregor and Jens Timmerman (New York: Cambridge University Press, 2012); and W. D. Ross, *The Right and the Good* (Oxford: Oxford University Press, 1930).

[13] For more on this, see Aristotle, *Nichomachean Ethics.*

[14] Scarbrough commenting: For the student and lay reader interested in learning more about ethical theory, I highly recommend the writings of Louis Pojman. I have to credit his work for bringing to my attention such a succinct articulation of the strengths and weaknesses of deontology and utilitarianism. Pojman, a prolific and well-respected moral philosopher of the twentieth century, effectively condensed, without oversimplifying, the exceedingly deep counterpoint of these ethical theories into a well-mediated, more accessible, introductory overview in his *Ethics: Discovering Right and Wrong*. The title itself was a purposeful counterpoint to his own teacher, also a renowned philosopher, J. L. Mackie's *Ethics: Inventing Right and Wrong*. For one's presupposition concerning whether morality is invented or discovered necessarily biases the debate over *telos*—thereby impacting the dialogue over virtue. For the reader so interested, I highly recommend the first and sixth editions of Louis P. Pojman, *Ethics: Discovering Right and Wrong*, (Belmont: Wadsworth, 1990)—the first edition, primarily for its helpful chart on p. 155, distinguishing between cognitivist and noncognitivist camps in light of the Fact-Value Problem.

[15] Matt. 5:21-22, 27-28.

[16] Aristotle, *Physics* II.3; *Metaphysics* V.2.

17 Michael J. Sandel, *Justice: What's the Right Thing to Do?* (New York: Farrar, Straus and Giroux, 2009), 207.

18 While it is possible for even villains to demonstrate virtues (e.g., fortitude), the villainous cannot *be* "virtuous" for they know not justice.

19 Howard Ashman and Alan Menken, "Something There," in *Beauty and the Beast*, dir. Gary Trousdale and Kirk Wise (Burbank: Walt Disney Studios, 1991).

20 *Beauty and the Beast*, dir. Bill Condon (Burbank: Walt Disney Studios, 2017).

21 Stephen Schwartz and Alan Menken, "The Bells of Notre Dame," in *The Hunchback of Notre Dame*, dir. Gary Trousdale and Kirk Trousdale (Burbank: Walt Disney Studios, 1996).

22 Lin-Manuel Miranda, Opetaia Foa'i, and Mark Mancina, "Know Who You Are," in *Moana*, dir. Ron Clements and John Musker (Burbank: Walt Disney Studios, 2016).

23 William J. Devlin, "Knowing Who You Are: Existence Precedes Essence in Moana," in *Disney and Philosophy: Truth, Trust, and a Little Bit of Pixie Dust*, ed. Richard B. Davis (Hoboken: John Wiley and Sons Ltd, 2020).

24 Lin-Manuel Miranda, Opetaia Foa'i, and Mark Mancina, "I Am Moana (Song of the Ancestors)," in *Moana* (2016).

25 See Plato, *Phaedrus* 253d-256e and *The Republic* 580d-e, 588b-589e.

26 See Aristotle, *Nichomachean Ethics* II.5-6, 1108b11-1109b26.

27 While this might seem utilitarian, Aladdin's actions are contrary to the expectations of the majority; his motive seems closer to deontology in seeing the poor as intrinsically valuable ends-in-themselves.

28 *Aladdin*, dir. Ron Clemens and John Musker (Burbank: Walt Disney Studios, 1992).

29 *Cinderella*, dir. Kenneth Branaugh (Burbank: Walt Disney Studios, 2015).

30 Again, this may appear utilitarian, but Robin's motive stems from more of a Natural-Law-Theory perspective concerning individual property rights and an unjust order. (For more on this, see chapter 13, "On Justice." For more on natural law, see: Aquinas, *Summa Theologica* 2.91.2, 2.94.4).

Chapter 4

1 Gammon, 9.

2 Alister E. McGrath, *Narrative Apologetics* (Grand Rapids, MI: BakerBooks, 2019), 30.

[3] Joseph Campbell with Bill Moyers, *The Power of Myth*, ed. Betty Sue Flowers (New York: Anchor Books, 1991), 60.

[4] Aquinas, *Summa Theologica* 1: q.5, a.4, ad.1.

[5] Roland Gammon, *Faith is a Star* (New York, NY: Dutton, 1963), 8.

[6] For more on this, see James W. Sire, *The Universe Next Door*, 5th ed. (Downers Grove: IVP Academic, 2009), 39-46; and Gregory Koukl, *The Story of Reality* (Grand Rapids: Zondervan, 2017), 25, 38, 47.

[7] Gal. 5:16-17, 22-24; Rom. 7:18-23; Titus 2:11-12; Prov. 16:18; Matt. 23:12; Luke 18:14; James. 4:6; Phil. 2:3-9; and Rom. 12.

[8] Eph. 6:10-11; 2 Cor. 10:4-5; James 4:7.

[9] Eph. 6:12.

[10] John 8:44.

[11] Isa. 14:12–14.

[12] 1 Pet. 4:8; 1 John 4:8.

[13] Matt. 6:21.

[14] 1 Pet. 5:8.

[15] Ward, 14.

[16] Ibid., 16.

[17] Gen. 3.

[18] Rev. 22:3.

[19] Perhaps there is even room here for a subtle polemic against magical/religious pluralism. While many characters may wield magic (spiritual knowledge?), there is a big difference between Elsa or Merlin and Shadow Man or Madam Mim. Not all magic (spiritual "truth") is in fact good/right, but only that which aligns with the Good. *The Black Cauldron* even goes as far as to envision some magic as the harbinger of hell on earth.

[20] For a fascinating Platonic perspective, see Nathan Mueller and Leilani Mueller, "Breaking the Spell: *Beauty and the Beast* and Plato's Prisoner," in Davis, *Disney and Philosophy*, 177-83.

[21] Larry Morey and Frank Churchill, "Someday My Prince Will Come," in *Snow White and the Seven Dwarfs* dir. David Hand, William Cottrell, Wilfred Jackson, Larry Morey, Perce Pearce, and Ben Sharpsteen (Burbank: Walt Disney Studios, 1937).

[22] Pinsky, 25.

[23] Ibid., 56.

[24] Luke 15: 3-6.

[25] Ps. 8:4.

[26] Luke 15:3-7; John 10:11.

[27] Pinsky, 77.

[28] Eph. 6.

[29] C. A. McIntosh, "How to Convince Sleeping Beauty She's Not Dreaming," in Davis, *Disney and Philosophy*, 95-105.

[30] Pinsky, 78.

Chapter 5

[1] Belle means "beautiful;" Tiana means "princess;" Simba means "lion;" Mufasa means "king;" etc.

[2] Daniel J. Levitin, *This is Your Brain on Music: The Science of a Human Obsession* (New York, NY: Dutton, 2006), 229-31.

[3] Monique Wonderly, "Children's Film as an Instrument of Moral Education," *Journal of Moral Education* 38, no. 1 (2009): 7-9.

[4] B. Edward McClellan, *Moral Education in America: Schools and the Shaping of Character from Colonial Times to the Present* (New York: Teachers College Press, 1999).

[5] Annalee R. Ward, *Mouse Morality: The Rhetoric of Disney Animated Film* (Austin: University of Texas Press, 2002): 5.

[6] Mark I. Pinsky, *The Gospel According to Disney: Faith, Trust, and Pixie Dust* (Louisville: Westminster John Knox Press, 2004), 27.

[7] Elisabeth Schellekens, *Aesthetics & Morality* (New York: Continuum, 2007).

[8] Amanda Rutherford and Sarah Baker, "The Disney 'Princess Bubble' as a Cultural Influencer," *M/C Journal* 24, no.1 (2021). Accessed October 7, 2021 from https://journal.media-culture.org.au/index.php/mcjournal/article/view/2742.

[9] Frank Thomas and Ollie Johnston, *The Illusion of Life: Disney Animation* (New York: Walt Disney Productions, 1981), 445.

[10] Ibid., 417.

[11] Ibid., 35.

[12] Leslie A. Zebrowitz and Joann M. Montepare, "Social Psychological Face Perception: Why Appearance Matters," *Social and Personality Psychology Compass* 2, no. 3 (2008), 1497-98.

[13] Ibid.

[14] Ibid.

[15] Ibid.

[16] Gammon, 8.

[17] Pinocchio was hanged in his original narrative, and Mulan killed herself in a 17th century retelling of her 6th century ballad. Although such things are part of reality, however, their complexity convolutes moral accessibility.

[18] "Picture Perfect: The Making of Sleeping Beauty," disc 2, *Sleeping Beauty*, platinum ed., DVD, dir. Clyde Geronimi (Burbank: Walt Disney Studios, 2008).

[19] Victor Hugo's *Notre-Dame de Paris* is considered an artistic defense of Gothic architecture. Disney's realistic depiction of Notre Dame's splendor helps to that end.

[20] There *are* problematic non-idealistic/socio-cultural depictions in Disney's history (e.g., crows in Dumbo).

[21] Disney has no obligation to draw characters in realistic rather than idealistic ways. It is the parent's prerogative to teach his or her child, through Disney, that it is her heart which makes the princess beautiful.

[22] Consider, e.g., how *anime* artists often draw eyes purposefully to express character/personality.

[23] See, e.g., Edwardo Pérez, "From Snow White to Moana: Understanding Disney's Feminist Transformation," in *Disney and Philosophy: Truth, Trust, and a Little Bit of Pixie Dust*, ed. Richard B. Davis (Hoboken: John Wiley and Sons Ltd, 2020), 72-73.

[24] Abraham Kuyper, *Wisdom and Wonder: Common Grace in Science and Art*, ed. Jordan J. Ballor and Stephen J. Grabill, trans. Nelson D. Kloosterman (Grand Rapids: Christian's Library Press, 2011), 130.

[25] Ibid., 133.

[26] Ibid.

[27] Maeve Louise Heaney, *Music as Theology: What Music Says About the Word* (Eugene: Pickwick Publications, 2012), 187.

Chapter 6

[1] For more on "kingdom" as the main theme of the Bible see: Gregory Koukl, *The Story of Reality* (Grand Rapids: Zondervan, 2017), 47.

[2] Matt. 5:29.

[3] Matt. 16:24-26.

[4] Matt. 22:37-40.

[5] Matt. 15:15-20.

[6] Prov. 21: 3; Jer. 7:22-23; Ps. 50:9-13, 51:16-17; Hos. 6:6; Mic. 6:7-8; Mark 12:33; Heb. 10:1-22.

[7] Rev. 7:9.

[8] Rev. 19:16.

[9] John 1:12.

[10] Ezek. 36:26.

[11] John 14:15, 23; Rom. 6:17-18; 2 John 6.

[12] Rom. 6:14; Gal. 3:23-25.

[13] 1 John 4:21.

[14] John 3:3; 2 Cor. 5:17; 1 Pet. 1:3-5.

[15] Plato's perspective on justice as involving a struggle within the soul is especially reminiscent of Rom. 7:14-24. For more on Plato's compatibility with Christianity, see Augustine's *City of God*. For more on the compatibility of Aristotelian thought, see Aquinas's appreciation of Aristotle and Aquinas's contribution to Christian ethics. We are speaking here primarily of Plato's and Aristotle's moral philosophy. The extent to which either philosopher is compatible with Christianity in other areas of thought has historically been, and still remains, a point of dispute. For a helpful resource on the influence of each philosopher upon the history of theology, see: Diogenes Allen and Eric O. Springsted, *Philosophy for Understanding Theology*, 2nd ed. (Louisville: Westminster John Know Press, 2007).

[16] This idea is echoed by Nietzsche in *Thus Spoke Zarathustra* and *Beyond Good and Evil*. For more on this, see also: Paul Copan, *Is God a Moral Monster?* (Grand Rapids: Baker Books, 2011); Charles Taylor, *A Secular Age* (Cambridge: Harvard University Press, Belknap Press, 2007), 244-47; and Luc Ferry, *A Brief History of Thought: A Philosophical Guide to Living*, trans. Theo Cuffe (New York: HarperCollins, 2011), 71-78. In Ferry's words, Christianity "opened a chasm in the philosophies of Antiquity and dominated the Occidental world for nearly fifteen hundred years" (p. 53). "In direct contradiction [to the ancient Greek understanding], Christianity was to introduce the notion that humanity was fundamentally identical, that men were equal in dignity.... Christianity revolutionized the history of thought. For the first time in human history, liberty rather than nature had become the foundation for morality" (pp. 72-74). Thus, agapism is directly related to the idea of intrinsic human worth, which grounds the language of individual rights and due dignity. For more on the inability of modern, post-Christian theories to ground naturalistic claims to rights, see Alasdair MacIntyre, *After Virtue: A Study in Moral Theory* (University of Notre Dame Press, 1981); and Nicholas Wolterstorff, *Justice: Rights and Wrongs* (Princeton: Princeton University Press, 2008). Citing a letter from 1809, wherein John Adams insists that the Hebrews "have done more to civilize man than any other nation," Copan notes the significance of the Hebrew culture's countercultural emphasis upon a robust form of monotheism—a single, personal, creative authority from whom all goodness comes and to whom all honor is due—and an ethics that flowed out of that understanding. For the early Christians—understanding the events reported in the Gospels and the eyewitness testimony of a resurrected Christ as both the capstone to Old Testament prophecy and the cornerstone to Old Testament theology—a teleologically-informed biblical worldview and *thankfulness* for Jesus's sacrifice naturally overflowed into applications of love (charity/hospitality), forgiveness, and social justice. Says Copan, "Historians have documented that the values of human rights, tolerance, social justice, and radical reconciliation are the legacy of the Christian faith, not some Enlightenment ideals" (Copan, 117-18). He concludes, "Advocating human rights, democracy, political freedoms, concern for the poor: These themes are rooted in the biblical ideals that all humans are made in God's image, that they have dignity and worth, and that they are equal before the law" (Copan, 219). While many religions have stressed a justice that is due God or the gods, and many religious and ethical systems have accounted for a sort of Golden Rule, the Christian heritage stands out in its emphasis upon intrinsic human rights, a due-dignity to all image-bearers. Similarly, while many in the ancient world understood justice as "giving to each one his or her due," the idea that a general acknowledgement of basic human rights/dignity was due to each person of each culture and class, equally, was largely inconceivable. Whether advocating systems of health care and education, defending human equality, or condemning injustices against human life, the

historical impact of a sacrificial, other-serving ethics, which grew out of classical Christian theology, is undeniable, incomparable, and immeasurable.

[17] See Augustine, *City of God* 14.28.

[18] See Immanuel Kant, *The Grounding of the Metaphysics of Morals* (1785), section 1, paragraph 2.

[19] Abortion, for instance, kills one human being (an end in him/herself) in the name of loving another human being as an end in herself, thereby raising questions as to the nature of love and the very grounding for human value.

[20] Phil. 2:3-7, James 2:1-8, 1 John 4:7-8.

[21] 2 Cor. 5:20.

[22] Matt. 5:44; John 15:13.

[23] 2 Cor. 3:18, 5:17.

[24] Rom. 8.

[25] Matt. 7:21-23.

[26] Kristen Anderson-Lopez and Robert Lopez, "Show Yourself," in *Frozen II*, dir. Chris Buck and Jennifer Lee (Burbank: Walt Disney Studios, 2019).

[27] *Soul*, dir. Pete Docter (Burbank, CA: Walt Disney Studios, 2020).

[28] 1 Thess. 5:18.

[29] Gen. 3:6.

[30] Rom. 7.

[31] Phil. 4:8-9.

[32] Søren Kierkegaard, *Works of Love*, trans. David F. Swenson and Lillian Marvin Swenson (Princeton: Princeton University Press, 1949), 68; 157-65.

[33] For more on the concept of a teleological imperative, see: Oskar Gruenwald, "The Teleological Imperative," *Journal of Interdisciplinary Studies* 19, no. 1 (2007): 1-18.

Chapter 7

[1] Stephen Schwartz and Alan Menken, "That's How You Know," in *Enchanted*, dir. Kevin Lima (Burbank: Walt Disney Studios, 2007).

[2] C. S. Lewis, *Mere Christianity* (San Francisco: HarperCollins, 2001), 136-7.

[3] Augustine, *City of God* 14.28; *On Christian Doctrine* 3.10.15-16.

[4] 2 Cor. 5:20.

[5] Col. 3:2.

[6] Ps. 16:11.

[7] Heb. 11:1-3.

[8] 1 Cor. 13.

[9] 2 Cor. 11:14.

[10] John 15:13.

[11] Jer. 17:9.

[12] 1 John 4:18.

[13] Standing in contrast to Calvinism's emphasis on God's sovereignty and Arminianism's emphasis on human free will and responsibility, Molinism attempts to reconcile this tension through modal reasoning.

[14] E.g., Josh. 24:15.

[15] For more on this, see R. Zachary Manis, "Could God Do Something Evil? A Molinist Solution to the Problem of Divine Freedom," *Faith and Philosophy* 28, no. 2 (2011): 209-223.

[16] Kristen Anderson-Lopez and Robert Lopez, "Do You Want to Build a Snowman?" in *Frozen*, dir. Chris Buck and Jennifer Lee (Burbank: Walt Disney Studios, 2013).

[17] Francis A. Schaeffer, *The God Who is There*, in *Francis A. Schaeffer Trilogy* (Wheaton: Crossway Books, 1990), 158.

[18] Phil. 4:8.

Part III

Chapter 8

[1] Roland Gammon, *Faith is a Star* (New York: Dutton, 1963), 8.

[2] Ibid.

[3] Gammon, 8.

[4] Some theologians might wish to push back here: If man's natural impulses are often evil and wicked, then this caliber of collective impulses will require conditioning by either common or special grace. Our emphasis, at the moment, however, is on Disney's vision in particular and a general sense of the ever-after which resonates with Disney's viewers.

[5] Stephen Schwartz and Alan Menken, "The Bells of Notre Dame" in *The Hunchback of Notre Dame*, dir. Gary Trousdale and Kirk Trousdale (Burbank: Walt Disney Studios, 1996).

[6] Wyndy Corbin-Reuschling, *Reviving Evangelical Ethics.* (Grand Rapids: Brazos Press, 2008), 132.

[7] John Warwick Montgomery, *Human Rights and Human Dignity* (Grand Rapids: Zondervan, 1986), 78-80.

Chapter 9

[1] Robert B. Sherman and Richard M. Sherman, "That's What Makes the World Go Round," in *The Sword in the Stone*, dir. Wolfgang Reitherman (1963)

[2] Douglas Kellner, "Toward a Critical Media/Cultural Studies," in *Media/Cultural Studies: Critical Approaches*, ed. Rhonda Hammer and Douglas Kellner (New York, NY: Peter Lang Publishing, 2009), 6.

[3] Robert T. Craig and Heidi L. Muller, *Theorizing Communication: Readings Across Traditions* (Thousand Oaks, CA: Sage Publications, 2007), 59.

[4] Annalee R. Ward, *Mouse Morality: The Rhetoric of Disney Animated Film* (Austin: University of Texas Press, 2002): 5.

[5] "Discrimination," like "social justice," is equivocal. In the sense of discernment/distinction/differentiation, discrimination is unavoidable in moral decision-making (when we choose true/good we necessarily discriminate against false/bad). Mistreatment of persons *is* a valid concern, *but only if* egalitarian justice is grounded. To equate *moral* discrimination necessarily with hate/violence/injustice is problematic.

[6] An impoverished gay woman who is also a racial and religious minority has at least a five-way intersection of minority/marginalized perspectives (racial, religious, gendered, sexual, impoverished). Some believe she would thus be more qualified to speak of truth/knowledge and justice for the marginalized than would a more "narrow," "oppressor's" perspective (e.g., wealthy, white, straight, Christian, male). As an example of this type of claim in critical scholarship, see Kate

Lockwood Harris, "Re-situating organizational knowledge: Violence, intersectionality and the privilege of partial perspective," *Human Relations* 70 no. 3 (2017).

Chapter 10

[1] *Peter Pan*, dir. Clyde Geronimi, Wilfred Jackson, and Hamilton Luske (Burbank: Walt Disney Studios, 1953).

[2] Mark Pinsky reviews a number of pro/contra perspectives in the debate, beginning in the 1960s, about Disney, values, and education, and especially concerning Disney's marketing strategy of substituting magic for religion. Mark Pinsky, *The Gospel According to* Disney (Louisville: Westminster John Knox Press, 2004), 4-9. See also p. 240.

[3] Pinsky, 15-16

[4] Ibid, 17.

[5] Citing animation authority John Culhane, Pinsky elaborated, "'Walt wanted to communicate with a global audience.... He wanted to communicate with a multicultural audience.' Thus the choice was made to keep the films accessible and relevant to children from both inside and outside the Judeo-Christian tradition in order to pass through a minefield of conflicting sensibilities. Yet since ancient times, dramatists have seen the need for a sometimes unexpected device to intervene and resolve plot conflicts.... Magic, Disney apparently decided, would be a far more universal device to do this than any one religion.... But there is also a key theological dimension to Disney's choice of magic over religion." Pinsky 2004, 4.

[6] Francis A. Schaeffer, "The God Who is There," in Francis A. Schaeffer Trilogy (Wheaton: Crossway Books, 1990), 144.

[7] Albert Camus, *The Myth of Sisyphus and Other Essays*, trans. Justin O'Brien (New York: Vintage Books, 1991). In the opening pages, addressing "absurdity and suicide," Camus claims that because the only real problem is suicide, the meaning of life—determining what makes life worth living—is the most important question of philosophy (p. 3). He unpacks the idea that "the absurd depends as much on man as on the world" (21); it is "born of this confrontation between the human need and the unreasonable silence of the world" (28). He concludes that the struggle itself to make life meaningful is enough to bring a sense of contentment in continuing the struggle.

[8] While eighteenth-century writers like Jeremy Bentham asserted that human rights are nonsense-talk, and twentieth-century thinkers like A. J. Ayer added that our moral utterances mean little more than "Yay" or Boo," nineteenth-century thinkers

like Feuerbach, Marx, and Freud (along with Bentham before them) either attempted to rid discourse of what they considered to be the religious disease (in Bentham's case), or attempted to explain it away as psychological phenomena functioning like an opiate for the (implicitly ignorant) masses. Add to this the larger philosophical struggles of the Enlightenment heritage. As the supposed chasm widened between our knowledge and ability to speak of the material and the immaterial, philosophers began to dig at the inevitable conclusions which follow from the mechanistic nature of a matter-only reality: what room is left for human freedom and why think a "mind" is really anything more than a by-product of material processes occurring in the body? The latter casts doubt on the real existence of the soul, the "I" of which Descartes said we could be certain. Yet the "I" is that which is most central to any sense of identity, and identity is necessary for drawing out purpose and significance. Thus, it is not difficult to draw lines from this problem, which has come to be known as the "ghost in the machine," and the loss of freedom (by way of determinism) to the existentialist assertion of absolute freedom in the face of absurdity (to choose one's own purpose and meaning) and the controversial neo-existentialist emphasis on an absolute freedom to determine the purpose and nature of sex and gender identity.

[9] This speaks to the power of nostalgia, a longing to re-live the meaningful, but the meaningful experiences which we long to relive are often meaningful precisely because they point to something bigger than experience per se.

[10] T. Z. Lavine, *From Socrates to Sartre: The Philosophic Quest* (New York: Bantam Books, 1984), 261-321.

[11] In *The Essence of Christianity*, Feuerbach claimed that God is merely an outward projection of an idealized humanity. In *The German Ideology* (1845), under the heading "First Premises of Materialist Method," Marx argued that metaphysical ideas like morality and religion are just "phantoms formed in the human brain;" consciousness is ultimately the product of material conditions of the times. See Ludwig Feuerbach, The Essence of Christianity, 2nd ed., trans. Marian Evans (London: Trübner & Co., Ludgate Hill, 1881), 226; and Karl Marx and Frederick Engels, The German Ideology, ed. C. J. Arthur (New York, NY: International Publishers, 1970), 47.

[12] Lavine, 261-321; Frederick Copleston, "Modern Philosophy: From the French Revolution to Sartre, Camus, and Levi-Strauss," *A History of Philosophy*, vol. 9 (New York: Image Books, 1994), 55-73; Gordon H. Clark, *Thales to Dewey: A History of Philosophy* (Grand Rapids: Baker Book House, 1980), 468-85.

[13] Karl Marx and Friedrich Engels, *The Communist Manifesto*, trans. Samuel Moore, ed. Joseph Katz (New York: Pocket Books, 1967), 57-59; See also, Clark, 477-84.

14 See: Rolf Wiggershaus, *The Frankfurt School: Its History, Theories, and Political Significance*, trans. Michael Robertson (Cambridge: MIT Press, 1995).

15 Thomas Hobbes, *Leviathan 1. 14.*

16 E. O. Wilson, "Sociobiology and Ethics," in *Ethical Theory: Classical and Contemporary Readings*, 6th ed., ed. Louis P. Pojman and James Fieser, (Boston: Wadsworth, 2011), 639.

17 Michael Ruse, "Evolution and Ethics: The Sociobiological Approach," in Pojman and Fieser, *Ethical Theory*, 652.

18 See: R. Scott Smith, *In Search of Moral Knowledge: Overcoming the Fact-Value Dichotomy* (Downers Grove: InterVarsity Press, 2014), Loc. 1923-97, Kindle.

19 Norman L. Geisler and Frank Turek, *I Don't Have Enough Faith to Be an Atheist* (Wheaton: Crossway, 2004), 187.

20 Ruse, 652.

21 Geisler and Turek, 187-89.

22 Ibid., 188.

23 Ibid., 189.

24 *Zootopia*, dir. Byron Howard and Rich Moore (Burbank, CA: Walt Disney Studios, 2016).

25 See: Smith, Loc. 2076-2132.

26 Here, morality is relative to human nature rather than perspective; remove human beings and you remove moral obligation. Contrast this, however, with theistic narratives which include created *immaterial* beings (e.g., angels) also morally bound by a teleological order.

27 Smith, Loc. 2091.

28 Elliot Sober, "Prospects for an Evolutionary Ethics," in Pojman and Fieser, *Ethical Theory*, 6th ed., 667.

29 Bertrand Russell, "A Free Man's Worship," in *Ethical Theory: Classical and Contemporary Readings*, 3rd ed., ed. Louis P. Pojman, (Belmont: Wadsworth, 1998), 646.

30 George Mavrodes, "Religion and the Queerness of Morality," in Pojman and Fieser, *Ethical Theory*, 6th ed., 607-608.

31 American Anthropological Association, "Statement on Human Rights," *American Anthropologist* 49, no. 4 (1947): 542, 539-43.

[32] Louis P. Pojman, A Defense of Ethical Objectivism," in *Moral Philosophy: A Reader*, 4th ed., ed. Louis P. Pojman and Peter Tramel. (Indianapolis: Hackett Publishing Company, Inc., 2009), 38-52.

Chapter 11

[1] See: Bradley A. U. Levinson et al., eds., *Beyond Critique: Exploring Critical Social Theories and Education* (Boulder: Paradigm Publishers, 2011); Ben Agger, *Critical Social Theories*, 3rd ed. (New York: Oxford University Press, 2013); Thomas S. Popkewitz and Lynn Fendler, eds., *Critical Theories in Education: Changing Terrains of Knowledge and Politics* (New York: Routledge, 1999); James Bohman, "Critical Theory," *The Stanford Encyclopedia of Philosophy* (Winter 2019), ed. Edward N. Zalta, https://plato.stanford.edu/archives/win2019/entries/critical-theory/; Claudio Corradetti, "The Frankfurt School and Critical Theory," *The Internet Encyclopedia of Philosophy*, ed. James Fieser and Bradley Dowden, https://www.iep.utm.edu/frankfur/; Ann S. Beck, "A Place for Critical Literacy," *Journal of Adolescent & Adult Literacy* 48, no. 5 (2005): 392-400; Consider also the description of UC Berkley's Program in CT, which identifies "contemporary forms and modes of critical theory" as "including critical race theory, post-colonialist theory, feminist critique, gender studies and queer theory, and the diverse approaches to critique arising with and after structuralism and poststructuralism." September 12, 2020, https://criticaltheory.berkeley.edu/.

[2] Heather Davidson et al., "Power and Action in Critical Theory Across Disciplines: Implications for Critical Community Psychology," *American Journal of Community Psychology* 38, no. 1-2 (2006): 36.

[3] William A. Gorton, "Philosophy of Social Science," *The Internet Encyclopedia of Philosophy*, ed. James Fieser and Bradley Dowden, https://www.iep.utm.edu/soc-sci/.

[4] Arnold Farr, "Herbert Marcuse," *The Stanford Encyclopedia of Philosophy* (Summer 2020), ed. Edward N. Zalta, https://plato.stanford.edu/entries/marcuse/; Kim Díaz, "Paulo Freire (1921—1997)," *The Internet Encyclopedia of Philosophy*, ed. James Fieser and Bradley Dowden, https://www.iep.utm.edu/freire/; Paulo Freire, *Pedagogy of the Oppressed*. (New York: Continuum, 2005); Allen, Amy, "Feminist Perspectives on Power", *The Stanford Encyclopedia of Philosophy* (Fall 2016), ed. Edward N. Zalta, https://plato.stanford.edu/entries/feminist-power/; Özlem Sensoy and Robin DiAngelo, *Is Everyone Really Equal? An Introduction to Key Concepts in Social Justice Education* 2nd ed. (New York: Teachers College Press, 2017).

[5] Gorton, "Philosophy of Social Science;" Gutting, Gary and Oksala, Johanna, "Michel Foucault", *The Stanford Encyclopedia of Philosophy* (Spring 2019), ed. Edward N. Zalta; https://plato.stanford.edu/entries/foucault/; Mark Kelly, "Michel Foucault

(1926–1984)," *The Internet Encyclopedia of Philosophy*, ed. James Fieser and Bradley Dowden, https://www.iep.utm.edu/foucault/.

[6] Quoted in Gerald Turkel, "Michel Foucault: Law, Power, and Knowledge," *Journal of Law and Society* 17, no. 2 (1990), p. 179.

[7] Friedrich Nietzsche, "The Transvaluation of Values," in Pojman, *Ethical Theory*, 3rd ed., 162.

[8] Lavine, 219-223.

[9] Friedrich Nietzsche, "Beyond Good and Evil," in Pojman and Tramel, *Moral Philosophy*, 123-130.

[10] Freire, 56.

[11] Kate Lockwood Harris, "Re-situating Organizational Knowledge: Violence, Intersectionality and the Privilege of Partial Perspective," *Human Relations* 70, no. 3 (2017): 264.

[12] David K. Naugle, *Worldview: The History of a Concept* (Grand Rapids: Eerdmans, 2002), 102.

[13] Marcel Stoetzler and Nira Yuval-Davis, "Standpoint Theory, Situated Knowledge and the Situated Imagination," *Feminist Theory* 3, no. 3 (2002): 315-333.

[14] T. Bowell, "Feminist Standpoint Theory," *The Internet Encyclopedia of Philosophy*, ed. James Fieser and Bradley Dowden, https://www.iep.utm.edu/fem-stan/.

[15] Classical virtue ethics understood morality as tethered to *essentialism*—the belief that humans have an essence/nature/telos. Existentialists rejected this, insisting we are free to assert our own truths concerning our essences/identities, and to define our own values accordingly.

[16] Gorton, "Philosophy of Social Science."

[17] Ibid.

[18] For example: Elizabeth Bondy, Elizabeth Burt, and Priscilla V. Bell, "Cultivating Critical Social Justice Literacy: Surfacing and Examining Candidates' Embodied Knowledge," *The New Educator* 18, no. 1-2 (2022): 27-41; Kathryn Sorrells, *Intercultural Communication: Globalization and Social Justice* (SAGE Publications, Incorporated, 2020); Elizabeth McGibbon and Sionnach Lukeman, "Critical Social Justice: The Moral Imperative for Critical Perspectives in Nursing," *Witness: The Canadian Journal of Critical Nursing Discourse* 1, no. 1 (2019): 3-12; Sensoy and DiAngelo, *Is Everyone Really Equal?*; David O. Stovall, *Cultivating Social Justice Teachers: How Teacher Educators Have Helped Students Overcome Cognitive Bottlenecks and Learn*

Critical Social Justice Concepts (Stylus Publishing, LLC, 2013); Madonna G. Constantine, Sally M. Hage, Mai M. Kindaichi, and Rhonda M. Bryant, "Social Justice and Multicultural Issues: Implications for the Practice and Training of Counselors and Counseling Psychologists," *Journal of Counseling & Development* 85, no. 1 (2007): 24-29. Kathy Hytten, "Education for Social Justice: Provocations and Challenges," *Educational Theory* 56, no. 2 (2006): 221-236.

[19] Sensoy and DiAngelo, 20.

[20] Ibid., 50.

[21] Ibid., 20.

[22] Ibid.

[23] Ibid., 51, 54-55, 57.

[24] Ibid., 54.

[25] Ibid., 53.

[26] Ibid., 54.

[27] The negativity associated with colonialism is the idea of imposing ideologies, cultural values, and behavioral prescriptions/expectations upon other cultures/worldviews that did not want them. Is this not what CSJ does by attempting to seize influence in various areas of society from the academy to the corporate boardroom in an effort to assert the values of CSJ and de-emphasize any contrary values of the heretofore mainstream—even to publicly shame those who reject some of the values, expectations, and ideology of CSJ? Is CSJ not attempting to "colonize", so to speak, the mainstream's perspective of what should be understood as right or normal?

[28] Sensoy and DiAngelo, 57.

[29] Ibid., 185.

[30] Ibid., 207.

[31] Ibid., 180, 85-86, 145.

[32] Ibid., 145.

[33] Ibid., 94.

[34] Ibid., 205.

[35] Ibid.

[36] Ibid., 206.

[37] A. J. Ayer, *The Central Questions of Philosophy* (New York: William Morrow, 1973), 235.

[38] Smith, Loc. 2496.

Chapter 12

[1] *Alice in Wonderland*, dir. Clyde Geronimi, Wilfred Jackson, and Hamilton Luske (Burbank: Walt Disney Studios, 1951).

[2] Jack Feldman and Tom Snow, "One of Us," in *The Lion King II: Simba's Pride*, dir. Darrell Rooney (Burbank, CA: Walt Disney Studios, 1998).

[3] Tevin Campbell, "I 2 I" in *A Goofy Movie*, dir. Kevin Lima (Burbank, CA: Walt Disney Studios, 1995).

[4] Paul M. Gould, *Cultural Apologetics: Renewing the Christian Voice, Conscience, and Imagination in a Disenchanted World* (Grand Rapids: Zondervan, 2019), 36-37.

[5] C. S. Lewis, *The Magician's Nephew* (New York: HarperCollins, 1983), 136.

[6] *Beauty and the Beast*, dir. Bill Condon (Burbank: Walt Disney Studios, 2017).

[7] For more on this, see chapter one.

[8] By "hate crimes" we mean crimes against intrinsic human dignity through an assault upon one's (1) life; (2) free will/conscience; or (3) property. We do *not* mean: (1) attacking one's beliefs/ethics or refusing to affirm a belief as correct; (2) limiting one's questionable actions (freedom to act); or (3) denying one the right to a property or privilege that was not clearly/unquestionably already due him/her.

[9] Gary Chapman has insightfully connected anger to an indignation for injustice. It may be misdirected, as we may be incorrect about the details surrounding an offense or the appropriate course to justice. Nevertheless, when we feel *wronged* or believe someone else to have been wronged, we respond in indignation and our protest can even manifest itself in our physiological responses. Gary Chapman, *Anger: Taming a Powerful Emotion* (Chicago: Moody Publishers, 2015), 20-23.

[10] Joseph Zornado, *Disney and the Dialectic of Desire: Fantasy as Social Practice* (Cham: Palgrave Macmillan, 2017), 1-28.

[11] Cf. the parable of The Blind Men and the Elephant.

[12] Wart did not possess a *right* to free/accessible education. Still, Merlin's deed was *good*.

[13] Lin-Manuel Miranda, "What Else Can I Do?" in *Encanto*, dir. Jared Bush and Byron Howard (Burbank, CA: Walt Disney Studios, 2021).

[14] Prov. 27:17.

[15] Colleen Flaherty, "Blowback Against a Hoax," *Inside Higher Ed*, June 23, 2020, https://www.insidehighered.com/news/2019/01/08/author-recent-academic-hoax-faces-disciplinary-action-portland-state; Helen Pluckrose, James A. Lindsay, and Peter Boghossian, "Academic Grievance Studies and the Corruption of Scholarship," *Aero*, June 23, 2020, https://areomagazine.com/2018/10/02/academic-grievance-studies-and-the-corruption-of-scholarship/.

[16] The view that truth means that which *corresponds* to reality (the way things actually are), in contrast to the view that truth amounts to whatever *coheres* to our other beliefs about reality, or whatever works.

[17] As Boghossian describes it, in Culture War 1.0, Christians and atheists appealed to objective knowledge, truth (corresponding to reality), and to *reason* in debate over the existence of God; Culture War 2.0 largely writes off such an appeal as a form of western oppression and prefers silencing opposition over debating. Peter Boghossian, "Welcome to Culture War 2.0: The Great Realignment," *The American Mind*, June 23, 2020, https://americanmind.org/salvo/welcome-to-culture-war-2-0/.

[18] Simon Blackburn, *Truth: A Guide* (Oxford: Oxford University Press, 2007), 31.

[19] It must be *defined* because it cannot be *known* or *discovered* if immaterial things like Moral Law/Truth are ultimately non-existent.

[20] Arguments for abortion/euthanasia demonstrate how the skewing of lines impacts not only questions of right-to-alleged-distribution, but also right-to-life/death.

[21] Lin-Manuel Miranda, "We Don't Talk About Bruno," in *Encanto*.

[22] Jeremy E. Scarbrough, "Facing the Void," (unpublished poem, Nov. 11, 2017).

Chapter 13

[1] Richard M. Sherman and Robert B. Sherman, "The Age of Not Believing," *Bedknobs and Broomsticks*, dir. Robert Stevenson (Burbank: Walt Disney Studios, 1971).

[2] William Lane Craig, *Reasonable Faith: Christian Truth and Apologetics*, 3rd ed. (Wheaton: Crossway, 2008), 173-75.

[3] Richard Taylor, *Ethics, Faith, and Reason* (Englewood Cliffs: Prentice-Hall, 1985), 83-84.

[4] Gregory Koukl, *The Story of Reality* (Grand Rapids: Zondervan, 2017), 35.

[5] Angus J. L. Menuge, ed. *Legitimizing Human Rights: Secular and Religious Perspectives* (New York: Routledge, 2016), 1.

[6] Louis Pojman, "On Equal Human Worth: A Critique of Contemporary Egalitarianism," in *Equality: Selected Readings*, ed. Louis P. Pojman and Robert Westmoreland (New York: Oxford University Press, 1997), 283.

[7] Ibid. 294.

[8] Ibid.

[9] Ibid. 296.

[10] Ibid. 295.

[11] Ibid. 296.

[12] William Uzgalis, "John Locke," *The Stanford Encyclopedia of Philosophy* (Spring 2020), ed. Edward N. Zalta, https://plato.stanford.edu/entries/locke/.

[13] Alasdair MacIntyre, *After Virtue: A Study in Moral Theory*, 3rd ed. (University of Notre Dame Press, 2007), 71.

[14] Ibid., 69.

[15] Ibid., 67.

[16] See "Science," *Dug Days*, directed by Bob Peterson (Burbank, CA: Walt Disney Studios, 2021).

[17] Scarbrough commenting: For if God created me to exist, I cannot say "I have a right to live" as if, were God to require my life from me today, God would be guilty of denying my right—I have no *right* to exist, but it is indeed a privilege, and if a privilege given by God, then this may imply something as it relates to social order. Yet, if by "I have a right to life" is really meant, "no other human has a right to take my life from me," (assuming this assertion fits the frame and is grounded in the metanarrative), this seems to make more sense. Nor do I clearly have a "right" to live according to my own ideals of pleasure, or even to claim just anything as my property. Yet, if a right to liberty or the pursuit of happiness is to mean that no other human has a right to bring clear and intentional harm to me as I pursue my own happiness, or to coerce me to confess belief in something that is contrary to my moral convictions; if a right to property simply means, *if* something is indeed mine (though this is, admittedly, a deeper question), then no other human has a right to take it from me; then again, assuming such assertions fit the frame and ground themselves within a metanarrative, this seems to be more intelligible. The

point, then, is that the positive assertion that something is due me is less obvious than the negative claim that what is understood to be mine ought not to be taken from me without good reason.

[18] Paul Copan, "Grounding Human Rights: Naturalism's Failure and Biblical Theism's Success," in Menuge, *Legitimizing Human Rights*, 16.

[19] Paul Copan, *Is God a Vindictive Bully? Reconciling Portrayals of God in Old and New Testaments* (Grand Rapids, MI: Baker Academic, 2022), 59.

[20] Ibid., 62.

[21] Stanley I. Benn, "Rights," in *Encyclopedia of Philosophy*, Vol. 7, ed. Paul Edwards (New York: MacMillan, 1967), 197-99.

[22] Classical philosophy often referenced the idea that the universe is rationally ordered, and that human society should reflect this order in some capacity. The apostle Paul pressed into this conviction; "When Gentiles who do not have the Law do instinctively the things of the Law ... they show the work of the Law written in their hearts, their conscience bearing witness." (Rom. 2:14-15, NASB).

[23] Aquinas, *Summa Theologica* 2-1.91.2, 2-1.94.4.

[24] Copan, *Is God a Vindictive Bully?*, 58.

[25] Pojman, 295.

[26] Julian (Flavius Claudius Julianus), *The works of the Emperor Julian*, Vol. 3, trans. Wilmer Cave Wright (London: Heinemann, 1913), 71.

[27] Luc Ferry, *A Brief History of Thought: A Philosophical Guide to Living*, trans. Theo Cuffe (New York: HarperCollins, 2011), 72-74.

[28] Uzgalis, "John Locke."

[29] Stephen Schwartz and Alan Menken, "God Help the Outcast," in *The Hunchback of Notre Dame*, dir. Gary Trousdale and Kirk Trousdale (Burbank: Walt Disney Studios, 1996).

[30] Koukl, 70-72.

[31] Louis P. Pojman, "The Case Against Moral Relativism," in *The Moral Life: An Introductory Reader in Ethics and Literature*, 2nd ed., ed. Louis P. Pojman (Oxford: Oxford University Press, 2004), 179. See also Louis P. Pojman, "A Critique of Ethical Relativism," in Ethical Theory: Classical and Contemporary Readings, 6th ed., edited by Louis P. Pojman and James Fieser (Boston: Wadsworth, 2011), 49-50.

[32] David Baggett and Jerry L. Walls. *Good God: The Theistic Foundations of Morality* (Oxford: Oxford University Press, 2011), 47.

[33] Luke 10:27.

[34] See, e.g., *Qur'an* 2.190; 2.276; 3.32; 3.57; 3.140; 4.36.

[35] Acknowledging Islam's shared understanding with biblical theism concerning the sovereignty of God—in so far as an "infidel" or "sinner" is one who has freely rejected God's authority and denied his due respect—there is nonetheless division over God's nature/character. Moreover, many have argued that only a trinitarian view can completely ground a God-is-love claim. Theology of the Trinity targets the God-is-love question; if love requires exchange/action, God could not be loving *before*/apart from creation *unless* God were able to share a loving communion with different persons within the singularity of his absolute being. See Koukl, 111; C. S. Lewis, *Mere Christianity* (HarperCollins, 2001), 174.

[36] While one is free to reject any given evidence as unconvincing, it is foolish to insist that there is no evidence, for evidence abounds in a plethora of arguments from causation, being, design, consciousness, and universal convictions regarding justice and a desire to experience goodness, beauty, and a sense of purpose, etc.

[37] Acts 28:24-28; Rom. 1:18-25; Zech. 7:12; Jer. 3:20, 31:31-32; Hos. 11; 2 Chron. 36:15-16.

[38] John 15:19.

[39] Acts 2:42-46.

[40] Matt. 22:36-40.

[41] In bringing law and commandment together under the prescription to love, is Jesus not hanging the foundation of morality upon an *obligatory commandment* to love one another? Actually, he seems to be offering a practical precept rather than an injunction *per se*. He is directing our attention to a teleological intention (God's will for the created order, what is appropriate, and therein what is best for us), which requires a sense of honor or respect due to one another and fidelity due to God as King. There is a sense of due-ness and so it does carry an obligatory force in the sense of self-control, but Jesus is simultaneously *calling* us to go beyond mere self-control here. Thus the profundity and beauty in simplicity of such a general rule for living well, for living in accordance with God's will, and for living in harmony with one another. As Copan observes, "To some degree, the Mosaic "law" is more like "wise instruction" than a legal code. The word *torah* is often translated "law," but it means "teaching" or "instruction." To a certain extent, the Mosaic law was like other ancient Near Eastern law collections.... Unlike our modern Western legal

system, ancient Near Eastern rulers and judges didn't refer to these collections as legal manuals." This does not mean, he clarifies, that the law has nothing to do with moral commands. "If wisdom is the skill for living, fulfilling certain *practical moral* duties will be required for living wisely. Parents begin with duties in teaching their children moral virtue and character formation. These aren't separate. Even so, we can derive basic commands, ethical duties, and moral priorities from collections of wisdom." [Paul Copan, *Is God a Vindictive Bully?*, 51-52]. Likewise, Jesus does not seem to be stressing Mosaic commands *per se*, but summarizing the moral wisdom revealed in the Old Testament, as succinctly found in the *Shema* (Deut. 6:4) and applied socially in the latter part of Lev. 19: 18. Love involves an acknowledgement of something or someone's value and requires an act of will rather than emotive reaction. Sometimes loving one another means considering what is good for others even if we do not really like them. Yet while a basic sense of respect for one another (self-restraint) might be mandated, since love requires action and sometimes asks us to practice what lies contrary to our will, love as a *free* expression of gentleness and service may be prescribed as a *precept* for living well—a call to aim for the orientation of heart and mind that is *best* for one's soul and for social harmony—but it cannot be commanded as injunction, without minimizing free will and potentially turning a faith-based theology into a works-based theology.

42 Matt. 20:13-15. Understandably, many political disagreements come down to questions of who actually owns rights to what property. Yet all disagreements over property rights appeal to an ideal of due respect, which is based upon an assumption of intrinsic dignity as an essential property of humanness. Thus, although justice extends to material conditions, it begins with immaterial preconditions.

43 James 3:16.

44 Aleksandr I. Solzhenitsyn, The Gulag Archipelago 1918-1956: An Experiment in Literary Investigation, I-II, trans. Thomas P. Whitney (New York: Harper and Row, 1974), 168.

45 Consider the sobering words of George Steiner: "We know that a man can read Goethe or Rilke in the evening, that he can play Bach and Schubert, and go to his day's work at Auschwitz in the morning." George Steiner, Language and Silence: Essays 1958-1966 (London: Faber, 1967), 15.

Chapter 14

[1] Admittedly, as with artistic perspectives, there may remain an ethical question concerning whether the exposure of some moral perspectives is suitable for children.

[2] From Marco Antonio de Dominis's *De Repubblica Ecclesiastica* (1617), and a 1627 tract by Rupertus Meldenius.

[3] We do not *teach* our children to assert themselves in disrespect, deceit, envy, and aggression, and *we* need not be taught to subvert the needs of others to our own desires, to love gossip and schadenfreude, or even, at times, to act unlovingly toward the very ones whom we love most; these things come naturally.

[4] Numbers 15, though the verse has a particular context, suggests that even a wrong done in ignorance can incur a sense of guilt, and, importantly, that the guilt of *some* is attributed to the entire congregation. Additionally, the forgiveness of God is extended to the entire congregation in light of the priest's propitiation. This passage seems to be dripping with symbolism as it relates both to Genesis and the gospel.

[5] Harold L. Willmington, *Willmington's Guide to the Bible* (Carol Stream: Tyndale House Publishers, 2011), 558.

[6] Lewis, 122.

[7] Rom. 2-3; Gal. 3.

[8] Craig, 173.

[9] Gal. 5:22-23.

[10] DC Talk, "What If I Stumble," *Jesus Freak* ForeFront Records, 1995, CD.

[11] Brennan Manning, *The Ragamuffin Gospel* (Colorado Springs: Multnomah Books, 2005), 2.

[12] Jer. 29:7.

[13] 1 John 4:7-21.

[14] The question raised here is "Can I be good without God?" and there are three possible answers. First, if one means "Can I be good if God does not exist?" then (1) the answer is no, because "goodness" as matter of fact becomes unintelligible nonsense; for there is no real measure for goodness; there is only need, desire, privilege, preference, and power. On the other hand, one might mean, "Can I do and be good, even, supposing for the sake of argument that God *may* exist, if I either reject God's authority over my life, choose not to believe in Him, or simply ignore the question altogether?" In this case, there are two possible, tiered, responses: First, if God made us in His image—to reflect His goodness—then it is no surprise that all human beings have a potential for doing good. So, (2) here the answer is a qualified yes. However, *reflecting* goodness is not actually the same as *being* good. If Jesus was correct, in that, while a secondary reflection of goodness may involve how we treat others, the primary reflection of goodness involves our direct position of

thankfulness and respect in relation to God, and a sense of due worship owed by us to God, then this ultimate requirement is not one that a non-believer could satisfy. Ultimately, then, (3) the more pointed, though unfortunate conclusion would seem to be, no.

[15] Rom. 8; Rom. 12.

[16] 1 Thess. 5:18.

[17] 1 Pet. 2:15.

[18] Heb. 10:10-24.

[19] Mic. 6:8 NASB.

[20] Matt. 25:34-40.

[21] Cornelius Plantinga Jr., Not the Way It's Supposed to Be: A Breviary of Sin (Grand Rapids, MI: William B. Eerdmans, 1995), 10

[22] Isa. 59:8-9; 14.

[23] Rom. 7:15-20.

[24] Matt. 4:17.

[25] David Zippel, Matthew Wilder, and Jerry Goldsmith, "Reflection," in *Mulan*, dir. Barry Cook and Tony Bancroft (Burbank: Walt Disney Studios, 1998).

[26] Stephen Schwartz and Alan Menken, "Colors of the Wind," in *Pocahontas*, dir. Mike Gabriel and Eric Goldberg (Burbank: Walt Disney Studios, 1995).

[27] George MacDonald, "The Fantastic Imagination," in *The Light Princess, and Other Fairy Tales* (Digireads.com Publishing, 2009), 7.

[28] Pinsky 2004, 1-2

Chapter 15

[1] Elton John and Tim Rice, "I Just Can't Wait to Be King" in The Lion King, dir. Rob Allers and Rob Minkoff (Burbank, CA: Walt Disney Studios, 1994).

[2] John 8:44.

[3] Eph. 6:12.

[4] James H. Cone, *God of the Oppressed* (Maryknoll: Orbis Books, 2018), 9.

[5] Ibid., 32.

[6] Ibid., 74-75.

[7] Ibid., 86.

[8] James Cone, "Black Liberation Theology, in its Founder's Words," interview by Terry Gross, *National Public Radio*, 2008, retrieved October 10, 2020, https://www.npr.org/templates/story/story.php?storyId=89236116.

[9] Ibid.

[10] Ibid.

[11] Gen. 16:13-14.

[12] Isa. 7:14.

[13] Christopher J. H. Wright, *Knowing Jesus Through the Old Testament* (Downers Grove: IVP Academic, 1992), 36.

[14] Ibid., 29-30.

[15] Ibid., 84.

[16] Gustavo Gutiérrez, *A Theology of Liberation: History, Politics, and Salvation,* trans. Sister Caridad Inda and John Eagleson (Maryknoll: Orbis Books, 1988), 174.

[17] Millard J. Erickson, *Christian Theology,* 2nd ed. (Grand Rapids: Baker Academic, 1998), 1017.

[18] Ibid.

[19] Ibid., 608-11.

[20] Matt. 5:17-48.

[21] Ps. 51:14-17; Luke 15:17-24; Ps. 138:6; Isa. 57:15; 66:2; 1 Pet. 5:5.

[22] Ps. 34.

[23] Matt 16:24-27; Luke 14:27.

[24] Ps. 13:1-2; Hab. 1:2; Rev. 6:10.

[25] Num. 14:18; also consider Gen. 15:16.

[26] Deut. 10:17-18; 27:19.

[27] Lev. 25:35-38.

[28] Lev. 19:15; Deut. 16:19.

[29] 1 Cor. 15:12-19.

[30] C. S. Lewis, *The Lion, the Witch, and the Wardrobe,* in *The Chronicles of Narnia* (New York: HarperEntertainment, 2008), 146.

[31] Lewis, *Mere Christianity,* 51-52.

[32] Mark 12:28-34; Matt. 7:12.

[33] King insisted that the silence of good people can be just as harmful as the hateful actions of bad people. Martin Luther King Jr., "Letter from Birmingham Jail," in *Why We Can't Wait* (New York: Signet Classics, 2000), 99.

[34] Matt 16:25-27; Matt. 6. In the same passage wherein Jesus stressed the value of giving to the poor—having just "upped the ante" on both the demands of moral perfection and the expectations of love—he emphasized the need to seek *heavenly, not* earthly, rewards. In fact, the emphasis upon ministering to the needy was not, at that moment, on social justice at all; it involved *the condition of one's heart* while serving *in order to be seen* as a lover of justice in the eyes of the community.

[35] John 16:33.

[36] John 15:18-21.

[37] Rom. 8:28.

[38] Luke 10.

[39] 1 John 3:18.

[40] Jer. 29:7.

[41] *Tinkerbell and the Legend of the NeverBeast,* dir. Steve Loter (Burbank: Walt Disney Studios, 2014).

[42] Lewis, *Mere Christianity,* 65.

[43] Gal. 5:13.

Illustration by Arthur Rackham, from "Snowdrop" in
Snowdrop & Other Tales *(1920) by the Brothers Grimm*

VOLUME II:

Disney
& THE MORAL IMAGINATION

Disney

& THE MORAL IMAGINATION

Edited by Jeremy E. Scarbrough

HIGH BRIDGE BOOKS
HOUSTON

Prologue

W hat has Disney to do with apologetics? In many ways, it is easy to approach a volume like this. Disney lore is rich with ethical and aesthetic food for thought, lending itself naturally to theological reflection. It is also difficult, precisely because of the nature of culture wars.

The emphasis of Disney films on traditional family values has long won the hearts and support of American conservatives. Yet some have accused Disney of replacing God with magic, or moral responsibility with individual self-empowerment.[1] Mark Pinsky has even detailed disputes between conservatives and Disney in the 1990s over employee benefits and theme-park policies concerning homosexuality.[2] While the propagandizing of questionable ethical perspectives through children's films *would* warrant cultural collision, attacking Disney as a non-religious corporation over how it ought to handle its own business beyond film was a more difficult battle. While some conservative concerns are understandable, the God-and-culture-as-antithesis approach, in this case, was more disheartening than helpful. Others criticize Disney's long-standing emphasis upon traditional values or mainstream western perspectives. Some hold Disney morally accountable either for a general lack of racial or cultural representation or for historical cases of misrepresentation. Annalee Ward has attempted to balance this challenge; "Dismissing Disney films critically as hegemonic agents of self-interested consumeristic values that communicate patriarchal, racist, hierarchical, and antiauthority visions of morality misses powerful dimensions of prosocial morality and aesthetically delightful animated art."[3] Critical antitheses abound.

Some challenge that Disney heroines are too sexualized for young viewers. Others take no issue with princess form or attire, but question whether Disney-princess motifs communicate that finding "the one" and establishing adult relationships are the key to the good life—whether or not it may be included in the good life, the critique is that young girls need not be concerned with such things. Still others demand that Disney ought to feature under-represented LGBTQ+ perspectives. This, of course, stands in tension with the two prior critiques, which raise concern regarding any potential for over-sexualizing young viewers or making them more body conscious. Add to this the point that aesthetic appreciation—and, with it, cultural appropriation—often walks a fine line between familiarity and offense, idealization and ignorance, or contrast and controversy.

This problem becomes increasingly complicated when attempting to appeal to a global audience. How does one create a global culture (for example, Disney Culture) with a single canon (for instance, animated Disney lore) without offending anyone? Thus, while writing about Disney is easy, writing in a way that speaks to as many critics as possible is difficult. Despite being a flashpoint for the culture war, or even perhaps because of it, Disney provides rich fodder for considering the human condition, and it is the aim of this volume to draw out that dialogical richness.

The Disney Legacy

Walt Disney revolutionized the history of animation and music with the debut of *Steamboat Willie* in 1928. In addition to the first cartoon with fully synchronized sound, he gave us the first cartoon in full color (1932) and the first animated feature film (1937). Disney continued to produce a wide variety of commercial goods, and he had his hands in numerous projects from television to theme parks. Still, while his theme parks continue to bring great joy to many people, and though many of his other classic cartoons and live-action film projects may hold a special place in many viewer's hearts, the cornerstone of Disney's legacy seems to be the continued success of its growing cannon of animated feature films and live-action animated films. Disney's animated narratives—whether short, "silly" symphonies or full-length features—seem to possess a unique sort of magic able to capture and enrapture our moral imagination and aesthetic sensibilities. Moreover, I think it is safe to say that the *most* beloved Disney films are musicals—whether fully animated films like *The Lion King* and *Frozen*, animated live-action like *Mary Poppins* and *Bedknobs and Broomsticks*, or live-action films like *The Newsies* and *Descendants*—and I think there is something to that. The music of Disney has enchanted generations, and I submit that the removal of music from Disney's expansive history would reduce a trove of treasured experiences to a collection of well-drawn but comparatively lackluster amusements.

So, Disney may offer an array of allures, yet it seems to be the very things that launched Walt's career—the animated feature and a unique approach to music—which continue, nearly a century later, to serve as effective instruments of enchantment. Of course, music and animation are not unique to Disney; other films employ these things. Nevertheless, Disney set the bar in exemplifying how the right balance between animation, music, and storytelling can create an aesthetic experience so powerful as to become transformative. And so, no matter where one falls on the spectrum between fans and critics, what seems undeniable is that Disney is a cultural force that has shaped the imagination of generations and audiences around the world. This unique aesthetic common ground opens up much ground for apologetic dialogue and inquiry.

Aim, Approach, and Intent

Building off my prior work on Disney's grand moral narrative, the ability of the Christian vision of reality to enfold Disney stories, and the power of Disney lore when used to supplement the doing of moral apologetics,[4] this project approaches Disney as doorway to dialogue on issues of ethics, aesthetics, and theology. Although my own agenda in that work may not necessarily reflect the views of other contributing authors in this volume, that apologetic interest has nonetheless shaped the assembly of these chapters. These essays will ponder the aesthetic power of storytelling, live-action animation, and music to enrapture our imagination, even presenting the moral argument in a language that goes beyond propositions and grips us at our deepest convictions, and they will examine themes of theology and moral formation within particular Disney narratives: the problem of evil in *Cinderella*; a portrait of redemption in *Tangled*; the nature and process of salvation in *Pinocchio*; the human condition *in Raya and the Last Dragon*; questions of faith and charity in *Beauty and the Beast*; and other avenues of exploration across additional cherished films, such as *Moana, The Lion King, Hercules, The Jungle Book*, and more.

The reader should understand that—notwithstanding the valid point that the issues of past ignorance and insensitivity is a dialogue worth having[5]—this volume approaches Disney's established and well-received narratives through a lens of aesthetic appreciation—and this is not to be misconstrued as sympathizing with Disney on such issues of insensitivity. Rather, the aim of this volume is an exploration of moral consonance, not dissonance. One need not support all that Disney stands for in order to appreciate, to find aesthetic value and productive moral dialogue within, Disney features—especially those from 1937 to 2021. This is a book about Disney stories, and more importantly, a greater story which enfolds Disney lore.

Regarding the theological framework, some essays are more broadly monotheistic, while others are more explicitly concerned with a Christian perspective. Still, there are many observations herein that lend themselves well to broader inquiries in monotheism, generalized themes in systematic theology, and explorations in aesthetics. While the volume is accessible to anyone interested in ethics and theology, several chapters may warrant the attention of arts educators and philosophers of aesthetics, and the overall work will be of particular significance to one interested in Christian theology and apologetics—especially apologetics and the arts.

The overall vision of the volume is one of interdisciplinary studies. For some, that is a well-appreciated and liberating form of scholarship. For others, this can be confusing. Is it philosophy? Is it theology? Is it apologetics? Is it aesthetics? The answer is, yes. Some chapters dig more at theological concepts, while others draw out the philosophical. Some are primarily interested with broader aesthetic questions, the theological significance of such questions, and the connection between aesthetic sensitivity and the moral imagination. While all essays, in some way, approach Disney through a lens of cultural apologetics—using pop-culture and the arts to explore or explain issues at the intersection of moral philosophy and theology—some essays engage more purposefully in theistic apologetics—using the arts to press into one's deep existential conviction that God is there. Both approaches intersect with, or capitalize upon, moral apologetics. What all chapters herein share is an interest in the moral imagination—how the authors' given areas of interest (philosophy, theology, or aesthetics) overlap with moral questions as presented in Disney's canon of animated classics.

As it is interdisciplinary, this volume is intended for anyone who is interested in interdisciplinary studies and the intersection of philosophy, theology, and the arts—especially for one who is interested in the connection between pop culture and apologetics. This work is intended to be presented at the "high popular" level. That is, it is written for a popular (not academic) audience, yet it is written in the hope of engaging academic and layperson alike. In the words of William Irwin, editor for the Blackwell Philosophy and Pop Culture Series:

> We are not aiming for the scholarly innovation of academic journal articles, nor are we producing classroom lectures. Rather, we are aiming to create a sense of discovery..... Admittedly, there is some risk of [sending the message that this is 'all you need to know'], but it is the same risk that we take in teaching Introduction to Philosophy. The clear message of the intro course and of most public philosophy is that this is *not* all you need to know, but rather that this is an introduction, one that will hopefully prompt you to want to know more.[6]

This applies not only to moral philosophy, but also to theology, apologetics, aesthetics and the study of pop culture. Similarly, this work does not presume to say all that can and should be said; its aim is to prompt further inquiry.

A word of caution is in order for some Christian readers. One should avoid reading into Disney films literal prescriptions and ideologies that are not explicitly intended, though the drawing out of worldview applications implicitly embedded, or issues potentially suggested, is a worthwhile endeavor for fostering inquiry and dialogue—as this volume demonstrates. Christians should refrain from expecting all Disney films to "give the gospel;" it was not Walt's intent to do so. This of course does not mean that the truth of God—in which Walt believed—cannot be found, nor that narratives cannot point to the gospel. Yet, as Francis Schaeffer wrote, "We must never forget that the first part of the gospel is not "Accept Christ as Savior," but "God is there." Only then is one ready to hear God's solution for man's moral dilemma."[7] In so far as some chapters carry an apologetic concern, readers should understand that the primary apologetic concern therein is not Christian evangelism *per se*, but theistic pre-evangelism—arguing that Disney features press powerfully into deep convictions concerning higher moral truths, which often align strikingly with the Christian narrative.

Overview of Essays

This volume is divided into two sections. The first section explores the power of stories and the arts to speak to our moral and theological imagination. The focus here is on aesthetics, with an eye toward moral and theological significance. In that way, these essays exemplify imaginative and aesthetic apologetics. Holly Ordway argues that imagination is essential to moral judgment, as stories offer unique opportunities for vicariously experiencing the effect of moral choices and acquiring a broader sense of moral meaning. Subsequent chapters unpack Ordway's premise and apply it to other aspects of the Disney oeuvre. Joel Paulus explores live-action animated musicals as a means of speaking to our desire for transcendence while communicating something about our need for a mediator. Doug Powell considers music's ability to communicate something about the objectivity of beauty by tapping into our desires and emotions. Rounding out this first section are paired chapters by D. J. Culp and I that consider the role of music in the moral imagination and how Disney masterfully leverages that potential.

Part II then investigates theological questions concerning moral formation, identity, and the human condition. Authors in this section investigate the moral formation and theological development of specific characters within particular narratives, expanding the apologetic discussion further. Shawn White insists we can learn a great deal about character formation, especially as it concerns the struggle between pride and humility, if we look to Pinocchio, Merida, Pocahontas, Aladdin, and Mulan. Miguel Benitez Jr. argues that Disney princesses are purposefully drawn to signal something about virtue, holiness, and the acquisition of a beautiful soul. Timothy Bartel presents Rapunzel's story as an artistic rendering of humanity's deception and redemption, closing with a profound observation concerning art's mediating role in communicating something about truth and identity. Sean Hadley explores *Moana*'s depiction of the moral tensions of lived communities, as morals are informed by one's story, yet one's culture may contain many competing narratives.

Eric Williamson and Russell Clayton unpack what Disney presents as the "good life," and how that stacks up against a Christian vision. Paul Miles presents *Pinocchio* as a portrait of spiritual deadness and a study in soteriology, while Mark Linville unpacks the nature of moral formation within this classic tale. John Weitzel analyzes Disney's retelling of *Hercules*, arguing that this polytheistic narrative actually bespeaks the conviction of a grand moral order lying above the Greek Pantheon, and ultimately champions a Christian, rather than Homeric, conception of virtue. Lori Peters considers what hope looks like in a world fraught with pain and conflict as depicted in *Cinderella*. Josh Herring approaches *The Lion King* through a Kierkegaardian lens, as Simba wrestles with the tension between his desire for the aesthetic level of existence and his calling to embrace the ethical. Zachary Schmoll and Neal Foster explore two perspectives on hospitality in *Beauty and the Beast*.

Whereas Schmoll reads this beloved tale in light of the parable of the Good Samaritan, pondering the practice of hospitality as a preparation for one's growth into something more, Foster questions whether Beast, in light of hospitable actions which accompany his moral development, qualifies more as a Kierkegaardian knight of faith or a knight of infinite resignation. The work concludes with my own reflection on faith, hope, and the human condition in *Raya and the Last Dragon*.

Tale as Old as Time

A common belief underlies all these chapters. In an "age of not believing"[8] sometimes what we need is not new information and better arguments, but a new perspective—an opportunity to look again, in a new and imaginative way, at something we have seen many times before; to ponder anew an old familiar tale; to consider the stories we are given as attempts to communicate something meaningful about the human experience, before simply writing them off as mere children's entertainment or compartmentalizing them so quickly into "fiction" and in opposition to "fact." Perhaps when we look on old tales with fresh eyes, there may be "something there that wasn't there before."[9] In *The Sword in the Stone*, Merlin attempts to offer Wart a good education, yet he goes about this not through teaching systematized methods for analyzing the world, but rather by expanding Wart's perspective to see the fantastic within the familiar. Wart had no doubt seen squirrels, fish, and birds, time and again. And yet he had never thought to *see as* the squirrel, the fish, or the bird. It was through enchanting the ordinary—engaging the imagination and appealing to Wart's direct experience—that Merlin was able to teach the young king-to-be how to see more clearly and consider more carefully the characters and problems before him. So too, Pocahontas asks John Smith to consider nature from nature's perspective, and to learn to see people as "people," even when they neither look nor act like him.

Fantasia helped many children and adults to *see* Baroque, Classical, and Romantic music of the 1600-1800s in a new and engaging way. In *The Emperor's New Groove* (2000), Kuzco had "seen" the peasants in his kingdom prior to his transformation into a llama, but this new outlook offered new insights into the richness of their narratives, and also into the depravity of his own heart. Rapunzel similarly had seen the lights of the annual festival for years, but by stepping into that part of her culture to know it better, she gained a deeper insight into her own identity. This volume likewise invites the reader to revisit tales as old as 1937 to see these narratives anew; to consider the power of imagination and the extent to which the good and the beautiful, moral conviction and aesthetic allure, bespeak something of the deeper truths embedded within the background of Disney's celebrated narratives; and to approach a handful of these narratives on their own terms yet in the light of an enfolding tale as old as time itself.

Notes

[1] See Mark Pinsky, *The Gospel According to* Disney (Louisville: Westminster John Knox Press, 2004), 4-9.

[2] Ibid., 240-61.

[3] Annalee R. Ward, *Mouse Morality: The Rhetoric of Disney Animated Film* (Austin: University of Texas Press, 2002), 135.

[4] Jeremy E. Scarbrough with Pat Sawyer, *Disney as Doorway to Apologetic Dialogue* (Houston: Moral Apologetics Press, 2023).

[5] E.g., the depiction of crows in *Dumbo*, stereotypical caricatures of Native Americans (*Peter Pan*) and East Asian peoples (*The Aristocats* and *Lady and the Tramp*). Disney animators could have certainly made some better choices along the way. There is also some controversy regarding the choice of a monkey for the jazz-loving King Louis (*The Jungle Book*).

[6] William Irwin, "Writing for the Reader: A Defense of Philosophy and Pop Culture Books," *Essays Philos* 15 (2014): 178-79.

[7] Francis A. Schaeffer, "The God Who is There," in Francis A. Schaeffer Trilogy (Wheaton: Crossway Books, 1990), 144.

[8] Richard M. Sherman and Robert B. Sherman, "The Age of Not Believing," *Bedknobs and Broomsticks*, dir. Robert Stevenson (Burbank, CA: Walt Disney Studios, 1971).

[9] Howard Ashman and Alan Menken, "Something There," in *Beauty and the Beast*, dir. Gary Trousdale and Kirk Wise (Burbank, CA: Walt Disney Studios, 1991).

Part 1

IMAGINATIVE AND AESTHETIC APOLOGETICS:

Exploring Disney's Moral Magic and Narrative Power

1

Imagination, the Incarnation, and the Moral Power of Storytelling

Holly Ordway

W hat does the phrase "Moral theology" suggest? Probably something serious and stern; perhaps abstract and philosophical; certainly, it points to things weighty and intellectual. What comes to mind with 'Walt Disney'? For most people, very different ideas: frivolity, play, humor, silliness. To say that something is "Mickey Mouse" is to say that it's trivial, amateurish. Here we might well observe that the modern cultural disconnect between reason and imagination is fully presented. Morality is considered a serious and important adult concern, but entertainment, especially children's entertainment, is a secondary, even inconsequential, matter. This volume challenges such a division, and explores the ways in which moral theology sheds light on children's entertainment, and vice versa.

Disney animated films have been part of the childhood experience of multiple generations by now. The subject matter of the very first of these films, *Snow White* (1937), reminds us of an important point: that most of these films can be described as being, in some form, *fairy-tales*: that is, stories that draw us into another world, that evoke wonder (as well as terror and delight), that have a flavor of fantasy and magic, even without overt fantastic elements.[1] Fairy-tales have something elemental about them; most importantly for our purposes, they play a significant role in human moral development.

As G.K. Chesterton explains, the monsters and frightening events of fairytales are to be valued, not avoided. Children's fears, he says, are perfectly reasonable:

> They are alarmed at this world, because this world is a very alarming place. They dislike being alone because it is verily and indeed an awful idea to be alone. Barbarians fear the unknown for the same reason that Agnostics worship it – because it is a fact.... Fairy tales do not give the child his first idea of bogey. What fairy tales give the child is his first clear idea of the possible defeat of bogey.[2]

Cruelty and evil are not new concepts for any human being, of any age. That human beings have the power to hurt each other, whether by word or action, is something that every child learns very quickly. But that is, as Chesterton puts it, simply a fact about the world. How do we respond to that fact? In *One Hundred and One Dalmatians*, is Cruella de Vil, who steals the Dalmatian puppies in order to make a luxurious fur coat out of them, a figure to be admired for her initiative and sense of fashion, or despised for her cruelty and indifference to others? The story of St. George and the dragon teaches us not just that the dragon can be killed, but that it should be.

Stories have special power to move us. Indeed, arguably one of the greatest animated films ever made, *Toy Story*, puts this identity right in the title. From *Frozen* to *Finding Nemo*, *Aristocats* to *Aladdin*, *Peter Pan* to *Pinocchio*—these stories allow viewers to experience sympathy or dislike for characters; nervousness, suspense, relief, joy, or sorrow at the resolution of a plot. In a film, our reactions to the narrative and characters are strengthened and shaped by the visual elements and, very importantly, the music, as well. A film draws us in, gets us involved, on an experiential level.

Our response to the images we see and the stories we experience is an innate part of being human; people are not, and never will be, and indeed cannot be, purely rational and un-affected by emotion. (Indeed, if they were, they would have ceased to be fully human.) Stories have the power to shape our emotions, to teach us what we should feel about the various experiences and characters we are likely to encounter in the world. If there is such a thing as objective morality, then our emotions should be ordered to the right ends: we should love what is good, and fear what will truly harm us.[3] Stories—and especially the clear-cut, vividly told, elemental stories that we call 'fairy-tales'—both evoke emotion and help to orient that emotion toward certain ends.

And here we begin to see the reason why stories, whether in written or visual form, are so important to the moral theologian. Do we love what we ought to love, and fear what we ought to fear? Do we both know what is good, and love it? When emotion and intellect are in line, rather than at odds, with each other, and both are oriented toward the proper ends, then it becomes easier for the will to direct action toward the good.

Here we should pause, however, for a brief methodological consideration. Insofar as stories convey ideas related to moral theology, they do so in a way different from direct argument. Narratives convey meaning, but they do so in an imaginative, not a propositional, mode. Therefore, in order to analyze what that meaning is, and to consider whether it is true or false, presented well or presented badly, we need to approach the narrative on its own terms.

Etymologically, 'analysis' means the 'loosening' or 'breaking up' of a topic into smaller parts for study. We take a thing apart, to understand what it is made of, and how it works. This is a necessary and valuable process; we can learn a great deal from analytical study. But the technique of loosening-up, of taking-apart, has limits; it cannot tell us everything; in fact, it can sometimes prevent us from seeing the very thing we seek. Roger Lancelyn Green once remarked, regarding J. R. R. Tolkien's story *Smith of Wootton Major*, that "To seek for the meaning is to cut open the ball in search of its bounce."[4] This is, of course, a poetic exaggeration: seeking to understand the meaning of a story is a perfectly legitimate endeavor, and indeed Tolkien himself wrote to another friend, Clyde Kilby, explaining some of the allegorical meanings of the story. Green's point is that certain types of critical approaches are reductive and destructive of the very thing they seek to understand. Statistical analysis, for instance, can tell us how many different words Tolkien used, and the frequency with which he used them; we could make tables and charts; but such an approach would in the end obscure more than it revealed about the literary art of the story under consideration.

As we embark upon the *analysis* of moral theology and the work of Walt Disney, we should first consider how it is that stories work, before we begin to tease apart any given story into its constituent elements. Doing so will allow us to see the way that those parts relate to the whole. The rest of this essay will address one aspect of that whole: *how* stories function to create that sense of connection which makes them so effective for the shaping of the moral sense.

Imagination and the Creation of Meaning

The first step is to briefly consider how the imagination works in the process of meaning-making. At the most basic level, the imagination is what allows us to conceive an image in our minds—what J. R. R. Tolkien calls "the mental power of image-making."[5] Imagination is most often associated with images that do not exist in the physical world: things that are *imaginary*. However, the formation of mental images of non-existent things—such as mermaids, superheroes, or flying elephants—is only one part of what the imagination does. In reality, the imagination is a fundamental human faculty that assimilates sensory data into images, upon which the intellect can then act.[6]

C. S. Lewis writes that "reason is the natural organ of truth; but imagination is the organ of meaning. Imagination, producing new metaphors or revivifying old, is not the cause of truth, but its condition."[7] Michael Ward explains that "Lewis defines the opposite of meaning as not error but nonsense. Things must rise up out of the swamp of nonsense into the realm of meaning if the imagination is to get any handle on them. Before something can be either true or false it must mean."[8] When we watch a film, our senses of sight and hearing bring us colors, shapes, sounds, and motion, and our imagination attempts to use this information to create meaningful images. If there has been a technological glitch and what our senses bring us is a mere jumble of noise and color, we will have the data, but it will be *nonsense*; our imagination will not be able to get a grip on it, and present it to the intellect. Likewise, if the images presented are so far outside our experience and knowledge that our imagination cannot make any connections, the data will remain nonsense, meaningless.

But if the imagination is able to discern that the data is *not* nonsense, then, drawing on memory and intellectual knowledge, it will shape the data into meaningful images to present to the intellect. Only then can the intellect make judgments about that image: for instance, whether it could, or could not exist in real life; or whether the actions presented are, or are not, morally good. The reason cannot make judgments unless it has something meaningful to judge, and it is the imagination that constructs the meaning. The imagination, then, is an active and vital human faculty; and it is a necessary element in the process of making moral judgments. We must be able to perceive *that* a given action is meaningful, before we can begin to discern the extent to which it is good, or bad. As Ward points out, "Even a lie means something, and a lie understood as a lie can be most instructive. Only nonsensical things mean nothing."[9]

We have seen, then, that the imagination is an essential element of meaning-making, and that meaning is essential for the development of a moral sense. Imagination is a constructive, synthesizing faculty, which provides the reason with material that can be analyzed and judged. With this context for our exploration established, we turn now from the role of the imagination simply, to the role of stories as an imaginative form for the shaping of the moral sense.

Many people today are deeply suspicious about meta-narratives: any claim to the overall meaning or significance of our experiences. Faced with such claims, they will often retreat into relativistic responses: 'That's true for you, but not for me.' It is difficult to engage with underlying moral claims in this context. Here we should consider that although *meta*-narratives often provoke a response of rejection, *narratives* can provide a non-threatening means to present moral truth-claims. In the rest of this essay, we will consider some aspects of the incarnational quality of storytelling that make this possible.

Embodiment

As we have already noted, stories have the power to evoke emotion—and emotions are part of the experience of being embodied. When we feel, it is not possible to separate our mind from our body. Sorrow may be experienced as a tightness in the throat, a knot in the stomach, or a heaviness in the limbs; love, as a feeling of lightness, the heart beating faster, a thrill in the nerves, or a feeling of warmth. This emotional-physical response points us toward what is, for our purposes, the key feature of stories: that they are *incarnational*. As Shakespeare puts it in *A Midsummer Night's Dream*, "imagination bodies forth / The forms of things unknown, the poet's pen / Turns them to shapes, and gives to airy nothing / A local habitation and a name."[10] The key word is 'bodies forth.'

A story *embodies* an idea; it particularizes it, gives it form in specific images, characters, settings, and events. This sort of embodiment can happen in forms that are not specifically narrative, such as drama or lyric poetry, but it happens most fully in stories. Expressed propositionally, an idea remains abstract, and could potentially give rise to an enormous range of stories. When the idea is incarnated into a story, it becomes specific and therefore engaging; we experience this character, this location, this sequence of events, these colors and shapes. By the very limitation inherent in these specific choices of story, characters, and images, the truth becomes tangible, more accessible, and potentially transformative.

For instance, the idea of 'the love of parents for their children' could be discussed propositionally, without reference to any specific fathers, mothers, or children. But in *One Hundred and One Dalmatians*, we have a specific set of parents: the dogs Pongo and Perdita, and a specific litter of puppies, who face a very specific danger that calls forth the parents' heroic rescue. A story is in this way *incarnational*, in that the Imagination 'bodies forth' an idea into a particular story or image.

The specificity of a story means that there are many different ways to explore a given concept. Analytical language gives precision and concision to a concept, which is helpful and often necessary for clarity. But those very qualities can lead to oversimplification, or a failure to see the *meaning* of the concept: to use C. S. Lewis's expression from "Meditation in a Toolshed," if we only look *at* something, and not *along* it, in a participatory way, we will have only a partial picture. So, the very multiplicity of potential narrative expressions of an idea, which might seem like imprecision is, in fact, part of the value of story in coming to a full understanding of an idea.

We could say, as a propositional statement, that "the maturation involves understanding one's own identity and place in the community." What does that mean? We might consider how it unfolds in *The Sword in the Stone*, *The Little Mermaid*, *The Lion King*, *Pinocchio*, or *The Incredibles* – all very different ways of exploring the topic. And as we consider the topic from these different, embodied points of view, we will very probably find that the stories come to different conclusions about what is necessary for growth or valuable for identity. These insights, in turn, will help us to bring more nuance and depth to our understanding of our propositional statement. What does it mean to properly mature? How does the individual find the right place in the community? What is a healthy individual, and a healthy community? These questions cannot be resolved by any individual story, because each story is, as it were, an embodiment of a specific point of view and set of assumptions about what is good and healthy for an individual and a community. What the stories can do, and do well, is to bring those points of view to life and allow us to experience them — and perhaps to clarify what we mean.

The experience of being embodied includes the experience of inhabiting time: we experience our lives as a narrative, a sequence. The basic expectation of human beings is that our lives have a beginning, a middle, and an end that relate to each other in an intelligible way; as a result, we are highly responsive to having meaning expressed in a narrative form. In fact, the mental experience of 'making meaning' from the narrative elements that unfold in a story ("Oh, so that's why....") echoes and reinforces the ongoing discovery of meaning in our own lives. By providing a story that moves through time and takes the reader with the characters on the journey, a film becomes an incarnational experience: one that resonates with the viewer's own experience in living life, and one that invites connections between story and lived experience. We can see ourselves and other people in the characters and situations of the story, thus exploring moral ideas and challenges in a way that is engaging, yet safe because it does not directly impinge upon our own lives.

One key feature of narrative in this regard is it allows the viewer to vicariously experience the effect of moral choices. The depiction of meaningful choices, with their accompanying consequences, is one way that films can be *moral* without being *moralistic*: that is, to provide an embodied presentation of a moral truth, rather than a propositional statement of it.

For instance, in *Cars*, the young racecar Lightning McQueen is on track to become the first rookie to win the coveted Piston Cup. But in the crucial race itself, he gives up his certain victory in order to push another car, who has been sideswiped and crashed, over the finish line, so that he will be able to finish his last race and retire with dignity. Here we see real self-sacrifice: even with a race-winning future ahead of him, he can never again have the prestige of being the first rookie to win the Piston Cup. Similarly, in *Toy Story 4*, the cowboy toy Woody gives up his voice box to help another doll have a chance to achieve her dream of having an owner. The fact that this doll is unlikeable and has earlier tried to take the voice-box from Woody by force makes the scene all the more powerful: it embodies real forgiveness on his part, and real self-sacrifice, for he gives up something that has been part of who he is in all the films. It is a genuinely discomforting experience for the viewer. Both of these stories embody the idea of self-sacrifice in a way that is powerful precisely because it is specific to *these* characters, in *these* situations, making *these* choices with their consequences.

The more vividly realized and 'embodied' the world of the story, the more likely it is that the viewer will want to 'inhabit' that story and experience it imaginatively. Again, here we can see some of the appeal of 'tie-in' merchandise: dolls and toys that allow the child viewer to continue to have that story embodied, present in their lives, even though the film has an ending. The desire to revisit a story is natural: if it is richly meaningful, there is always more to be understood, more to be engaged with. A story that conveys truth and beauty will show more of its truth and beauty each time the reader comes to it, and in a different way, because the viewer will be different, coming to the text with new experiences, different moods, different questions.

Narrative and Moral Theology

Since films, in particular, are so vivid — and since children tend to watch animated films repeatedly — they can even become a form of vicarious experience themselves. Moral qualities are embodied and lived out; we observe what they look like, draw conclusions about whether these qualities are attractive or not, and what they might be like in our own lives. All villains, if they are effectively presented, have something attractive about them. The Wicked Queen in *Snow White* is elegant and powerful; Gaston from *Beauty and the Beast* is handsome. But as we see the way that their stories unfold, we also see, in clear terms, the effects of vanity, cruelty, arrogance, and egotism on other characters whom we have come to admire. In this way, the film both evokes emotions and allows for a response to the story that involves the intellect, as we make judgments about the characters' actions and the situation.

The moral sense is formed (or deformed) by discovering what sorts of actions are praised or punished, rewarded or ridiculed, presented as attractive or unattractive. In this process, the imagination is always working to create meaning with whatever materials are at hand, whether that material is from personal, direct experience, or from imaginative engagement. But some materials are richer than others, and can more immediately, fully, and robustly become meaningful. The arts are particularly significant in this regard because a film, a story, a poem, a painting, or a piece of music is deliberately designed by the artist to convey a certain meaning to the audience. Depending on the artist's intent, the nature of the content, and the context in which they are received, some stories present ideas and values that our fully formed moral sense would judge to be true and good, and others that we would judge to be false and harmful—and here we enter the rightful realm of analysis. As we do so, we should bear in mind that our analysis itself depends on the story itself being meaningful. Whatever we conclude about the moral truth-value of a film, we must reckon with it as story.

Notes

[1] See J. R. R. Tolkien's seminal essay "On Fairy-stories" for an in-depth exploration of the workings of fairytales and fantasy.

[2] G. K. Chesterton, "The Red Angel," in *Tremendous Trifles*, Project Gutenberg, http://www.gutenberg.org/ebooks/8092.

[3] See C. S. Lewis's *The Abolition of Man*. One of the questions for our day is, in fact, the question of whether there is such a thing as rightly ordered emotions. Lewis was prophetic in recognizing that those who would deny objective morality in general will often do so by attempting to break the connection between emotion and objective reality.

[4] Roger Lancelyn Green, qtd in J. R. R. Tolkien, *The Letters of J. R. R. Tolkien*, ed. Humphrey Carpenter (London: HarperCollins, 2006), 388.

[5] J. R. R.Tolkien, "On Fairy-stories," in *Tolkien On Fairy-stories*, ed. Verlyn Flieger and Douglas A. Anderson (London: HarperCollins, 2014), 59.

[6] See further, Holly Ordway, *Apologetics and the Christian Imagination: An Integrated Approach to Defending the Faith* (Steubenville: Emmaus Road, 2017).

[7] C. S. Lewis, "Bluspels and Flalansferes: A Semantic Nightmare," in *Selected Literary Essays*, ed. Walter Hooper (Cambridge: Cambridge University Press, 1969), 265.

[8] Michael Ward, "The Good Serves the Better and Both the Best: C. S. Lewis on Imagination and Reason in Apologetics," in *Imaginative Apologetics: Theology, Philosophy and the Catholic Tradition*, ed. Andrew Davison (Grand Rapids: Baker Academic, 2012), 61-62.

[9] Ibid., 62.

[10] William Shakespeare, *A Midsummer Night's Dream*, act 5, sc. 1.

2

Disney's Live-Action Animated Musical: A "Satisfactual" Glimpse of Transcendence

Joel W. Paulus

Walking along a wooded path on a gentle sunny day, Uncle Remus sings about the goodness he senses around him, but he is not alone. His joy is soon shared by a group of animated animals who join him in song. While such a scene would not play out in one's local park, film allows for such interaction between two worlds. As an innovator and leader in the field of animation, the Walt Disney Company stands out for effectively integrating 2-D animation with live action in memorable musical numbers. The "Zip-A-Dee-Do-Dah" scene from *Song of the South* (1946), which found 1986 to be its last US screen release, is still widely known by multiple generations. Similar scenes appear in other Disney films such as: *The Three Caballeros* (1944), *Mary Poppins* (1964), and *Bedknobs and Broomsticks* (1971).

The whimsical nature of these scenes, while entertaining on their own, are depictions of two distinct worlds combining without apparent conflict. A similar phenomenon occurs in scripture where the earthly and the heavenly—two distinct worlds—temporarily adjoin, blending in space and time without apparent conflict. Examining musical animated pieces in four Disney films offers an analogous glimpse of transcendence and morality between the real world and a hyper-real world which the character in question cannot reach on their own but must be taken there by faith through a mediator.[1] Disney's blended musical numbers resonate with the human condition of longing for more than the world presently offers by presenting a vision of something beyond the audience's present reality.

Is the appeal of blending live action with animation merely spectacle, or could it resonate with a core human desire? The Bible suggests an answer in its routine depiction of two worlds coming together, namely, a real world affected by sin, entropy, and physical limitations interacting coherently with a hyper-real world seemingly unaffected by those things. A key difference is that Disney stories do not have historical or philosophical moorings while the Bible has historical roots with verifiable people and places.[2] However, the commonality they share, the blending of two worlds, evokes something of a mystery to the human mind. Norman Geisler points out that this type of mystery invites reverence and awe, differing from the type of mystery that promotes solving a problem.[3] Likewise, the mystical nature of transcendence is to be enjoyed for what it is. Uncle Remus, who enjoys interacting with his animated surroundings rather than questioning it, depicts this well.

The Disney Animated Musical

The animated Disney musical is a form of musical theatre, namely, a story performed through dialogue, song, and dance. While any drama, music, and dance performance are singularly powerful communicative art forms, musical theatre productions layer all three in a sequence that accentuates the intermingling of reality and a heightened reality. Singing and dancing are activities in the real world, yet when characters break into song and dance these actions serve as a bridge between the real world and a hyper-real world. When Mary Poppins begins to sing "A Spoonful of Sugar" it signals that a real-world activity, namely tidying up one's room, will become a heightened experience gesturing to a reality beyond the character's current state.[4]

Music's expressive power reaches the heart and mind beyond the use of words. Emotional expressiveness in instrumental music affects the soul crossing cultural and linguistic boundaries. Melodies communicate in non-discursive ways. Words take on a heightened sense of expression when combined with music. Music allows for revelation and enhancement of a character's state of being introducing a hyper-realistic element of the musical theatre.

Disney's animated musicals employ the elements of musical theatre effectively in cinema. Animation allows for greater range of possibilities than live performance since animated characters are not bound to laws that govern the real-world. The animated worlds Disney produces are fictional, yet not completely un-real. They share the reality that people inhabit and know. Reality is represented in the animation, but the freedom of the animator exceeds the realm of possibilities — the freedom possible in the real world. Physical laws and properties such as gravity, color, and proportion are not bound in the animated worlds, yet resemble the actual world. Through animation, one can fly or breathe underwater without assistance.

Within the world of animation, physical laws find suspension from real world behavior. In animation characters and objects naturally bound by gravity can fly, animals can talk or even sing and dance. Morality, however, does not change between the worlds. Interactions between the characters, whether live-action or animated, operate within an objective moral standard. This shared element makes crossing between live-action and animation workable. An ethical standard makes sense of character and plot continuity in a radically different environment. Disney's crossing of live-action and animation in musical numbers demonstrate ethical transcendence and continuity between two worlds.

Live-Action Animation

With the 1944 release of *The Three Caballeros*, Disney presents the first combination of live action and animation in a feature film. Donald Duck and José Carioca interact with Aurora Miranda and her band in a musical sequence crossing between the real and animated worlds.[5] The whimsical number does not further the plot. However, this technique produces a convincing scene where two-dimensional animated characters interact with three-dimensional reality.

Such spectacle serves imagination and possibilities as one's mind entertains the blending of the animated and live worlds. In the live world, blending of animated characters with people is impossible, but through the art of the animated musical, Disney characters interact with humans with ease. Audiences delight in the notion, opening the mind to desire and enjoy a hyper-reality. The entertainment factor carries a sense of longing to experience what is being imagined.

Desire may be stirred in an audience in the sense the way C. S. Lewis describes longing for a place he's never been.[6] The longing Lewis writes of is a kind of desire for something not yet experienced, which prompts the individual to ponder why that is. According to the Bible, people are created to experience more than the fragmented joys and anxieties of this life. Since sin entered the world, a tension persists between the fallen-ness and the desire for goodness. Helmut Thielicke writes of this tension between what "is" and what "ought" to be.[7] Human beings face the reality of sin in contrast to a moral standard. The desire for what ought to be is hindered by the way things *are* in the fallen state. The desire, however, serves as the directive toward that other world where people are predestined to be morally complete. Musicals where live actors enter an animated, hyper-real world speaks to the desire in people to experience something beyond the limits of this world. While this desire for the intermingling of two worlds appears on a subtle level in *The Three Caballeros*, a clear example may be found in *Song of the South*.

Song of the South

One of the most iconic moments in the cannon of Disney musical animation happens when Uncle Remus bursts into an animated world while singing "Zip-A-Dee-Do-Dah" in *Song of the South*.[8] This film is not without controversy and the points surrounding its history is beyond the scope of this subject. Since this aspect of the film has been treated in other works, focus is strictly on the technical effect of combining live action with animation. The purpose of introducing this scene is not to dismiss the elements of the overall film raising issue since its release in 1947.[9] This musical sequence is one of the most technically innovative scenes, certainly for the time in which it was produced, and the effect still holds up over seventy-five years later.

The scene begins in the real world, during the night hours, when Uncle Remus tells a story to some children. He sets up the narrative with dialogue but when he sings the first note, everything becomes bright and colorful in a flash of light. At this point Uncle Remus appears in an animated world. He still addresses the children throughout changing from the real world to hyper-real world. As the story element continues, however, the animated world begins interacting with him. The singing animals and Uncle Remus carry on as if this is a normal occurrence.

During the movie's finale there is a reprise of the "Zip-Ah-Dee-Doo-Dah." With the introduction of music and singing, characters from the hyper-real world now enter the real world. At this point in the story, the children are interacting with the animated characters as if anthropomorphic animals were nothing unusual. Uncle Remus sees this, expressing delight and surprise while declaring through song that seeing the children interacting with the animated characters is true, actual, and "satisfactual." This indicates that the two worlds are now closer together than at first. Uncle Remus, originally a mediator into the animated world, contrasts with the end where the animated world is interacting with the children. This displays a glimpse of transcendence of how what is good and right can bind the real and hyper-real together. The end times (eschaton) will see the heavenlies and the created world come together.

Mary Poppins

In *Mary Poppins*,[10] two musical numbers share a scene where live action and animated worlds commingle. Mary takes Michael and Jane to the park where Bert is finishing some chalk drawings at the entrance. Bert introduces the idea of traveling to the various places he has drawn on the sidewalk. Suggesting they enter a chalk drawing Burt performs different gestures before attempting to jump in without success. Marry Poppins takes their hands and jumps in the drawing with ease. Mary acts as mediator bringing Bert and the children into the hyper-real environment they could never reach on their own.

The action of jumping with Mary into the chalk drawing is that which brings the real and hyper-real together. The world they now temporarily inhabit is such a heightened experience, that their expression of it goes beyond mere dialog. In the song, "Jolly Holiday,"[11] Bert and Mary explore the new environment while singing about one another's virtues, showing moral consistency in the hyper-real environment.

The characters, while inside the drawing, ride a carousel from which the horses detach riding them through the animated world. This event departs from real-world physical laws, yet the moral law continues. As they enter a horse race, rules of good sportsmanship apply as it plays out in the hyper-real world. Once Mary wins the race on her carousel horse, she is asked how she feels about winning. This prompts the song "Supercalifragilisticexpialidocious"[12] in which Mary and Bert express (through song and dance) how to communicate a situation so good, it takes something more than the ordinary means to convey it. The heightened experience in the drawing is brought short by the intervention of foul weather. Rain brings them back to the real world as the chalk washes away. The stark contrast between the hyper-real superlative and the fallen real world provides a glimpse of the way things could be compared to the way things are.

The desire and delight for the world of the hyper-real is carried into the real world. The children are excited about the possibility of revisiting the hyper-real, yet Mary, who took them there, is more concerned that they focus on the real world in which they presently find themselves. The experience for the children was transcendent, in providing a glimpse of what *could* be. The rain, metaphorically, re-introduced the inability for the characters in the real world to overcome it. The desire for being in another place that is free of trouble speaks to the desire for a goodness that is in alignment with the way things ought to be.

Bedknobs and Broomsticks

A seamless portrayal of live action and animation may be found in the 1971 Disney release *Bedknobs and Broomsticks*.[13] Three children, Charlie, Carrie, and Paul are sent to live temporarily with Eglantine Price near the coast in Pepperidge Eye. One night the children discover Miss Price flying on a broom and surmise that she is a witch. In order to secure the children's confidence, Miss Price offers them a traveling spell through a brass bed knob in the possession of the youngest child, Paul. Only Paul can unlock the bed knob's ability to make the bed travel anywhere. He then is the mediator, along with the bed, that transports the characters to an animated world.

The characters search for a spell engraved on the Star of Astoroth. Paul has a book about the Isle of Naboombu, a place ruled by animals, where the star is thought to be. Paul uses the bed knob to take everyone to Naboombu where they enter an animated world. An animated bear fishes them out of the lagoon, and attempts throwing them back upon their asking to see the king. Paul appeals to his book which says *anybody* can see the king; and that's the law. The bear acknowledges the law and obliges the humans, thus indicating a standard of rule in this hyper-reality.

To establish good terms with King Leonidas, who wears the star, Professor Browne agrees to referee a soccer game. The king cheats his way to victory and by allowing the win, Professor Browne gets close enough to Leonidas to take the star. Leonidas becomes angry discovering the star has been stolen, and chases after the human characters. In the animated world, stealing is recognized as a moral transgression, demonstrating universal moral standards remain consistent between both worlds.

Professor Browne places the star in his handkerchief for safe keeping, but when Miss Price asks for it upon their return to the real world, it vanishes—much to Professor Browne's surprise. Miss Price consoles him saying, "I should have realized that it would be quite impossible to take an object from one world into another." The words are revealed by Paul from his book about the island. In contrast to transcendent morality between the Island of Naboombu and the real world, this demonstrates division between the two. The object itself cannot cross between the two worlds, but immaterial moral principles can.

Theologically Speaking

Transcendent experience and objective morality are two aspects exemplified by combining live action with animation. Crossing the created world and the supernatural world resembles crossing live-action into the hyper-real animated world, a glimpse of transcendent experience. Biblical instances of the supernatural and created world interacting include God walking and talking with Adam in the Garden of Eden, and when God speaks with Moses through a burning bush. The presence of God and the heavenlies participates symbolically through the design of the wilderness tabernacle and temple. Jesus, who is fully God and fully human, fulfills the law and is the epitome of heaven on earth. He equally participates in both worlds and repairs the breach between them. The transfiguration recorded in the Gospels offers an overt instance of blending the two worlds—the real world and a super-real world.[14] This may be said to be an intermingling of the created world and the supernatural world as Jesus reveals his Divinity.

Human experience of this two-world intermingling happens in a limited and temporary manner. Paul describes a man caught up to the third heaven.[15] He saw things that he could not explain, yet was able to interact with the environment, at least in a sensory way. The descriptions in the Bible of the supernatural interacting with the natural world are temporary events that reflect a desire for the fallen creation to have a restored relationship with the whole of God's Kingdom. This anticipates the time when God and humankind share the same space. Morality remains the similarity between the old creation and the new. The laws of the created order will be different as evidenced by glorified bodies in a redeemed environment, but the moral law stays the same between both worlds.

Notes

1 The use of transcendence here falls within the definition offered by Jeremy Begbie when he writes, "[T]ranscendent signals what lies 'beyond' something 'here'... [T]ranscendence is obviously a correlative or relational term; it presupposes a reality to be transcended, as well as some kind of limit or boundary to that reality." Jeremy Begbie, *Redeeming Transcendence in the Arts: Bearing Witness to the Triune God* (Grand Rapids: Eerdmans, 2018), 5.

2 For more information on this see Norman L. Geisler and William E. Nix, *A General Introduction to the Bible* (Chicago: Moody Press, 1986).

3 He goes on to say, "It would appear that there is a place for both the intellectual and the mystical." Norman Geisler, *Systematic Theology, vol. 2, God and Creation* (Minneapolis: Bethany House, 2003), 252.

4 Richard M. Sherman and Robert B. Sherman, "A Spoonful of Sugar," in *Mary Poppins* (1964).

5 *The Three Caballeros*, dir. Norman Ferguson, Clyde Geronimi, Jack Kinney, Bill Roberts, and Harold Young (Burbank, CA: Walt Disney Studios, 1944).

6 Lewis, C. S. *The Weight of Glory and Other Addresses* (San Francisco: HarperSanFrancisco, 2001), 29-31.

7 According to Thielicke, the world's fallenness involves not only the evils that human beings *do*, but also the idea that they have been *transplanted* into a place of good *and* evil, being *and* ought. Thus, there is no longer 'has' or 'is;' but only 'ought.' The struggle one faces between 'is' and 'ought' can only be overcome by a love that liberates and inclines one toward God's will. See Helmut Thielicke, *Theologische Ethik*, vol. 2, Part 1 (Tübingen: J. C. B. Mohr, 1955), 442.

8 Ray Gilbert and Allie Wrubel, "Zip-Ah-Dee-Doo-Dah," in *Song of the South*, dir. Harve Foster and Wilfred Jackson (Burbank, CA: Walt Disney Studios, 1947).

9 For more information, see Jim Korkis, *Who's Afraid of the Song of the South? And Other Forbidden Disney Stories* (Orlando: Theme Park Press, 2012).

[10] *Mary Poppins*, dir. Robert Stevenson (Burbank, CA: Walt Disney Studios, 1964).

[11] Richard M. Sherman and Robert B. Sherman, "Jolly Holiday," in *Mary Poppins* (1964).

[12] Richard M. Sherman and Robert B. Sherman, "Supercalifragilisticexpialidocious," in *Mary Poppins* (1964).

[13] *Bedknobs and Broomsticks*, dir. Robert Stevenson (Burbank, CA: Walt Disney Studios, 1971).

[14] Matt 17:1-8; Mark 9:2-8; Luke 9:28-36.

[15] 2 Cor. 12:4.

3

Beauty and the Beat

Doug Powell

When *Steamboat Willy* premiered on November 18, 1928, it was a Copernican Revolution in the world of animated film. Never before had events and character actions been synchronized to a musical soundtrack. For almost eight minutes the fusion of motion and music gave even the most absurd gags of the cartoon a reality that enabled the film to transcend being a kinetic comic strip and come alive to have a profound impact on the moviegoers. Over the next few years other Disney innovations such as color and the multiplane camera added to the reality of their animations, but they were merely technical advances. In addition to the technical triumph of *Steamboat Willy*, music became an important factor in the development of personality animation as well as a tool for advancing the narrative. Thoughts and emotions of characters were conveyed not only in expressions and body language, but in the music that accompanied them, which was just as descriptive as the drawings. Disney artists Frank Thomas and Ollie Johnston wrote, "The effect of absolutely everything being related to the musical beat became so well developed that, in the musical world, 'Mickey mousing' became the name for music that accented or echoed every action on the screen."[1]

When Walt[2] combined these and other advances to create the first feature-length animation, *Snow White* (1937), he continued to redefine and expand what music could do. According to Walt, "There's terrific power to music...[T]he minute you put music behind (these pictures) they have life and vitality they don't get in any other way."[3] He was also very intentional about how the music should be used. "The music has to supply something that would ordinarily be supplied with dialogue and a more gripping story."[4] Under Walt's direction, the film's three composers created leitmotifs—themes for each of the major characters—a technique borrowed from opera that was just starting to be used in the composition of film music and has since become standard practice in movies.

The queen's evil character is conveyed not only in her appearance, but in her menacing leitmotif. Snow White's leitmotif is melodious and innocent. The magic mirror's leitmotif is mysterious, while the Dwarfs' is playful. The leitmotifs serve as an interpretive grid woven into a soundtrack designed to articulate the story while evoking the appropriate emotional response. Walt's push for realism led him to create "a new way to use music—weave it into the story so somebody doesn't just burst into song."[5] In fact, the soundtrack is such an integral part of the film that less than one minute of its running time lacks a musical score, with the longest stretch of non-music lasting only twenty-two seconds. The result was an emotionally powerful experience that left many in the audience tearing up at a cartoon. And this was Walt's stated goal. "The most important aim of any of the fine arts is to get a purely emotional response from the beholder."[6]

Snow White became a template for the classic Disney movie. Although Walt continued to experiment and push the bounds of what the medium could do, *Pinocchio* (1940), *Fantasia* (1940), *Dumbo* (1941), and *Bambi* (1942) all employed the same techniques, creating a palette of tools that defined Disney movies and influenced the animated films that followed. But although animation styles changed, the use of music to tell the story as much as the drawing—making them almost inextricable—has remained a constant. It was such a unique aesthetic that composer Jerome Kern called Walt's approach to his soundtracks, "the 20th century's only important contribution to music."[7]

Kern's extravagant claim notwithstanding, Disney's employment of music is a main characteristic of its films. And one of the primary reasons is that it guides the audience in how to recognize virtue—or the lack of it—in the characters. When Ursula sings "Poor Unfortunate Souls" in *The Little Mermaid* (1988), or Scar sings "Be Prepared" in *The Lion King* (1994), or Oogie Boogie sings his song in *The Nightmare Before Christmas* (1993) there is no mistaking the evil intent of the villains. But singing villains in Disney films are rare, leaving the songs to the protagonists and their sidekicks.[8] Yet through leitmotifs and illustrative scores, the villain is never mistaken musically. Whether Shere Khan is prowling near Mowgli in *The Jungle Book*, man is in the forest in *Bambi*, Jafar is plotting in *Aladdin* (1992), or Hades is simmering in *Hercules* (1997), we know the villain through music, but not through songs they themselves sing. This musical moral distinction is most obvious in the closing sequence of *Fantasia*, where Walt intentionally juxtaposes Mussorgsky's *Night on Bald Mountain* (a tone poem depicting a witches' sabbath worshipping the devil) with Schubert's "Ave Maria" (based on a Catholic prayer) as a contrast of evil and good, with good triumphing in the end.

Music acts on an intuitive level, the whole creating something more than its components, giving it an ineffable quality that evokes emotions while communicating aesthetically. In fact, as a non-musician, Walt acted purely on intuition when he grasped what music could convey and leveraged it as a storytelling element. Characters who are good and desire truth are rendered with a harmonious melody in a major key, and resolve in a strong and obvious tonic. But characters who are evil or dubious are cast in minor keys, or with dissonance, instilling a sense of unease. The few instances villains are not depicted in darker tones are when they are employing sophistry, painting bad as good for the purpose of deceit, such as Honest John's "An Actor's Life for Me" in *Pinocchio*, or "Gaston" in *Beauty and the Beast*.

By designating beautiful music to good and true characters and situations while applying dark and unsettling music to malevolent characters and events, Walt appealed to an objective standard of beauty. Just as virtue and truth are clearly distinguished and universally recognized in Disney movies, so is beauty. Beauty is not relegated to the status of mere opinion, and the music would lose its logic apart from an objective standard of beauty because of what it signifies and how it communicates the narrative.

What makes this important is the implication it has. Although these standards are depicted in the fantastic worlds of animated films, they are part of our reality as well, and are indeed what makes us care about the story at all. The goodness, truth, and beauty we see in *Snow White* are the same not only in every other animated Disney film, but in the reality we live in as well. Disney's reliance on these standards—as well as the audience's intuitive recognition of their import—requires transcendent principles: an objective truth, goodness, and beauty that govern our world and give us reason to believe in a God who authored them.

To understand why, we first need to understand the nature of an objective standard. If someone claimed to be ten feet tall, you probably wouldn't believe them. If they insisted you prove them wrong, the best way to go about it would be to use a ruler to measure their height. When the ruler showed the person was not ten feet tall, you wouldn't mistrust the ruler, you would reject the claim. That is because the ruler is the standard by which distance is measured. The ruler is used to determine if the claim matches the object. If it does, the claim is true; if not, the claim is false. This is Aristotle's correspondence definition of truth.[9] Or, as wise Uncle Remus sings in *Song of the South* (1946), "It's the truth, it's actual. Everything is satisfactual."[10] In other words, truth is when a claim or a belief matches the way the world actually is. An objective standard is what we use to determine if there is a correspondence.

There is an interesting relationship between the true and the good such that when you have one, you have the other. When our beliefs correspond with the way the world is, then we have truth. That being the case, it means our minds are functioning properly, working as they were designed to do, which is good. And the result of proper intellectual function is a benefit, which is also good. On the Christian view, because God is sovereign over all things and makes them what they are, everything that is true and good has God as its ultimate source. Both truth and goodness are linked by God's nature.

Where does beauty fit in to this? Imagine your favorite Disney film animated with stick figures in environments of line drawings accompanied by a soundtrack composed of a single note. Same exact story. It's true in the sense that the drawings really exist and reflect in a fundamental way the nature of the world. It's good in the sense that the animation is done with such excellent craftsmanship that the characters move fluidly and create the illusion of life-like interaction in that world. It functions as animation.

With that in mind, think about that same Disney film in the way it was released. They both reflect reality, and they are both functionally sound. In other words, both are true and good. They tell the same story. So, what does the Disney version have that the stick-figure version lacks? What makes people watch the Disney version repeatedly when they would never be interested in watching the stick-figure version?

The answer is that the Disney version has something excellent about it that the stick-figure version does not. And that excellence is pleasing to us. The excellence doesn't make the story any truer or the animation function better from a technical standpoint. The excellence we intuit isn't necessary for it to function as an animation. However, the excellence does attract our attention, and even commands it because we get such pleasure from it. This excellence we are recognizing is what we call beauty. In fact, when we try to think of someone standing before a clear example of beauty such as the Grand Canyon and not apprehending its beauty, we do not think there is no beauty in the Grand Canyon; rather, we think there is something wrong the person who can't see it. In fact, its beauty is so self-evident that Walt created two shorts about what one called "nature's masterpiece": the Donald Duck cartoon *Grand Canyonscope* (1954), and the Oscar-winning, live-action *Grand Canyon* (1958).

Beauty, then, is a kind of excellence that is pleasing to our senses and is not necessary to how something works. This brings us to the old saying that "beauty is in the eye of the beholder." But is something beautiful simply because it is pleasing? The answer is *no*.

If beauty was in the eye of the beholder then the concept of beauty would lose its meaning. When someone called something beautiful, they would not be saying anything about the object, only about their opinion of the object. Think of it this way: when the evil queen in Snow White asks the mirror on the wall who the fairest in the land is, she is not asking the genie in the mirror his opinion. She is asking for an evaluation based on an objective standard. That is precisely what upsets her when she is not named the fairest. Otherwise, the queen would simply dismiss the judgment by saying, "Well, that's just *your* opinion."

How do we determine if something is beautiful or not? We all have an intuition that gives us the ability to recognize beauty. But being pleased by something we see or hear is not enough to call it beautiful. We can always take pleasure in ugly things. That is why we also have to develop that intuition and nurture it so that it matures. And we do this through experience and education. This is no different than the intuition we all possess about right and wrong. We can always take pleasure in bad and wrong things. But part of growing up and maturing is developing that intuition so that we can better recognize what is right and order our lives around it. To do that we need experience with it and education about it. To say that beauty is in the eye of the beholder confuses an opinion about something with the thing itself.

Interestingly, what is considered beautiful in one culture or society is often different from another culture or society. Some offer this as evidence that beauty cannot be objective. They say that if beauty was objective then there would be much more similarity from culture to culture. They say the difference in what is considered beautiful from culture to culture shows that each culture creates its own standard of beauty, therefore it cannot be objective.

There are two problems with this view. The first is that a disagreement about something does not mean there is no right answer. If you were playing a sport with some friends and you disagreed about the score, would that mean there is no actual score, no objective standard of scorekeeping? Obviously not. It would merely show that there was a disagreement about the score. Just because there is a difference in what is beautiful in different cultures does not mean there is no objective beauty.

The other problem is that objective beauty does not mean things must look or sound in only one certain way. Think about chocolate again. How many kinds of chocolate are there? A great many! Dark chocolate, milk chocolate, white chocolate, orange chocolate, cherry chocolate, mole, to name a few. Does the fact there are difference instances of chocolate mean there is no standard for chocolate? No, it means there is a variety of chocolate. Chocolate can appear in all sorts of different ways and still be chocolate. Or think about morality again. How many things are morally good? Telling the truth, helping those in need, compassion, love: it is hard to even think about how you would name them all. But does that mean there is no objective moral standard? Again, the answer is no. These examples show that there is great variety in how that objective standard applies to the world. And the same with beauty. There are countless beautiful things in this world, and the thing that unites them is an objective standard of beauty.

This is where personal taste comes in. Beauty is not in the eye of the beholder, but personal taste is. Just because objective beauty exists does not mean you cannot prefer one instance of beauty over another. Just as experiences of goodness and beauty vary, so too do personalities. No two people are exactly the same in every way. Our likes and dislikes are an important part of what make us individuals. The existence of objective beauty does not mean that everything should look the same or sound the same and that we should all like the same things. But we should be able to recognize and acknowledge beauty even when it is not our cup of tea. Preferring one instance of beauty to the another doesn't mean denying the beauty of the other, only that it does not suit your taste. The beautiful things in this world are united by an objective standard of beauty.

Thinkers such as Plato, Augustine, Thomas Aquinas, Jonathan Edwards, and C. S. Lewis are but a short list of the philosophers who have similarly argued for objective beauty, and many philosophers throughout history have insisted that objective beauty points unavoidably to the nature of a personal God—and is particularly powerful evidence for the God of the Bible. Although they approach the argument in different ways, the basic shape of the case is the same.

Objective standards are not the kinds of things that change. They are tools we use to evaluate or measure things, and a ruler that changes is not a ruler at all. Particular facts, such as whether Pinocchio is a boy or a puppet, might change from being true to false because of a change in circumstance, but truth itself does not change; he is one or the other. The same is true for beauty. Particular things might go from being beautiful to not beautiful, but the objective standard of beauty itself does not change. And like goodness and truth, it is measured in quality, not quantity. They have no limits. There is not even a point in time where they did not exist. If there were, then there would be a time when truth or goodness did not exist, which is impossible. Objective standards necessarily exist because of the impossibility of the contrary.

The source of goodness, truth, and beauty is personal since it provides the tools for how we comprehend and evaluate the world and our experience in it. But is this personal source a part of the world or separate from it? If it was a part of the world it would be finite since the world came into being and is always changing. The person, therefore, must be separate from the world, or transcendent. What kind of person is infinite, unchanging, and transcendent? That is a big part of the classic definition of God.

There is no evidence that Walt Disney himself articulated the source of objective beauty in this way, and his Congregational faith seemed nominal at best and most likely didn't provide for him the structure of the argument made above. However, given his use of music to connect goodness, truth, and beauty, he does appear to have intuitively grasped that these principles are objective standards.

He unwittingly proved that when he previewed *Steamboat Willy* five months before its premier to test out his theory of the impact of synchronized sound. Walt and the four others who made up Disney studios at the time invited their wives and girlfriends to the showing. The soundtrack had not been recorded yet, so as the animation was projected, Walt and the others performed the music and sound effects to the best of their abilities. Ub Iwerks, the principal animator, said, "I never saw such a reaction in an audience in my life...The scheme worked perfectly. The sound itself gave the illusion of something emanating directly from the screen."[11] It was Walt who brought the animation to life while at the same time being transcendent from it. He was the transcendent source, mirroring the creator/creation distinction foundational to the biblical worldview.

The truth is that Pinocchio was never more self-deceived than when he sang, "I've got no strings to hold me down."[12] He is correct that strings do not hold him down. However, he is self-deceived if he believes he's got no strings to hold him *up*—the strings of goodness, truth, and beauty. The reality so highly sought by Walt in his animated films resulted in a paradigm that communicates the same truths about God's world as the world they reflect, regardless of whether that was his intention.

Notes

[1] Frank Thomas and Ollie Johnston, *The Illusion of Life: Disney Animation* (New York: Abbeville Press, 1981), 288.

[2] In this essay, "Walt" refers to the man, while "Disney" refers to the company—a helpful distinction borrowed from: Neal Gabler, *Walt Disney: The Triumph of an American Imagination* (New York: Knopf, 2006).

[3] James Bohn, *Music in Disney's Animated Features: Snow White and the Seven Dwarfs to The Jungle Book* (Jackson: University Press of Mississippi, 2017), 106.

[4] Ibid., 106.

[5] Gabler, 192.

[6] Ibid., 172.

[7] Christopher Finch, *The Art of Walt Disney: From Mickey Mouse to the Magic Kingdoms and Beyond* (New York: Harry N. Abrams, 1973), 124.

[8] In a conversation on January 31, 2020, Mike Narwoki, co-creator of Veggie Tales, told me that he had received complaints from parents about "The Bunny Song" from the *Rack, Shack and Benny* episode. Apparently, kids loved the song so much they sang it for fun, thereby embracing the very opposite of the moral lesson of the show.

[9] Aristotle, *Metaphysics* 4.7.1. [Not to be confused with Aristotle Bolt, antagonist of *Escape to Witch Mountain* (1975)].

[10] Ray Gilbert and Allie Wrubel, "Zip-a-Dee-Doo-Dah," in *Song of the South*, dir. Harve Foster and Wilfred Jackson (Burbank, CA: Walt Disney Studios, 1946).

[11] Gabler, 118.

[12] Leigh Harline and Ned Washington, "I've Got No Strings," in *Pinocchio*, dir. Ben Sharpsteen and Hamilton Luske (Burbank, CA: Walt Disney Studios, 1940).

4

The Moral Magic of a Disney Musical

Jeremy E. Scarbrough and D.J. Culp Jr.

Walt Disney grew up regularly attending his local Congregational church, and as an adult he habitually drove his daughters to Sunday School.[1] Reflecting on his own life, career, and religious experience, he stated, "All I ask of myself is to live a good Christian life and toward that objective I bend every effort in shaping my personal, domestic and professional activities and growth."[2] Yet, though it is continually concluded by Disney scholars and authors that Walt did in fact believe in God and prayer, it seems that there was never an intent, neither implicitly nor explicitly, to proselytize any one religion in his films.[3] There is, however, one common theme that can be found in nearly every Disney cartoon or feature film—overcoming evil with good.[4] As Disney films have become renowned for their musical accompaniment, and since it was music with which Walt revolutionized the world of animation, this raises questions about a potential connection between the felt experiences of moral conviction when watching a Disney film and the aesthetic power of a good Disney musical to draw us into that experience or affect that moral conviction in any way.

The musical canvases heard by countless audiences throughout the twentieth and twenty-first centuries were composed and constructed with focused specificity and identifiable emotional intent based upon the characters, events, and actions within the animation sequences. Walt Disney believed that musical scores have the potential to elevate audience experience, provided that the music was intentionally composed for that purpose[5]—an approach that, up to that point, had been overlooked by the entire industry. The introduction of sound films occurred during 1928, at the same time Walt was starting afresh with a new character, Mickey Mouse (originally named 'Mortimer'). One of the first sound cartoons in history, *Steamboat Willie* (1928) acted as a sort of "proof of concept" for Walt and sounding board for market approval.[6] This offers much insight into the viewing experiences of American and soon-to-be international audiences—unless they were familiar with Walt's short lived 1st generation cartoon characters such as Oswald the Lucky Rabbit, audiences were only (barely) accustomed to sound films and, therefore, were entirely ignorant of any cartoon experience other than that of silent cartoons accompanied by incidental music. Furthermore, Walt's approach to hustling his cartoons kept him primed for another historical opportune moment—the end of Felix the Cat. As the primary animator of Felix, Hal Walker, states, "Disney put us out of business with his sound."[7] It is this innovation that also forced all other cartoon companies to begin to follow suit, clearly giving Walt and his crew the upper hand.

Musicians and composers hired by Walt Disney during the early years of the company's second iteration had a very specific role to fill. Their job as composers was to determine how music could best serve the animation sequences, which acted as their primary source of inspiration. It should be noted that the quality of musical composition in these instances was not based on the various artistic contributions by the composer. Rather, the quality of the music was determined by its level of emotional effect on Walt Disney, the animators, and the composers when paired with the animated scene. Therefore, the music and animation of Disney shared a symbiotic relationship. In the case of smaller length cartoons, the music was primarily composed to specifically accommodate the individual characters and events. Melodies were deemed inappropriate if they did not emotionally accentuate the events on screen. Walt Disney held the same standard of emotional congruency in his full-length feature films. An exemplary instance where music and animation align and elevate the aesthetic experience of the viewer is near the end of *Pinocchio* (1940). After sacrificing his life and saving Geppetto's, Pinocchio's body begins to glow and the voice of the Blue Fairy can be heard restating the conditions for becoming a real boy: "Prove yourself brave, truthful, and unselfish, and someday you will be a real boy."[8] The Blue Fairy instructs the marionette in flesh to rise, and a new lyric can be heard, "When your heart is in your dream, no request is too extreme." This particular moment demonstrates the care taken to establish congruency between the two forms of Disney art: animation sequence and music.

Connecting with the Audience: Program Music and Leitmotif

When discussing the approach to animation sequences for *Fantasia* (1940), Walt was keenly aware of his lack of understanding of art music—European musical traditions of the 1600 – 1900s, composed by trained musicians such as Bach, Mozart, and Beethoven; music that is historically considered to be of a higher, more complex, aesthetic value when compared to folk music traditions. "Our object is to reach the very people who walked out on this 'Toccata and Fugue' because they didn't understand it. I am one of those people; but when I understand it, I like it!"[9] Speaking and collaborating in great detail with conductor Leopold Stokowski, Walt's undertaking was very much rooted in his own ability to understand art music selections for *Fantasia*.[10] Assuming that general audiences would largely be unaffected—bored, rather—by art music, Walt decided that referentialism would be the most accessible and effective means of translating an understandable musical message. Referential music (music that refers to ideas beyond the sounds themselves), as demonstrated in program music (instrumental music that is composed for the purpose of portraying emotions, events, scenes, or extra-musical ideas[11]), was the key to the planning process that the Disney animation studio used to ensure audience enjoyment, beginning even with *Steamboat Willie* and the *Silly Symphonies* (1929-1939), but magnified exponentially with *Fantasia*.

Walt heeded the advice of Stokowski and extensively listened to preexisting art music compositions to familiarize himself with composer trends, music period idiosyncrasies, and melodic and harmonic attractiveness. In doing so, Walt Disney and his animation company began to utilize one of the most effective compositional tools contributed by Richard Wagner, the leitmotif.

According to Frank Thomas and Ollie Johnston, in their book on Disney animation, Walt's view on music was that it was "undoubtedly the most important addition [to be made] to the picture. It can do more to bring a production to life...than any other single ingredient."[12] In light of this historical backdrop and the significant role that music may play in attuning the viewer to the narrative, what impact might Disney's musical narratives have upon the viewers' moral imagination? What is the moral magic of a Disney musical?

Aesthetic Sensibilities

Disney's contribution to film aesthetics and American music education cannot be overstated. *Steamboat Willie* transformed the animated film industry with sight-sound synchronization,[13] and "Mickey Mousing," influenced even the "father" of (live-action) film music Max Steiner.[14] The *Silly Symphonies*, along with works like *Fantasia, Peter and the Wolf*, and *Sleeping Beauty* made art music more accessible, sharpened our appreciation for program music, and brought to life the leitmotif as never before. Moreover, Disney works are replete with exposure to well-composed vocal harmonies—including polyphonic duets and ensembles of the *Opera buffa* style. Still, there was more going on in Disney's music than sound-experimentation and western music education. Disney purposefully sought to immerse one in an imaginative experience that would highlight "those virtues that make both children and adults attractive," and remind us "that good can always triumph over evil."[15] So what makes this music so attractive, and how might it expand our understanding of the good?

The first thing to note is the general significance of Broadway, which seems to have become so successful precisely because it serves as a sort of mediation between worlds of musical difference. In one sense, it is largely a pop musical style, easily accessible to the common folk; in another, it is often so well-orchestrated, and accompanied by witty and artistic lyricism, that it might be better understood as variant of the English operetta. So, the first point of significance—an aesthetic anchor seemingly shared by the musical genre as a whole—involves Disney's balance between a backdrop of well-composed harmonic progression and lyrically artistic, pop-infused hooks that drive the drama forward, while also successfully getting "stuck in our heads." Yet, whereas the musical already holds a certain sense of power in presentation, the animated musical is able to go beyond this and draw our attention more explicitly and artistically to key features which we are meant to notice.

This mediation is no small detail since a key feature of music's cognitive appeal involves finding the *just-so* balance between the familiar and the fascinating. Psychologically, we seek a meaningful aesthetic equilibrium between simplicity and complexity—and these relate to familiarity. We tend to reject extreme simplicity *and* extreme complexity, while unfamiliarity can lead to frustration, thereby hindering appreciation.[16] According to Daniel Levitin, "At a neural level, we need to be able to find a few landmarks in order to invoke a cognitive schema."[17] While the arts are powerful in that they "can connect us to one another, and to larger truths about what it means to be alive and what it means to be human,"[18] there is nevertheless a sense of safety and trust involved as we allow composers and performers to take us beyond ourselves—a vulnerability rarely entrusted to strangers.[19] With Disney, the visual holds our interest and the tuneful marks expectation while we are subtly immersed in an experience that introduces us to nuances of western art music and other music cultures of the world.

Jazz and the folk ballad were two of the most important ingredients in the history of the American music phenomenon. Seemingly aware of this, Richard and Robert Sherman began to explore the power of pop music and folk jingles in the late 1960s and early 1970s. *The Sword in the Stone, The Aristocats,* and *The Jungle Book* all exemplify this jazz/folk infusion. *Robin Hood* captured the spirit of the folk music revival with songs by Country singer Roger Miller. Emphasis on animation and musicals declined in the 1970s. The point is that every successful Disney animated classic up to that point seems to have capitalized on this infusion of pop-music quite purposefully—except for *Sleeping Beauty*, which nonetheless added lyrics to create an iconic pop-esque song out of Tchaikovsky's catchy waltz.

It was in the late 1980s when Disney began to understand the need for, and capitalize upon, that Broadway balance of art music with a pop/folk-infusion.[20] Indeed, Disney was so aware of adolescents' desire for musical expression that the All-New Mickey Mouse Club (1989-1995) regularly featured music videos, and the Disney Channel formed its own pop group, *The Party*,[21] featuring six of the cast members. *Oliver & Company* placed a spotlight on Billy Joel in 1988, but it was *The Little Mermaid* that set a new precedent of fusing pop-like arias together with a backdrop of artistically orchestrated accompaniment. The films that followed this "Renaissance"—*Beauty and the Beast, Aladdin,* and *The Lion King*—are among the most celebrated of Disney treasures. Though released through Touchstone Pictures, due to darker content, Tim Burton's (1993) *The Nightmare Before Christmas*—

featuring Danny Elfman's musical mind—quickly became, and remains, a cult classic. With the rise of Pixar, *circa* 2000, interest in animated musicals again declined, but a new line of animated musicals, beginning with *Enchanted* (2007) and *The Princess and the Frog* (2009) rekindled this affinity within the decade. (It might well have been the success of the live-action Disney Channel Original Movie *High School Musical* (2006) which reminded Disney of just how much fans hungered for music).

It was Alan Menken and Howard Ashman who brought the Disney musical to its new level of pop-art fusion, during the 1990s, and Disney musicals continued to seek this artistic balance thereafter—coupling the compositional genius of Hans Zimmer with Elton John in *The Lion King*; featuring Phil Collins in *Tarzan*; Pairing Randy Newman's songwriting with jazz, gospel, zydeco, and Broadway styles in *The Princess and the Frog*; bringing Menken back to work with pop-icon Mandy Moore in *Tangled*;[22] spotlighting Broadway singers Idina Menzel and Kristen Bell over a collaboration of talented songwriting and film scoring in *Frozen*; and combining respected film composition with reputable Broadway song-writing and an award-winning South-Pacific pop-fusion group to bring us the musical treasure that is *Moana*. The key to this musical success seems to lie within an artistic pairing of popular hooks with well-composed harmonic progressions. According to philosopher Roger Scruton, well-composed music—driven by a motion that invites us to move with it in a sort of transcendental dance—involves a sense of openness and awareness of otherness, whereas some forms of pop music, created primarily for consumption, force one to submit merely to a pulse without a partner. The point is that a well-composed music (art or pop) offers an organic sense of motion, and Disney's pop-art-synthesis capitalizes on just that.[23]

A second, related point also begins with Broadway. This involves cultural exposure. One of the most striking features of the 1943 classic *Oklahoma!* was its aim for aesthetic authenticity surrounding its depicted music cultures—its groundbreaking inclusion of farm dance and cowboy ballads. Similarly, Disney has a gift for contextual immersion. In *The Princess* Frog, for instance, we are exposed to the southern draw; the love for beignets; the fascination with voodoo; economic struggle and social differentiation; but also, the racial integration at the heart of New Orleans; and all that *jazz*—that musical meeting point which transcends difference and division. Understandably, the extent and accuracy of cultural representation in Disney films has drawn criticism. Still, however imperfect, or even problematic, some of

Disney's attempts may have been, and however long it may have taken for Disney to become more purposeful and sensitive in its cultural representations, it is worth noting that, historically, Disney seems to have led the way in cultural exposure through animated musicals.

The significance of this aesthetic enculturation should not be overlooked. For if musical exposure to other cultures holds a potential for the expansion of empathy, then it may also play a role in enlarging moral sympathy and imagination. In 1942, Disney attempted to expand U.S. sensitivities to Latin American culture, combining live action with animation and music to celebrate community over diversity in *Saludos Amigos*. Moreover, in the 1990s Disney began a purposeful expansion in its storytelling, to become more inclusive of multiple, though archetypal, perspectives—and the music helped! In *The Hunchback of Notre Dame*, we are introduced to both aesthetic variables and social injustices involving the Gypsy culture. *Mulan* shows us that, if "Be a Man"[24] is to be the mantra of strength, then perhaps a girl with a courageous heart and an eye toward the good can better exemplify what some men ought to be. We are exposed to gender norms foreign to us, yet not so foreign. Additionally, we are exposed to East Asian pentatonic scales and unique timbres reminiscent of Chinese opera and traditional styles.

The Little Mermaid presented the metaphor of two worlds to teach us about judging before understanding, and about love's power to transcend difference—while also introducing us to Caribbean instrumentation in "painting" the oceanic context. Music can also be used as a means to enculturation through lyrical artistry that paints the traditions or tensions of a given context, and we see this in Ursula's eloquent account of gender tensions when she says things like, "On land it's much preferred for ladies not to say a word" and "It's she who holds her tongue who gets a man."[25] *Aladdin* introduced us to Arabia, to socioeconomic inequalities, to a non-western princess, and to Middle Eastern scales with appropriate melodic manipulations. *The Lion King* created in us an awe for the African landscape, its diversity, and the uniqueness of its vocal timbres, harmonies, and polyrhythms— the native musical tongue is the first thing we hear. We see similar subtleties of suggestive enculturation[26] in other films such as *Pocahontas*, *Frozen*, and *Moana*—expanding our empathy and aesthetic sensitivities to Native American, Norwegian, and Oceanic music cultures, language, and perspectives (*subtly* challenging the nature of gender roles, "true love," tradition, and, in *Pocahontas*, "savagery"). *Encanto* has been similarly praised for its attention to culturally significant details, and the music plays a role in providing a glimpse into both Colombian folk elements and pan-Latin musical diversity.

Moral Sensitivities

Disney has clearly capitalized on these areas of aesthetic psychology and musical enculturation. While there are a number of ways in which music is tethered to the moral imagination, we submit that Disney exemplifies the ability of aesthetic experience to serve as metaphor for moral dialogue, as well as a potential for a subliminal expansion of empathy through musical encultura-tion. Disney's appeal to the musical vernacular is a noteworthy point of mediation between aesthetic tastes and traditions.[27] This integrative approach offers a metaphor for moral dialogue.

Scholars have noted the power of artistically challenging an audience's perspective without frustrating them.[28] As explained above, simplicity and complexity, and especially unfamiliarity, can potentially hinder aesthetic appreciation. Consider, for example, songs which many viewers consider to be dark, suspenseful, or creepy—such as "Pink Elephants on Parade" from *Dumbo*, "Savages" from *Pocahontas*, "Heffalumps and Woozles" from *Winnie the Pooh*, or "Hellfire" from *The Hunchback of Notre Dame*. Now, contrast these with the soundtrack from *The Black Cauldron*. Although the latter was well-composed, the former examples were more musically accessible for many viewers because they were presented in song with pop-like hooks, catchy rhythmic passages, or clear and enjoyable melodic and bass lines discernable even amidst passing dissonances and chordal tensions. Might this be why *The Black Cauldron* tends to be a lesser celebrated film, though still an appreciated part of Disney lore? While its soundtrack did contain melodic content, it did not strike many as a significant part of Disney's musical heritage. Yet this is not because the soundtrack was instrumental; the magic seems not to lie in "song" per se, but, rather, in song-like musicality. Thus, one wants to "sing" along (in jazz-scat fashion) to the theme song from *Pirates of the Caribbean*.

So too, moral dialogue often calls for a sort of conversational finesse in speaking with charity and conviction, in acknowledging our agreements while also addressing our perspectival differences. In a sense, because of its palatable presentation, Disney can teach us to bear patiently with aesthetic differentiation in order to come together and enjoy the points of aesthetic unity that we share. The art-music enthusiast may not care for certain pop-like simplicities yet can appreciate their relationship to an overall compositional complexity. The lover of pop may not appreciate structural significance, yet they do enjoy the progressing sense of emotive power felt beneath that hook. The former may prefer soundtracks like that of *The Black Cauldron*, while the latter may prefer "Oo-de-Lally" from *Robin Hood*. Yet both can appreciate the pop-like song with well-composed accompaniment like *Aladdin's* "A Whole New World." In the same way, when we dialogue about ethics, we come from different worldviews with different values, expectations, presuppositions, and language. If progress is to follow, we must learn to begin with those points of agreement in order to mediate the language between worldviews and work together toward a harmonic progression. (Still, this can only come once we concede—whether we understand it or not—an underlying moral structure and teleological order).

Disney's approach to music enculturates us subtly, without overwhelming us with unfamiliarity. It moves us—expanding our awareness and empathy toward other aesthetic perspectives, or at least our tolerance of aesthetic otherness. Because there remains a sense of pleasure and familiarity, we seem to attain a sense of patience and charity, while exposed to nuances of the unfamiliar. Disney musicals can also remind us that, despite the relativity of aesthetic taste and tradition, a universal conviction nevertheless remains concerning beauty; all musical expression is an attempt to embody this conviction—though from unique perspectives—and at some level, this embodied experience moves us all.

Moral Apologetics and the Disney Musical

Walt changed the world of animated storytelling with sight-sound synchronization. Not only did he use music to bring the drama to life; he also used animation to enhance music's referential potential. Thus, part of the power of an animated musical, as exemplified by Disney, involves this synchronized symbiosis. However, it seems the more significant variable in Disney's example for approaching animated features involves the inclusion of popular hooks with a well-composed accompaniment, and a delicate balance between the musically foreign and the familiar. Using the aesthetic allure of the former, Disney is able to leverage the latter to introduce new and foreign perspectives more powerfully. More needs to be said about music's referential power, but this essay has argued that Disney's careful approach to animated musicals can exemplify the need for apologetic dialogue to balance winsome allure with patience and charity. It also testifies to the value of cultural apologetics—doing apologetics through pop-culture artifacts. Though we share the grand narrative of the human condition, our individual narratives must have some level of allure and aesthetic accessibility if they are to communicate any sense of cross-narrative significance, and it is through this accessibility that we expand our perspective concerning humanity and the human condition, and begin to see more clearly similarities between our individual narratives.

Notes

[1] Walt Disney, "Walt Disney on Divine Inspiration," *Guideposts*, June 1949, Retrieved on June 5, 2022 from: https://www.guideposts.org/better-living/entertainment/movies-and-tv/guideposts-classics-walt-disney-on-divine-inspiration.

[2] Ibid.

[3] Mark Pinsky, *The Gospel According to Disney* (Louisville: Westminster John Knox Press, 2004), 20.

[4] Ibid., 2.

[5] Frank Thomas and Ollie Johnston, *The Illusion of Life: Disney Animation* (New York: Abbeville Press, 1981), 294.

[6] Neal Gabler, *Walt Disney: The Triumph of the American Imagination* (New York: Knopf, 2006), 116. It was during a random conversation with his brother Roy that Walt spawned the idea of fixing sound to cartoon film. Though Walt was certainly not the first person to have the idea, as Warner Bros. and Universal were also working on plans for combining sound with cartoon, Walt was all too familiar with the streamlined cartoon qualities of his contemporaries. Walt and his employees used *The Jazz Singer* (1927)—the first feature-length film with synchronized dialogue— as their methodological inspiration for coupling music with animation.

[7] Ibid., 128.

[8] *Pinocchio*, dir. Ben Sharpsteen and Hamilton Luske (Burbank, CA: Walt Disney Studios, 1940).

[9] Thomas & Johnston, 295. Walt used himself as the primary reference source for gauging the level of audience acceptance as he most certainly associated himself with the general public when concerning knowledge of art music.

[10] Ibid.

[11] See, e.g., "The Old Mill," *Silly Symphonies,* Directed by Wilfred Jackson (Burbank, CA: Walt Disney Studios, 1937). This cartoon includes a severe thunderstorm, during which the music is composed specifically for the purpose of portraying that storm to such an extent—the idea is—that one could visualize the storm even without the animated depiction given. In this scene, the music and animation work together uniquely, signaling a new era of both program music and animation.

[12] Thomas & Johnston, 285.

[13] Jon Newsom, "A Sound Idea: Music for Animated Films," *The Quarterly Journal of the Library of Congress* 37, no. 3/4 (1980): 283-84.

[14] Mervyn Cooke, *A History of Film Music,* (Cambridge: Cambridge University Press, 2008), 89, 92.

[15] Roland Gammon, *Faith is a Star,* (New York: Dutton, 1963), 8.

[16] Daniel J. Levitin, *This is Your Brain on Music: The Science of a Human Obsession* (New York: Dutton, 2006), 229-31. This applies to education as well.

[17] Ibid., 231.

[18] Ibid. 238.

[19] Ibid., 237.

[20] Cooke, 294.

[21] "Positive Attitude Reflects Today's Youth."

[22] Glenn Slater's and Alan Menken's "Mother Knows Best"—with reprise!—is a great example of the Broadway fusion. *Tangled,* dir. Nathan Greno and Byron Howard (Burbank, CA: Walt Disney Studios, 2010).

[23] Roger Scruton, "Music and Morality" *American Spectator* 43, no. 1 (2010): 42-45.

[24] David Zippel and Matthew Wilder, "I'll Make a Man Out of You," in *Mulan,* dir. Barry Cook and Tony Bancroft (Burbank, CA: Walt Disney Studios, 1998).

[25] Howard Ashman and Alan Menken, "Poor Unfortunate Souls," in *The Little Mermaid,* dir. Ron Clemens and John Musker (Burbank, CA: Walt Disney Studios, 1989).

[26] Critics might challenge that a film cannot *wholly* enculturate us, and the resulting appropriation is problematic, but the one who is quick to cry "misappropriation" needs to understand something about aesthetic appreciation. *Any* exposure (even if limited or less than ideal, so long as the misrepresentation is not egregious or harmful) *can* be beneficial to appreciation—and appreciation is essential to charity.

[27] In the early 1900s, Zoltan Kodály stressed the importance of folk music as key to learning about culture, mood, and perspective in Hungarian children's education, just as Fred Rogers, in the late 1900s, understood melody as key to memory and defended *accessible* music as significant in American childhood education.

[28] Kenneth Walden, "Art and Moral Revolution," *The Journal of Aesthetics and Art Criticism* 73, no. 3 (2015): 289.

5

Nostalgic Deliberation and the Moral Imagination: Music's Referential Power

Jeremy E. Scarbrough

Disney has long exemplified music's power to resonate with the aesthetic sensibilities of many viewers. I submit that many Disney films also resonate with our deep moral convictions, and this is precisely because Disney has long valued music's *referential* potential. When Elsa sings of her wrestling with a call "into the unknown," in *Frozen II*,[1] we sense that something appropriate is happening in the musical accompaniment, as the changes in instrumentation, the pauses, and the pulsing bassline all draw our attention toward a seeming sense of rightness, suggesting direction toward an end of our desire. The power builds with her anticipation and excitement at the thought of finding something she senses is missing, while the dancing of the strings in syncopated fashion effectively paints a picture of Elsa's racing heartbeat, and begins to quicken ours as well. The coalescing of two very different voices into one accord communicates something of a discord set right. What is pulling at us in all of this is not necessarily an ideal of beauty, but a desire for order and a reaction of aesthetic approval to an experience of well-ordered motion. This, as I have argued elsewhere, is because music is able to communicate to us subliminally that there is a meaningful grand order to be known, a way it ought to be, and this enraptures our desire.[2] Many premodern thinkers similarly believed that music's greatest value lies in its ability to draw our rational attention to higher things. Alas, this perspective changed over time, in the history of western aesthetics.

Following the Enlightenment, mainstream academic circles of thought increasingly began to marginalize music's relationship to higher things. With reference marginalized, aestheticians argued over whether aesthetic value was the product of the art object and experience itself or one's subjective feelings toward it. With the possibility of reference to goodness beyond the art object removed, it is no surprise that subjectivism won out. If there is no ultimate thing to be valued, then how could aesthetic value amount to anything more than subjective preference? (As it relates to this chapter, if music does not refer to any objective truth beyond itself then it cannot press into one's moral conviction). This was the ideology *en vogue* with which C. S. Lewis took issue in *The Abolition of Man*. He encountered textbooks teaching children that a man who calls a waterfall sublime may appear to be saying something about the waterfall, but "Actually... he was not making a remark about the waterfall, but a remark about his own feelings."[3]

Yet, in contrast to many mainstream academic perspectives, Walt Disney understood that there is a unique power in music's ability to refer our attention to ideas beyond the music itself, and even beyond the animation. Because Disney films are able to exemplify music's referential power, they are also able to open the dialogue to ponder the question of just how deep music's meaningful references can go. While some argue that the "magic" of Disney is merely that of nostalgia, there is something historically distinct and undeniably powerful about Disney musicals. I submit that, in many cases, Disney fans think first of the *musical* treasures and secondarily of the narratives attached to them—or the lessons attached to the narratives. After all, many of Disney's beloved narratives are not new tales, but old ones reimagined and musically embodied—and it is this musical reimagining that has enchanted us so. This chapter explores how Disney films exemplify music's referential power, and I suggest that music can play a meta-referential role in speaking subconsciously to our deepest moral conviction that there is a way-it-ought-to-be, thereby appealing to our theological imagination. It will first be helpful, however, to review some of the differing perspectives on musical reference.

Musical Reference

For Plato and Aristotle, music somehow relates to the harmonic order that permeates our meaningful world, and because musical temperament or expression somehow relates to our own emotional temperament, music is somehow connected to the acquisition of temperance, and therefore a stepping-stone to moral virtue. Plato distrusted music's emotional power, stressing instead its ability to prepare the mind for rational inquiry. To Plato's point, while the *Encanto* song "Surface Pressure" is clearly about the weight of shouldering a responsibility to meet familial expectations, if one is so moved by the alluring rhythmic drive and melodic dance of the vocals that one misses the most theologically and morally significant point—that Luisa Madrigal carries the moral burden of a works-centered identity, seeing herself as only instrumentally valuable, "worthless if [she] can't be of service"[4]—then perhaps the music is distracting one from the deeper contemplation which ought to be taking place. Aristotle, on the other hand, appreciating the fact that music moves both body and soul, and acknowledging a greater value within the pleasurable experience, saw the contemplation of emotional ordering—the intellectual pleasure—as the noble end of music. Walt Disney was clearly concerned with prompting viewers to ponder good and evil, but, in a more Aristotelian manner, he also valued music's potential for dramatic effect and emotional impact.

For both Plato and Aristotle, despite differences, while musical *enjoyment* is directly connected to emotional experience, this enjoyment is nevertheless tethered to an awareness of a higher order reflected within the artistic imitation. (Disney explored this fascinating connection between mathematical order, the arts, and aesthetic qualities in nature, in the 1959 film *Donald in Mathmagic Land*). As Aristotle realized, by nature, we desire understanding, and knowledge presupposes order. We delight in imitations and expressions of order precisely because we desire to know it more intimately.[5]

With time, following the rise of secular humanism in the 1700s, an empiricist slant began to encourage the view that (1) nothing exists beyond the material universe and so (2) we must reject any appeal to *telos* (an ultimate, objective sense of order, meaning, and purpose). Value language, therefore, only refers to physiological effect, psychological experience, socio-cultural context, or an art-object's structural significance, but not to anything truly meaningful referenced beyond. By the twentieth century, there was a standing dichotomy in U.S. philosophies of music and music education.[6] While programmatic or socio-cultural reference remained of interest to some, and instrumental references (art's ability to serve as means to another end, such as moral education) remained of interest to others, mainstream theories saw increasingly less need for discussing musical reference. Music's value, it was believed, must lie either within its *formal* qualities alone (the beautifully designed object produces pleasurable effects within us, and so we value its structurally meaningful arrangement of signs) or in its *expressive* qualities (we value not the object itself, but rather the emotional experience expressed or the special *"buzz"* that we experience when encountering an object).

The view that music's greatest value lies beyond form and experience *per se* and within extra-musical symbolism was largely ignored in mainstream twentieth-century analytic thought.[7] Yet it survived in the twentieth-century film industry. Francis Schaeffer once argued that a robust theology understands that art celebrates the entire human person—emotion, intellect, and imagination.[8] Reference, then, is a natural, even significant, part of aesthetic experience. Understanding this, Disney capitalized on the power and potential of musical reference. Valuing artistic imagination over trained interpretation, *Fantasia* showed that even absolute music provokes the imagination, and that musical and visual references can enhance one another.

Referential symbolism can be simple or complex, and it is applied in a number of ways in programmatic music. It may involve *intra*-musical, diegetic motifs (music within the narrative, heard by the characters), such as the festival music which moves Rapunzel to dance in *Tangled*, or Naveen's cover of Dippermouth Blues which catches Louis's attention in *The Princess and the Frog* . Or it may involve *inter*-musical ideas (referencing extant ideas, or motifs). For example, there is a musical reference to "Dies Irae" in *The Hunchback of Notre Dame,* as Frollo condemns a Gypsy.[9] Though it is a lyrical reference, and not the iconic musical motif, the *Dies Irae* chant, meaning "day of wrath," has a long history of musical significance. (A reference to the iconic musical motif can be heard in "King of Pride Rock" from *The Lion King* score,[10] as the long-awaited return of the rightful king is also a day of judgment for those who brought injustice to the Pride Lands). Another example can be seen at the beginning of *The Three Caballeros,* when there is a musical reference to the theme song from its preceding film, "Saludos Amigos."

Finally, program music is especially known for its *extra*-musical symbolism. This may include *leitmotifs,* imitating sounds of nature, word painting; or musically significant cultural representations—whether foreign or nationalistic. When Mary Poppins sings "the medicine go down"[11] for the second time, in each chorus, her pitch slides downward. In this case, the word painting is clear. In other cases, it may be more suggestive. At the end of "Let It Go,"[12] when Elsa belts, "Let the storm rage on!" we notice that her vibrato has built increasingly throughout the song and she is now "letting it go" — that is, the fullness of her voice. Indeed, now it seems to be "raging like a storm," as she continues to sustain that powerful note. The programmatic concerns of Disney's origins continued throughout its history, and its repertoire is replete with referential symbolism.

While examples abound, *Frozen II* offers the best insight. In this film, the fifth spirit has its own *leitmotif*, as does the river — supported by strings that paint a musical portrait of its currents.[13] In "Into the Unknown," the melody brings to life Elsa's struggle with safety and adventure. Vocally, steps are always safer than leaps, though some leaps are safer than others. The chorus begins, "Un-known," with a leap to the octave (the safest musical leap). Then Elsa repeats this, leaping to the step just beyond, but quickly sliding back to her "safe place." The third time presents a new boldness as she leaps with abandon, well beyond the safety of the octave and "into the unknown" stratosphere.

There is also an interesting symbolism in the fifth spirit's four-note motif. As it turns out, the composers were purposefully attempting to imitate an ancient Norwegian technique that shepherdesses would use to call their livestock home. Usually sung very high with a yodel-esque release, these short motives, called *Kulning* — well known to those animals acquainted with the one calling — would reverberate throughout the mountains, calling livestock home from great distances.[14] The greatest moment of symbolism occurs in the song "Show Yourself," with the coming together of *leitmotifs* (since the river is key to the spirit's location) and within the growing statement of power (both orchestral and vocal) at the song's climactic ending, as Elsa embraces a newfound truth concerning her connection to the fifth spirit. Until this point, the gentle call always presented itself (in another's voice) with minimal vibrato, but now, as Elsa accepts the fullness of her power and purpose, we hear this motif transformed by the fullness of her own unmistakable timbre and vibrato.[15]

Music and the Moral Imagination

Disney films illustrate well music's referential power in general, but there is still a deeper potential for reference which I believe many Disney musicals exemplify—a reference to our own convictions of and desire for moral order. Like characters who realize they are actually part of a larger narrative, we are moved by the musical experience to question our context as it resonates with a profundity concerning the human condition. Music appeals to our moral and theological cognition in two ways—one is imaginative—an appeal to the head, with references to various imaginative possibilities, or possible aesthetic worlds—while the other is an intuitive appeal to the heart—with reference to the fingerprint of our actual object of desire. The former involves the imaginative power of the arts in general. The latter targets music's ability to refer, beyond sensation, to a deep-seated (subliminal) conviction of cosmological order and teleological *just-ness*—a properly basic belief that there *is* a way-it-should-be, that such should-be-ness is good, that we want more of it, and that our desire somehow corresponds to things set right.

Since the Enlightenment, music's moral potential and place in western education has been justified primarily in one of two ways. In one sense, many believed that music has an ineffable, intrinsic value that will somehow rub off on us as we expose ourselves to it.[16] In another sense it was believed that we will become better citizens the more we experience growth, unity, and teamwork within smaller social settings, and musical ensembles are an effective means to this end. Both views are narrow. As defended by Elisabeth Schellekens, perhaps aesthetics and morality are in fact the same, rather than distinct philosophical spheres,[17] and so music's connection to moral theology involves both aesthetic and moral sensibilities. She argues that art is capable of imparting moral knowledge, that this is entwined with its intrinsic value, and that any inability to see this intersection of goodness and beauty may say more about *us* than it says about the actual nature of the good and the beautiful.[18]

Schellekens insists that the essential variable connecting the aesthetic to the moral is imagination. Once the aesthetic qualities are perceived "the imagination can create a narrative around the elements we are given which helps us to make sense of all of an artwork's aesthetically relevant features, and thus to make a judgment about its aesthetic value."[19] In the song, "Let It Go," when Elsa exclaims "Here I stand!" there is a standing power in her voice, as it word-paints a sense of descent—as if she is putting her foot down... and indeed she does, emitting frozen fractals from the force of her stomp. As she begins to erect her palace of isolation by the sheer force of her determination, the spreading of icy filigree is depicted symbolically in the piano while the orchestral accompaniment illustrates both a quickening pulse of excitement and the power of Elsa's magical outbursts. The lyrics, the musical accompaniment, and the visual art all work together in a powerful way to provide us with the elements to bring the narrative to life, allowing us to experience Elsa's strong feelings of freedom and anticipation. The experience is so rich that we are also able to perceive aesthetic qualities of this experience and to deliberate about Elsa's feelings, her icy artistry, and the appropriateness of her actions in isolating herself.

Perhaps this is why Monique Wonderly has argued that film is the ideal platform for developing empathy and expanding moral reasoning skills in children. Narratives help us to ponder the human condition, and animated characters are more accessible than literary figures. If music, an organic expression in time, similarly carries a sort of narrative potential—as exemplified by programmatic instrumental music—then perhaps her insights for films connection to moral deliberation may offer application to music as well. Wonderly likens a good narrative's educational power to philosophical thought experiments, which challenge students to imagine situations beyond their current levels of reasoning.[20] Therefore, the way in which our imagination constructs a context and perspective for aesthetic evaluation may be profoundly intertwined with our moral imagination. Schellekens expounds:

> In moral deliberation, we employ our imagination to create scenarios that enable us to investigate the various courses of action and decisions available to us.... [We build narratives, or thought experiments] through which we can envisage the possible outcomes and consequences of a range of actions and decisions before settling on any particular one. So, in advance of making one's mind up... we need to conjure up imaginative settings in which these various possibilities are acted out since doing so can help us see which action or decision leads to the best result. Somewhat similarly, evaluating a work's overall aesthetic character often involves creating a narrative, perhaps even a plot or storyline, which gives the aesthetic qualities a context in which they can be compared and possibly ranked.[21]

This is easy to conceptualize with film, but it also applies to music. *All* musical ideas are referents—to formal qualities; to experience (emotional, physiological, imaginative, or meta-cognitive); to social, cultural, and political contexts; or to something else—and these imaginative acts of envisioning form and fit, evaluating aesthetic significance, and reconstructing meaningful contexts all seem to engage and develop the same cognitive faculties necessary for and involved in moral deliberation.

A crucial factor in imagination involves the lived experience. Rather than merely "seeing" a work, we piece it together as we live through it. This piecing together involves rational and emotional consideration, contrast and judgement. We deliberate precisely because we do not see clearly,[22] as when we ponder whether Alice really visited Wonderland or whether she was just dreaming. And we use our imaginations to ponder other perspectives, as when *Pocahontas* prompts us to question both the definition of a "savage" and whether one is necessarily more knowledgeable of truth simply because one has encountered more perspectives ("You've been so many places/ I guess it must be so"[23]). The importance of aesthetic experience, Schellekens concludes, "seems to consist in the way it keeps our minds open, so to speak, in prompting us to bring our imagination into play in considering the objects and situations that confront us."[24] This sits well with Nicholas Wolterstorff's theory of art as world-projection.[25] As summarized by Steven Cowan and James Spiegel, art imitates God's creative nature by "fashioning a world for public appreciation."[26] I have argued elsewhere that they may also serve to present us with questions, rather than beauty *per se*. In this sense, the arts are not merely for appreciation of a beauty inherent to the object, but also for contemplation of meaning beyond it.[27]

In *Sleeping Beauty*, the musical piece entitled "Maleficent's Evil Spell" presents a sort of musical "world" in which there is an interplay of the alluring and the repulsive.[28] A three-note musical motif beckons "Au-ro-ra" in a seemingly soft and inviting manner, yet it is presented in a bitonal pair — the second presentation of motif is a half-step removed from the first, thereby creating an air of dissonance although the two melodic fragments are not played at the same time, and so they are not clearly perceived as incompatible. Aurora's ascent up the stairway is accompanied by a growing sense of dissonance and a looming rhythmic restlessness, climaxing in a fully diminished chord. In this musical "world," we face questions of aesthetic order and appropriateness, or excellence. Is a world like this palatable, desirable, or even tolerable, or does it give us a sense that something is not as it should be? Perhaps this music picture is even theologically symbolic. Do we find allure in what should be repulsive because we cannot quite make out the cognitive, moral, or spiritual dissonances? Do we find our aesthetic appetites restless because we are enchanted by diminished caricatures of goodness, unable to satiate our desire? Art objects are thought experiments exploring the nature of reality (including order and meaning) and questions of the human condition (existential significance). Moreover, music is especially potent in its ability to embody our own feelings and consequently facilitate reflection.

The second paradigm of cognitive reference involves the significance that lived experience plays in exposing intuition. Music is the most organic ingredient in aesthetic experience—moving hearts to know and long; arguably, all artistic expression imitates musical movement in some way. While ancient Western philosophers suggested that music attunes us to a harmonic cosmological order,[29] ancient Eastern philosophers offered an important piece of that puzzle. As Ming Dong Gu explains, ancient Chinese thought understood a deep connection between music and desire. Life begins with desire, and desire is a fundamental variable in suffering. As loss leads to desire, we sense estrangement from the good, yet this desire is insatiable. This is similar to C. S. Lewis's appeal to *Sehnsucht* (a deep insatiable, yearning)[30] in that all the arts are expressions of human disposition and our search for a substantive form of fulfillment. Music, then, offers unique access to this deep sense of loss.[31] It has a potential to appeal to our heart with the deepest sort of reference—a theologically-intuitive desire which bespeaks a greater beauty that we were meant to know—and when this artistic ordering of musical intuition is crafted in a palatable way, this occurs most potently.

Because music is effective in rousing our sense of desire, it is also able to speak to our sense of loss. This may happen through a building tension followed by silence—as with the moment Bambi's mother dies—or a noticeable change in tone and orchestration—as with the death of Bing Bong, from *Inside Out*. Because loss is not something one "gets over" but rather something that one learns to live through by carrying yesterday's joys into tomorrow's journeys, loss can even be experienced, alongside hope, in lighthearted moments and motifs. This is captured well in the theme song from the film *Up*.[32] The same tune that is tethered to innocence, companionship, and hope, once slowed down and stripped to a sole piano, is able to communicate loss, fear to move on, caution in doing so, and even fatigue from trying to cope. Yet, precisely because of its connection to hope and companionship, it is able to portray a new companionship, and with it a new strength for adventure and a new sense of hope.

While it can be tempting to assert moral truth as relative to culture, Lewis powerfully revealed that all cultures in fact share a universal conviction that there is such a thing as justice—a way it should be.[33] While we differ on what is due and to whom, we are confident that something is due to someone, and justice involves this objective sense of order. This is a conviction of the deepest sort. If the aesthetic and moral spheres are intertwined, then this same conviction bleeds over in some way into our aesthetic knowing as well. While there is relativity surrounding tradition, there is also consensus concerning beauty as meaningful and somehow connected to the good life—a way-it-should-be. Music refers our cognitive awareness to both art-object and a sense of order beyond it. As Aristotle noted, we possess a desire to know *and* a conviction that there *is* an orderliness to be known. Music may involve pleasure, but it also evokes a passion for justice in a robust and teleological sense.[34] When the tritone (historically known as "the interval of the devil") is played just before the bear attack in *The Fox and the Hound;* when we hear the alarming brass accompanied by frantic stringed instruments as the headless horseman chases Ichabod; and especially when we experience musically the Horned King calling forth the Army of the Dead from the Black Cauldron; we know something is not quite as it ought to be. When we *hear* Simba take his place in "Circle of Life (Reprise)," we sense that something *is* as it should be. There is a felt sense of rightness and goodness.

Some insightfully attribute Disney's magic to a nostalgia for restoration (a desire to recover something lost), but then attack such fantasy as perpetuating indoctrination into an allegedly archaic narrative of power (that of religion and outdated virtues) as a form of social control and capital gain.[35] Some critical theorists might have us reject such narratives because they are asserted to be the cause of social injustice, and since nostalgia begs us to return to the narrative and seek the sort of world prescribed therein, it should be rejected as well. The problem is that limiting restorative nostalgia to this lens does not account robustly enough for the human aesthetic experience.[36] As Elizabeth Butterfield has written, "I am optimistic enough about my own free will and self-awareness to suspect there is more to my love for Disney than indoctrination."[37]

Butterfield suggests that perhaps we escape into Disney fantasies because the "real world" is not as it should be. She posits that some virtues—like justice, hope, and kindness—are "really worth believing" and "Disney can inspire us to bring the magic home and make the world as it should be."[38] Perhaps Disney fantasies are so powerful precisely because they ring true with our deepest intuitions. Concerning the animated musicals, perhaps the music moves us most deeply, precisely because musical form references our conviction of a deeper order. This indeed awakens a nostalgia within us, and it is indeed restorative. For despite our contemporary rejections of objective truth and telos (a way-it-should-be), our deeper convictions of an actual beauty reflected within a grand order moves us to know and to want to know.

Aesthetics Apologetics: Musical Intuition and Moral Deliberation

If our sensitivities to beauty and to order are connected, then musical experience is profoundly connected to moral cognition and theological imagining—to an intuitive awareness of referential just-ness (a sense-of-things-as-they-should-be). Prerequisite to understanding any connection between goodness, beauty, and moral excellence is an intuitive awareness of order and significance, and perhaps estrangement and the potential for restoration as well. As I have argued elsewhere, juxtaposing the perspectives of Maeve Louise Heaney, Hans Urs von Balthasar, and Pierangelo Sequeri,[39] "perhaps music is not so much an object as it is the *transformation of subjects*. It is an embodiment of *logos*,[40] revealing our *instinct of order*[41] and enrapturing hope...[42] precisely because it speaks to one's convictions of a teleological justice, and a potential for knowing its realization."[43]

We are moved to hope in an ability to grasp goodness by "I am Moana (Song of the Ancestors)," for example, as the protagonist's perspective is transformed by a deeper sense of identity.[44] Realizing that "scars can... reveal just who you are," she discovers a light of intuition and, with it, direction for setting things as they ought to be. "I know the way," she now boldly sings. Her transformative conviction and strength to hope become our own as the accompaniment builds and she finds the fullness of her voice, because we too are moved by the seeming right-order and emotional appropriateness of the music, and by the seeming goodness in finding one's identity, strength, and purpose in relation to something that is bigger than oneself.

Music is an encounter with emanating projections of divine goodness which expose our convictions and awakens within us an insatiable desire for something this world cannot satisfy. Music is thus a powerful apologetic that we are meant for another world.[45] Disney musicals exemplify the power of an imaginative environment wherein one experiences profoundly this spiritual conviction—as the music, animation, and narrative all work together to engage the imagination in complex ways that expand one's ability for greater moral deliberation concerning such conviction.

Notes

[1] Kristen Anderson-Lopez and Robert Lopez, "Into the Unknown," performed by Idina Menzel featuring AURORA (Aurora Aksnes), in *Frozen II*, dir. Chris Buck and Jennifer Lee (Burbank, CA: Walt Disney Studios, 2019).

[2] Jeremy E. Scarbrough, "Music and Justice: A Teleological Philosophy of Music Aesthetics," *Journal of Interdisciplinary Studies* 34, no. 1 (2022): 11-42.

[3] C. S. Lewis, *The Abolition of Man* (New York: HarperOne, 1974), 2.

[4] Lin-Manuel Miranda, "Surface Pressure," in *Encanto*, dir. Jarod Bush and Byron Howard (Burbank, CA: Walt Disney Studios, 2021).

[5] Mary B. Schoen-Nazzaro, "Plato and Aristotle on the Ends of Music," *Laval théologique et philosophique* 34, no. 3 (1978): 264-65, 268-70. For more on Plato's perspective, see *Timaeus* 42; and *The Republic* 3:401-02, 411-12; 4:424-25; 7:521-22. For more on Aristotle's perspective see *Politics* 8:1339-1340; and *Metaphysics* 1:1:980

[6] For more on the history of music and aesthetics, see Andy Hamilton, *Aesthetics and Music* (London: Continuum International, 2007). For more on the historical dialogue concerning ethics and aesthetics, since there is a connection between the two and since our conclusions concerning the nature of value language impacts both areas of inquiry, see Elisabeth Schellekens, *Aesthetics & Morality* (New York: Continuum, 2007). For more on the two dogmas of musical modernism and the twentieth-century debate between formalism and expressionism, see Jeremy Edwin Scarbrough, "The Historical Impact of Philosophical Naturalism on American Aesthetic Education: Bennett Reimer's Philosophy of Music Education as Aesthetic Education" (PhD diss., University of Mississippi, 2015), 57; and Hamilton, 85-6.

[7] Reference is unavoidable. One of the issues that has plagued modern philosophy is the fact that when we experience the world, we find ourselves experiencing our idea of the world at the very same time. (So how could we ever know we experience *the world as it is* rather than merely *our idea of the world*?) The problem is that *all* ideas are referents. The question is, to what do they refer?

[8] Francis Schaeffer, *Art and the Bible* (Downers Grove: InterVasirty Press, 2006), 16.

[9] Stephen Schwartz and Alan Menken, "The Bells of Notre Dame," in *The Hunchback of Notre Dame*, dir. Gary Trousdale and Kirk Trousdale (Burbank, CA: Walt Disney Studios, 1996).

[10] Hans Zimmer, "King of Pride Rock" (score), in *The Lion King*, dir. Roger Allers and Rob Minkoff (Burbank, CA: Walt Disney Studios, 1994).

[11] Richard M. Sherman and Robert B. Sherman, "A Spoonful of Sugar," performed by Julie Andrews, in *Mary Poppins*, dir. Robert Stevenson (Burbank, CA: Walt Disney Studios, 1964).

[12] Kristen Anderson-Lopez and Robert Lopez, "Let It Go," performed by Idina Menzel, in *Frozen*, dir. Chris Buck and Jennifer Lee (Burbank, CA: Walt Disney Studios, 2013).

[13] Kristen Anderson-Lopez and Robert Lopez, "All is Found," performed by Evan Rachel Wood, in *Frozen II* (2019).

[14] Kristen Anderson-Lopez and Robert Lopez, "Ep. 6: 'Frozen' Notes: The Songs and the Songwriters," interview by Ginger Zee, *Inside Frozen 2*, ABC, December 25, 2019, podcast audio, 22:23, https://abcaudio.com/podcasts/inside-frozen-2/.

[15] Kristen Anderson-Lopez and Robert Lopez, "Show Yourself," performed by Idina Menzel and Evan Rachel Wood, in *Frozen II* (2019).

[16] Michael L. Mark, *Music Education: Source Readings from Ancient Greece to Today*, 4th ed. (New York: Routledge, 2013), 111-12.

[17] Schellekens, 4.

[18] Ibid., 90-91, 98.

[19] Ibid., 142.

[20] Monique Wonderly, "Children's Film as an Instrument of Moral Education," *Journal of Moral Education* 38, no. 1 (2009): 7-9.

[21] Schellekens, 142.

[22] Ibid. 144.

[23] Stephen Schwartz and Alan Menken, "Colors of the Wind," in *Pocahontas*, dir. Mike Gabriel and Eric Goldberg (Burbank, CA: Walt Disney Studios, 1995).

[24] Schellekens, 145.

[25] See Nicholas Wolterstorff, *Art in Action: Toward a Christian Aesthetic* (Grand Rapids: Eerdmans, 1980).

[26] Steven B. Cowen and James S. Spiegel, *The Love of Wisdom* (Nashville: B&H Academic, 2009), 428.

[27] See Scarbrough, "Music and Justice" (2022).

[28] George Bruns, "Maleficent's Evil Spell" (score), in *Sleeping Beauty*, dir. Clyde Geronimi (Burbank, CA: Walt Disney Studios, 1959).

[29] Schellekens, 15.

[30] C. S. Lewis, *Surprised by Joy* (New York: Harcourt, Brace and World, Inc., 1955), 17-18. See also Alister McGrath, *The Intellectual World of C. S. Lewis* (Oxford: Wiley-Blackwell, 2014), 106.

[31] Ming Dong Gu, "The Ethical Turn in Aesthetic Education: Early Chinese Thinkers on Music and the Arts," *Journal of Aesthetics Education* 50, no. 1 (2016): 98-104.

[32] Michael Giacchino, "Married Life," in *Up*, dir. Pete Docter (Burbank, CA: Walt Disney Studios, 2009).

[33] See Lewis' *The Abolition of Man*, 16-18; and Appendix.

[34] Another aesthetic variable unaddressed here is that of appreciating excellence in craft or performance. Note, however, that this too appeals to the intuition of justice/due-ness because we acknowledge a sense of respect and admiration *due* a creator in light of the creation. Here there is a complementarity between both the imaginative (world-projection as imitating a Creator) and intuitive (the passion for justice) explicated above. From the perspective of a Christian theology, the arts (whether presented as an assertion of order and significance or an exploratory question concerning order and meaning) are an expression of the *imago Dei*. This too can be seen as a reflection of justice in the most robust sense, if it is true that we were made to bear likeness to God. For more on this, see Scarbrough, "Music and Justice" (2022).

[35] Joseph Zornado, *Disney and the Dialectic of Desire: Fantasy as Social Practice* (Cham: Palgrave Macmillan, 2017), 1-28.

[36] Why think that restorative aesthetics and deep longing would cease in a Marxian utopia?

[37] Elizabeth Butterfield, "How I Learned to Stop Worrying and Love Disney: Marx and Marcuse at Disney World," in *Disney and Philosophy: Faith, Trust, and a Little Pixie Dust*, ed. Richard B. Davis (Hoboken: John Wiley and Sons Ltd, 2020). 248.

[38] Ibid., 256.

[39] Maeve Louise Heaney, *Music as Theology: What Music Says About the Word* (Eugene: Pickwick Publications, 2012), 220.

[40] Ibid., 142.

[41] Ibid., 205.

[42] Ibid., 188.

[43] Scarbrough (2022), 38.

[44] Lin-Manuel Miranda, Opetaia Foa'i, and Mark Mancina, "I Am Moana (Song of the Ancestors)," in *Moana* (2016).

[45] See Lewis' argument from desire: C. S. Lewis, *Mere Christianity*, (San Francisco, CA: HarperCollins, 2001), 136-7.

Part 2

EXPLORING QUESTIONS OF THEOLOGY AND MORAL FORMATION WITHIN DISNEY STORIES.

6

Marionettes, Moral Excellence, and Characters Worth Imitating

Shawn White

Stories serve a great role in their ability to communicate truth through entertainment. As Queen Elinor taught Princess Merida: "Legends are lessons. They ring with truths."[1] Stories have a way of not just teaching us moral lessons, but also providing us exemplars whom we should either emulate or avoid. Through the medium of animated film, Disney has told some of the most magnificent and memorable stories of our time. As we take a tour through a handful of Disney's most beloved stories, we will encounter the internal struggle between pride and humility.

According to the Bible, this battle between pride and humility is as old as this world's first human inhabitants and is central to the human condition. Adam and Eve lived humbly before God in the Garden of Eden, and yet it was pride that severed that relationship, resulting in an expulsion from Paradise. Moreover, as we read the Christian scriptures, we learn humility plays an important part in reuniting us with our Creator. However, in our current time, humility is neither a well-understood nor a well-received virtue. Even in the 1700s, philosophers like David Hume saw humility as a weakness and a vice. Hume labeled humility, fasting, celibacy, and other acts as "monkish virtues" which "stupify the understanding and harden the heart, obscure the fancy and sour the temper," and therefore, should be placed "in the cata-logue of vices."[2]

Opposite David Hume, medieval philosopher Thomas Aquinas thought humility to be a subspecies of the cardinal virtue temperance and that humility is in healthy tension with the virtue of magnanimity.[3] Temper-ance is the virtue which deals with having self-control over one's appetites and desires. It requires wisdom, or prudence, to know one's limitations with the fortitude and courage to act upon and keep oneself in check so as not to exceed one's own boundaries. Thus, according to Aquinas, "Humility re-strains the appetite from aiming at great things against right reason: while magnanimity urges the mind to great things in accord with right reason. Hence it is clear that magnanimity is not opposed to humility: indeed they concur in this, that each is according to right reason."[4] Aquinas further says that "just as it belongs to magnanimity to urge the mind to great things against despair, so it belongs to humility to withdraw the mind from the in-ordinate desire of great things against presumption."[5] Christian author G. K. Chesterton sums it up nicely, by writing, "humility was largely meant as a restraint upon the arrogance and infinity of the appetite of man."[6]

Still, humility is a tough virtue to place firm boundaries around. There are a wide variety of theories—including Aquinas's defense of the twelve degrees of humility[7] and Nicholas Bommarito's perspective on "Modesty and Humility."[8] On professor Nancy Snow's "Proper Limitations-owning" view,[9] humility is understood as having "the awareness of and concern about your limitations to have a realistic influence on our attitudes and behavior. At the heart of this realism is a perspective gained through accurate appraisal of your limitations and their implications for your circumstances, attitudes, and behaviors."[10] In other words, as articulated by Norvin Richards, "humil-ity...coexists appropriately with positive feelings about oneself, feelings founded not in error—as with the improperly proud—but in self-knowledge."[11] Thus, on this view of humility, not only is there a proper knowledge of self, but action must also accompany that knowledge once it has been judged by the intellect; as mentioned earlier, humility must accord with right reason.[12] Moreover, humility is crucial to a Christian apologetic today as it gives us the right posture and attitude we ought to carry into our conversations with those we interact with on a daily basis.

Pinocchio

Snow's insight raises an interesting question. If an individual lacks the requisite self-knowledge, is pride or humility even possible? In Disney's *Pinocchio*,[13] for instance, we find that Pinocchio is incapable of pride and humility due to his epistemic ignorance and lack of life experience. Arguably, his humility does not make an appearance until we near the end of the film. Rather, Pinocchio is a case study in the formation of humility in his character. When the Blue Fairy grants life to Geppetto's marionette, she tells Pinocchio that in order to complete the transformation into a real boy, it will require him to be brave, selfless, and truthful. The path to bravery and selflessness is partially found in putting others before oneself. Similarly, the path to truthfulness is pre-conditioned by an attitude of humility. But at the time Pinocchio is first brought to life, he lacks the self-awareness and self-knowledge which would allow him to be either humble or proud. This will come through life-experiences and learning one's boundaries. What is refreshing about Pinocchio is he learns from his mistakes. In other words, he is open to correction, even if he is not open to instruction. But one gets the sense that Pinocchio's lack of taking instruction from Jiminy Cricket or Geppetto is not due to any prideful rejection, but rather due to his ignorance which allows him to be persuaded by any passing wind that blows.

When the negative consequences of teaming up with Stromboli begin to dawn on Pinocchio, when he loses his freedom by being locked in a cage, then he learns why the choices he made were bad. This realization causes a change in Pinocchio, leading him to reject a shortcut to fame and fortune. It no longer becomes a temptation he will succumb to because he now has the proper knowledge from his life experience to put up healthy boundaries. His experience teaches him discipline and equips him with knowledge to make better decisions. Admitting his mistakes is the beginning of the formation of humility in his character.

The next temptation Pinocchio is faced with is pleasure. While pleasure in and of itself is a good, like any good that is left unchecked and allowed to run wild, it can quickly turn dangerous and even deadly. In the case of Pinocchio, his time on Pleasure Island does nothing to help him on the journey to become a real boy. In fact, it has quite the opposite effect as wild pleasure begins to turn him into a braying donkey. Thankfully, the beginning of the transformation scares Pinocchio straight and with Jiminy Cricket's help, he is able to escape Pleasure Island and return home. Pinocchio's experiences with Stromboli and Pleasure Island begin to cultivate humility within his character. The small fact that in both situations Pinocchio accepts the help of Jiminy Cricket is a tacit recognition that his limitations are real, and he must rely on others to survive. Finally, Pinocchio owns up to the truthfulness of his past mistakes and limitations. If Pinocchio were proud, he would not see himself as needing help; accepting help would be a sign of weakness. Pinocchio's experiences, however, are making him wise enough to see that this is not the case.

This emerging humility serves Pinocchio well as he arrives home, discovering that Geppetto is gone and that he and Jiminy will need to perform a rescue mission of their own. Hereafter, Pinocchio exhibits real bravery and unselfishness. As a result, in his ultimate act of humility through self-sacrifice, Pinocchio gives his life to save Geppetto. When the lifeless wooden marionette washes up on shore, he is brought back home where his final transformation occurs. Because he was brave and unselfish and truthful, the Blue Fairy brings Pinocchio back to life, while also transforming him from a wooden puppet into a living boy. In seeking to become more virtuous over time, he finds that he has also become more human by the end of the film.

Merida

The consequence of being transformed into something less human, such as Pinocchio becoming a donkey, is an even more pronounced theme in the Disney film *Brave*. *Brave* is a lush computer animated film set in a fictional medieval Scotland with fantastic scenery and memorable characters throughout. In this film Princess Merida is constantly in conflict with her mother Queen Elinor. In a rash act of defiance, Merida takes her sword and slashes the family tapestry, cleaving her mother's image from the family, and then she runs away into the forest. While in the forest, she encounters a witch who provides her with an enchanted cake. Once eaten, it will "change" the person who consumes it, and Merida is desperate to change her own fate by changing her mother's control.

Merida returns home and offers Elinor the cake as a false peace-offering, believing that it will simply change the Queen's point of view. Surprisingly, however, it completely changes her mother; Elinor transforms into a giant black bear. While the external transformation is nearly instantaneous, there is an internal transformation taking place as well, as Elinor has moments wherein her humanness seems to briefly disappear, leaving only bear-like instincts and actions. In a joint search for the cure, Merida and Elinor discover they must be reconciled by the second sunrise or else the transformation will be permanent, and Elinor will be forever a bear, losing all trace of her humanness.

An additional complication arises when Merida's three younger brothers also eat the cake, and they turn into little bear cubs. This is often the sad fact about vices such as pride. We might think that they will harm no one except the person infected, yet vices can have unforeseen results that effect even the most innocent of people. Moreover, vices such as pride erode relationships, one's own character and, as seen in both *Pinocchio* and *Brave*, one's own humanity. These illustrations seem to be echoes of the pride which drove Nebuchadnezzar into being an animal until he humbled himself before God.[14] The species of pride in *Brave* is a lack of intellectual humility. Intellectual humility is a type of open-mindedness where we are able to retain our convictions while at the same time listening and seeking to understand another's perspective. This is not open mindedness in the extreme where we abandon any and all convictions and accept another's perspective without justification.

This kind of pride is what prevents Elinor and Merida from having a healthy relationship as mother and daughter. Elinor prioritizes decorum and status over her daughter's desires and feelings. Merida prioritizes her desire for independence from the trappings of royal life over her mother's allegiance to tradition. This stubbornness is present in each of them, as they are both blinded to one another's point of view. Neither is capable of empathy in this state. In essence, they lack the intellectual humility which creates space for open-mindedness and empathy. It is only after the witch's spell takes effect that both are able to lay aside their own interests and work together. When they are finally able to let go of their pride, it is only then that they are able to reconcile by truly listening to one another. This act of humility breaks the witch's spell and reunites, not just mother and daughter, but the family and the community. For Queen Elinor and Princess Merida, humility is the path to relational restoration, healing, and a return of their humanity.

Pocahontas

A stellar example of intellectual humility is portrayed in the character of Pocahontas.[15] In this film, suspicion abounds from two groups, the Native

American Powhatan tribe and the English settlers from the Virginia Company. The Londoners are on a mission to find gold in the New Country, and they come armed to protect themselves from the "savages." The Powhatans are leery of these new people and also consider *them* savages. In the course of a chance meeting between the Englishman Captain John Smith and Chief Powhatan's daughter Pocahontas, they begin to form a relationship as they attempt to understand each other's differences and similarities. Later, when the warrior Kocoum spies Pocahontas and John Smith kissing, he attacks the Englishman partly out of jealousy. This skirmish ends with John Smith's good friend Thomas shooting and killing Kocoum and John Smith being taken captive by Powhatan tribesmen.

Chief Powhatan is furious at the death of Kocoum and decides to rally the men for battle against the English, but not before he plans on executing John Smith. Pocahontas intervenes and is able to convince the English and her father to not only call off the battle but also to spare John's life. The Chief agrees. However, the greedy and arrogant Governor Ratcliffe is not so easily swayed by Pocahontas, and he fires his musket at Chief Powhatan. Seeing what is happening, John Smith steps in front of the Chief and takes the bullet from Ratcliffe's rifle. The tribesmen arrest Ratcliffe, attend to John's wound as best they can, and release him back to his people.

Pocahontas's intervention is worthy of our attention. She exemplifies intellectual humility in her appeal to her tribe and the English colonists. Unlike Pinocchio, who suffered from actual ignorance, the Powhatans and Englishmen suffered from pride-induced ignorance. Their ignorance prevents them from adopting the rival groups perspective, and results in each group seeing and treating the opposing group as savages. But Pocahontas understands that resting in one's ignorance leads to hatred and death. Thankfully, she is able to convince both parties that there is much good her people can learn from the English, and much good the English can learn from the Powhatans. Thus, Pocahontas's humility leads to other moral goods that are beneficial to both groups: benevolence (the Powhatan tribe caring for the wounded John Smith), altruism (sharing of goods between the two communities), and co-existence in a blended and shared community. Again, these are echoes of Christian values and way of life.[16]

Aladdin

Pride can do more than just prevent us from listening to one another. *Aladdin* is a cautionary tale wherein pride is the downfall of several of the characters.[17] Pride can cause us not to see things as they really are and to miss the hidden value because of one's presumption and arrogance. Pride can also result in objectifying others and using them as means to ends rather than ends in themselves. Further, it can cause us to put on false airs in order to gather to ourselves underserved status and praise. When pride reigns nothing is as it seems. All of these dangers are present in *Aladdin*, and yet, in the end, it is the humble who triumph.

The manifestation of pride in the form of devaluing and objectifying others is represented in the relationship between Jafar and Aladdin. In the course of trying to find the magic lamp, it is revealed to Jafar that Aladdin is a "diamond in the rough," and this is exactly what Jafar needs to enter the cave of wonders and complete his selfish scheme. Jafar is only after the lamp, and cares nothing for Aladdin beyond Aladdin's ability to retrieve the lamp. Jafar thinks nothing of sacrificing Aladdin's life on the altar of his own selfish desires. Jafar's pride makes him incapable of appreciating Aladdin as a person of worth or to care about his virtuous qualities beyond serving his own needs. To Jafar, Aladdin is disposable. This is typical of Jafar and how his pride has shaped his relationships with those around him: The Sultan, Princess Jasmine, and the Genie.

Though Aladdin is prophesied to be the diamond in the rough, he must battle his own species of pride, that of being something he is not. Aladdin is a street kid who dreams of becoming a prince and living in the palace. Along the way, he meets Princess Jasmine and falls in love. He believes she will not accept him for who he is, and so, when he encounters a magic lamp, he wishes to become a wealthy and powerful prince. The Genie grants Aladdin his wish and externally transforms him into Prince Ali. With this significant socio-economic upgrade, Prince Ali seeks to woo Princess Jasmine into choosing him for her husband. While initially hesitant, Princess Jasmine keeps Prince Ali at a distance even though there is something the Princess finds familiar about him that eludes her.

As Aladdin's duplicity unravels and his real identity becomes known, Jasmine is heartbroken. Not because she wished him to be wealthy and powerful, but because Aladdin was not honest with her. He pursued her with right motives yet through wrong means. Aladdin wanted Jasmine to fall in love with him, yet he placed external appearances above character. Still, his most serious crime was that he exchanged humility for pride. Instead of accepting who he was and finding value in that, he elected to be something he was not and falsely peddled a duplicitous identity as his true self. It is not until Aladdin humbles himself through an act of self-sacrifice that he finally wins Princess Jasmine's heart completely. After letting go of the external things—being content with himself—and giving the Genie his promised freedom, Jasmine chooses to marry Aladdin. Although this reward was not the reason for Aladdin's choosing humility, doing so worked in Aladdin's favor. Still, not everyone appreciates a humble person.

Mulan

Of all the characters analyzed in this essay, Mulan[18] might represent humility in its most beautiful light. Her entire story is one of self-sacrifice, even at the expense of cultural norms, for she must be brave enough to transcend her honor/shame culture in order to do what is ultimately right. She surreptitiously takes her father's place in fulfilling his military service when the Huns invade China. She does this by cutting her hair short and disguising herself as a boy in order to fit in with the rest of the warriors. Her true identity is discovered after a battle wherein she nearly single-handedly defeats the Huns by causing an avalanche. During the battle she is wounded and while she is being attended to, Mulan is found out to be a woman disguised as a man. Though she has saved her people, she is shunned and stripped of her military service with orders to return home. On her return she learns that the Hun leader, Shan Yu and some of his key men somehow escaped during the avalanche. Since everyone thinks them dead, the Huns have devised a plan to infiltrate the palace and capture the Emperor. With this knowledge, Mulan makes her way to the men she served alongside to warn them, but they refuse to listen to her.

Once again it falls to Mulan to save the day. She convinces a few of the men to follow her and together they thwart the attack, rescue the Emperor and save China from the Huns. The Emperor presents Mulan with Shan Yu's sword, a huge honor for her and her family. When she returns home, she presents her father with the sword, less concerned about the accolades and rewards she has received and more grateful simply to return home. Mulan lives a life of consistent self-sacrifice manifested in repeated acts of bravery and courage to save her friends, her emperor, her countrymen, and her family. Her humility functions as a precursor to these other virtuous acts. Of all the characters discussed, Mulan exhibits a healthy and proper disregard for herself and how she is perceived, and she is most concerned with everyone else's well-being, despite the social cost. This is truly a mark of deep-seated humility forged in her character.

Conclusion

In our image-conscious culture, in which we continually craft seemingly perfected, though often deceptive, identities to portray on social media, it seems tragically apparent that we are all too eager to exchange any honor to be earned in humility for the adoration and affirmation of strangers. True humility brings with it a level of disinterestedness in those opinions due to holding a healthy self-image and a fairly accurate assessment of self-worth. One aspect of humility lies within the possession of a realistic self-image— not thinking or projecting an image that is too high (pride) or too low (false modesty). Self-editing is a bottomless abyss, and no one can live up to the false images they create.

This is where these Disney stories can help us. How does one begin to cultivate a life of humility? Imitate Pinocchio: who learned from his mistakes, learned to respect his own limitations, and was open to seeking truth, even if it was at times painful. How does one learn to live well with others, both those we call family and those who are strangers? Look at the examples of Queen Elinor, Princess Merida, and Pocahontas. They show us how to listen with an open-mindedness that promotes empathy and peaceful co-existence alongside those with whom we may not always agree. Disagreement does not need to dissolve into discord. How do we rest in our true self-worth? Learn from Aladdin that the effort to put on false airs about oneself eventually unravels. It is better to be as honest with oneself and others as possible, because integrity will carry one far in life.

Why should we choose humility, in a culture that encourages us to look out for number one? Mulan shows us that selflessness is far better than selfishness. She quietly and consistently chose to serve others over her own needs. She continued to do the right thing, even in the face of scorn and ridicule, and in the end, she was richly rewarded. Just as the apostle James beseeched his listeners to "humble yourselves before the Lord, and he will lift you up,"[19] so too a mere marionette, two princesses, an orphan, and an unexpected warrior have creatively called us to consider the beauty and power of a life that exemplifies humility over self-interest. Additionally, these lessons can greatly benefit our applied apologetics. When Peter tells us to "set Christ apart as Lord in your hearts and always be ready to give an answer to anyone who asks about the hope you possess. Yet do it with courtesy and respect, keeping a good conscience,"[20] he is reminding us to engage with others from a posture of humility. This is a virtue that ought to be central in our approach with those who believe differently than us.

Notes

[1] *Brave*, dir. Mark Andrews and Brenda Chapman (Burbank, CA: Walt Disney Studios, 2012).

[2] David Hume, *An Enquiry Concerning the Principles of Morals*, ed. J. B. Schneewind, (Indianapolis: Hackett Publishing, 1983), 73-74.

[3] Aquinas, *Summa Theologica* 2-2.161.1.

[4] Ibid., 2-2.161.1.3.

[5] Ibid., 2-2.162.1.3.

[6] G. K. Chesterton, *Orthodoxy*, (Baton Rouge: Mud House Art and Literature, 2017), 44.

[7] Aquinas, *ST* 2-2.162.4.4.

[8] Nicolas Bommarito, "Modesty and Humility," *The Stanford Encyclopedia of Philosophy* (Winter 2018 Edition), Edward N. Zalta (ed.), accessed April 25, 2020, https://plato.stanford.edu/archives/win2018/entries/modesty-humility/. See specifically Sections 2 (Doxastic), 3 (Non-Doxastic), and 4 (Epistemological).

[9] Nancy E. Snow, "Humility," in *The Journal of Value Inquiry* 29, no. 2 (1995): 206-207.

[10] Ibid., 210.

[11] Norvin Richards, "Is Humility a Virtue?," *American Philosophical Quarterly* 25, no 3, (July 1988): 258.

[12] Aquinas, *ST* 2-2.161.1.3.

[13] *Pinocchio*, dir. Ben Sharpsteen and Hamilton Luske (Burbank, CA: Walt Disney Studios, 1940).

[14] Dan. 4.

[15] *Pocahontas*, dir. Mike Gabriel and Eric Goldberg (Burbank, CA: Walt Disney Studios, 1995).

[16] Acts 2:5-9, 41-42.

[17] *Aladdin*, dir. Ron Clements and John Musker (Burbank, CA: Walt Disney Studios, 1992).

[18] *Mulan*, dir. Barry Cook and Tony Bancroft (Burbank, CA: Walt Disney Studios, 1998).

[19] James 4:10 (NIV).

[20] 1 Pet. 3:15, 16a (NET).

7

The Pretty Princess: Disney's Theology of Becoming Beautiful

Miguel Benitez Jr.

D isney Princesses are the source of numerous controversies.[1] Do they contribute to patriarchal ideas? Are they, to the contrary, great symbols of feminism? Or is this, perhaps, a false dichotomy? Certainly, narratives do possess a formative power. Thus, the ultimate question is: in what ways are Disney princesses shaping the ideas of children? Answers to these questions are all worthy pursuits but, in this essay, I will seek to go down a less traveled road, that which deals with the beauty and moral virtue of the Disney Princesses. It is my contention that the outward beauty of the Disney Princesses is a visual metaphor or symbol pointing to the inner spiritual beauty that is tied to virtue. I will conclude by suggesting that once this view of beauty and virtue are established, an opportunity presents itself to point people to God. While Disney princesses may be admired for outward beauty, their tales show a deeper beauty to which physical beauty pales in comparison. As the prince was warned, before becoming a beast, *"beauty is found within."*[2] I submit that Disney princesses are drawn to signal holiness, such as we find in Tiana, Mulan, and Ariel. These outwardly beautiful princesses become more truly (inwardly) beautiful as they are shaped by lessons learned. Thus, the beauty *seen* in the beginning of the films is an artistic foreshadowing, signaling something about the princesses' character and their journey toward becoming more truly beautiful.

Beauty

First, some delimitations might prove helpful. I am not asserting what Disney *meant* to convey; I am suggesting an interpretive lens that might aid in teaching children about what Disney tales *can* convey. I acknowledge that there are harmful ideas that may have influenced and misinformed our culture's philosophy and theology of beauty. The interpretation I am offering assumes that such superficial stereotypes of beauty are not the whole story. The problem with many cultural ideals and prescriptions of physical beauty is that they presuppose there is no real ideal of beauty if it cannot be defined empirically. So, beauty must therefore be purely subjective. While beauty is a complex subject to pin down, this conclusion is problematic.

The question "what is beauty?" is one with which philosophers have wrestled for millennia. I do not claim to offer the final word here, but I think there are some helpful things we can say about it. First, beauty is, in some sense, objective; for though we point to different things and call each "beautiful," we are certain that we are stating something of substance—that "beauty" ought somehow to be understood as universally intelligible. Beauty is transcendental, like truth and goodness which are often associated with it. It is something that is not merely tied to a physical object; it is something that points beyond itself. Beauty is often said to "move us," which raises the question, "toward what are we moved?" This also means beauty is not merely a matter of taste or opinion. There is an objective element to beauty.

Saint Augustine points out that when we have a favorite actor, whose performance art we are fond of, we make arguments, we try to persuade those whose opinions differ from ours.[3] It seems odd to try to convince someone of something that is merely a matter of taste and that has no ultimate standard. To give another example, consider a red rose and a rat carcass being devoured by maggots. Which of these are more beautiful? Most people, regardless of race, gender, or time, would choose the flower, even if they found maggots devouring a rat to be more interesting. This strong intuition is reason to consider the possibility of beauty as objective.

Second, beauty is not primarily physical. In the Bible, the psalmist declares his desire "to gaze upon the beauty of the LORD."[4] If God is spirit[5] and not merely *an* example of beauty, but *the* example of beauty, then it seems that beauty is not primarily physical, but spiritual. Some may point to the fact that the Psalmist intentionally uses the word "gaze," perhaps alluding to some physical manifestation—something like the beatific vision. However, the very next line reads, "to inquire in his temple." This word inquire is also translated as "meditate". This suggests that what is taking place here is a rational process—it is not a physical manifestation that is beautiful, but God's attributes that are beautiful. The beauty of the temple, the physical, points to the higher beauty of the Lord, which is not physical.

To attach God's beauty to mere physical manifestation seems to reduce the significance of this passage. If God is only beautiful in physical manifestation, if such a manifestation is taking place, then God is not beautiful in nature. This would suggest that God can be both beautiful and not beautiful. Moreover, without God serving as the ultimate standard for beauty, it seems the psalmist's declaration of God's beauty is merely a matter of taste—meaning that someone is not wrong if they find God to be ugly. Both issues are problematic as the psalmist is declaring something about both God's nature and how we ought to think of God. Understanding that beauty is not primarily physical, but spiritual, opens the door for interpreting the beautiful depictions of the Disney princesses. As I will argue below, we see this in the life of Mulan, in which Mulan's growing in beauty has nothing to do with her appearance, after all she's depicted as beautiful the whole movie, but rather it has to do with her growth in virtue. While physical beauty is real and exists, spiritual beauty is a greater beauty.

Plato similarly declares, "the beauty of the mind is more honorable than the beauty of the outward form."[6] Diotima, Socrates's teacher, states that beauty is objective. She states that one would be "foolish .... not to recognize that the beauty in every form is one and the same!"[7] Similar to the Christian tradition, Diotima finds that all beauty is connected in that it points to or comes from the ultimate source of and standard for beauty. This view helps make sense of the fact that a person, a flower, a song, a play, and a painting can all be beautiful despite these various objects being incredibly different from each other. Also relevant is Diotima's discussion on beauties serving as "steps." She says that one goes "from one to two, and from two to all fair forms, and from fair forms to fair actions, and from fair actions to fair notions, until from fair notions he arrives at the notion of absolute beauty, and at last knows what the essence of beauty is."[8] Diotima asserts that to love the soul, to recognize the beauty of the soul, is greater than the love of the body.

Thus, one can surmise from this that the beauty of the soul is a "higher" kind of beauty.

Aquinas also observes this connection between beauty and the spiritual. "Spiritual beauty consists in a man's conduct or actions being well-proportioned in respect of the spiritual clarity of reason. Now this is what is meant by honesty, which we have stated to be the same as virtue; and it is virtue that moderates according to reason all that is connected with man. Wherefore honesty is the same as spiritual beauty."[9] Here Aquinas ties beauty to honesty, virtue, which leads us to beauty and its relation to holiness.

Third, beauty is connected to holiness. This may initially seem like a leap, but there are good reasons to see this connection. For example, consider question ten from the Westminster Shorter Catechism: "How did God create man?" The response states, "God created man male and female, after his own image, in knowledge, righteousness, and holiness, with dominion over the creatures."[10] The three-fold description of humanity consisting of knowledge, righteousness, and holiness corresponds to the traditional transcendentals of goodness, truth, and beauty. Knowledge corresponds with truth, righteousness with goodness, and holiness with beauty.

In the Scriptures, time and time again when people encounter God's presence, the proclamation made is "holy". This further suggests this connection between holiness and beauty. Theologian John-Mark Miravalle writes, "When people pursue truth, they will be conformed to truth by becoming knowledgeable. When people pursue goodness, they will be conformed to goodness by becoming morally upright."[11] What of the person who pursues beauty? It seems to follow the person who pursues beauty, conforms to holiness.

Two common biblical uses of *holiness* deserve attention. Holiness can refer to a "separateness" or being set apart from the common. In this way God is said to be holy in that God is completely separate or distinct from his creation. Humans can also be separate or set apart by their deeds, by the life that they lead. Beauty sets apart, separates things from the common. Miravalle argues, both order and surprise are important aspects of beauty,[12] yet the quality of order, or fit, receives more attention than the significance of surprise. That said, considering beauty is associated with words like "wonder," "amazement," "breathtaking," and "speechless," surprise seems to play a key role in making beautiful objects stand out. Similarly, beautiful people—people with beautiful souls—stand out or "surprise" us through their virtue and conduct.

Holiness can also be used "in the sense of transformation of the total person."[13] The apostle Paul declares, "let us cleanse ourselves from every defilement of body and spirit, bringing holiness to completion in the fear of God."[14] Holiness is often used in the sense of sanctification, or the transformed life that leads to eternal life.[15] This also ties into the idea of being made anew.[16] Many "coming of age" stories may tie in closely. In this sense then we can say that holiness, sanctification, or being made anew are the process of becoming beautiful. Likewise, when beauty accomplishes its purpose, it points to the holy.

Now we turn our attention to the princesses and their journey of becoming beautiful. Remembering that these films are made for children, the beauty of the princess is an indication to the child, that special attention should be given to this character throughout the film. In what follows, I will present case studies of three princesses—Tiana; Mulan; and Ariel—to draw out the points I have explained above.

Tiana And What's Most Important

Tiana, the princess from *The Princess and the Frog*, shared her father's dream of opening their own restaurant. Despite her father's efforts and incredible work ethic, his dream never became a reality. Along with passing his dream and work ethic to his daughter, Tiana's dad also cautioned her to never lose sight of what is really important. While the context contains clues, what is "really important" is not explicit until much later in the movie.

Tiana works two jobs, skips out on hanging out with friends, and sacrifices everything to reach her goal of owning a restaurant. Tiana finally makes enough money to make an offer on a very modest, run-down restaurant. Her mother visits to share this momentous occasion and in passing mentions that it is a shame Tiana is having to work so hard, to which Tiana replies, "I gotta make sure all Daddy's hard work means something." Tiana's mother becomes visibly upset and replies, "Daddy may not have gotten the place he always wanted, but he had something better... he had love." Tiana's mom tells Tiana that she wants her to have love as well. It is in this context that Tiana begins to sing "Almost There."[17] Taken in context, this is a song of ambition, and tunnel vision, and signifies that Tiana has missed something important.

Tiana encounters a frog and in a dramatic twist of the famous fairy tale—rather than the frog, Prince Naveen, becoming a prince, Tiana becomes a frog. As Tiana and Naveen go on their adventure to try to become human again, Tiana is resistant to both fun and, more importantly, love. Tiana and Naveen are led to Mama Odie, a blind Voodoo priestess, who tells Tiana, "You want to be human but you're blind to what you need." The irony of a blind woman telling Tiana she's blind to what she needs indicates that Tiana does not need something physical; but rather, something immaterial, or spiritual. For Tiana to figure this out, she will need to "dig a little deeper."[18]

What Tiana needs is elucidated toward the end of the film when she is forced to choose between owning her own restaurant, after her previous purchase fell through, and Prince Naveen, the man she loves. Here it becomes clear that what Tiana was missing is the spiritual virtue of love. The apostle Paul lists the spiritual virtues as faith, hope, and love, declaring that the greatest of these is love.[19] Tiana exhibits faith, (though not explicitly in God) in herself, in wishing upon a star, and in the values she learned from her father. She was also driven by hope; she hoped her own restaurant would give meaning to her efforts—and her father's. However, her father, her mother, and even Mama Odie realized that Tiana lacked the greatest virtue, love. Tiana's outward beauty may be understood as a metaphor for the greater cultivation of beauty inside of her. Her transformation from frog back to human further symbolizes spiritual transformation. Tiana grows in holiness, and as such grows in beauty.

Mulan Brings Honor to Us All

A second Disney princess whose external beauty points to spiritual beauty, is Mulan.[20] In Mulan one finds a virtuous young woman, despite being initially shown to be a bit awkward, clumsy, and immature. Near the start of the film, Mulan prepares to meet the matchmaker in hopes of finding a husband. Girls in Mulan's culture are taught that the greatest way to bring their families honor involves conforming to society's ideal of a good wife: "A girl can bring her family great honor in one way, by striking a good match and this could be the day."[21]

Mulan's meeting with the matchmaker is disastrous due to her clumsiness and her "lucky" cricket. The matchmaker screams that Mulan may "look like a bride," but that she will never bring her family honor. While the matchmaker condemns Mulan's seeming inability to conform to what is expected of young women in her culture, even her harshest critic acknowledges her outer beauty. Mulan proves to be a princess of great virtue by the end of the film. As Cardinal Newman states, "There is a physical beauty and a moral: there is a beauty of person, there is a beauty of our moral being, which is natural virtue; and in like manner there is a beauty, there is a perfection, of the intellect."[22] Mulan exhibits these various aspects of beauty as she grows and changes as a person.

After her disastrous meeting with the matchmaker, Mulan and her father sit outside where he observes the beautiful blossoms that surround them. He points out a single blossom, not yet fully bloomed, and states that when it does, it will be the most beautiful of all. This foreshadows Mulan's "blossoming." Note that Mulan's father is connecting the idea of her growing in character, maturing as an adult, increasing in virtue with becoming beautiful. Mulan's becoming beautiful is not a physical change, but a moral or spiritual one.

A virtue that sets Mulan apart which deserves particular attention is fortitude. Fortitude is tied to the idea of endurance and resiliency in the face of danger. As the Huns invade, the emperor decrees that every imperial family must send one male representative to fight in the war. Mulan's father, Fa Zhou, has no son, therefore despite being elderly and physically limited, he agrees to go. The night before he is to leave for training, Mulan steals Fa Zhou's papers and takes his place posing as his son. Mulan acknowledges that one of her motives involves self-discovery, but the major motivating factor is the desire to protect her father from a war in which he would almost certainly die.

Despite the impression that Mulan is not like the other women and has now chosen to go off to war, this need not be seen as a lack of femininity, but rather a broader understanding of it. Mulan is not like the guys; she struggles to play by their rules. The irony of the song "I'll Make a Man out of You"[23] is that Mulan is not a man, nor becoming a man, but rather, she relentlessly grows in her talents, skills, and abilities as a woman to get the job done. Mulan and her fellow soldiers find themselves heavily outnumbered by the Huns, yet with her quick thinking and courage she executes a plan that saves them all. Ping, Mulan's male persona, is declared the bravest of them all. Mulan is injured in battle which exposes her identity. Only then is her true identity as both feminine and having fortitude, being beautiful and brave, revealed.

At the end of the film, as a kind of bookend to Fa Zhou's comment about Mulan being a late blooming blossom, the King tells Li Shang, "The flower that blooms in adversity is the most rare and beautiful of all." Here again,

Mulan's blooming beauty is referenced not in the context of physical beauty, but in the context of her becoming beautiful morally and spiritually because she has faced adversity with great courage.

Ariel as Rebel Mermaid

Of the princesses I am surveying, Ariel may be the most controversial, especially when considering what is traditionally seen as virtuous. Ariel is disobedient, rebellious, self-absorbed, irresponsible, and an overall bratty teenager. Breaking from traditional Disney princesses, Ariel is more assertive and active. For some this transition is seen as a positive attribute, while for others this is negative. Either way, few would likely hold Ariel up as an example of virtue. While Ariel is not as virtuous as the princesses discussed above, Ariel does grow. Ariel learns the cost of immaturity and rebellion. She grows as she moves toward the golden mean between rashness and cowardice, the virtue of courage.

Ariel gets into trouble when she strikes a deal with Ursula in order to become human to win Prince Eric's heart. Ariel has three days to get Eric to give her true love's kiss, so she and her friends attempt to make this happen. Initially she appears to be on the verge of success, but Ursula thwarts her plans by posing as a human. Ariel runs out of time and now belongs to Ursula. This is where Ariel's growth can be observed.

Ariel sees not only that her immaturity and rebellion have landed *her* in a lot of trouble, but also that her behavior has negatively affected others. When King Triton, her father, attempts to save her, we see Ariel's regret, her change of mind, or repentance on display. She apologizes and asks her father's forgiveness. Triton had to exchange himself for his daughter's freedom. This sets Ariel off into a mode that is much more mature and courageous. Rather than acting for her own desires, she was now acting to save those she loved. At the end of the movie, Ariel is shown to become inwardly beautiful in her repentance and courage, something her outward beauty pointed to all along.

Beauty in a Fallen World

Another important lesson is drawn from *The Little Mermaid* when one considers Ursula as a kind of counterexample to the princesses discussed above.

Ursula is a hideous character, inside and out. To be clear, to say that Ursula is ugly does not necessitate believing that fat equals ugly. While some believe that Disney perpetuates the idea that skinny is pretty and fat is ugly, this is not necessarily so, as many fuller-bodied characters throughout Disney tales—from fairy godmothers to Pooh-bears—are depicted as good, admirable, and lovely rather than *ugly* or *hideous*. Ursula on the other hand is disordered; she is clearly, though for reasons difficult to delineate, drawn as ugly on the exterior—and this is artistically intended to point to a wickedness on the inside. However, Ursula changes her outward appearance to a more attractive form as she tries to fool Eric into marrying her. Does this not show that beauty is in fact only skin deep—that it is physical beauty which attracts the prince? Certainly, the beauty *she* possesses while in human form should in no way be seen as an indication of holiness or virtue. This does raise one final and important issue when exploring the theology of beauty.

The author of Proverbs in the Bible warns his audience about the dangers of beauty. He states that charm can be deceptive, and beauty is vain.[24] He goes on to warn about the seductive power of certain beautiful people that must be resisted.[25] Ursula serves as a warning that there are exceptions to the rule and in a fallen world, outward beauty does not always correspond to inward beauty. It does not take much time watching the news or scrolling through headlines on the internet to see that this is so. Some of the stars in Hollywood, often praised for their looks, show lives marked by immorality and vice. When Ursula dons a deceptive form, placing Eric under a spell to hinder him from recognizing Ariel's inner beauty, she reminds us that in a world where things are not always as they *ought* to be, outward beauty does not always point to the beauty of the soul. In a broken world sometimes, what passes for beauty can be deceiving. Sometimes, ugliness hides in such a way that can appeal to our tastes. Despite deceptive exceptions, like Ursula's, in understanding the view of beauty that has been presented above, there is reason to believe that there is great reward in becoming more inwardly beautiful. Disney princess stories can serve parents well in understanding that beauty is tied to character, character is formed by each along our own journey, within our own stories, and it is the beautiful soul, not the physically acclaimed form, which connects character to the good life and the ever-after.

Conclusion

I have suggested viewing Disney princesses through a lens of redemption. These princesses, if seen as visual metaphors for virtue or holiness, can serve as instructional guides to children in forming their views of what is truly beautiful—teaching them that true beauty lies within. Beauty of persons is at a higher level when it points to a person's virtue or holiness. Once this aspect of moral philosophy is understood, an opportunity presents itself to speak to an even deeper lesson in moral theology, for when a person's virtue or holiness stands out, when it separates them from the common and the usual, that is when beauty is fulfilling its ultimate purpose, of pointing to the source of all beauty, the beautiful God who has created beautifully.

Notes

[1] This essay is dedicated to my pretty princess, my daughter, Gabriela.

[2] *Beauty and the Beast*, dir. Gary Trousdale and Kirk Wise (Burbank, CA: Walt Disney Studios, 1991).

[3] Augustine, *On Christian Doctrine*, 1.29.30.

[4] Ps. 27:4.

[5] John 4:24.

[6] Plato, *Symposium*, 210b-210c.

[7] Ibid., 210a-210c.

[8] Ibid., 211c-211e.

[9] Thomas Aquinas, *Summa Theologica* 2-2.145.2.

[10] *Westminster Shorter Catechism*, Question 10.

[11] John-Mark L. Miravalle, *Beauty: What it is and Why it Matters* (Manchester: Sophia Institute Press, 2019), 35.

[12] Ibid., 32-35.

[13] J. R. Williams, "Holiness," in *Evangelical Dictionary of Theology*, 2nd ed., ed. Walter A. Elwell (Grand Rapids: Baker Academic, 2001), 563.

[14] 2 Cor. 7:1.

[15] Rom. 6:22.

[16] 2 Cor. 5:17.

[17] Randy Newman, "Almost There," in *The Princess and the Frog*, dir. Ron Clements and John Musker (Burbank, CA: Walt Disney Studios, 2009).

[18] Randy Newman, "Dig a Little Deeper," in *The Princess and the Frog* (2009).

[19] 1 Cor. 13:13.

[20] While Mulan may not be a princess by position in the movie, she is still considered a Disney Princess by the franchise.

[21] David Zippel and Matthew Wilder, "Honor to Us All," in *Mulan*, dir. Barry Cook and Tony Bancroft (Burbank, CA: Walt Disney Studios, 1998).

[22] John Henry Newman, *The Idea of a University*, ed. Martin J. Svaglic. Notre Dame: University of Notre Dame Press, 1982: 86; as found in Stratford Caldecott, *Beauty for Truth's Sake: On the Re-enchantment of Education*. Grand Rapids: Brazos Press, 2009: 28.

[23] David Zippel and Matthew Wilder, "I'll Make a Man Out of You," in *Mulan* (1998).

[24] Prov. 31:30.

[25] Prov. 6:25.

8

The Lost Princess: The Theological Anthropology of Disney's Tangled

Timothy E. G. Bartel

To those interested in the conversation between theology and the story-worlds of Disney, the *Rapunzel* fairy tale is instructive. This story was made famous by the Brothers Grimm in their early nineteenth-century collection of German folk tales. In the Grimm tale, a pregnant couple make a deal with a witch named Gothel ("godmother" in German)—they trade their future daughter for the rampion plant in Gothel's garden. The girl, who is named "Rapunzel" after the plant she was traded for, lives in a tall tower, which is only accessible by climbing the girl's very long hair. A wandering prince finds out the tower's secret, climbs to Rapunzel, and becomes her lover. When Gothel finds out about the two, she cuts Rapunzel's hair, abandons her in the wilderness, and lures the prince into the tower where she reveals that his love is gone. In despair, the Prince falls from the tower and is blinded. He wanders the wilderness until he discovers Rapunzel, who heals his eyes with her tears, and the two are finally together at last.[1]

This story, filled as it is with themes of exchange, imprisonment, struggle, and the healing power of love, would become one of the most popular fairy tales in nineteenth and twentieth century culture. It has been retold in both serious poems and jovial spoofs, until it finally received the Disney treatment in 2010's animated musical *Tangled*. Far from being a mere parody or modish updating of the Grimm fairy tale, *Tangled*, as developed by Glen Keane, is a film that preserves the major thematic heart of the Grimm tale, and, through significant changes, magnifies the ethical themes of the original tale into a theological vision of human identity.

In his influential study of fairy tales, *The Uses of Enchantment*, Bruno Bettelheim argues that the Grimm version of Rapunzel features patterns of selfishness followed by growth: "Both Rapunzel and the Prince have to undergo a period of trial and tribulation, of inner growth through misfortune — as is true for many heroes of fairy tales."[2] These patterns, Bettelheim argues, prove instructive to the reader of the tale, especially in childhood: "The child is unaware of his inner processes, which is why these are externalized in the fairy tale and symbolically represented by actions standing for inner and outer struggles."[3] Thus the story of Rapunzel can be pedagogical tool for the young reader: they are able to see in the characters the failure and growth that is taking place within the maturing human self. Though Bettelheim does not discuss the theological implications of the ethical themes in the Rapunzel tale, an investigation of the development of Disney's *Tangled* reveals that the filmmakers discerned theological possibilities within the Rapunzel tale, especially in its themes of exchange and magical healing

Disney's *Tangled* and the Grimm Tale

In 2010, Disney released *Tangled* as its 50th animated feature.[4] With *Tangled*, Disney discovered a new, winning formula for animated musicals; *Tangled* is set in the same type of medieval fairy tale world as *Snow White* and *Beauty and the Beast*, but it uses 3D computer animation as its medium, a first for a Disney animated musical. The man most responsible for the creation of *Tangled* is Glen Keane, a veteran of Disney's Renaissance films, who had been working on *Tangled* since 1996. In a 2010 interview, Keane explained the development of his project:

> I started developing this story in '96 while I was doing "Tarzan" and "Treasure Planet" and then started to work on it in 2002 full-time. At that point, the studio was looking for more of a twist on the fairy tale. That was the way the wind was blowing

and I put up my sails and blew in that direction. That version was called "Rapunzel Unbraided" and I worked on it for three years. It was a fun, wonderful, witty version and we had a couple of great writers. But in my heart of hearts I believed there was something much more sincere and genuine to get out of the story, so we set it aside and went back to the roots of the original fairy tale.[5]

Inspired by the success of more cynical children's films like *Shrek* (2001), Disney was attempting to throw off its overly sincere image. But it was sincerity that Keane most wanted to show in a Rapunzel film, and it was this more "sincere and genuine" vision that won out. Keane credits the turn toward sincerity in the final film to "the sensibility of [co-directors] Byron Howard and Nathan Greno, who have this really, really, deep, deep love of the sincerity of Disney films."[6] This sincerity and loyalty to the legacy of classic Disney musicals helped lead to the success of *Tangled*, and warranted Disney's rejuvenated output of computer animated, princess-focused musicals like *Frozen* (2013) *Moana* (2016), and *Frozen II* (2019).

The opening scene of Tangled begins with a voice-over: "This is the story of how I died," says the narrator. The voice is that of Flynn Rider, who will be the main male protagonist of the film. "Don't worry," he continues, "this is actually a very fun story, and the truth is, it isn't even mine. This is a story of a girl named Rapunzel, and it begins with the sun. Now, once upon a time a single drop of sunlight fell from the heavens."[7] This opening is a bold choice on the filmmakers' part, not just from a narrative standpoint but also because it casts a dark frame for the rest of the story. This story will end in, or at least include, death.

In Rider's story of the sun, a "single drop of sunlight" falls to earth, and where it falls there grows a "magic golden flower." This flower possesses a heavenly origin and contains the power "to heal the sick and injured" when a song is sung in its presence. We then see an old woman, who Rider calls "Mother Gothel," who finds the plant and sings a song which repeats the lines "Flower, gleam and glow... Bring back what once was mine."[8] As she sings, Gothel's wrinkles and white hair are magically replaced by smooth skin and dark locks. Though this story does not contain any exact parallels to the opening of the Rapunzel tale other than the name Gothel, the observant viewer can see parallel ethical themes emerging. We have the theme of healing drops, which appear, with Rapunzel's tears, at the end of the original tale. And we have a woman who seeks out a plant, this time growing in the wild on the edge of a seaside cliff, not in her neighbor's garden. But we see the woman hide the plant under a basket, and Rider, still narrating, tells us that instead of sharing the magic of the flower, Gothel hides it and keeps it to herself.

Here, then, we have a recognizable version of the witch from Grimm's tale: a woman involved in magic who in some way seeks to possess a valuable, desirable plant.[9] But the film makes clear that the magic flower does not belong to Gothel in the way the rapunzel plant belongs to the Witch in the Grimm tale. From the outset, then, Gothel cannot be wronged in the way that Grimm's Witch can be. If another woman desires the flower, she will have just as much right to it as Gothel.

Another woman *does* end up taking the plant: a pregnant queen who is dying, and whose subjects discover the flower, having heard of its healing powers. The queen's subjects uproot the flower, steep it in water, and the resulting poultice, when drunk, heals the queen. She gives birth to a girl with long golden hair and names her Rapunzel. Rapunzel is connected to the plant not just because she is traded for it, as in the Grimm tale, but because she is imbued with the same heavenly, golden, healing power that the plant possessed. Seeking revenge for the loss of the flower, Gothel sneaks into the castle while the king and queen sleep. Finding that Rapunzel's hair possesses the flower's magic, Gothel steals the girl and locks her in a tower. We also see that Rapunzel's hair only works its magic while attached to Rapunzel's head. Her hair turns brown and ordinary when cut. Gothel would have preferred the hair without the girl. This is unlike the witch in the Grimm tale, who *does* seem to actually want the child—a child who, incidentally, has no apparent magical value.

From these prologue scenes, we can see that Disney's *Tangled* has retained the basic exchange plot of the Grimm tale—a pregnant couple take a plant from Gothel and Gothel takes their baby—but the magic element of the final scene of the Grimm tale has been expanded backward into each element of the story from the opening. There is still a plant, but it is a *magic* plant from the heavens. And there is still a baby, but she is a *magic* baby—what's more, she's a princess, not the daughter of commoners. Also, the reason Gothel steals and locks away the girls is because she is useful for magic, not because of the more mundane reason that the Grimm's tale implies, namely that Gothel wants to keep her safe from men, now that she is an adolescent.

The whole first half of the Grimm tale is paralleled by the brief opening prologue, leaving room for the bulk of *Tangled* to dramatize the story of

Rapunzel and the Prince. And it does, with some notable exceptions. After the prologue the film jumps to Rapunzel before her eighteenth birthday, and we are made familiar with her life: having lived in the tower since infancy, Rapunzel seems to have mastered all domestic and many fine arts: she cooks, she sews, she cleans, she reads, she does ballet, she plays chess and guitar, she is a masterful painter and singer, and on top of all this, she has made her incredibly long hair into a prehensile appendage, using it with finesse as a grappling hook, whip, and, of course the rappelling rope of the original tale, by which Gothel reaches her. Gothel, we learn, makes sure Rapunzel is materially cared for, but she belittles and humiliates Rapunzel in her interactions with her, and prioritizes Rapunzel's hair over her person. She even calls Rapunzel "my flower." To Rapunzel this may seem like a term of endearment, but we as the audience know it is an example of Gothel only prizing Rapunzel for the power of the flower that she now possesses.

Unsurprisingly, Rapunzel desperately wants to leave the tower, but Gothel will have none of it. What Rapunzel most wants to discover is the nature of the floating lights that she sees on the horizon every year on her birthday. We as the audience know that they are a tribute of floating lanterns commemorating the lost princess, which is offered by the king and queen every year. Rapunzel is drawn to these lights; they are even featured in her paintings, but she does not understand them.

When we meet the young man who will be the suitor of Rapunzel, he is not a prince at all. He is the narrator of the prologue, the outlaw Flynn Rider, who finds and climbs Rapunzel's tower with no knowledge at all that there is a girl within it. He is merely outrunning the palace guards, who are chasing him because he stole a crown from the castle—a crown that, we slowly learn, belongs to the lost princess of the kingdom: Rapunzel herself. Flynn climbs the tower using arrows, and upon entering is immediately knocked unconscious by a terrified Rapunzel. While Flynn is unconscious, Rapunzel finds the crown in his satchel, and almost has a moment of recognition when she puts on the crown and looks in the mirror—the music swells, there is a look of enlightenment on her face—but in the next moment she disregards it. Once Rider comes to and finds himself securely tied up in Rapunzel's hair, he finds himself presented with a new sort of exchange: she will give him "his" crown back if he will take her to see what she calls the "floating lights." Looking at Rapunzel's painting of the lights that she indicates on her wall, Rider tells her that the lights are "the lantern thing they do for the princess." After some further reluctance, Rider agrees to Rapunzel's deal.

The bulk of the rest of the film is the adventure that Rider and Rapunzel have, in which they meet a motley crew of pub-lounging brigands and stay one step ahead of Rider's former band of thieves, the palace guards' clever horse Maximus, and, eventually, a vengeful Gothel. As they explore the kingdom, Rapunzel has two things reinforced: that though the world is indeed dangerous, she can survive and even flourish in it, and that the healing power of her magical hair can help many people, not just Gothel. Further, she sees a whole society whose iconography and cultural artifacts are organized around the magic of the sun-flower and a sorrow over the lost princess. Sun-like flower emblems abound: on the armor of the palace guards, on the palace flags, in the cobblestones of the streets, and, most significantly, on the floating lanterns that are released by the thousands on the night of her birthday.

Of course, Rapunzel and Rider begin to fall in love, but their happiness is interrupted by Gothel, who catches up with them, delivers Rider over to the authorities to be hanged, and takes Rapunzel back to the tower. Rapunzel, despairing for Rider's life, not to mention her own freedom, begins to put together the pieces of what she has experienced: the sorrow of the kingdom, the lantern ceremony's coincidence with her birthday, the sun-flower imagery all over the kingdom, and her own memories from infancy of seeing that same flower imagery; all these point to the truth, which she finally and boldly declares to Gothel: "I am the lost princess." Rapunzel has realized her own identity. She is not, like in the Grimm tale, a child of commoners, willingly given up. She is the daughter of the king, deceived to believe she was of little worth except for her hair, which could only be used to serve—and preserve—her captor and deceiver. *Tangled*, then, gives Rapunzel a hidden identity, one of great dignity, royalty, and worth, and sets her on a journey to discover her true identity and to confront the great deceiver who has imprisoned and used her.

The astute reader will have begun to see the rich theological suggestiveness in Keane's and Disney's re-imagining of Rapunzel, and the climax of the film only adds to this theological suggestiveness. Rider is saved by a newly sympathetic Maximus the horse with the help of the well-meaning brigands. Rider speeds to Rapunzel's tower, and calls out the immortal line: "Rapunzel, let down your hair!" Down comes Rapunzel's hair, and up climbs Rider, but it is—as in Grimm—all a ruse. Rapunzel is not gone, but she is in chains, and Gothel steps from the shadows and mortally wounds Rider with a knife.

Now we see what Rider promised us in the beginning: this is indeed the story of how he died.

Rapunzel, knowing the power she possesses, makes a final exchange with Gothel. If Gothel will let her heal Rider, she will go away with Gothel and serve her forever. Gothel agrees, and Rider is faced with a choice: whether or not to let the woman he loves doom herself to save him. In his dying act, Rider slices off Rapunzel's hair, causing a chain reaction of death: Rapunzel's hair loses its magic, darkening to a dull brown; Gothel loses her youth, wrinkling and writhing in agony, then tripping and falling out of the tower to her death; and Rider himself dies, having saved Rapunzel from her captor and deceiver. As Rapunzel cradles her dead love, she begins to cry — and to sing. And finally, the magic of the original tale is enacted: the song reminds us of the power of the sun-flower: "heal what has been hurt... save what has been lost." Rapunzel's tears, as they fall on Rider's face, briefly glow in the shape of the sun-flower. Rider is restored to life, and it seems that the film will now end.

But there is one last reconciliation, one last healing to be enacted, and it is the most important—and perhaps the most moving—of all. We see the king and queen, in great sorrow, wordlessly encouraging one another to leave their chambers and face another day. A guard, in a state of awe, bursts in, and, speechless, merely nods to them and gestures toward the door. The king and queen rush out to a balcony, where Rapunzel and Rider stand expectantly. The reunited family embrace, and we see the true and final reconciliation; for, while she was lost, Rapunzel was not the only one who lived in a deprived state. The whole kingdom had been in a state of loss and incompleteness, both for the present and for the future. But now the lost princess has returned to her own true identity, and to her proper place in the kingdom.

The Theological Anthropology of *Tangled*

If Bettelheim is correct, and fairy tales teach children about their own selves, placing internal struggles and truths into external realities and characters, then *Tangled* can be read as a story about the deception and redemption of humanity. Glen Keane was the first to give a theological interpretation to *Tangled* story. Jordan Poblete writes,

When animating the opening sequence of *Tangled*, Keane thought of.... James 1:17, saying "Every good and perfect gift is from above, coming down from the Father of the heavenly lights." He continued saying that truth "...is this amazing source of life and beauty and transformation. That's something I believe in my own life. And with the characters I've animated, I've always tried [to animate in a way] that reflects my own spiritual life.'"[10]

Keane confirms the intentionally heavenly nature of the magic in the sun, the sun-flower, and Rapunzel's hair and tears. Further, he points to truth as the element that transforms Rapunzel from a frightened and self-doubting captive to a royal and illumined woman, with the power of healing in her very body. The connections between truth and light are prevalent within the film, both in the aforementioned sun-imagery throughout the kingdom, and, most memorably, in the song Rapunzel and Rider sing while they watch the floating lantern ceremony: "And at last I see the light, and it's like a fog has lifted / And it's warm, and real and bright, and the world has somehow shifted."[11] The shift that seems to be in "the world" is more accurately a shift that has happened in Rapunzel and Rider; they have come to a new under-standing of their own identities and how they fit into the world.[12] For Rapunzel, this will prove to be a realization that the whole kingdom—the whole world, even—is organized around the hope that she will return to her identity.

In Romans, St. Paul writes, "For the creation waits with eager longing for the revealing of the children of God; for the creation was subjected to futility, not of its own will but the will of the one who subjected it, in hope that the creation itself will be set free from its bondage to decay and will obtain the freedom of the glory of the children of God."[13] In these two verses can be found most of the major thematic elements of *Tangled* we have been discussing: a realm eagerly waiting for the revelation of a child, the experience of bondage to decay and futility that coexists with the hope for freedom, and, finally, the possibility of glorious children of God who, having been freed, bring freedom.

St Basil the Great, a fourth century theologian, expands on this Pauline vision. In his first "Treatise On the Origin of Humanity," he insists on the inherent dignity of the human being. "Know your own dignity!" he urges his audience.[14] Further, he explains that this dignity is due to humans being created in the image and likeness of God: "In our initial structure co-

originates and exists our coming into being according to the image of God....
And in giving us the power to become like God he let us be artisans of the
likeness to God, so that the reward for the work would be ours."[15] To drive
home this final point, Basil provides a brief catechism. "How do we come to
be according to the likeness? Through the Gospels. What is Christianity?
Likeness to God as far as is possible for human nature."[16]

For Basil, humans are created as beings of special dignity, and with free
will in order to become like God through a Christian life grounded in the
truth of the New Testament Gospels. Because of the fall, humans often forget
this inherent dignity and the call to become like God. This is why, according
to both St Paul and St Basil, we need the gospel of Christ: He is "the way,
and the truth, and the life,"[17] and through the salvation that Christ offers, the
formerly deceived human can be transformed into one of the "children of
God." This heavenly identity is the true nature of all humans according to St.
Basil. Keane's grounding of Rapunzel's identity in a royal, and, ultimately,
heavenly source, follows the basic contours of Pauline and Basilian theology.
Because each human was created by God in God's image, they have a heavenly origin, and are called to become more and more heavenly, more and
more like God.

By the end of *Tangled*, Rapunzel's body literally exudes heavenly, healing light, and heals all it touches. According to Christian theology, what Rapunzel becomes is what all humans should become: beings resembling their
heavenly origin, spreading the light and truth of their heavenly source to
all—even and especially to the dead, who, Christian doctrine reminds us, can
be raised.

Conclusion: The Witness of Art

Tangled is a film full of art, and it is through art that the major transformation
of the tale takes place. The film is itself, of course, a piece of art, but it is also
about an artist and how she comes to understand her true identity through
art. Rapunzel is a painter, and she paints not only lovely scenes of nature and
star charts, but also, as the centerpiece of her tower, she paints a girl with
long golden hair sitting in a tree looking at the strange floating lights; it is
herself, contemplating a mystery. Part of what draws Rapunzel and Rider
together is that Rider can interpret Rapunzel's art properly. It is through his
interpretation of her art that she first learns of the lost princess. Further,
when the duo gets to the city, Rapunzel interacts with the inhabitants of the

city through art; she draws a huge, ornate sun-flower, and as she does, she observes another piece of art—a mosaic of the king and queen and herself as a small child. When Rapunzel has her realization of her true identity as the lost princess, it is through reflecting on her recurring motif of the sun-flower in her own paintings, connecting it to the sunflower motif she saw all over the kingdom, and, finally, correctly identifying the little princess in the mosaic as herself.

Just as art plays a pivotal role in Rapunzel's transformation, it can play an important role in how Christians communicate heavenly truth to the world. In the fairy land of *Tangled*, truth is communicated through art. And we, the viewers, live in a fairy land not so different from that of Rapunzel. Though we find no glowing hair nor magic sunflowers in our world, we do still find truth through art—in this case, through an animated musical about a lost princess who can be understood to stand for all of us: lost, but not wholly; still able to discern, through the beauty of story, our original, heavenward call.

Notes

[1] Brothers Grimm, *Selected Tales*, trans. David Luke (New York: Penguin, 1982), 66–69.

[2] Bruno Bettelheim, *The Uses of Enchantment* (New York: Vintage, 1976), 149.

[3] Ibid., 149–50.

[4] *Tangled* was released after a decade in which Disney had largely abandoned the princess-focused musicals that had defined the studio in the 1990s. From 2000–2008, Disney released no animated features that focused on princesses. Instead sarcastic adventure comedies dominated, with features like *The Emperor's New Groove* (2000), *Home on the Range* (2004), *Chicken Little* (2005), and *Meet the Robinsons* (2007).

[5] Glen Keane, "Interview: Glen Keane of Tangled," interviewed by Nell Minow, Movie Mom (blog). November 4, 2010, https://moviemom.com/interview-glen-keane-of-tangle/.

[6] Ibid.

[7] *Tangled*, dir. Nathan Greno and Byron Howard (Burbank, CA: Walt Disney Studios, 2010).

[8] Glenn Slater and Alan Menken, "Healing Incantation," in *Tangled* (2010).

[9] Is Disney's Gothel a witch? She obviously involves herself in the usage of Rapunzel's magical hair, but she does not seem to otherwise use magic, as does *Sleeping Beauty*'s Maleficent or *Snow White*'s evil queen.

[10] Jordan Poblete, "Half Disney Animator, Half Preacher," *The Disney Examiner*, June 29, 2015, http://disneyexaminer.com/2015/06/29/half-disney-animator-half-preacher-glen-keane-animation-as-ministry/.

[11] Glenn Slater and Alan Menken, "I See the Light," in *Tangled* (2010).

[12] Though this paper does not focus on Rider, it is significant that over the course of the film his growing love for Rapunzel allows him to reveal his true name and backstory.

[13] Rom. 8:19–20 (NRSV).

[14] Basil the Great, *On The Human Condition*, trans. Nonna Verna Harrison (Crestwood: St Vladimir Seminary Press, 2005), 43.

[15] Ibid., 43–44.

[16] Ibid., 45.

[17] John 14:6.

9

I Am Moana: MacIntyre's Virtue Theory and the Reality of Animated Morality

Sean C. Hadley

D
isney's animated features often explore the tension of lived communities, whether it's a fiery Scottish princess displeased with her
mother's approach to politics (*Brave*) or the fear-based threat of war
between English colonists and Native Americans (*Pocahontas*). The plot
might even write itself *ad nauseum*: the scene opens on a young, impression-
able character, the plot challenging a previously held idea, someone from a
competing community becomes involved, and the primary actor must make
a choice regarding the kind of person they wish to be from that moment forward. The artists and storytellers who worked on these films did not invent
this structure, though. For what Aristotle wrote of tragedy holds true in all
story–telling: the "greatest means of emotional power are components of the
plot-structure."[1] Well–established plot–structures are more than mere convention, though that might be powerful enough on its own; arcs of story–
telling are passed on from generation to generation, creating an unbroken
(even if sometimes shifting) understanding of what it means to tell a story of
moral worth.

First-century BC Roman poet Horace wrote that all "good writing" stems from moral sense, and the Bible provides a plethora of stories which fit this mold nicely.[2] Hans-Georg Gadamer similarly observed, pagans and Christians have long known that stories reinforce the morality of ages past, while also allowing for the "before and after to form a unified flow of experience."[3] This story–telling aspect of human culture plays a key role in understanding any moral tradition, for the audience only recognizes the answer to the question, "What am I to do?" if they first understand, "Of what story or stories do I find myself a part?"[4] While modern film making has rendered many children's movies into little more than sugar–coated propaganda, there are some animated films which accomplish something more. By exploring the idea of blending competing visions of the moral life, more than other family-oriented studios, Disney animated films engage moral traditions in significant ways.

Though sometimes viewed as saccharin—oversimplifications of what Alasdair MacIntyre calls emotivism (the view that moral statements refer only to subjective feelings, and not to objective truth)—certain Disney films actually suggest complex moral tensions, rooted in an older understanding of what it means to be "happy" or to be a "good citizen." Consider *Fantasia 2000* (1999). This update, blending musical scores and animated shorts, is not merely "feel good" entertainment; the film suggests something about communal roots, something metaphysical, that shapes the basics of all moral decision making. Such animated features take elements from multiple cultures and blends them to craft a moral vision. *Fantasia 2000* presents these amalgamations in the most startling of ways, as Edward Elgar's "Pomp and Circumstance" accompanies Donald Duck on the Biblical Ark, and Igor Stravinsky's "The Firebird" provides the background of a mythic Sprite who restores a devastated forest. In both instances, the art forms fuse to communicate something about the story in view, which is both emotional and moral. "Pomp and Circumstance," with its grandiose notes, draws upon Donald's comic attempts to corral the animals.[5] Disney enjoys the juxtaposition of things unalike, but always tending toward a moral aim in line with current cultural concepts of right and wrong.

Of all their most recent films, Disney's *Moana* (2016)[6] embodies the tension between the metaphysical and physical claims on morality in a way most clearly aligned with MacIntyre's thesis. This movie does not simply uproot the old to replace it with the new, but the opposite; Moana revives an older understanding in order to better serve her community's present circumstances. In fact, the story employs the same process of how to evaluate competing moral claims as outlined in Alasdair MacIntyre's virtue theory. In rejecting emotivism and encouraging both an adaptability to circumstances and connection to the past, *Moana* restores "intelligibility and rationality to our moral and social attitudes and commitments" in a way that few films can.[7] What processes lead Moana to the complex moral understanding that MacIntyre describes, and what competing moral claims of the physical and metaphysical realities find expression in her story? MacIntyre's Christian view of morality helps us to see *Moana* through the lens of a well-ordered, thoughtful, virtuous life.

Defining Morality

Alasdair MacIntyre's virtue theory draws from his study of Aristotle and Christian ethics. First, MacIntyre identifies the moral theory of emotivism, and its various implications: "Emotivism is the doctrine that all evaluative judgements and more specifically all moral judgements are *nothing but* expressions of preference, expressions of attitude or feeling, insofar as they are moral or evaluative in character."[8] It is not just that such a philosophy describes a singular preference for moral judgement, however. For "emotivism is thus a theory which professes to give an account of *all* value judgements whatsoever."[9] The emotivist thus claims to explain all morality as mere feeling but does so with "no rational history in its transitions from one state of moral commitment to another."[10] This view finds expression in the "follow your heart" mantra that permeates children's literature and entertainment. Moral decision making for the emotivist depends entirely upon the individual's mood and context; there can be no objective standard outside of the moral agent to inform their actions.

The second of MacIntyre's points is that the history of moral development is a back-and-forth, with competing traditions constantly pushing against on one another to determine the right course of ethical action. However, it is not a case of *alien* cultures, for "if two moral traditions are able to recognize each other as advancing rival contentions on issues of importance, then necessarily they must share common features."[11] Such ethical contentions exist within different generations of the same culture, just as much as when two foreign cultures meet one another. And such interaction is important, for "nothing precludes the discovery that the rival tradition offers cogent explanations of weaknesses, of inabilities to formulate or solve problems adequately, of a variety of incoherences in one's own tradition for which the resources of one's own tradition had not been able to offer a convincing account."[12]

MacIntyre's thesis aims to show that any "theory of moral reality" is going to be "*the best theory so far* [emphasis in original]."[13] The constant tension exhibited between competing moral claims, such as those between *Moana*'s characters on the island of Motunui, lead the viewer to try making sense of moral action in the present. This is something that Disney movies have not always portrayed well. But this does not negate the presence of morality in Disney movies. Annalee Ward, a professor at the University of Dubuque who has written on morality in Disney's films, argues that, the notion that a Disney film "may entertain by virtue of being a narrative" but nevertheless "promotes certain values over and against others."[14] And this sentiment is writ large in the American population, who see Disney's stories as moral in their essence.[15] MacIntyre's approach to moral theory can help Christians make sense of films that seem to be engaging pagan gods on the surface, but are ripe with apologetic promise.

Moana's Moral Compass

The 2016 film, *Moana*, offers a peculiar look into the notion of virtue theory and moral tensions. To understand the importance of *Moana*, it is helpful to know something of how the story progressed, as well as to recognize the directors' progression from their earlier films. The problems of competing moral claims manifests in Disney animated films in a couple of primary ways, with either one generation's virtues upending the earlier or one culture's morality subsuming another. Consider the moral conclusions of *Aladdin* (1992) and *Pocahontas* (1995) as examples. Aladdin's presence in the palace results in the rewriting of a long-standing tradition, while Pocahontas aids John Smith's journey toward understanding the virtues of her people. *Moana* tackles both, set within the context of the culture of Pacific Islanders and their deities.

Making a Disney movie about the mythology and Polynesian culture is sufficient to raise red flags, as Disney's track record rates poorly when representing cultures outside the Western tradition. The first screenwriter, Taika Waititi initially signed on to the project to "help try and make this not a bad film."[16] Though his script served primarily to show the eventual filmmakers what direction the humor could reasonably take, Waititi spoke of the final product as something "good." John Musker and Ron Clements, long-time Disney storytellers, spent considerable amounts of time learning from locals and natives from whom the world *Moana* is something lived.[17] The two directors spent three weeks traveling among "Fiji, Samoa, and Tahiti," learning from "linguists, archeologists and navigators." The story of Moana is born out of more than a passing fancy; the movie expresses the interaction of one culture seeking to understand another.

Such seeking would not typically describe the Musker and Clements films of the past. *The Little Mermaid* (1989) and *The Princess and the Frog* (2009) are well-received films, but not seen as the merging of horizons between competing moral claims. Musker and Clements' take on the Hans Christian Andersen classic is held up as the prime example of a culture gone awry, adding "Sebastian the singing crab and the bikini-clad Ariel" in lieu of the original's "child's Easter sermon"[18] These films typify the emotivist claims that the right thing tends to be the one that "feels" right, whatever that may be. Even here, characters change and develop, for the notion that children's stories are natural venues for the passing on of virtues has permeated Disney films over the decades.[19] But the moral development is typically in one direction, with the clearly right thing to do established early on in the story, without moral exploration. As Monique Wonderly, professor of philosophy at UC San Diego, has highlighted, Disney films often treat their child audiences on a superficial level, ignoring that children make complex moral choices every day, requiring "only that we properly guide and equip them."[20]

Musker and Clements have oversimplified ethical choices in their plots before, allowing the supernatural to steer the otherwise self-seeking characters towards the right. Triton transforms Ariel into a human, and a kiss makes Tiana human again. In reaction to this, viewers might reject the metaphysical, arguing that "realistic" portrayals of morality best develop children into ethical agents. MacIntyre's virtue theory does not require this materialist account, though, and Disney's films are rooted in the mixed world of the natural and supernatural. *Moana* demonstrates that the invocation of the divine may be a better aid for stimulating the moral imagination.[21] Going further, *Moana* seemed to the directors as something more than the standard characters they had previously crafted.[22]

Clements's invocation of Joseph Campbell's hero's journey suggests that stock, shallow characters are not sufficient for the story *Moana* tells.[23] But it also is a call back into older plot forms. The problem does not lie with stock characters, for such are a part of the elements that Aristotle elucidated, and

MacIntyre notes that their presence in "Japanese Noh plays and English medieval morality plays" enable audiences to understand the plot and development of the story.[24] To go deeper with the plot-structure, which will also allow deeper moral development, *Moana* needed to recover more traditional ways to communicating action and character.

Moana, Maui, & the Ocean

Moana's island life has more in common with Ancient Greece than the modern world might, which situates her more closely to a classical conception of morality as well. In such a small, tightly woven village, Moana's questions of what to do in the face of complex moral choices find answers within the "rich stock of descriptions available" to her as she defines her life "in terms of the life of the community."[25] The communal life around her helps Moana define herself in simple, straightforward ways. But when crisis comes to her people, Moana's virtues come into conflict with the twin tensions of her life: the divine calling to action and the physical needs of a people. The audience learns early in the film that the Ocean has chosen Moana for action, though only after she demonstrates her virtue by preserving the life of a newly hatched sea turtle. Moana's father whisks her away from the sea and reminds her that no one leaves Motunui, which establishes the ethical conflict for the young protagonist: will Moana choose the pragmatism of her father, Chief Tui, or the supernaturalism of her grandmother, who opens the film as she narrates the fall of Maui?

Musker and Clements accomplish much in the opening minutes of the film, establishing vital contextualization for understanding the ethical course of Moana's journey. This finds resonance with MacIntyre's concept of tradition, for "the injunctions 'Be virtuous,' 'Be courageous,' 'Be great-souled,' 'Be liberal' do not tell us what to do in the sense of what to aim at; they rather tell us how we should behave in the pursuit of our aim, whatever it is."[26] The audience, like Moana, needs a full picture of the competing traditions on Motunui to know what Moana's moral aim *ought* to be.

The refrain of the film's first full song encourages Moana to "find happiness right where you are," as Moana learns all there is to know about the life of her people.[27] At least, all that her father can teach her, though his rejection of the older ways limits his wisdom. Musker claimed that "the theme of the movie is like, 'Listen to your inner voice, it's all inside.'"[28] But what is the source for this inner voice? The directors found that making such a theme prominent needed an anchor of some kind, resulting in the creation of the grandmother "who's tied to the older traditions" of Motunui's culture.[29] This dual authority in Moana's life creates the tension needed to propel her along the way, reminiscent of Moses' parting encouragement for the Israelites to "Remember the days of old."[30] It is through the closest of neighbors that the individual and the group must confront what constitutes the common good.[31]

Consider the competing aims of life as explained by various characters in film. Moana's grandmother speaks of death as a natural part of life, while her father touts the concept of paradise on this earth. For Tui, Motunui is sufficient for the aims of life, and he considers no afterlife in his formulations; Tui's concerns are perpetually those of the moment. Both Chief Tui and Maui, a demigod, use the coconut to exemplify their views of the world. Tui denies the metaphysical while relishing in those divine gifts; Maui on the other hand cherishes his own divine reputation more than anything else, forgetting the *reason* he gave coconuts to humanity in the first place. Moana seems to constantly choose between the two opposing views of life, but her pursuit of the good enables her to bring these perspectives together.

Even early in the film, when she is attempting to meet the expectations of her people, Moana argues with her father publicly, insisting that the one rule, "no one goes beyond the reef," is invalid because of its age and practicality. While this shows her rejection of tradition, it is better understood as exposing the empty adaptations that have overcome deeper traditions that once governed the people of Tui and Moana. Tui has succumbed to the emotivist claim, allowing his feelings of guilt to dictate his concept of morality. Musker and Clements are on to something powerful in this scene, but struggle with the constant tug of a present day emotivist culture. Moana's mother steps in to provide the cliché "follow your heart" dictum that characterizes the directors' previous films. But the heart of the film lies elsewhere, just as Moana's heart longs for what her deity *desires*. Her sense of right and wrong creates a struggle, not because she is subject to her passions, but because the divine has informed her passions. Her own family does not understand this, except for her grandmother.

This role of the supernatural guides the moral development of the story. Though nebulous at times, the deities of *Moana* do not need clear definition for the audience to discern their essential role in the story. Moana regularly interacts with divine characters, often without any sense of shock or surprise, despite her father's classification of such things as "legends." Exactly where one draws the line of doubt and faith in the world of *Moana* is unclear, but one thing is certain: Moana believes in the metaphysical because she engages it regularly. This is what has linked her to the morality of the past. Even after she almost drowns, Moana's discussion with the Ocean suggests a superficial doubt, not something that has shaken her core.

Though frustrated when stranded on Maui's island, she quickly recognizes that what she thought was misfortune was in fact part of a divine fulfillment of her request. Moana likewise experiences a spiritual awakening upon discovering the large canoes of her ancestors, connecting her to the past in a deeper way than her father has ever known. Even after Tui reveals that he knew the boats of their ancestors existed, he does not express a desire to return to the old ways, but instead regrets that he not burned the relics of the past sooner. Moana does not challenge the way of life of her people in radical ways, but she calls them back in a deeper, more metaphysical way of understanding who they are and how they ought to live.

The plot revolves around Moana's sense of social place, and this concept of vocation gives life the sort of "moral particularity" that makes virtuous action possible.[32] Compare her with the self-centered actions of Maui. The heart of Te Fiti, stolen by Maui as a "gift" to humanity, creates problems instead of alleviating them, because the stone possesses power that humanity ought not to have: "the power to create life itself." Maui does not understand the need for divine prohibitions on such unfettered power, and it is that recklessness which prompts the encroaching darkness in the film. Again, Maui follows the emotivist line of thinking, and the consequences are dire. The monster Tamatoa also pursues emotivist ends. His obsession over his appearance and his material wealth presents itself as a contrast to the "follow your heart" motif scene earlier. But even here, the audience would be wise to bear the larger plot–structure in mind. When Tamatoa points to Moana's "heart," he is pointing to the heart of Te Fiti. He pays lip service to the emotivist claim of subjectivity and preference as the core of decision–making, but he ends up pointing the film's protagonist beyond herself and back to the divinity who commissioned her labor. Moana, even amongst the divine, receives a cautious encouragement that there is more to understanding virtuous action.

While Moana relishes in knowing her history, Maui actively tries to forget his own. When he does finally relent to Moana's pestering, his story reveals that he, like Tui, has forgotten the aspects of his past which make him who he *ought* to be. His actions are an intermingling of selfish desires and selfless actions, a conflict which results in the final overstep that set the movie's plot in motion. Only by acknowledging this, does Maui begin to re-gain the divine powers granted to him by the gods, which simultaneously allows him to fulfill his calling alongside Moana. For both characters, obedi-ence to their gods marks their path towards salvation. It is again the meta-physical reality bearing down on the physical, enabling virtuous action. As Maui explains to Moana, even "wayfinding" consists of "knowing where you are by knowing where you've been." Wayfinding, then, is more than *mere* navigation. This blending orients Moana towards courageous actions, which Maui's choices come to reflect, particularly when he puts himself in harm's way to protect the young girl.

Moana's ability to recognize the duality of Te Kā and Te Fiti and what she must do to save her dying world, as well as to understand what the Ocean deity sought to teach her all along, stems directly from her grasp on the stories told by her grandmother. Moana has internalized the stories of her people to the point that those stories guide her actions; she embodies the traditions of the past at her own peril. These memorized patterns of life prove to be the very thing which will deliver Moana, Maui, and all the people of Motunui. The parting shot of the film, from atop of Motunui, reveals the conch shell in place of where Moana's stone should have been. The visuals of the scene embody the very merging of moral traditions that Moana's ac-tions have wrought, with obedience to the divine leading the way

Conclusion

Intentional or not, *Moana* provides an apologetic for the beauty of traditions and morality in a pop culture format. When chief Tui declares that the Heart of Te Fiti, "is just a rock," the audience knows he is wrong and therefore primed for conversations about the moral nature of this world. The rival moral traditions on display connect to the culture they represent, but they embody the larger understanding of competing claims and the power of nar-ratives to aid the imagination in ethical development, confirming that the mouth only confirms what is in the heart.[33] MacIntyre warns that if we "de-prive children of stories.... you leave them unscripted, anxious stutterers in their actions as in their words."[34] *Moana* avoids the pitfalls of emotivism, while recognizing the importance of competing moral claims. This is the ul-timate "thank you" of the film that anchors the entire discussion in the metaphysical. Knowing where you are by knowing where you were turns out to be the only way forward.

Notes

[1] Aristotle, *Poetics* 1450b.33-35.

[2] Horace, *Ars Poetica* 309-310.

[3] Hans-George Gadamer, *Truth and Method*, 2nd ed., trans. Joel Weinsheimer and Donald G. Marshall (London: Bloomsbury, 2013), 285.

[4] Alasdair MacIntyre, *After Virtue*, 3rd ed. (Notre Dame: University of Notre Dame Press, 2007), 216.

[5] It is also worth remembering Aristotle's definition of the comic: "a mimesis of men who are inferior, but not in a way which involves complete evil.... the comic is constituted by a fault or mark of shame, but lacking in pain or destruction," (Aristotle, 1449a.31-36).

[6] *Moana*, dir. Ron Clements and John Musker (Burbank, CA: Walt Disney Studios, 2016).

[7] MacIntyre, 435.

[8] Ibid., 11.

[9] Ibid., 12.

[10] Ibid., 33.

[11] Ibid., 276.

[12] Ibid., 276-77.

[13] Ibid., 277.

[14] Annalee R. Ward, "*The Lion King*'s Mythic Narrative: Disney as Moral Educator," *Journal of Popular Film & Television* 23, no. 4 (1996): 172.

[15] Ibid., 174.

[16] Taika Waititi, "Taika Waititi on Shaking Up Thor and Being a Hollywood Outsider: 'They Take This Stuff So Seriously,'" interview by Elle Hunt, *The Guardian*, March

21, 2017, https://www.theguardian.com/film/2017/mar/21/taika-waititi-on-shaking-up-thor-and-being-a-hollywood-outsider.

[17] Ron Clements and John Musker, "*Moana* Directors Reveal How the Story Changed," interview by Carolyn Giardina, *The Hollywood Reporter*, November 25, 2016, https://www.hollywoodreporter.com/behind-screen/moana-directors-reveal-how-story-changed-950468.

[18] Charles Elder, "Why Kids Need (and Want) Fairy Tales," *Alberta Report*, October 5, 1998, 47.

[19] Monique Wonderly, "Children's Film as an Instrument of Moral Education," *Journal of Moral Education 38*, no. 1 (2009): 1.

[20] Ibid., 3.

[21] This runs counter to Wonderly's thought but has more in common with the historical representation of moral literature.

[22] Clements and Musker, "*Moana* Directors Reveal."

[23] Ron Clements and John Musker, "*Moana* Directors Talk the Film's Influences and Fun References," interview by Fred Topel, *Den of Geek*, November 21, 2016, https://www.denofgeek.com/movies/moana-directors-talk-the-films-influences-and-fun-references/.

[24] MacIntyre, 27.

[25] Alasdair MacIntyre, *A Short History of Ethics: A History of Moral Philosophy from the Homeric Age to the Twentieth Century*, 2nd ed. (Notre Dame: University of Notre Dame Press, 2002), 103.

[26] Ibid., 86.

[27] Lin-Manuel Miranda, Opetaia Foa'i, and Mark Mancina, "Where You Are," in *Moana* (2016).

[28] Ron Clements and John Musker, "Interview: *Moana* Directors John Musker and Ron Clements on Making Their First CG Movie," interview by Jack Giroux, *SlashFilm*, November 23, 2016, https://www.slashfilm.com/moana-john-musker-and-ron-clements-interview/.

[29] Ibid.

[30] Deut. 32:7 (NASB).

[31] Alasdair MacIntyre, *Ethics in the Conflicts of Modernity: An Essay on Desire, Practical Reasoning, and Narrative* (Cambridge: Cambridge University Press, 2016), 185-86.

[32] MacIntyre, *After Virtue*, 220.

[33] Luke 6:45.

[34] MacIntyre *After Virtue*, 216.

10

The Bare Necessities of Augustinian Virtue

Eric Williamson and Russell Clayton

The *Jungle Book* is an animated motion picture released by Walt Disney Productions in 1967.[1] Although the film was based on Rudyard Kipling's book, Walt Disney, in producing what would be his last film before passing away, demanded that his version omit dark themes associated with Kipling's writing, opting instead for a feel-good family musical adaptation.[2] Thus, the original composer, Terry Gilkyson, was replaced by long-time Disney composers the Sherman Brothers in an effort to bring a "Disney touch" to the movie's soundtrack.[3] Walt's vision for a feel-good animated film led to financial success. By 1968, a year after opening, *The Jungle Book* had grossed domestically $11.5 million[4]; the equivalent of present day $95 million. Providing further evidence of the film's success, Disney has re-released the original version in theatres several times since its initial 1968 release, and filmed a "live action" re-make of the film in 2016, which won an Oscar the following year.[5]

Although Gilkyson was replaced, his song, "The Bare Necessities,"[6] was retained and was nominated for an Academy Award for Best Original Song in 1967. The song is sung by Baloo the Bear, whose primary role is to raise a feral orphan boy (Mowgli) once he leaves the wolf family who raised him for

10 years. Given the success of the film, and the significance of "The Bare Necessities," we believe an apologetic response is fitting. Our analysis will use concepts from the song and scenes from the film to reveal where Baloo's moral philosophy demonstrates virtues expressed in Augustine's thought in contrast with Epicurus, who might appear to be a stronger candidate for Baloo's lifestyle.

The lyrics nicely portray Baloo's positive outlook. Contrasted with other characters, Baloo seems to live the good life. Where Bagheera is shackled by duty, King Louie overextends. In contrast, Baloo is the hipster—the quintessential worry-free protagonist. Bagheera even calls him a "shiftless, stupid jungle bum." Baloo befriends Mowgli to show him how to live the good life. From his perspective, the good life is one that enjoys the jungle. Worries and stress should be discarded. Baloo shows Mowgli the necessities to live the good life, which is the happy life. In some ways, Baloo could be taken to be an Epicurean figure.

There are several points of connection between Baloo and Epicurus. Epicurus (341–271 BC) taught that pleasure is the greatest good and pain should be avoided.[7] A successful navigation of life's challenges results in the greatest amount of pleasure. Baloo seems to personify this thought by teaching the values of the simple life. The Epicurean method calculates pleasures. Eating is good, but gluttony leads to pain. Like Epicurus, Baloo teaches Mowgli to avoid excessively filling his life with pleasures. Many of his expressions line up with Epicurean philosophy: Do not worry about life; do not take more than you need; be self-sufficient. Similarly, the "man cub" should follow Baloo's style and "rest at ease."

Epicurus had a garden outside of Athens where his students conversed about the happy life. They discussed many things, including friendship. Epicurus considered friendship to be one of the greatest assets for the happy life. When looking at the bear and the "man cub," we can see Baloo's jungle as the Epicurean garden. As much as there are similarities, we contend that Baloo's moral philosophy strongly harmonizes with Augustinian concepts, particularly in the areas of happiness and friendship. While some of Baloo's ideas may suggest Epicureanism, some of his actions stand in noteworthy contrast to Epicurean thought.

Happiness

Like Baloo, Augustine (AD 354-430) believed that the world is good. Anything that exists possesses goodness. He didn't mean that everything has the same level of goodness. Many things in the world are not equal.[8] There are superior things.[9] Yet, inequality does not eliminate the good in inferior things. Individually, things are good in themselves. Looking at all things together, Augustine sees everything as very good, which informs his morality.[10] He believes the natural beauty and order of the world must be within the makeup of humans, having "rhythm, poise, symmetry, and beauty" in their "precise proportions."[11]

They are not only beautiful in their design and complexity.[12] Everyone possesses a degree of goodness. According to a "gradations" of good, humans have a higher value than other things that are good. One aspect of their higher value is that their goodness has the potential for progression. This will also factor into Augustine's moral theory. Not only are humans good, they also aim at the good. It's impossible for them to not shrink from misery.[13] However, there are problems in the good world. Similar to Augustine, Baloo teaches Mowgli to distinguish the good from the bad.

The story shows that Baloo sincerely values Mowgli. One of the subplots involves Bagheera taking the boy back to the man-village. The wolf council decides to return him because they can't protect him. Even under the protection of the pack, the man cub stands in danger of Shere Khan. Mowgli doesn't want to go to the village, even telling King Louie he'll do anything to stay. Both Bagheera and the council believe Mowgli wouldn't last a day.

In contrast, Baloo teaches Mowgli to take care of himself. The bear sees that the boy needs help and teaches him to fight. Bagheera concedes that Baloo is building Mowgli's confidence, which the panther finds unnecessary. In a degree of foreshadowing, Baloo and Mowgli's first encounter parallels their meeting with Shere Khan. In the latter scene, Baloo contrasts the wolf pack's decision. They understood that the tiger would destroy Mowgli and anyone protecting him. Encountering Shere Khan, Baloo nobly confronts the tiger. It is even noted that everyone runs away from Shere Khan. Instead, Baloo stands firm to defend his friend. Baloo will ultimately see that the village is a safer place for Mowgli; yet he also sees Mowgli's potential.

From the beginning, Baloo instantly becomes Mowgli's protector. He teaches him to fight as well as how to survive on the bare necessities. He also steps in to save Mowgli from the monkeys. We see another example of

Baloo's care in the foil of King Louie. The orangutan and bear do share some traits, such as their affinity for scat singing (vocally immolating trumpet or saxophone riffs). Where they differ is truly stark. Louie wasn't interested in Mowgli. His only interest was in getting man's "red fire." Louie merely promises to keep the boy on the premise that Mowgli could tell him how to obtain fire. Conversely, Baloo's protection demonstrates the intrinsic worth he saw in Mowgli.

Misery

Baloo's instructions imply that there are wrong paths to happiness. Baloo tells Mowgli to forget about his anxieties; some routes won't lead to the happy life. Augustine agrees. He and Baloo are realists. They talk about *real* good and *real* evil. There is pain in the world. Where Baloo tells Mowgli how to avoid the obstacles of the prickly pear, Augustine experienced his own prickly pears. When he was young, he stole pears.[14] Later, he wrestled with these actions. Pears are good, eating is good, but stealing is wrong. He wondered why he did it. He was not starving; he did not even eat the pears. In his analysis, Augustine goes beyond the natural problems found in the world and observes psychological problems. Baloo implies this internal problem by advising Mowgli to reject some of his inclinations. This is not just a battle between the spirit and the flesh. Augustine finds the spirit to be at fault too. A major theme for Augustine is conflicting desires, which he frequently calls, "double-hearted." He was in disagreement with himself. He believed that everyone aims for happiness—everyone loves the good and will do what they can in order to achieve or obtain the good. However, Augustine experienced torment and misery in following his ambitions. In his younger days, he wanted notoriety and acclaim. He found this path to be bitter and far from happiness. Seeing a beggar, Augustine understood that the beggar was happier because his goal was easier to obtain. Augustine describes his ambition in terms that sound like panic attacks; he was directed by the "destructive fever of worry."[15] Even if it were a fleeting happiness, at least the beggar could get what he wanted.

Baloo also offers a message of contentment. The lyrics to "The Bare Necessities" teach Mowgli that happiness surrounds him in the jungle by way of provision. Rather than struggling for things that are out of reach, the man cub needs to realize that he doesn't need them. This realization will produce contentment. This idea is the essence of the song, which illustrates

Augustine's conflict of desires. Mowgli will be happier once he finds contentment and solace with the provisions of the jungle, which is Baloo's "backyard." Mowgli can find food under rocks, in trees, and on shrubs. In a deeper way, he has found a friend in the bear; however, they will ultimately have to part ways.

The idea of fleeting happiness is Augustine's central point. After a close friend died, Augustine wrote, "Misery befriends the temporal." The nature of our existence is wrapped in time, so misery is inevitable. The good things in the world are naturally temporal. They will fade. For Augustine, evil is not a thing; it is the deprivation of the good. When fruit ripens, it is at the height of its goodness. When it begins to decay and rot, it is the depriving of the good. The evil isn't a thing—just the lessening of the good. There is good but it is fleeting. Augustine sees the turning from good as a turn from oneself, approaching "nothingness."[16]

How can Augustine make sense of the good together with pain? He believes it's natural to aim at happiness. Everyone is born with this sense of self-love. Humans are slaves to their own desires. It is the war within. Desires can be met, but it is temporary. When our happiness is found only in these things, then happiness is ephemeral. "Things rise and things set: in their emerging they begin as it were to be, and grow to perfection; having reached perfection, they grow old and die. Not everything grows old, but everything dies. So, when things rise and emerge into existence, the faster they grow to be, the quicker they rush towards non-being. That is the law limiting their being."[17]

Augustine turned to philosophy for help. Philosophy was believed to be the hunt for happiness.[18] He felt that any philosophy that didn't aim at the happy life was not a legitimate philosophy. Augustine saw the enduring problem of philosophies in their persistent disagreement.[19] They disagreed on the good and virtuous. He categorized twelve different philosophies based on how each saw the good and how to achieve it.[20] He found their arguments weak because they didn't address the power of vice and the problem of temporality.

The virtuous life is always in the presence of vice, constantly battling vice. Augustine saw that virtue was good, but philosophers attributed too much to them, overlooking vice. He also found the virtuous life lacking because it may aim at the self and not the good. "False" temperance produces vanity because it is not truly aimed at the good but at promoting the self. Such hubris just represses errors for the sake of other errors.[21] Furthermore, the point of disagreement was not just among the philosophers, but it persisted with the self. "This debate in my heart was a struggle of myself against myself."[22]

Augustine also found that philosophers had not settled the problem of temporality. We crave the eternal because we know the pain that comes from loss. Recall, he believed that misery is friendship with mortality. In contrast, happiness is found in eternity.[23] We naturally long to live but we don't live long. This foreshadows the angst of some modern philosophies and their focus on death. Friedrich Nietzsche described a similar drive when he considered the beauty in the world and questioned, how could he *not* "lust for eternity" — concluding with impassioned confession, "O eternity, I love you!"[24]

This isn't his final word on the matter. Like Baloo, Augustine is no defeatist. He is simply emphasizing a point that resonates with Baloo's perspective. Good does exist and we should turn to the good, but how is this possible when we are prone to latch on to temporal goods? Augustine reexamines the nature of virtue in the light of his understanding of human nature.

Virtue

If we naturally seek good, and happiness, how can we avoid misery? After all, true philosophy should be on the prowl for happiness. Baloo does not articulate the challenge in this precise way. Instead, he teaches Mowgli that the good life is attainable. Is this just another dead-end philosophy from Augustine's perspective? Baloo's distinctive approach can be seen from a different angle. Rather than preaching self-help, his teaching and actions display a theme found in Augustine's approach to the happy life.

Augustine believes particular good things produce happiness. There *is* disagreement about what makes us happy, but we know that happiness is the aim. Using his idea of different degrees of good, there must be the greatest good (as well as the worst evil). Happiness, then, is found in the greatest good. The happy life is rightly ordered to the good. "The Bare Necessities" emphasizes this aspect of how to live in the world. Lesser goods should not be promoted over greater goods. Baloo believes that everything has its proper place in the jungle. As Baloo implies, it is the aim or nature of bees to provide honey, and it is the purpose of honey to sustain other forms of life, such as bears and man-cubs. When Mowgli understands this point, he can then rightly fit within the good. This is the good life.

Augustine phrases the loss of temporal goods as a form of punishment when we overemphasize the value of temporal objects. Rightly using temporal things for an eternal purpose is rewarded with eternal happiness. "The man who makes bad use of them is captivated by his love for them and is entangled by them. In other words, he becomes subject to things which should be subject to him, making these goods his goal when really, his true good should consist in assigning them their proper place and use."[25] For Augustine, we can't blame the things but the people who misuse them.

Augustine assumes his view is common sense; we know the right order of many things and understand their proper use. Experience gives us these clues. The problem is overcoming inner conflict, leading us in different directions. Pain and suffering result from "misplaced love" in the mind.[26] When someone is sick, they can't heal themselves. Because the person's health is at risk, no one can pull themselves up by the bootstraps. The reasonable act is to seek outside help—get a physician! Augustine hurls this objection against philosophies that insist on riding virtues to freedom. "No one can deny that this life however blessed spiritually, physically, or economically, is, by comparison, most miserable."[27] It is only reasonable that the inferior requires assistance from the superior.

This concession is the first virtue for Augustine, acknowledging inability. In essence it is humility. Aside from humility in abilities, the virtuous person is humble in desires. The drive for excessive wealth only drives us to anxiety because it is fleeting. Do not worry about poverty; it will not last either. Riches may sound sweet, but the trouble they bring is not.[28] Humility involves the intellectual virtue of understanding. Passing goods easily blind pain and, most importantly, unhappiness.[29] The acquisition of understanding is painful, but learning to love the highest good will ultimately elicit comfort. The happy life shows fortitude in the ongoing battle over a fixation with lesser goods, but the reward remains an eternal good.

The happy life is also a life at peace. Worry develops when our soul is "weighed down" by "inferior" material goods.[30] Thus, peace isn't the highest good rather it is the disposition toward the good. In this way, our pleasure isn't the highest good.[31] Because "peace is the calm that comes from order," unhappiness follows from disorder. Momentary happiness for the miserable is due to enslavement to worry and pain because their happiness isn't connected to order, giving them peace, rather their happiness or peace is detached from the order of nature.[32]

The happy life is comprised of these virtues. Augustine abstracts these virtues from the beatitudes in the Sermon on the Mount.[33] He sees obedience as the "mother" of all virtues.[34] The good is loved, so virtuous obedience is done in love. He deduces, "virtue is the perfect love for God."[35] In another way, Augustine unites obedience and love, where love corrects faith and hope. When loves are misguided, faith and hope will be misplaced.[36] Love must be placed in the highest good, just as faith and hope are placed there as well. There is one more virtue for Augustine. In line with the beatitudes, he lists mercy as a virtue. The merciful individual is one who saves others from misery—a trait demonstrated in Baloo's actions.

Friendship

Baloo and Augustine also focus on the theme of friendship. Baloo's friendship with Mowgli is one of the highlights of *The Jungle Book*. Baloo takes it upon himself to instruct Mowgli because he connects with and cares for "little britches." Up to this point, Baloo's traits have overlapped with Epicureanism. It is at the conception of friendship that his actions do not line up with this philosophy. Epicurus did see friendships as essential for the happy life. The most important element is the "acquisition of friends."[37] Friends bring protection and comfort: physical and psychological happiness. Epicurus states, "Nothing enhances our security so much as friendship."[38] However, the question of Epicurean friendship has been a point of debate.

Tim O'Keefe argues that Epicurus and his followers are inconsistent. They can't propose a selfless friendship given the tenets of their egoistic philosophy.[39] On the other hand, Matthew Evans contests that an Epicurean can sacrifice for a friend, without the hope that the friend will return the favor. However, Evans's argument does not ultimately reduce to selflessness because the one who's sacrificed expects the favor in return.[40] David O'Connor argues that Epicureans own their egoism, seeing friendship as truly hedonistic. Friends are valuable for they bring the beneficial goods of comfort and tranquility.[41]

In her comprehensive study, Catherine Wilson has covered issues such as politics, romance, and science through the lens of Epicureanism. Concerning friendship, she argues that it, along with wisdom and morality, is based on self-interest. The Epicurean does not "admire" sacrifice when it inflicts "fear, pain and death" upon herself. "He can see no moral goodness" in this action.[42] The Epicurean prefers compassion, but it must be grounded on "self-approval, and a fear of others and the pain of a bad conscience."[43]

While it is beneficial to have friends, Baloo's view goes deeper. The good he finds transcends his own happiness; he wants Mowgli to have happiness too. In contrast, Epicurean friendship is based on self-preservation and advantage. This sort of friendship is similar to Kant's shopkeeper who only charges fair prices for self-preservation and advantage rather than out of honesty and fairness. Kant claims that we cannot trust the shopkeeper, but he might be reliable.[44] Trust goes beyond self-preservation and self-intent. Baloo displayed a friendship that went beyond Epicurean concerns. Mowgli could rely on Baloo, but he could also trust him.

Most importantly, Baloo finds value *in* Mowgli, not in some benefit gained from befriending him. He shows the highest sense of friendship when he puts his own life in danger to save Mowgli. Although Shere Khan does not slaughter Baloo, the bear certainly risks his life. This trait matches Augustine's concept of mercy. Augustine sees virtue as a right relationship with God, thus it will be a right relationship with the world, including how we treat others. The happy life is helping others. What follows is that we show love for others. We naturally love what is good.[45] If humans are good, then we should love others. Augustine's moral theology takes the natural trait of self-love and shows how that love applies to others.

Self-love is an inborn trait. Infants show distress when they do not get what they want; they are immediately relived when they do. Augustine observes this in adults as well. It is an inherent mechanism, not something learned. Neither is it simply for survival because this self-love will go beyond what is necessary for survival. Thus, pleasure cannot be the highest good. Otherwise, every virtue would have to bow to its authority. Justice would make way for pleasure, which would inevitably lead to injustice.[46] In this way, obedience and love show a striking similarity. We obey what we love, cutting corners for it. (Obeying what we fear is self-love.) Augustine believes that we must be taught other forms of love.

He divides love into four categories: what is higher than us; what is the same; what is near; what is beneath.[47] Self-love satisfies the love of the same and beneath, meaning that we love our soul and our body. The soul is greater than the body because it controls the body. We lack the love for God (the above) and love for others (the near). Because these loves are not natural, they need to be taught and demonstrated. For Augustine, the beatitudes are virtues that demonstrate this love. If mercy aims to free others from misery, then its aim is to bring happiness. He sees the act of instruction as an act of mercy: Love for teaching will increase with love for students.[48] Likewise, Baloo persistently helps Mowgli in his actions and instruction.

Genuine mercy is sacrificial because it shows a higher degree of love for others.[49] Augustine believes that the greatest example of loving friendship is Jesus's sacrifice. This shows mercy to those who cannot help themselves, and thus, try to remedy their misery. Likewise, the film sets the stage for this aspect of friendship when Shere Khan finally encounters Mowgli to destroy him. However, Baloo interrupts his plans. In this scene, Mowgli witnesses the true nature of friendship in Baloo's sacrifice. Bagheera explains what has happened and understands that this is the greatest expression of friendship. He quotes John 15:13, describing what Baloo had accomplished for Mowgli. It's not based on utility, but on love. Similarly, Augustine says, "Lust diminishes as love grows."[50] In this way, the same love for the self should be extended to others. It would be wrong to love only people who are good. Rather, we should love everyone for their own goodness, whether they are good or have the potential for good.[51] Sacrificing the self is the ultimate love for others. Baloo's instruction and actions represent this Augustinian moral view.

Conclusion

Baloo's character shows a positive outlook on the jungle. The world is good, and it is good to have friends. Yet life requires instruction on how to live and how to achieve the happy life. While there is bad in the world, that does not mean that happiness is unattainable. To be sure, his views strongly resemble Epicureanism. Both teach that a life of enjoyment is free from craving things that are not necessary. Those who can live on necessities become self-sufficient and free from the anxieties that result from excessive desires. Instead of focusing on the bad, happiness embraces the good in the world. These ideas also appear in Augustine's writings. Additionally, we see that love is a crucial trait for Baloo's happy life. It is here that Baloo parts ways with Epicureanism and reflects Augustine's moral philosophy.

Would Augustine agree with us? Would he find Baloo to be virtuous? Would Augustine even watch a Disney film? We submit that he *would* agree, as well as watch the film with us. Augustine wrote about using the good in order to enjoy the greatest good. He found many things useful, alluding to this in the notion of "plundering the Egyptians"[52] —referencing the idea that the Israelites took Egyptian goods when leaving Egypt. Augustine understood this to mean that everything is useful, when used rightly and not self-indulgent. We believe he would draw the same points from Baloo's bare necessities.[53]

Notes

[1] *The Jungle Book*, dir. Wolfgang Reitherman (Burbank, CA: Walt Disney Studios, 1967).

[2] Wendy Mead, "The Inside Story of Rudyard Kipling and 'The Jungle Book.'" Biography, accessed May 11, 2020, https://www.biography.com/news/the-jungle-book-rudyard-kipling-facts, 2019.

[3] Robert B. Sherman and Richard M. Sherman, "Interview with the Sherman Brothers," *The Jungle Book* (soundtrack), Walt Disney Records, 1997, CD.

[4] "Big Rental Films of 1968". *Variety*. January 8, 1969. p. 15.

[5] https://www.oscars.org/oscars/ceremonies/2017

[6] Terry Gilkyson, "The Bare Necessities," in *The Jungle Book* (1967).

[7] Epicurus, *The Epicurus Reader: Selected Writings and Testimonia*, trans. and ed. Brad Inwood (Indianapolis: Hackett, 1994).

[8] Augustine, *The Enchiridion* 12.

[9] Augustine, *Confessions* 7.12-13.

[10] *The Enchiridion* 10.

[11] *City of God* 22.24.

[12] Ibid., 10.13.15.

[13] *The Enchiridion* 105.

[14] *Confessions* 2.4.9-13.

[15] Ibid., 6.6.9.

[16] Augustine, *City of God* 14.13.

17 Ibid., 4.10.15.

18 *City of God* 8.8.

19 Ibid., 19.

20 Ibid., 19.1-3.

21 Augustine, *City of God* 1.28.

22 *Confessions* 8.11.27.

23 *The Enchiridion* 20; *City of God* 14.25.

24 Friedrich Nietzsche, *Thus Spoke Zarathustra*, ed. Adrian Del Carlo and Robert Pippin. (New York: Cambridge University Press, 2006), 184-87.

25 Augustine, *The Free Choice of the Will* 1.16.33.

26 *City of God* 22.22.

27 Ibid., 19.20.

28 Augustine, *On the Beatitudes* 1.2.

29 Augustine, *On Continence* 3.7.

30 *City of God* 10.14.

31 Placing pleasure as the highest good troubles Augustine. He states that "the mobs" will only look to the government for protecting their pleasures. Anyone who goes against this decadence will be "branded as a public enemy, and should he attempt to interfere with them, let the mob be free to hound him to death." Ibid., 2.20.

32 Ibid., 19.13.

33 The virtuous person is poor in spirit, meek, and mourns the loss of temporal goods. The virtuous person has fortitude in hungering for righteousness and will be at peace in a rightly ordered character because the virtuous person loves goodness. Augustine, *On the Morals of the Catholic Church* I.6; Augustine, *The Sermon on the Mount* 1.2-5.

34 *City of God* 14.12.

35 *On the Morals of the Catholic Church* 1.15.

36 *The Enchiridion* 117.

37 Diogenes Laertius, *Lives of Eminent Philosophers* 10.148

38 Ibid.

[39] Tim O'Keefe, *Epicureanism* (New York: Routledge, 2010).

[40] Matthew Evans, "Can Epicureans Be Friends?" *Ancient Philosophy* 24 (2004): 407-24.

[41] David K. O'Connor, "The Invulnerable Pleasures of Epicurean Friendship," *Greek, Roman, and Byzantine Studies* 30, no. 1 (2005): 165-86.

[42] Catherine Wilson, *How to Be An Epicurean: The Ancient Art of Living Well* (New York: Basic Books, 2019), 107.

[43] Ibid., 145.

[44] Immanuel Kant, *Groundwork of the Metaphysics of Morals*, ed. Mary Gregor and Jens Timmermann. (New York: Cambridge University Press, 2012).

[45] Augustine, *On the Trinity* 8.3.4.

[46] *City of God* 5.20.

[47] Augustine, *On Christian Doctrine* 1.45.

[48] Augustine, *On the Catechizing of the Uninstructed* 10.14.

[49] *City of God* 10.6.

[50] *The Enchiridion* 121.

[51] *On the Trinity* 8.6.9.

[52] *On Christian Doctrine* 2.

11

Sin, Salvation, and the Human Condition in *Pinocchio*

Paul Miles

The Bible records the creation, fall, and future of humanity, so many theologians read it as the primary source for questions such as: What am I? Why is the world so messy? Is there a way out of this mess? It happens that Disney's *Pinocchio* depicts another story of origin, fall, and redemption—that of a wooden puppet who strives to become a real boy. *Pinocchio* is fiction—this puts it in a different genre from the Bible—but it is more than just a cute story. It is an epic myth that shaped a culture by tackling some of life's biggest questions from an American perspective.

A comparison of the views presented in *Pinocchio* and the Bible shows a contrast in the doctrines of anthropology (the doctrine of man), hamartiology (the doctrine of sin), and soteriology (the doctrine of salvation). Both sources recognize that man has shortcomings that must be resolved, but one ultimately sees the solution as being a path of self-improvement while the other teaches a salvation by grace.

Anthropology and Hamartiology: The Doctrines of Mankind and Sin

Origin stories introduce ideologies of God and the human condition. When the audience meets Geppetto, he is a lonely old man with nobody to keep him company except for Figaro the cat and his goldfish, Cleo. Neither Figaro nor Cleo has the capacity for speech, but Geppetto paints a mouth on the lifeless Pinocchio and sings, "Little do you know and yet it's true/That I'm mighty proud of you."[1] That night, Geppetto wishes upon a star, and while he sleeps the Blue Fairy visits him to animate his wooden puppet. The Bible depicts God and human origin in a different light. Unlike Geppetto with his pets, the God of the Bible had perfect fellowship within the three Persons of the Trinity before He created man.[2]

In the subsequent scenes of *Pinocchio* and in the ensuing parts of the Bible, narratives and doctrines unfold that propose two contrasting ideas of the human condition. Here are some considerations of conscience, deadness, and eternal destination.

Man's Conscience of Sin

The first thing that the Blue Fairy says is a declaration of morality and reward, "Good Geppetto, you have given so much happiness to others. You deserve to have your wish come true." Likewise, her instructions to Pinocchio are a promise of reward contingent upon moral virtue:

> BLUE FAIRY. Prove yourself brave, truthful, and unselfish, and someday you will be a real boy... You must learn to choose between right and wrong.
> PINOCCHIO. Right and wrong? But how will I know?
> BLUE FAIRY. Your conscience will tell you.
> PINOCCHIO. What are conscience?

At this point in the conversation Jiminy Cricket interrupts, "A conscience is that still, small voice people won't listen to. That's just the trouble with the world today."[3] The Blue Fairy appoints Jiminy to be Pinocchio's conscience and guide. From there, Jiminy should stay with Pinocchio as a continuous witness to what is right and wrong.

In the Bible, God puts Adam and Eve in a garden with the command to work and keep the garden and not to eat from the tree of the knowledge of good and evil.[4] They eat the fruit and gain the knowledge of good and evil, thus replacing their innocence with conscience. This conscience serves as a guide for them and their posterity, but human conscience serves humanity poorly; everyone follows his conscience and soon "the wickedness of man *was* great in the earth... every intent of the thoughts of his heart *was* only evil continually."[5]

In the Bible, whenever people lived the Blue Fairy way, with conscience as their guide, disaster ensued. Even after God selected a people to exemplify his moral expectations—after establishing both Abrahamic and Mosaic covenants—the book of Judges repeatedly reports that everyone continually did what was right in his own eyes. For a biblicist, conscience is not the best guide for leading people in righteousness, but rather helps lead people to God as they realize their shortcomings. Paul writes, "For when Gentiles, who do not have the law, by nature do what the law requires, they are a law to themselves, even though they do not have the law. They show that the work of the law is written on their hearts, while their conscience also bears witness, and their conflicting thoughts accuse or even excuse them on that day when, according to my gospel, God judges the secrets of men by Christ Jesus."[6]

Conscience helps man recognize morality even without divinely revealed Scripture. As Zane Hodges says, "Paul did not hold a view of total depravity that precluded him from seeing any morality at all outside the explicit observance of the law. Instead, he acknowledges such morality as evidence of the work of the Creator God."[7] The fallen conscience has apologetic value because it drives people to explore its source. Who else could hardwire man with a sense of right and wrong except God, the designer and definer of morality Himself?

Disney interrupts the logical and biblical path from conscience to Savior and instead foreshadows the Postmodern appeal to subjectivity, as the Blue Fairy's mandate declares that the difference between a human and wood is that the human follows his conscience. An observant eye will notice that Disney externalizes sin by creating distance between Pinocchio and his conscience whenever there is a temptation, such that Pinocchio only fails when Jiminy is absent. Pinocchio makes his first bad decision on his way to the first day of school. Jiminy is running late, so Pinocchio goes to school *alone* and Honest John and Gideon manipulate him to become a performer in

Stromboli's theater. Afterward, Pinocchio and Jiminy run home together, but Gideon stops Pinocchio and Jiminy keeps running. The conscience, in the form of Jiminy, has already been separated when Honest John tricks Pinocchio into boarding the carriage to Pleasure Island. Pinocchio befriends Lampwick at the front of the carriage and meanwhile, Jiminy is sitting underneath, coughing from the dust. When they arrive at the island, Pinocchio and Lampwick "tear the joint apart," as Jiminy runs around looking for him. Jiminy eventually finds an inebriated Pinocchio and storms off in outrage leaving Pinocchio to become a donkey in his absence. Throughout the whole movie, Pinocchio succumbs to temptation only when his conscience, Jiminy Cricket, is separated from him.

A presupposition in Disney's *Pinocchio* is that man is essentially good and so he only needs his conscience, but at the same time, Disney depicts the world as a fundamentally dangerous and evil place where most people are villains. The Bible agrees that the world is evil, but one reason for the world's condition is that it consists of wicked humanity, "Every one of them has turned aside; They have together become corrupt; *There is* none who does good, No, not one."[8] The biblical worldview consistently explains sin in terms of the macro-narrative, that the world is fallen, and in terms of the micro-narrative, that the individual humans of the world are sinful. Disney recognizes the obvious, that the world is full of villains, but falls short on the micro-level, not realizing that *everyone is sinful by nature* and needs divine intervention.

Man's Deadness in Sin

A biblical understanding of sin involves a separation of humans from their Maker; in theological terms, they are born spiritually dead. Biblical death is described in terms of separation, rather than nonexistence. Physical death is not ceasing to exist, but rather it is a separation of the body from the soul or spirit.[9] Likewise, spiritual death does not mean that mankind is spiritually nonexistent, but rather that there is an inherent separation from God. This spiritual separation is why God warns Adam when He says, "of the tree of the knowledge of good and evil you shall not eat, for in the day that you eat of it you shall surely die."[10] Adam did not physically die when he ate the fruit,[11] but he did become spiritually separated from God. This separation has been passed along, as the Bible says, "through one man sin entered the world, and death through sin, and thus death spread to all men."[12] Paul reminds the Ephesians and Colossians that, before believing in Christ, they were dead in trespasses and sins.[13] Spiritual death is our default, because "in Adam all die."[14]

From his creation, Pinocchio is condemned to live forever as a wooden puppet until his own merit saves him, allowing him to become a real boy. Salvation through self-merit is not biblical Christianity, but, interestingly, *Pinocchio* recognizes the need to be saved from an imperfect body. The Bible says that after Adam sinned, "The Lord God said, 'Behold, the man has become like one of Us, to know good and evil. And now, lest he put out his hand and take also of the tree of life, and eat, and live forever' — therefore the Lord God sent him out of the garden of Eden."[15] An intentional peculiarity occurs in the text of verse 22. God begins to say, "And now, lest he... live forever" but the sentence is never finished, nor should it be, because the idea of a man living forever, trapped in a fallen body, is so awful that it is unspeakable. Instead, God removes man from the tree of life and allows him to die physically to release him from his body.

Because of his Adamic lineage, man is dead and entirely hopeless of repairing his separation from God. The only exception is Jesus, who was not born spiritually dead, but rather came into the world in a state of perfect fellowship with God. In the Bible, the Creator becomes flesh to save creation, but in the final scenes of *Pinocchio*, the creation (Pinocchio), saves the creator (Geppetto), to become flesh. On the biblical view, while the sin barrier between God and men is addressed in light of Christ's sacrifice, the issue of free will remains; men and women are still spiritually dead from birth unless they accept the offer of a new life from their creator.

Soteriology: The Doctrine of Salvation

Disney brings about salvation in the one grand event of Pinocchio's death and resurrection after rescuing Geppetto. After proving his maturity, Pinocchio is rescued from his donkey-puppet body into the new body of a real boy. This is quite different from the Bible's presentation of salvation, which consists of three phases: salvation from the penalty of sin (justification); salvation from the power of sin (sanctification); and salvation from the presence of sin (glorification). Each of these doctrines should properly be distinguished in order to contrast more deeply the biblical view of salvation with that presented in Disney's *Pinocchio*.

Justification: Being Born Again

Justification is the first phase of salvation, and it occurs at that moment when someone first believes in Christ alone for eternal life. The Blue Fairy requires Pinocchio to conform to the virtues of a real boy while he is still a puppet, but God does not expect a person to behave like a Christian when he is still dead in trespasses and sin. The Eastern Orthodox theologian, Vigen Guroian, summarizes Pinocchio's path to righteousness: "In the Disney animation, real boyhood is bestowed on Pinocchio as a reward for being good by the Blue Fairy with a touch of her magic wand; or, as the Blue Fairy herself says, because Pinocchio has proven himself 'brave, truthful, and unselfish.' In Disney's imagination this is magic. In theological terms this is works righteousness."[16] The notion of works-righteousness is entirely foreign to the Bible, which states, "Now to him who works, the wages are not counted as grace but as debt. But to him who does not work but believes on Him who justifies the ungodly, his faith is accounted for righteousness."[17]

Justification is called a past-tense salvation because it is a salvation that has already happened for those who have believed in Christ, hence Paul's words to the believers in Ephesus: "For by grace you have been saved through faith, and that not of yourselves; *it is* the gift of God, not of works, lest anyone should boast."[18] Justification is only the beginning of the Christian's new life in Christ and it carries ramifications for the present and future. On the significant soteriological issue of faith vs. works, then, Disney's *Pinocchio* does not align with the Christian perspective; it implies that the second birth is contingent upon a person's own works as opposed to the biblical view that the only thing that a person can and must do to be born again is to believe in God's Son for eternal life.[19]

Sanctification: Becoming a Mature Believer

Sanctification is the second phase of salvation. It is a present-tense salvation because it is a process which involves the Holy Spirit's on-going work within the believer's life. Sanctification is God's will in the life of the believer, and it involves a sense of growing into the sort of person who develops habits of abandoning sin and pursuing holiness.[20] However, it is still possible for a believer's current experience to be characterized by sin. The Christians in Corinth are a glaring example of justified people struggling with carnality as Paul rebukes them as "babes in Christ."[21] The Christian is only able to grow *after* being born again; indeed, the entire "born again" imagery falls apart if the child must grow before even being born.

Pinocchio's story is backward because to be born again, he must first grow into the Blue Fairy's virtues. Instead of trying to earn justification, the Christian receives eternal life as a gift. After receiving this gift of a second birth, the Christian is free to grow in holiness with virtues being a result. Paul says, "Walk in the Spirit, and you shall not fulfill the lust of the flesh. For the flesh lusts against the Spirit, and the Spirit against the flesh; and these are contrary to one another, so that you do not do the things that you wish... But the fruit of the Spirit is love, joy, peace, longsuffering, kindness, goodness, faithfulness, gentleness, self-control. Against such there is no law."[22] The fruit of the Spirit is neither a requirement for justification, nor is it even a test to know if someone has been justified, but instead the fruit is the result of the sanctification process. This process can only begin after the new birth and the believer will never entirely be free from the power of sin while living in a sinful body, hence the need for glorification.

This concept of sinful flesh is captured, to an extent, in Collodi's original book, which marks key moments in Pinocchio's maturity by the removal of his 'flesh.' Disney redacts this point from the film's parallel narratives and thus remains consistent with the ideology that man is inherently good. Collodi's Pinocchio begins as a log who cries in agony as he is carved into a puppet, while Disney's Pinocchio comes to life by magic. Pinocchio's nose grows when he lies, so Collodi has woodpeckers chip the nose away, but in the Disney version, the Blue Fairy painlessly shrinks the nose with magic. When Collodi's Pinocchio becomes a donkey, he is cast in the sea to drown and fish eat his donkey flesh away, but Disney's Pinocchio, who only sprouted the ears and the tail of a donkey, is magically recovered because of his virtue.

Disney appears to be externalizing evil in a contemporary reaction to Collodi's depiction of sinful flesh. In Disney's system, growth and self-improvement come by listening to one's conscience. The Apostle Paul, however, insists "that in me (that is, in my flesh) nothing good dwells."[23] For Paul, sin includes an internal struggle with the flesh and so he issues the order, "present your bodies a living sacrifice, holy, acceptable to God, *which is* your reasonable service. And do not be conformed to this world, but be transformed by the renewing of your mind, that you may prove what *is* that good and acceptable and perfect will of God."[24]

Laying aside the significant differences about the second birth, perhaps a slight parallel can be drawn between maturity in *Pinocchio* and the Christian life. As the Christian grows, he becomes less dependent on himself and his own sense of right and wrong, and he becomes more dependent on God and the Bible. Charles Ryrie puts it well, "Spirituality is a grownup yet growing relation to the Holy Spirit."[25] At the end of the movie, Pinocchio learns that Geppetto is in Monstro's belly and decides to save him. Jiminy warns him about the danger, but Pinocchio chooses to be brave and attempt a rescue, nonetheless. This marks a point of maturity for Pinocchio as he no longer needs his conscience to do the right thing. When Monstro swallows Pinocchio, Jiminy is stuck outside. It is during this separation that Pinocchio courageously starts a fire inside the whale, gets sneezed out, and even continues to rescue a drowning Geppetto. Before this, Pinocchio's separation from his conscience only led to failure, but finally, Pinocchio can choose the Blue Fairy's virtues without depending on conscience. Perhaps this is in line with the original book, because "For Collodi, real boyhood is not so much a reward as it is the visible sign of a moral task that has been conscientiously pursued."[26]

The Christian walk is far removed from most of the *Pinocchio* mythos, but there is still that element of maturity that manifests when one chooses what is right even amidst hazards. Instead of following his own nature like Pinocchio, the Christian grows by laying aside the flesh and walking by the Spirit. Disney is correct in the summation that a mature human can overcome his feelings of hesitation to achieve virtue. In Pinocchio's case, the virtues are bravery, truthfulness, and unselfishness, but for the Christian, maturity is sanctification as he grows in relation to the Holy Spirit. While biblical virtue is different from Pinocchio's, there is still a similar quest to overcome the conscience of self-interest to pursue something greater.

Glorification: Receiving a New Body

Glorification is salvation from the *presence* of sin, when the believer leaves his sinful body and receives a glorified body in the presence of the Lord.[27] In the Old Testament, Job says about his future glorification, "For I know *that* my Redeemer lives, and He shall stand at last on the earth; and after my skin is destroyed, this *I know*, that in my flesh I shall see God."[28] Job believed in his Redeemer (justification), and therefore he *knew* that he would see God in new flesh (glorification). Pinocchio only received the body of a real boy, but the Christian will have a glorified body like Christ's. "For our citizenship is in heaven, from which we also eagerly wait for the Savior, the Lord Jesus Christ, who will transform our lowly body that it may be conformed to His glorious body, according to the working by which He is able even to subdue all things to Himself."[29]

After the resurrection and before Jesus ascended to heaven, He had a glorified body that could suddenly appear in a room, but was still flesh and bones that could eat and drink.[30] Such is the believer's anticipation, as Paul writes, "For we were saved in this hope, but hope that is seen is not hope; for why does one still hope for what he sees? But if we hope for what we do not see, we eagerly wait for *it* with perseverance."[31] In English, people often say "hope" when they want something that is unlikely, but the Greek has a different connotation. The words that Paul uses for "hope" are *elpis* and *elpizo,* which imply a confident expectation because we know that we will be glorified and we "eagerly wait for *it.*"

There are several Bible passages which include all three phases of salvation in one context,[32] but for brevity's sake, only one will be brought out here. "If then you were raised with Christ [at past justification], seek those things which are above [in current sanctification], where Christ is, sitting at the right hand of God. Set your mind on things above [in current sanctification], not on things on the earth. For you died [at past justification], and your life is hidden with Christ in God. When Christ *who is* our life appears, then you also will appear with Him in glory [at future glorification]."[33]

The film historian, Douglas Brode, has noted that after watching *Pinocchio*, children may "perceive themselves as being in some way incomplete, needing to prove themselves before being accepted as humans in the fullest sense,"[34] but the Christian who has already been justified does not need to prove himself, because he has the righteousness of Christ Himself credited to him (indeed, his journey to Christianity included the recognition that he could not be good enough). His goal in sanctification is to grow in his relationship with the Holy Spirit, not self, and since all believers still struggle with sin, sanctification looks quite different in one Christian's life as compared to another's. While sanctification may fluctuate due to a Christian's success or failure, glorification is God's work and therefore is an inevitable result of justification for all Christians.

Conclusion

The human experience features a constant interaction with morality that is etched into the conscience, bearing witness to God's existence and mankind's condition. This spiritual deadness cannot be overcome by effort and ultimately results in eternal separation from God. This chapter has contrasted Disney's *Pinocchio* with a biblical perspective concerning issues of sin, salvation, and the human condition. There is significant disagreement on the issue of salvation through works vs faith, yet there is an interesting alignment concerning the idea that the maturing individual—growing ever more "real"—begins to rely less on conscience *per se* and more upon something else. The human condition is actually much worse than Pinocchio presents it, but the reward of becoming a real boy pales in comparison to God's promise of eternal life to anyone who believes in Him!

Notes

[1] Ned Washington and Leigh Harline, "Little Wooden Head," in *Pinocchio*, dir. Ben Sharpsteen and Hamilton Luske (Burbank, CA: Walt Disney Studios, 1940).

[2] Gen. 1:1–25; John 1:1.

[3] In the movie, *Snow White and the Seven Dwarves* (1937), the dwarves (all except Dopey) proclaim, "Jiminy Crickets!" when they come home and notice that someone is already there. The interjection, "Jiminy Cricket!," used as an expletive, is a euphemism for "Jesus Christ." In *Pinocchio*, Jiminy calls conscience that "still, small voice," which is a biblical term for God's voice (1 Kings 19:12) . Perhaps Disney is usurping God with conscience in Pinocchio's introduction to Jiminy.

[4] Gen. 2:15–17.

[5] Gen. 6:5. Unless otherwise noted, Scripture quotations come from NKJV.

[6] Rom. 2:14–16 (ESV).

[7] Zane Hodges, *Romans: Deliverance from Wrath* (Corinth: Grace Evangelical Society, 2013), 1441–43, Kindle.

[8] Ps. 14:3; cf. Ps. 53; Rom. 3.

[9] Gen. 35:18; Eccl. 12:7; Phil. 1:23.

[10] Gen. 2:17.

[11] Gen. 5:5.

[12] Rom. 5:12.

[13] Eph. 2:1; Col. 2:13.

[14] 1 Cor. 15:22.

[15] Gen. 3:22–24.

[16] Vigen Guroian, *Tending the Heart of Virtue: How Classic Stories Awaken a Child's Moral Imagination* (New York: Oxford University Press, 1998), 42.

[17] Rom. 4:4–5.

[18] Eph. 2:8–9.

[19] John 3:3–18.

[20] 1 Thess. 4:3–8.

[21] 1 Cor. 3:1–4.

[22] Gal. 5:16–17, 22–33.

[23] Rom. 7:18.

[24] Rom. 12:1–2.

[25] Charles Ryrie, *Balancing the Christian Life* (Chicago: Moody Publishers, 1994), 13.

[26] Guroian, 42–43.

[27] 2 Cor. 5:8.

[28] Job 19:25–26.

[29] Phil. 3:20–21.

[30] Luke 24:36–43.

[31] Rom. 8:24–25.

[32] Others include Rom. 5:1–2, 13:10–11; Eph. 2:5–10; Phil. 3:7–11; 1 Thess. 1:8–10; Titus 2:11–13; 1 John 2:28, 3:1–3.

[33] Col. 3:1–4.

[34] Douglas Brode, *From Walt to Woodstock: How Disney Created the Counterculture* (Austin: University of Texas Press, 2004), 184.

12

On Becoming a Real Boy: Conscience and the Formation of Character

Mark D. Linville

isney's Geppetto is a kind old gentleman who, despite his white hair, seems somehow to have retained the heart of a child. This skilled woodcarver's shop is filled with carved wooden clocks, toys, music boxes, and other contrivances that would delight any village child who visited. He creates Pinocchio in order to "bring a little joy to every heart" as we learn from the song that he sings. But though he also sings to this "little wooden head" that "I'm mighty proud of you,"[1] he longs for a child of his own—a "real boy"—whom he can love as a son, and who will love him as a father.

Of course, even before Geppetto made his wish he was able to work the strings and make his wooden puppet behave as he wished, as when Pinocchio is made to dance and even to nod his approval of his chosen name. But Geppetto longs for the real love that only a real boy can give. And so, this is the wish that he makes upon the Wishing Star as he retires to bed. As he sleeps, that star descends, taking the form of the Blue Fairy, who stands by his bed and speaks: "Good Geppetto, you have given so much happiness to others, you deserve to have your wish come true."

With a touch of the Fairy's wand, the wooden boy comes to life. But as wonderful as an animated marionette may be, it falls short of the object of Geppetto's wish for a real boy. Pinocchio is granted the gift of life, but that life has a purpose beyond the living itself, and that purpose involves the fulfillment of both Geppetto's dream and Pinocchio's own potential of being a real boy.[2] Pinocchio is importantly like us, for we, too, have been brought to life for a purpose, and that purpose involves our one day becoming real persons. As we shall see, such a purpose is not only a salient feature of the human Good Life, but it points beyond itself to the Artisan who created us for such.

Am I a Real Boy?

The Fairy explains to Pinocchio, "To make Geppetto's wish come true will be entirely up to you. Prove yourself brave, truthful, and unselfish, and someday you *will* be a real boy." But why would she leave the fulfillment of Geppetto's wish—a wish that he "deserves" to have fulfilled—"entirely" in these freshly carved and painted wooden hands and this little wooden head? Why not make Pinocchio into a real boy with the simple wave of a wand? We might have thought that, for anyone capable of granting "the gift of life" to a puppet made of pine, the additional step of substituting flesh and bone for pine and pins would be small potatoes.

The answer, I think, is in the Fairy's explanation that connects *being a real boy* with *being good*. She implies that the latter is necessary for the former, and whether Pinocchio is *good* is entirely up to him. Magic can bring a puppet to life, rendering it conscious and able to speak. Magic might even be able to make that puppet *behave* in some desired manner. But were Pinocchio's behavior the work of a Fairy's wand rather than his free will, then the wand would be a mere upgrade from the artisan's paddle, operating wirelessly and by wizardry, and Geppetto *already* had a puppet.

Magic abounds in Fairyland, and it often contravenes what we *might* otherwise have mistaken for natural and inviolable laws. With a word or a wave, pumpkins turn into coaches, princes become toads, puppets of pine awaken to conscious life. These things do not happen every day around here. But even magic must operate within certain necessary constraints, as G. K. Chesterton explains.

For instance, if the Ugly Sisters are older than Cinderella, it is (in an iron and awful sense) NECESSARY that Cinderella is younger than the Ugly Sisters. There is no getting out of it.... If Jack is the son of a miller, a miller is the father of Jack. Cold reason decrees it from her awful throne: and we in fairyland submit. If the three brothers all ride horses, there are six animals and eighteen legs involved: that is true rationalism, and fairyland is full of it.[3]

Even in Fairyland it is one thing to claim that a pumpkin has been transformed into a coach. The claim will be received with unblinking credulity. It is quite another thing to claim that the coach has wheels made of square circles. Even in Fairyland this will be scorned for the sheer nonsense that it is. They do not doubt rumors of a spell that makes the victim do the precise bidding of the conjurer for they have encountered witches and wizards, but they will scoff at any suggestion that the victim thereby does that bidding freely.

The act in that case is compulsory, and, therefore, involuntary, as Aristotle would say. This is because "the moving principle is outside," or "the cause is in the external circumstances and the agent contributes nothing."[4] An act is *voluntary* only if "the moving principle is in the agent himself."[5] Geppetto was proud of Pinocchio as he danced the lifeless puppet about, but this was, of course, pride in his own skill as a woodcarver. This is different in kind from the pride that one might take in a son's good character or satisfaction in his love.

If, later in the story, Pinocchio is rightly praised for his courage and appreciated for his love in rescuing Geppetto from the belly of a whale, then it was up to Pinocchio whether to attempt the rescue. Interestingly, the very word *character* is from a Greek word that refers to a tool used for engraving or carving. As skilled as Geppetto was in carving Pinocchio's body, it was entirely up to Pinocchio to carve his own character,[6] whether good or bad, and this is achieved by learning to choose between right and wrong.

Not even the Blue Fairy can do that for him. She could bestow the Gift of Life, but as an old saying has it, character is a victory, not a gift. Of course, she enlists Jiminy Cricket to be Pinocchio's conscience, but it remains for Pinocchio to heed the advice of that conscience and choose accordingly. For Pinocchio, the guiding and goading counsel of conscience replaces the inexorable determination of the puppeteer's strings. Conscience is the mark of the moral agent, who is graced with free will and charged with the responsibility of making the right moral choices and cultivating the virtues. Because being a real boy requires being good, the Fairy had no choice but to leave the fulfillment of Geppetto's wish up to Pinocchio, for, necessarily, it is a task that none other than he can accomplish.

How to Become a Jackass

But what shall we make of the alleged connection between *being good* and *being real*? After all, the story has its villains—Honest John, Stromboli, and the Coachman, for instance—who are as *real* as any of the heroes, but they are anything but *good*. Why does the Fairy lay down this condition of being brave, truthful, and unselfish as prerequisite to Pinocchio's becoming a real boy?

Aristotle observed that "the many" seem to prefer "a life suitable to beasts," and he was speaking specifically of those who "identify the good, or happiness, with pleasure," whose chief aim is a life of enjoyment and who are "quite slavish in their tastes."[7] A life suitable to beasts is a life unworthy of a human person. We have been made for nobler ends and our very nature is defined by them. We flourish insofar as we align our lives to those ends, thus fulfilling the potential of our nature as humans and, indeed, becoming *fully human*.

The thrills of Pleasure Island seem perfectly suited to the people that Aristotle had in mind. The attraction of that place is stated succinctly by Pinocchio himself: "Being bad's a lot of fun." Why concern yourself with being brave, truthful or unselfish if those things get in the way of *fun*? After all, as Lampy says, "A guy only lives once!" And Pleasure Island is the perfect place for those who are slavish in their tastes because there are absolutely no rules or restrictions standing in the way of the unbridled pursuit of selfish pleasure. "They say it's a swell joint. No school, no cops. You can tear the joint apart and nobody says a word," Lampy tells Pinocchio on their way there. And there are no demands or expectations. "Loaf around. Plenty to eat. Plenty to drink. And it's all free!" He was right. "Eat all you want. Stuff your face. Be a glutton!" says the announcer at one attraction, encouraging one of the Seven Deadly Sins. "Come in and smoke your heads off. There's nobody here to stop you!" says another, as a giant, mechanical wooden Indian scatters cigars like a sower going forth to sow.

Even that still small voice of conscience, in the person of a cricket, is an unwelcome killjoy. "You mean to tell me you take orders from a grasshopper?" Lampy exclaims just before sending Jiminy careening into the corner pocket along with the Eightball. The evil Coachman laughed with derision at the "stupid little boys" that he had lured there. "Give a bad boy enough rope and he'll soon make a jackass of himself," he chuckled. If a life given to pleasure is *slavish* and *suitable for beasts*, then those "bad boys" suffered the natural consequences, for they were transformed from boys to donkeys and then sold into slavery as beasts of burden.

The fate of these bad boys reinforces the connection between being a real boy and being good. In order to *become* a real boy Pinocchio had to learn to choose right over wrong and to cultivate the virtues. By spurning all such instruction, boys who already *were* quite real lost their humanity to become enslaved jackasses. Nor did the sneering Coachman escape similar consequences, for he had become a monster and thereby lost his own humanity. It is worthy of note that Pinocchio barely escaped the same fate by finally following the dictates of his conscience: "This way, Pinoch! It's the only way out!"

The boys had foolishly believed that freedom is freedom from rules or restraint and that liberty is license, and so they threw off all authority and all rules and restrictions as unwanted shackles and obstacles to their happiness. Lampy and his comrades resent authority and discipline as the confining walls of a prison. Chesterton suggested that they are, in fact, the protective walls of a playground where danger lurks on the other side.

> We might fancy some children playing on the flat grassy top of some tall island in the sea. So long as there was a wall round the cliff's edge they could fling themselves into every frantic game and make the place the noisiest of nurseries. But the walls were knocked down, leaving the naked peril of the precipice. They [the children] did not fall over; but when their friends returned to them they were all huddled in terror in the center of the island; and their song had ceased.[8]

Chesterton's island might originally and aptly have been named "Pleasure Island" for the uproarious fun that the walls originally permitted within their boundaries. But once the walls were removed the fun was over and the terror begun. And like those children on Chesterton's island, the boys-become-donkeys huddled together in terror in the center of Pleasure Island. They, too, had stopped their singing, having begun braying.

They longed for the protection—along with the authority—of their homes. And the walls that then enclosed Pleasure Island were truly the walls of imprisonment and slavery. "Shut the doors and lock 'em tight!" the Coachman orders his apelike goons. True freedom is indeed the freedom to pursue happiness, but true happiness is enjoyed when the character that we carve for ourselves conforms to the Good.

Conditional Joy

The first step, then, in fulfilling Geppetto's wish is to confer upon the puppet certain properties and capacities necessary for that purpose. Pinocchio is given the gift of life, not an end in itself but a necessary condition for a kind of *probation* to qualify for something far more wonderful. To be the *kind* of thing that is capable of forming a moral character requires moral agency. To this end Pinocchio became a living being. He may no longer need the marionettist's strings, but his gift of life itself came with strings of a different kind attached.

Like all good fairy tales, *Pinocchio* includes not only a fairy but also one of the great precepts by which all of Fairyland is governed, what Chesterton called the *Doctrine of Conditional Joy*. Some great happiness is promised, but the fulfillment of that promise and the enjoyment of that happiness is conditional. Pinocchio may become a real boy, fulfilling Geppetto's wish, but only if he learns to choose between right and wrong and thus proves himself to be of good character.

Pinocchio's temptations must be understood against the backdrop of this purpose and the conditions of the promise. When Jiminy found Pinocchio in the pool hall on Pleasure Island he exclaimed, "So this is where I find you! How do you ever expect to be a real boy?!" Honest John tempted Pinocchio with "an actor's life" and "the easy road to success," with all of the rewards of fame—silk and silver, gold and diamonds. But this celebrated life *essentially* required that Pinocchio *remain* as he was, a wooden puppet who could dance about without any need of strings. Were he to become a *real* boy, he would be out of work, for *real* boys who can hop about are far less a novelty than a mere puppet that can behave very much *like* a real boy. It is thus the temptation not only to abandon the very purpose of the Blue Fairy's "gift of life," but to twist that gift into the service of a lesser and ignoble end.

And so, the temptation involves selling out and settling for a mere semblance of the genuine life offered to him. It is to trade a life as a real boy, a beloved son and the fulfillment of Geppetto's fondest wishes, for that of a slapstick sideshow freak, thus throwing away the chance at *real* life in exchange for whatever coins may be tossed his way. This exchange is a theme as old as time. To "worship and serve the creature rather than the Creator" is akin to the beastly mistake of those "vulgar types" that Aristotle described, who identify the good with pleasure, except that the former error is even more slavish.

Pinocchio's circumstances are similar to our own. Through some deep magic the breath of life was breathed into lifeless dust, and we have awakened, blinking, to conscious existence. "Every instant of conscious life is an unimaginable prodigy," Chesterton observed,[9] and if we saw things as they are, we would be no less astonished at consciousness in people than Geppetto was upon discovering that his wooden puppet had come to life. Like Pinocchio, we have been granted that gift for a higher purpose and the promise of a greater and richer reality of which the world around us is little more than a dim reflection. And we are similarly tempted to abandon the hope of "infinite happiness" for the sake of fleeting pleasures and impermanent things, neither marveling at the gift nor considering that it may have been granted for a nobler purpose than satisfied desires. We risk missing the whole point of living, much like Tolstoy's tragic character Ivan Ilyich, who "saw clearly that [all that for which he had lived] was not real at all, but a terrible and huge deception which had hidden both life and death."[10] Where the heavens once inspired wonder,[11] we seem to be less mindful of such things. It is a tragic thing for the distractions of life to prevent us from seeing the gift of life.

The Cat Shall Kiss the Goldfish

We carve our characters by the choices that we make and the habits of thought and deed that we form from those choices, and that dynamic process is continual throughout our lives. The changes wrought may be imperceptible, like the growing of the grass beneath our feet, but each vicious choice compromises the character on which we are continually, if unconsciously, working. Each virtuous choice has the opposite effect of reinforcing the integrity of that character. It is entirely possible that ten years from now I may wake to the realization that I have become a "hellish creature" that I never consciously set out to be. And having become that sort of person, I may not even care, which is all the more tragic. Indeed, C. S. Lewis once suggested that "the doors of hell are locked on the inside,"[12] meaning that it is the natural habitat of those who have spent a lifetime making themselves hellish through their conscious choices, much as the beastly transformation of the boys is the natural consequence of their preference for a life suitable to beasts. Perhaps hell is not so much a place where people are *cast*—against their protests—as it is a place where they arrive as a result of the series of turns they have taken and doors they have opened over a lifetime.

As Lewis conceives things, we exist somewhere along a continuum between being and non-being. God is the source of all being, and the closer we draw to that source the more fully real we become. Hell is at the other end of the continuum and is "nearly Nothing." Heaven is more fully real—solid— than earth, while hell is even less substantial. And so, when Lewis speaks of our choices turning us into either a "heavenly creature" or a "hellish" one, we may understand him to be saying that we choose between being real and fading towards unreality. Further, God is himself the Good, the ground and source of all goodness. As one of Lewis' characters from *The Great Divorce* explains, "There is but one good; that is God. Everything else is good when it looks to Him and bad when it turns from Him."[13] Because being and goodness are both rooted in God, to grow towards the one is to grow towards the other; to turn from his goodness is to fade towards nonexistence.

The Blue Fairy invoked a deep and ancient truth in connecting *being real* with *being good*. *Pinocchio* resonates with the most fundamental truth of our own created being. The wooden boy proved himself brave and unselfish to the point of sacrificing his own life out of a love for him who had created him. And so, he had met the conditions of the joy that was promised.

As Geppetto was bent over in grief beside the lifeless puppet lying on the bed, a change came over Pinocchio, and the moment of despair turned to a time of joy and celebration. Even Figaro the cat and Cleo the goldfish could not resist the infectious joy that filled their home. Pinocchio was not merely restored to the life that he had lost, but the Blue Fairy's promise—and Geppetto's wish—was fulfilled. Pinocchio had become a *real boy*.

Notes

[1] Ned Washington and Leigh Harline, "Little Wooden Head," in *Pinocchio*, dir. Ben Sharpsteen and Hamilton Luske (Burbank, CA: Walt Disney Studios, 1940).

[2] Geppetto wished for a boy, hence our title. But the reader will naturally and rightly infer that the principles involved here apply equally to wooden girls who hope someday to realize their full humanity.

[3] G. K. Chesterton, *Orthodoxy* in *G. K. Chesterton: Collected Works*, vol. 1 (San Francisco: Ignatius Press, 1986), 253.

[4] Aristotle, *NE* 3.1.1110a - 1110c.

[5] Ibid.

[6] In our agreement with the Fairy on this point we need not discount the roles played by both "nature" and "nurture." C. S. Lewis distinguished between the "raw material"—such as our genetic makeup and the circumstances of our rearing—that each of us is given to work with and *what we choose to do with it.* "God does not judge [one] on the raw material at all, but on what he has done with it." The raw material is not up to us; what we do with it is entirely up to us. See C. S. Lewis, *Mere Christianity* (New York: HarperCollins, 2001), 91.

[7] Aristotle, *NE* 1.5.1095b.

[8] Chesterton, *Orthodoxy*, 258.

[9] Chesterton, *Heretics* in *G. K. Chesterton: Collected Works*, vol. 1 (San Francisco: Ignatius Press, 1986), 68.

[10] Leo Tolstoy, *The Death of Ivan Ilyich, trans. Louise and Aylmer Maude* (IAP: 2018), 92.

[11] Ps. 8:4. Some may disparage theistic belief for its origins in a pre-scientific "Bronze Age," but those rustic shepherds who lay upon the earth and gazed into the firmament may have understood life and death with a depth and breadth undreamt of by many myopic moderns.

[12] C. S. Lewis, *The Problem of Pain* (New York: Harper Collins, 1996), 130.

[13] C. S. Lewis, *The Great Divorce* (New York: Macmillan Publishing Co., Inc., 1946), 106.

13

Cosmology and Natural Law in Disney's Hercules

John L. Weitzel

U nderstanding the cosmology of a story's main character is important. While the nuances of cosmological study may differ between ancient and modern approaches, cosmology involves an inquiry into the nature and origin of the universe. Ancient inquiry has a particular interest in the connection between cosmology and anthropology—for example, religion and the genealogy of gods.[1] Such questions of origins and the human condition are foundational elements in any worldview as they influence one's perspective on the meaning of life. Disney's narration of the ancient Greco-Roman tale of Hercules begins with the retelling of an older story—a genesis. This cosmological context is important for understanding the subsequent story. It is in light of this backdrop that we meet the once-divine, now estranged, Hercules desperate to become a hero worthy of fellowship with the gods. The cosmology presented in Disney's *Hercules* (1997) actually suggests a deep awareness of God's natural law.

Disney's *Hercules* begins with the Muses singing a Gospel tune, "The Gospel Truth,"[2] which describes the chaos of the Titans and the role Zeus plays in quelling them and establishing order. Afterward, Hercules is born, which upsets the plans of Hades, the Lord of the Dead. After being poisoned by Hades' minions, Hercules is left at the door of two mortals with most of his godliness taken from him. Over time, Hercules finds out that he is not like everyone else. He is strong but clumsy and unfocused. One might even say chaotic. After his foster parents reveal that he is the son of Zeus, he seeks out his father-god in his temple. He learns from Zeus that only a *true hero* could live with the gods, so he seeks to go the distance to earn heaven. From his interaction with Zeus, he thinks that his true and only destiny is with his father in heaven, Mt. Olympus. Hercules is unaware of the chaos outside of himself, including the existence of Hades. He employs the aid of hero-trainer Philoctetes, who trains him to focus on the task at hand and to understand his purpose. Once he begins to understand who he is and what he can accomplish, he seeks out greater challenges. He meets Megara and falls in love with her, though this love is based on outward appearance.

Once he discovers the plot of Hades and the betrayal of Megara, he reevaluates his life and the meaning of heroism. Hercules acts virtuously as he risks his life by jumping into the River Styx to save Megara. He survives, much to the surprise of Hades. After he brings Megara's soul back to her body, he flies to Zeus' side to help defeat the Titans who escaped with the help of Hades. His reward for being a true hero due to his rescue of Megara by risking his life and saving Mt. Olympus, was eternal life with the gods. He chose instead to become mortal and be with Megara, since she could not enter heaven. Hercules, the true hero, finds true happiness in the arms of a mortal woman with an uncertain afterlife. He determines that this life was more important than an afterlife of glory with the gods. Fear of death, of eternity in the Underworld, or a life of struggle, did not deter Hercules. The following will describe cosmology and natural law, as found in the movie.

Cosmology

The Greeks' view of cosmology was that the universe is ordered and supernatural. Roles and attributes of the supernatural and humanity included beliefs about the origin of the universe, the origin of humanity, and the fate of humanity within a religious context. This order provided meaning, defined virtues, and structured society. Ancient stories of creation, floods, and heavenly battles are called myths. Though some may consider myths to be nothing but make-believe stories for amusement, they are much more than that. J. R. R. Tolkien found that "myths expressed far greater truths than did historical facts or events."[3] Bradley Birzer explains that "Sanctified myths, inspired by grace, served as an *anamnesis*, or a way for a people to recall encounters with transcendence that helped to order their souls and their society ... a brief view of heaven."[4] Mythologies, including creation narratives, provide language for discovering the cosmological structure of a given community. In creation myths there is a movement from chaos to order. In Greek myths, history "was often viewed as cyclical or nonteleological,"[5] for example a belief in reincarnation and life with limited or no purpose. By comparison, the creation myths in Genesis are unique in the ancient world as they were linear and teleological (purposeful). Therefore, from a Christian point of view, there is for each individual one life to live, and that life has inherent meaning and purpose.

Hercules is written within the cultural milieu of ancient Greek life in the hero genre, which, according to Dickerson and O'Hara "depend on Homer's two epics,"[6] the *Iliad* and the *Odyssey*. These authors show that Greek myths "meant thinking about everything from the nature of the universe to our deepest moral attachments and obligations."[7] The *Iliad*, for example, allowed its readers to "reflect on human life and its significance."[8] Even if life is short, it can still be significant if lived with honor. The character arc includes a stated desired goal on the part of the protagonist, a challenge to overcome, climax, and a realization about the self, as well as a circle back to the beginning, since great adventures "end with a homecoming."[9]

There is a compelling cosmology inherent in *Hercules*. As in creation myths, there is chaos, a battle between deities, and the creation of an ordered cosmos. Humans are created as part of this order and have a particular role to play. In Greek myth, humans are made from dust with an infused soul. After a life of serving the deities, they die and end up in the Underworld. This afterlife is dull and hopeless. For the protagonist, Hercules, there is instead a joyful afterlife awaiting.

The poets of ancient Greece had a different vision of the gods than some of the philosophers. Poets wrote of conflict or chaos in the heavens, similar to the chaos caused by Hades, each divine being jockeyed for position. Homer writes, "Dione the shining among divinities answered her (Aphrodite) 'Have patience, my child, and endure it, though you be saddened. For many of us who have our homes on Olympus endure things from men, when ourselves we inflict hard pain on each other.'"[10] For Homer and other Greek poets, the gods behave much as humans do. There are quarrels and conflicts, battles and side deals. The gods are not paragons of virtue and often ought not to be imitated. In *The Odyssey*, Homer writes of the goddesses Dione and

Aphrodite, along with the gods Poseidon and Hephaistos, in divine conflict about the bondage of Ares, "Poseidon ... kept entreating Hephaistos ... asking him to set Ares free ... 'Let him go, and I guarantee he will pay whatever you ask' ... Hephaistos answered: ... 'Poseidon, do not urge this on me ... To what could I hold you among the immortal gods, if Ares were to go off, avoiding both his debt and his bondage?'[11] Many philosophers, on the other hand, had a different view of the divine. Plato, for his part, writes, "The divine is beauty, wisdom, goodness, and the like."[12] In the divine there is only order, there is no chaos or conflict. The gods conduct their sacred duty with honor. Evil among human souls is not tolerated.

What is shared between the poet and the philosopher is the idea of destiny or fate, which controls the universe and whose laws must be followed. Plato writes, "there is a law of Destiny, that the soul which attains any vision of truth in company with a god is preserved from harm."[13] Inherent in this truth is the idea of the human soul being capable of being awarded companionship with the gods. A pure soul, one who emulates the gods, that is 'beauty, wisdom, goodness, and the like,' may hope to have a share in the divine light. Plato writes that it is "only the soul of a philosopher, guileless and true, or the soul of a lover, who is not devoid of philosophy, may acquire wings."[14] Those who do not live as a philosopher have their soul sent back to live another lifetime as a human or as an animal. In the *Republic*, Plato warns not to listen to the stories of the poets since they tend to lie about the gods. He writes that "surely God and the things of God are in every way perfect."[15] The afterlife for most mortals is a temporary way station, not necessarily an eternal dullness. Hercules' universe had a Mount Olympus as the home for the gods, and the Underworld, a place where the dead dwell. Heaven was a bright, colorful, and joyous place of multiple deities. The Underworld was a place of misery and under the control and responsibility of Hades.

Interestingly, it is the Fates—Lachesis, Clotho, and Atropos—that have ultimate control. One measures the thread of life, one spins the thread, and the other cuts the thread. Although not directly addressed in the movie, in mythology, the Fates even have control over the gods. The Fates of the universe, or destiny, are an eternal law. Evidence for this in the film is that in the end, the prophecy is fulfilled even though Hades tries to stop it. Fate was present from the beginning when the Titans ruled in chaos. Although not shown in the film, it is implied in the opening song, "The Gospel Truth," that any humans living on earth would have to deal with earthquakes, floods, volcanos, and vicious storms. Zeus conquered the Titans with his lightning bolts and banished them in prison.

In Ancient Near Eastern mythologies, the fates control the universe in what Yehezkel Kaufmann identifies as the "metadivine" realm, which is the essence of paganism. He writes, "The heart of the pagan idea, then, is the conception of a primordial, supradivine (metadivine) realm which is the womb of all being, contains the roots and patterns of all nature, and out of which the gods themselves have emerged."[16] In the cosmology of *Hercules*, the gods are not the ultimate power of the universe; that claim goes to the Fates. The Fates inform Hades about the prophecy, Hades attempts to thwart the prophecy, but in the end that which was prophesized came true. This is distinct from a Christian perspective, wherein the one God has control over the dispensation of time. Greek religion and Christianity both have prophets who speak about current events and predict future ones, especially if the people do not mend their ways, though there is significant difference concerning the ultimate power behind future events.

Natural Law

Judaism, Christianity, and Islam share a similar cosmology, and each include the Adam and Eve narrative. Jews and Christians have this story in the Book of Genesis and Islam has it in various surahs such as *Al Baqara* in the Qur'an. Inherent in this cosmology is the desire on the part of God to be in relationship with humanity and a drive on the part of humans to desire to be in relationship with their creator. Adam and Eve are created in God's image and likeness and are commanded to be fruitful and multiply,[17] that is to be in relationship with each other. God creates Adam "of the dust from the ground and breathed into his nostrils the breath of life."[18] Humanity was created to be in relationship with God. God's spirit dwells in people. Abraham, was called by God so that through him, "all the families of the earth shall be blessed."[19] In Matthew's gospel, magi or wise men (non-Jews) came from the east to seek him.[20] St. Paul in his letter to the Romans states that God's "invisible attributes, namely, his eternal power and divine nature, have been clearly perceived, ever since the creation of the world."[21] In the next chapter he writes that the law is "written on their hearts, their consciences ... and their thoughts."[22]

Augustine considered Plato to be someone who follows his conscience and seeks after a relationship with God, without hearing or knowing the law of Moses or the Gospel. In his *City of God*, he praises Plato and his "philosophy which has come nearest to the Christian faith."[23] He writes, "Plato determined the final good to be to live according to virtue, and affirmed that he only can attain to virtue who knows and imitates God, —which knowledge and imitation are the only cause of blessedness."[24] Certainly, Augustine knew that Plato was a polytheist and performed rituals to many gods. However, he recognized that he has a deep subconscious longing for true virtue, wisdom, and relationship with his creator. Aquinas identified this deep subconscious longing as an intuition of the *natural law*, which follows his understanding of Paul's claim in the book of Romans about the law being written on the hearts of all.[25] Therefore, all may come to know the objective truth concerning morality and immorality. This means that people are, by nature, aware of good and praiseworthy virtues.

Plato wrote of four basic virtues in his dialogues, justice, temperance, prudence, and courage. In his dialogue, *Laches*, Socrates and others attempt to define courage. The closest they come to a definition is "that courage is the knowledge of the grounds of fear and hope" and Laches distinguishes courage from "rashness and boldness, and fearlessness, which has no forethought."[26] Plato's *Republic* describes how the young must be trained properly, including in courage. One who is courageous must be "fearless of death" and learn to "honor the gods and their parents, and to value friendship."[27] The youth ought not to be taught, says Plato, "that the gods are the authors of evil" and "heroes are no better than men."[28]

Philoctetes trains Hercules to face the challenges of being a courageous hero both physically and emotionally. He sings to Hercules, "To be a true hero ... it's a work of heart, It takes more than sinew, Comes down to what's in you."[29] A similar sentiment is written by Homer in *The Iliad*. Here he writes of Idomeneus' speech to Meriones, describing the difference between warriors who are cowards and those who are brave. The coward's heart is frightened but the brave one's heart is not.[30] All the men in the battle were certainly strong of sinew, but not all were brave. Those who were frightened feared death and were less willing to sacrifice their life for honor, glory, or country.

Aristotle shifted the focus of Homeric heroism and sacrifice to the Noble Soul. Courage is the middle ground between fear and confidence. The courageous person, according to Aristotle, is one "who is fearless in the face of a noble death."[31] He calls those who are courageous, noble. One who is courageous does so, not for the same reason as Homer's ideal of bravery, but for the sake of honor itself[32] as an internal satisfaction or virtue and not for the external reward of praise from others.[33] One who desires to be courageous cannot be fearful or foolhardy, rushing into battle without preparation, even if confident. Part of living the good life or *eudaemonia*, is loving the self and being satisfied with life even if there is pain or suffering. The feeling of self-worth reflects living a virtuous life. Aristotle admits that "courage involves pain, and is justly praised; for it is harder to face what is painful than to abstain from what is pleasant."[34]

Hercules seems to move from a Homeric hero wanting the parades and adulation of the crowd, as well as the prize of a beautiful woman, to a more Aristotelian type of hero, who is virtuous for the sake of being a virtuous person. He first had to love himself for who he is and do the noble act because it was the noble thing to do. Megara demonstrates this to him by saving Hercules' life by risking her own. Aristotle teaches that someone who is good "should be a lover of self ... doing noble acts ... and if necessary dies for (friends)."[35] Hercules satisfies Aristotle's definition of courage. Jesus expands this from friends to neighbors, categories that include all people.[36]

As Hercules expands his understanding of the meaning of life, his worldview begins to reflect a deeper understanding of virtue. Thomas Aquinas writes of eleven virtues in his *Summa Theologica* and quotes Aristotle that "virtue, "like art is about difficult things."[37] One of the virtues he describes is fortitude, as one of the four cardinal or moral virtues.[38] He defines fortitude as "every virtue that strengthens the mind against the passions ... which strengthens against dangers of death."[39] For Aquinas, as for Aristotle, virtue must be taught and practiced so that it becomes a habit. The proper end or *telos* of virtues is charity.[40] Those that practice virtue, especially when the *telos* is charity, is doing so according to the natural law which is "the rational creature's participation of the eternal law" or Divine providence.[41] Hercules practiced doing good for personal gain at first. His desire was to be honored in the Homeric sense, with public praise. At the end of the movie his purpose for acting virtuously was charity, or love; this would follow Aquinas' *following the divine natural law*.

Hercules also gains a deeper value for self-sacrifice, a willingness to give up his own desires, even his life, for the benefit of another. Joseph Campbell relays a story of a police officer who rushes to the aid of a potential suicide victim, endangering his own life.[42] Further, Campbell discusses Jesus' commandment to "Love thy neighbor as thyself" and St. Paul's teaching that Jesus came to earth to serve, emptying himself of divinity, and accepting death on the cross.[43] This idea of self-sacrifice is common in real-life, myth, and movies. Dickerson and O'Hara compare *Beowulf*, the writings of Tolkien, and other fairy tales—especially about fortitude and wisdom. There is the act of self-sacrifice for the sake of honor and then the act with the "Christian sense of morality ... *eternal* values (and) .... *moral integrity.*"[44] The intent of the action and the consequences define the difference between self-sacrifice as a heroic action alone or as a salvific event with eternal consequences. For Hercules, his choice to live as a mortal is also a self-sacrifice. He gave up eternal life as a deity in order to be in relationship with Megara.

Herculean Arc

Hercules takes place at a particular time and in a particular space, when the gods and humans often interacted with each other. Throughout the movie, Hercules grows in knowledge about himself and even learns to love himself enough to care about others, which is charity. He shifts from love of self, to desire for relationship with his divine father, to love of honor, and finally love of other. He begins to see more than his own selfish ambition; he starts to see the world through the eyes of others. At the end of the movie, he stands ready to move from the role of hero as self-serving to a leadership role in his community. He sees Zeus's love for him and his own love for Megara as a parallel to how he should *love his neighbor as himself.*

At the beginning of the movie, Hercules' worldview is limited. Although he did briefly thank his foster parents for raising him, his focus was primarily on finding out where he belongs. His adolescence was chaotic as he was clumsy, but as the movie progresses, he becomes more adept at controlling his body and focusing on a particular task. A true hero is someone who can focus on a task without prejudice. His worldview expands when he interacts with Philoctetes and Megara. Certainly the introduction of Hades and his wrestling with various creatures teaches him some valuable lessons about the world as a place of danger and obstacles, both of which could be overcome.

His relationship with his father, Zeus, was one-on-one; his worldview limited to a dyad. The only way to achieve heaven was his own effort by showing Zeus that he is a true hero. It took several misadventures for him to learn to love like a god, in a Platonic, not a Homeric sense. He knew he was from Olympus and that he has the gift of strength but needed to learn in the face of danger. In his song, "Go the Distance," his concern is reaching Mt. Olympus with Zeus and having the admiration of the crowds, a Homeric hero's reward including his image on merchandise, and the woman of his desire. In Platonic terms he had the 'soul of a lover' and desires companionship with the gods. Furthermore, as if listening to Plato's advice, Philoctetes trains Hercules' body reminding his trainee that training is also a 'work of heart.' Also, he is courageous in the face of death. Furthermore, he satisfies Aristotle's Noble Soul teaching. He is 'fearless in the face of a noble death,' desires to live a virtuous life, and is willing to face pain for another.

From a Christian perspective, it may be said that Hercules is living a virtuous life and is on a path to understanding the Christian truth. As stated above, scripture teaches that God wants to be in relationship, that God's spirit dwells in all, and one's conscience and heart has God's law present. Just as Augustine saw Plato, so the viewer can see Hercules had a deep longing for true virtue, wisdom, and relationship with his creator. Hercules grows in virtue and relationship throughout the film, but he still needs to work on wisdom. Aquinas might say that he has found God's true nature through the natural law but only needs the revealed truth. He has only begun to understand that to live for others is the call of God. Hercules has fortitude and learns charity. At the end of the movie, he finally begins to live virtuously. That is, he begins to participate in the *eternal* law.

Notes

[1] Stanslaw Iwaniszewski, "Did I Say Cosmology? On Modern Cosmologies and Ancient Worldviews," in *Cosmology Across Cultures*, eds. José Alberto Rubino-Martin, Juan Antonio Belmonte, Francisco Prada and Anxton Alberdi (Astronomical Society of the Pacific Conference Series, Vol. 409, 2009), 103.

[2] David Zippel and Alan Menken, "The Gospel Truth," in *Hercules*, dir. Ron Clements and John Musker (Burbank, CA: Walt Disney Studios, 1997).

[3] Bradley J. Birzer, *Sanctifying Myth*, (Wilmington: Intercollegiate Studies Institute, 2014), 24.

[4] Ibid., 24.

[5] Matthew Dickerson and David O'Hara, *From Homer to Harry Potter* (Grand Rapids: Brazos Press, 2006), 103.

[6] Ibid., 95.

[7] Ibid.

[8] Ibid., 97.

[9] Ibid., 101.

[10] Homer, *Iliad* 380, in Mortimer J. Adler, Clifton Fadiman, and Philip W. Goetz, eds., *Great Books of the Western World*, 2nd ed., vol. 3, ed. (Chicago: Encyclopædia Britannica, Inc., 1990).

[11] Homer, *Odyssey* 345-350, in Adler, Fadiman, and Goetz, *Great Books*, vol. 3.

[12] Plato, *Phaedrus* 246, in Adler, Fadiman, and Goetz, *Great Books*, vol. 6.

[13] *Phaedrus* 248.

[14] Ibid., 249.

[15] Plato, *Republic* 381, in Adler, Fadiman, and Goetz, *Great Books*, vol. 6.

[16] Yehezkel Kaufmann, "The Biblical Age," in Great Ages and Ideas of the Jewish People, ed. Leo W. Schwartz, (New York: Random House, 1956), 10.

[17] Gen. 1:26-28.

[18] Gen. 2:7 (ESV).

[19] Gen. 12:3.

[20] Matt. 2.

[21] Rom. 1:20.

[22] Rom. 2:15.

[23] Augustine, *City of God* 8.8, in Adler, Fadiman, and Goetz, *Great Books*, vol. 16.

[24] *City of God* 8.9.

[25] Aquinas, *Summa Theologica* 2-1.91.2, 2-1.94.4, in Adler, Fadiman, and Goetz, *Great Books*, vol. 18.

[26] Plato, *Laches* 197, in Adler, Fadiman, and Goetz, *Great Books*, vol. 6.

[27] *Republic* 3.386.

[28] Ibid., 3.391.

[29] David Zippel and Alan Menken, "One Last Hope," in *Hercules* (1997).

[30] Homer, *Iliad* 277-287.

[31] Aristotle, *Nicomachean Ethics* 3.1115a5-35, in Adler, Fadiman, and Goetz, *Great Books*, vol. 8.

[32] *NE* 3.1115b11-13.

[33] Ibid., 3.1116a25-29.

[34] Ibid., 3.1117a36-38.

[35] Ibid., 9.11169a1-19.

[36] See Matt. 22:36-40 and Luke 10:25-37.

[37] Aquinas, *ST* 1-2.60.5; The quote from Aristotle is *NE* 2.3.1105a9.

[38] Aquinas, *ST* 1-2.61.1.

[39] Ibid., 1-2.61.3.

[40] Ibid., 1-2.65.4.

[41] Ibid., 1-2.91.2; 1-2.94.3.

[42] Joseph Campbell, *The Power of Myth* (New York: Anchor Books, 1991), 138-39.

[43] Ibid., 142.

[44] Dickerson and O'Hara, 320-21.

14

Ḟave Courage and Be Kind: Cinderella and the Problem of Evil

Lori A. Peters

isney's *Cinderella* provides a model of response to the problem of pain and suffering, as Cinderella also exemplifies the power and beauty of moral transformation through adversity. Cinderella's very attitude and actions demonstrate that her response is morally proper. Of course, her story should not be taken to imply that it is okay to ignore abuse or injustice, or to endure otherwise avoidable suffering. Cinderella 's tale does not diminish the anguish and emotional toll that suffering caused in her soul. Rather, her continuous acts of service and care for the animals of the house bring cheerfulness to an otherwise torturous situation. The problem of evil refers to the challenge that the existence of a loving, powerful, and all-knowing God is somehow incompatible with the reality of pain and suffering in the world. In a world wrought with evil and suffering, many cry out in anger at God or reject His existence. This anger or rejection is often tied to a deep pain and a lack of understanding about why a good God would allow anyone—especially seemingly good people—to endure bad things. There are various ways for the theist to respond to this challenge, but one of the most important points for understanding any theodicy is to understand that the world is broken. Alas, suffering has a way of bringing the existential (that which is felt and personal) and the logical (that which is abstract and rational) in tension with one another. It is for this reason that Disney's classic tale offers apologetic power. Even without abstract arguments, we *feel* that her situation is not right, and we sense that something about her character is morally commendable.

Cinderella provides not only a model of faith and fortitude in the face of injustice and suffering, but also an answer to the existential problem of evil and suffering—hope. While her enduring hope that dreams will come true is a questionable ideal, the act of placing one's hope in something better—a greater goodness beyond one's situation—is the foundation of the moral response to suffering. According to the Christian scriptures, it is the hope of Jesus and his promise to deal with injustice and to make new this broken world which serves as the ultimate theodicy. It is through such hope in a greater and forthcoming goodness that one can respond to real-world suffering in a manner like that so beautifully displayed in Walt Disney's Cinderella.[1]

Cinderella's Suffering

Disney's adaptation of the classic fairy tale opens with a young girl who has already lost her mother. After suffering the loss of a father as well, she is left with a selfish stepmother who acts cruelly toward anyone she believes to threaten the happiness and advancement of herself and her daughters, Drizella and Anastasia. Her cruelty and jealousy of Cinderella's beauty and gracious personality leads Lady Tremaine to lower Cinderella to the position of a scullery maid and servant. Cinderella's life becomes one of endless chores, abuse, false accusations, and gratuitous evil. The climax of the story truly displays the depth of depravity in Lady Tremaine's heart when she allows her daughters to assault Cinderella over a dress made of their scraps, thereby destroying Cinderella's opportunity to attend the ball which was intended for *every* eligible maiden in the kingdom. When Lady Tremaine realizes Cinderella is the unknown girl from the ball who received the prince's favor, she proceeds to lock Cinderella in her room, in the tower, to prevent her from having even a chance at happiness. Finally, when all seems lost for Lady Tremaine, she commits an act of treason by tripping the Grand Duke's assistant, causing the glass slipper to fall and break into a thousand pieces.

All this mistreatment is done to prevent Cinderella from receiving anything good in life and, especially, from marrying the prince. The suffering and injustice in Cinderella's tale are far more vivid for the adult viewer than for the child, but the evil of the stepmother's intentions and the goodness of Cinderella's responses are not lost on either viewer.

Cinderella's Response

It would be misleading to characterize Cinderella's response to her suffering as shallow or unreasonable. She often voices her anger and deep sadness, and she cried out in her grief not knowing when her wishes would come true. Yet, she neither seeks revenge nor acts angrily toward those who hate her. She even tells Bruno, the dog, that he should find a way to make peace with Lucifer, the cat—not just for his safety but because there must be something good about Lucifer to admire. Lucifer makes Cinderella's life miserable, and he antagonizes the other animals residing in and around the chateau. Yet even in this, Cinderella never mistreats the awful cat. Her kindness to all the animals, her family, and even Lucifer is a courageous act in the face of injustice.

She also treats her family with respect even though they are not blood relatives; she considers them all family. She seems to take care of her stepsisters with excellence and treats her stepmother with an unreciprocated respect. Cinderella also responds with kindness when falsely accused. When Gus the mouse is accidentally trapped under Anastasia's teacup, afraid to come out because of Lucifer, Cinderella is accused of deliberately placing Gus under the cup, as a mean joke. She begins to answer the charge, but then chooses to remain silent in the face of the accusation. When Lady Tremaine punishes Cinderella with an exorbitant list of chores, beyond her daily duties, Cinderella simply acknowledges her stepmother and begins the work without argument. It is only after Cinderella's dress (a gift from her only friends) is ruined by her stepsisters that Cinderella falls into despair and begins to doubt that her wishes will come true.

Cinderella's response to suffering brings to mind the example of Jesus. Though often remembered, in pop culture, primarily as a loving person who showed kindness to the marginalized, the historical Jesus faced accusations of false teaching and being demon-possessed. He often expressed frustration at both the hypocrisy of religious leaders and his disciples' inability to understand his teaching. His methods were often questioned, even by his mother and half-siblings.[2] He felt deep sorrow for Mary and Martha over the loss of their brother and for the city of Jerusalem as he saw her future. Jesus showed deep mercy and love for people who were living immoral life-styles, such as Zacchaeus, the tax collector, and the woman caught in adultery. He never once mistreated those who hated him, accused him of demon possession, or wanted to kill him. He wept in the garden the night before his crucifixion—grieving for what was yet to come. He suffered betrayal by two of his closest followers. He was arrested due to the betrayal of Judas, and Peter denied knowing Jesus, three times, out of fear and self-interest. Following his arrest, in all four Gospel accounts, Jesus refrained from defending himself or giving reasons for the false accusations of blasphemy and treason. He remained silent. Finally, he was willing to take all the suffering of humanity's due punishment (for injustices against God and one another) upon himself. Jesus understood suffering, false accusation, and persecution well, yet chose to demonstrate fortitude and love—thereby providing the ultimate example of courage and kindness in the face of great injustice. Thus, while Cinderella raises the bar for many viewers, even she is reaching for a standard modeled perfectly by Jesus.

Cinderella's Moral Transformation

In order to understand and appreciate Cinderella's moral transformation, a brief foray into the argument from evil is appropriate. Cinderella was a victim of the libertarian free will of her family. They chose to abuse the gift given by God—the freedom to choose for oneself whether to act in accordance with the Good or in antithesis to the Good (or even, in self-interest, at the expense of true goodness)—and Cinderella was the recipient of their wicked decisions. God is morally justified in allowing such evil because human beings are responsible for their own free choices. The question is rightly asked, why doesn't God stop evil, like the suffering Cinderella experienced? God's intervention to prevent all gratuitous evil, however, would ultimately come at the expense of free will.[3]

As a result of free will, horrific evils exist. Additionally, as with Cinderella, people who live with in accordance with goodness and justice still experience evil perpetrated by others who abuse the gift of free will. Cinderella endured abuse for no reason, and her kindness was often met with more cruelty as it shined a light on the darkness of her family members' souls. However, underlying this discussion is the question, how does one even know what evil is? It would seem evident that watching Cinderella's stepsisters treat her so unkindly is a glaring example of evil. Yet, the recognition of evil concedes a deeper conviction. There can be no objective notion of evil if there is no objective standard of good in which all thoughts and actions can be evaluated. C. S. Lewis adeptly argued that one can only understand a line as crooked by first knowing a straight line.[4] So, what would be the moral standard to which Cinderella or others could appeal in identifying her situation as unjust or wrong? It seems that gratuitous evil and suffering actually hint at the existence of God far more than they challenge his existence.[5] God is the only being that is wholly good and is the best way for people of all walks of life to verify their actions as moral. God is also the best explanation for why people, regardless of their beliefs, exemplify the desire for justice in the face of evil.

Cinderella clearly demonstrates a deep conviction of an objective moral standard, and her moral transformation takes place in light of this grounding. Moral transformation is the change in one's character and virtue resulting from following the moral standard.[6] Cinderella repeatedly responds toward her family with the moral values of kindness, forgiveness, and forbearance. Her situation provides the opportunity to exercise both her faith in the existence of an objective moral standard and her freedom in choosing to align her actions in accordance with that goodness. This moral response then provides the opportunity for Cinderella to become a better person. She *chooses* not to dwell in bitterness and anger but opens each day with singing and care for her animal friends. She tackles her chores earnestly and does not allow the chiming clock tower to ruin her day. Her cheerfulness does not mean she faces no disappointment, anger, or sadness. Instead, she chooses neither to dwell on nor to react to these anxieties, but to concern herself primarily with the Good. Her attitude strengthens her character and protects her heart from deep despair and bitterness.

Cinderella's transformation also strengthens her hope that dreams will come true. She continually chooses to believe in the hope that things will be better, and this drives her continual moral response to her family and situation. Her moral transformation reflects the caliber of character (revealed in Jesus) into which God calls us all to grow. Still, if God provides the perfect standard of justice by which all should live, then it would seem clear that rescuing the abused and bringing to justice the abuser would be the appropriate end to Cinderella's plight. We deeply long for a final justice, and the story of *Cinderella* indeed provides us this sense of satisfaction. Yet it is the nature of her character amidst suffering, and not simply the fact of her salvation, that makes her story so profound and her example so powerful. In short, we are amazed by her sense of hope—and that is the very thing she gives to *us*!

A Necessary Note on Abuse

As mentioned above, what Cinderella experienced was emotional and physical abuse, as well as neglect. As with parables, we need to take caution and not press the details beyond the narrative. However, given the argument that Cinderella's response to this abuse was moral, a clarification regarding abuse is necessary. Her fictional historical context is the 18th or early 19th century in a French-like culture. Historically, this was not a time where abused or neglected people, especially women, had the power or the resources to flee the type of abuse she experienced. In addition to the lack of resources for women, it appears that Cinderella experiences the bulk of the abuse as an older child and teen. Even when coming of age, she would have had limited, if any, chances to escape her family situation. At worst, she would have been able to marry a pauper or, at best, a merchant. However, given the vindictiveness of her stepmother, Lady Tremaine would have likely prevented anything from interfering with her ability to continue to abuse Cinderella (as many abusers do).

To be clear, this essay should not be construed as advocating that anyone should remain in an abusive situation, nor does it argue that injustice should be ignored. The moral response to injustice and abuse is to seek to rescue the abused and ensure justice is served to the abuser. For those who claim to follow Jesus, the Bible clearly teaches that evil is to be repudiated,[7] justice and mercy are to be pursued,[8] and that one should refuse to seek revenge, but rather seek the good for all.[9] [10] Additionally, nothing in Scripture states that someone without power or position is required to suffer under the abuse of another, whether in marriage or any other relationship. Even Jesus, when he told his follower to turn the other cheek, was not teaching that one must endure abuse. He was teaching a deeper truth concerning the goodness of forgiveness and the redemptive power of choosing to act in love rather than retaliation. His ministry to the marginalized, the abused, and victims of injustice, precludes the notion that Jesus taught to accept abuse. Thus, we are *not* to take from Cinderella's tale that abuse is necessary or ought to be endured if escapable. Rather, Cinderella offers a reflection of Jesus's teaching—that there are morally excellent ways to respond to anxieties amid suffering and toward others when one is mistreated—and she reminds us that goodness is somehow connected to such moral excellence.[11]

Hope

What fueled Cinderella's moral response to intense personal suffering? Hope: hope that one day things would be much better for her; hope that her dreams would come true; hope that her life would change. She expresses this hope in the opening scene, singing to her animal friends about dreams and wishes. She confides in them that if one simply keeps believing, one day, those wishes and dreams can come true.[12] As she sobbed in the garden after, her stepsisters' humiliating assault destroyed all hope of attending the ball, Cinderella claims no longer to believe—that belief is now useless. However, she did not actually lose hope. For her fairy godmother appears and informs Cinderella that if she had lost all faith, she, the fairy godmother, would have never appeared. Yet Cinderella's fairy godmother *does* appear and provides Cinderella the means and accouterments to attend the ball. Cinderella's hope carried her to the ball. Her hope would also carry to the ultimate fulfillment of her dreams.

Unfortunately, Cinderella is only a fairy tale. Her hope in something, someday, changing her life is a hope that wears thin on the soul without some evidence of its possible fruition. When enduring the sufferings of this world, either because of its brokenness or one's righteousness while living in it, there must be some other hope. Human beings repeatedly fail to progress to a moral ideal and are demonstrably lacking in a unified mission to abolish evil and suffering. It must be asked, then, is there really any grounding for hope? Can one find hope amid personal suffering without a promised fairy tale ending? In truth, she does not really need a Prince Charming who is conveniently privileged enough to be able to rescue her from circumstantial suffering, simply hiding her away from the reminders of her losses and injustices; she needs a Prince of Peace[13] who is ready to redeem what was lost, eager to serve justice, and able to provide a cessation to suffering. *True* hope should be built on nothing less.[14]

The Christian scriptures call us to be bearers (ambassadors) of hope for those around us who are desperate for hope yet cannot find it. Cinderella and her animal friends exemplify what it means to be a bearer of hope. Cinderella shared her hope with the mice, birds, and farm animals. However, her bearing of hope was far more than words and song—it was action! She provided clothing, food, and protection for her animal friends. Being a bearer of hope requires actions far more than just words. Cinderella experiences this from her animal friends in two crucial scenes. After receiving the punishment of more chores for the false accusation of playing a prank on Anastasia, Cinderella is left with no time to alter her mother's dress. Cinderella is unexpectedly surprised by her animal friends' fantastic work to alter and update the dress, raising her hope, once again, that she can attend the ball. Jaq and Gus bring the second act of hope as they steal the key from Lady Tremaine's pocket, to free Cinderella from the tower. Just when they reach the door, having brought the key up many flights of stairs, Lucifer traps Gus and the key under a cup as Cinderella watches with anticipation. The other mice and birds come to fight Lucifer, and eventually bring Bruno to chase Lucifer away. The mice give the key to Cinderella, and she escapes the tower to see the Grand Duke. Cinderella not only brings resolution, but she shares the evidence of her hope by producing the other glass slipper after the first breaks. She and her animal friends mutually provided practical ways not only to lift their spirits, but also to fuel their hope for a better life.

Much ink has been spilled concerning the argument from evil and answers abound as to why God allows evil and suffering. However, one must be a bearer of hope, and not merely a bearer of theodicy, if one wants to have an apologetic impact in the face of suffering. It is in one's response to another's suffering where hope is found. It is in the actions of a bearer of hope that the sufferer can see and taste a glimpse of hope. Those who know the true hope found in Jesus should listen, empathize, and provide practical help to those in pain—whether followers of Christ or not. Grief and suffering are no respecters of persons, and all need to know or be reminded of where true hope resides. Cinderella needed practical help to change her situation.

One does not need fairy tales to provide hope and help. People honestly do not want to know why they are suffering, but how to end it, change it, or prevent it. The most practical ways of being a bearer of hope are demonstrated in Cinderella's animal friends, who are there for her daily. It is when family members and friends carry one another's burdens in community, that hope is not lost, but rather is shared with those who need it most. Even more critical is presence. Not words. Not platitudes. Not theodicies. Presence. Hope can be felt and seen in the presence of a hope bearer. Cinderella's friends would sit with her, cry with her, and listen to her in her times of sorrow. Sometimes this is all they had to offer. In the preface of *Night*, François

Mauriac recounts hearing author Elie Wiesel describe the horrific hanging of a child in the concentration camp and his cries of where God could possibly be in the midst of such evil. Mauriac wanted to share his hope about God's love and grace, but instead wrapped his arms around Wiesel and cried with him.[15] Sometimes the simplest act of hope is to be present and grieve with those suffering.

Final Thoughts

It may not have been the intention of Disney to provide a moral answer to the problem of enduring suffering. However, in producing *Cinderella*, they did provide an inspiring model of suffering with grace and character. Cinderella took no further action or revenge on her stepmother or stepsisters after she married Prince Charming. One could imagine Lady Tremaine and her daughters sitting at the deteriorating chateau, with no servants, no horse, no dog, and no happiness, as they wallowed in the misery of their dark souls. Jesus had an answer, however, for how one should treat such people. He commanded his followers to love those who are considered enemies and pray for those who bring persecution.[16] No greater moral response, courage, or kindness can be found than in the example and teaching of Jesus. When we suffer injustices, with charity and fortitude—focusing instead on our faith in higher, excellent, praiseworthy truths[17]— we may also become bearers of hope to others who are suffering. *Cinderella* resonates with our sense of injustice and calls us both to love virtue and to help others. Her response to evil exemplifies the call of Christ to serve as ambassadors of hope to a world desperate for justice and to provide comfort to those who endure suffering and abuse...

Notes

[1] *Cinderella*, dir. Clyde Geronimi, Hamilton Luske, and Wilfred Jackson (Burbank, CA: Walt Disney Studios, 1950).

[2] Mark 3:21.

[3] Bruce A. Little, *A Creation-Order Theodicy: God and Gratuitous Evil* (Lanham: University Press of America, 2005), 162-63.

[4] C. S. Lewis, *Mere Christianity*, (New York: HarperCollins, 2001), 38.

[5] David Baggett and Jerry L. Walls, *Good God: The Theistic Foundations of Morality* (New York: Oxford University Press, 2011), 156.

[6] David Baggett and Jerry L. Walls, *God and Cosmos: Moral Truth and Human Meaning* (New York: Oxford University Press, 2016), loc. 5672, Kindle.

[7] Rom. 6.

[8] Mic. 6:8.

[9] 1 Thess. 5:15.

[10] Little, 116.

[11] In modern contexts, these evils should be battled with all the power of the justice system and all the compassion and protection that people can provide. No one should be expected to endure abuse for the sake of a family, but should be provided the resources and protection to flee from such horrors. The Church at large should be a safe haven for abused persons who desperately need love, compassion, and practical help to navigate leaving such a situation both literally and legally.

[12] Mack David, Al Hoffman and Jerry Livingston "A Dream is a Wish Your Heart Makes," in *Cinderella* (1950).

[13] Isa. 9:6.

[14] Jesus is not just the moral exemplar for how to endure evil and suffering—he is the remedy. He came to rescue humanity from the power of evil and death. He came to reconcile humanity to himself as their evil became a barrier to a genuine relationship with a holy God. He did not just die on the cross bearing the weight of all the evil humanity committed, but he conquered sin and death with the most climactic act in history—his resurrection. It is in his resurrection, for those who choose to experience the spiritual death and resurrection in following Jesus, that real hope can be found. The ultimate destiny for Christians is a bodily and glorified resurrection to dwell with God forever. Jesus was the unique agent of salvation and eternal life, through his death *and* his bodily resurrection. All hope for eternal life, hope to endure the sufferings of this world, hope to face the persecution of following Jesus, and to have abundant life, are found in his resurrection. The

resurrection signals a gratuitous good potent enough to provide a transformative hope for gratuitous evil and suffering worldwide.

[15] Elie Wiesel, *Night* (New York: Hill and Wang, 2006), xxi.

[16] Matt. 5:44.

[17] Phil. 4:8.

15

A Kierkegaardian Reading of *The Lion King*: Simba Becomes a Person

Josh Herring

D anish philosopher Soren Kierkegaard once suggested that, if he had a child, his parting wisdom would be that the greatest treasure of this life is not to be found in fortunes, honors, or titles, but within one's own inner self. For "there is an Either/Or there that makes a human being greater than [even] the angels."[1] By "Either/Or" Kierkegaard means an absolute moral choice. These words describe the value Kierkegaard placed on the human capacity to make choices. Unique among creation, humans have the ability to shape who they become through intentional, rational choices. This capacity for self-formation becomes the foundation of Kierkegaard's notion of ethical responsibility. The development of an ethical self appears, in Kierkegaard's thought, as the highest goal of life. Through the circuitous route of choices, the self develops a personality. Though most go through life without making such choices, drifting from circumstance to circumstance as life directs, a few individuals rise above the appearance of determinism and embrace the capacity for choosing who they will become.

The importance of making this choice is the theme of Kierkegaard's work, *Either/Or*.

Such a theme drives the plot of Disney's *The Lion King*. Raised in relative luxury with the expectation of exercising royal power, exile present Simba with the possibility of living a dissolute life. The heart of Simba's development lies in *choosing* to return to Pride Rock; in so doing, Simba illustrates the choice to live a life of responsibility. By pairing Kierkegaard and *The Lion King*, the reader is equipped to see the significance behind this beloved film.

Kierkegaard authored 25 books; of those, *Either/Or* is the most philosophical (ethical). *Either/Or* is a dialogue of letters between two characters, "The Aesthete" and "The Judge." Both characters speak to the ancient Socratic question: What constitutes the "good life"? The Aesthete lays out a "life-view" proposing the pursuit of momentary pleasure as the highest goal. His aesthetic leads him to advocate for seduction as the symbol of ultimate beauty. The Judge advocates a different "life-view;" he contends that true beauty is found in mundane moments that extend through time; his symbol for this kind of beauty is marriage. He recognizes that this kind of beauty is less exciting but claims that it is ultimately far more satisfying. The Judge conceptualizes their differences in urging the Aesthete to make a sincere choice; the following quote shows the difference between the substantive life urged by the Judge and the life of fleeting vanities pursued by the Aesthete.

> If you want to go on amusing your soul with the trifling of wittiness and the vainglory of the intellect, then do so. Leave your home, emigrate to Paris, devote yourself to journalism, court the smiles of languid women, cool their hot blood with the chill of your wit, let it be your life's proud task to dispel an idle woman's boredom or the gloomy thoughts of a burned-out sensualist; forget that you were a child, that there was piety in your soul and innocence in your thoughts; muffle every lofty voice in your heart, loaf your life away in the glittering wretchedness of social gatherings; forget that there is an immortal spirit within you, torture the last farthing out of your soul; and when your wittiness lapses into silence, there still is water in the Seine and gunpowder in the shop and travelling company for every time in the day.[2]

The choice the Judge presents is a choice between a substantive life, or a meaningless life. Perceiving the reality of the choice leads to making the right choice and cultivating a mature personality. "At the first moment of choice the personality seemingly emerges as naked as the infant from the mother's womb; at the next moment it is concrete in itself, and a person can remain at this point only through an arbitrary abstraction. ...the choice penetrates everything and changes it. Thus, his finite personality is now made infinite in the choice, in which he infinitely chooses himself."[3]

His emphasis on choice positions Kierkegaard as the perfect theoretician for *The Lion King*. *Either/Or*, in particular, illuminates through Simba's journey a crucial part of the human condition: our choices matter, and through our choices we create our future. In revealing this truth, *The Lion King* shows us both the nature of ethical self-development and the goal of education: education should enable the student to perceive him or herself and choose his or her inner infinity.

The Kierkegaardian *Lion King*

Kierkegaard describes movement between two different domains: the aesthetic, and the ethical. "The aesthetic, it was said, is that in which a person whereby he immediately is the person that he is; the ethical is that whereby a person becomes what he becomes."[4] In this movement, ethical development occurs. This shift from what one is to what one becomes Kierkegaard terms the ethical, and this journey describes the growth in Simba's personality across *The Lion King*. We first meet Simba as a young cub. He is enamored with being the "future-king," and his song "I Just Can't Wait to Be King" celebrates his excitement about exercising power (while simultaneously distracting guardian Zazu so that he and Nala can have an adventure in the elephant graveyard). Simba's initial understanding of kingship is disturbing—he envisions only the privileges of rank and the power of intimidation: "I'm brushing up on looking down / I'm working on my roar."[5] There are no restraints in this imagined future, no responsibilities, only privileges, pleasures, and commands.

Young Simba is implicitly contrasted with the older, wiser, much more responsible Mufasa. While Simba resists admitting his fear, Mufasa has no such problem. "I was [afraid] today. I thought I might lose you." Mufasa the wise king knows the fragility of life; he is unwilling to promise he will always be there for Simba, because he knows he will die. His role as king involves maintaining "the delicate balance" that allows all life to flourish in the Pride Lands. How will Simba grow into his potential such that he becomes a good king, rather than a tyrant like Scar? This question is the underlying theme controlling the narrative, and it is a primary question of education: how does the current generation pass on society to the young such that they appreciate and value what the previous generation stewarded? In answering the initial question, *The Lion King* offers an answer to the broader question of education. Kierkegaard writes, "Just as an heir, even if he were an heir to the treasures of the whole world, does not possess them before he has come of age, so the richest personality is nothing before he has chosen himself."[6] Simba has all the potential to be a good king of Pride Rock, but the route to fulfilling that potential involves making a choice between two different ways of life. In that choice, he chooses to become himself in his fullness.

Kierkegaard places an almost incalculable weight on the importance of the individual making choices. He writes that "in the choosing the personality declares itself in its inner infinity and in turn the personality is thereby consolidated."[7] Significant choices, what later thinkers termed "existential choices,"[8] that direct the course of the individual's life, allow for the abstract personality to become concrete. Kierkegaard contends that in such choices we develop ourselves into certain persons. Growing in personhood is a process of making such choices as life demands them. Throughout the first half of *The Lion King*, the audience sees Simba make choices: he chooses to take Nala to the graveyard; he chooses to believe Scar after Mufasa's death; he chooses to trust Timon and Pumbaa when he arrives in the jungle.

The first movement of the story focuses on Simba choosing to become a disciple of *hakuna matata,* Timon and Pumbaa's quasi-Epicurean "problem-free philosophy" that "means no worries for the rest of your days." Each choice is real, and it brings Simba's nascent personality further into existence. Kierkegaard describes this process, writing, "The choice itself is crucial for the content of the personality: through the choice the personality submerges itself in that which is being chosen, when it does not choose, it withers away in atrophy."[9] The person Simba has chosen to be, by the conclusion of the first movement of the story, is an Epicurean figure who perceives nothing greater than a pleasurable life with friends. Kierkegaard argues that "Every human being...has a natural need to formulate a life-view, a conception of the meaning of life and its purpose. The person who lives aesthetically also does that, and the popular expression heard in all ages and from various stages is this: 'One must enjoy life.'"[10] Simba currently enjoys his life—living in comfort, with plenty of food, water, and shade, is of greater value than worrying about the fate of the Pride Lands in the absence of Mufasa.

Nala's arrival changes everything. Simba chose to leave the Pride Lands because Scar told him Mufasa's death was his fault; "Run away, Simba! Run away, and never return." In the aftermath of his father's death, Simba abandons any responsibility for ruling Pride Rock. He embraces the life Timon and Pumbaa teach him—eating insects, romping through the jungle, living easy. Nala arrives, and suddenly his past returns. She tells him hyenas rule the Pride Lands, and that the lionesses are starving. Simba, now a young lion at the height of strength, feels an initial sense of responsibility, but then shakes his head.

> SIMBA. No! *Hakuna Matata!* Look—sometimes bad things happen, and there's nothing you can do about it!
> NALA. What's happened to you? You're not the Simba I remember.
> SIMBA. No, I'm not. You know, you're starting to sound like my father!
> NALA. Good; at least one of us does.
> SIMBA. You don't even know what I've been through!

Simba lopes off, angry but unable to articulate his anger. He has been asked to make a choice. From Nala's perspective, the choice is simple: Simba should return, and right what is wrong. For Simba, however, the choice involves more. "That which is to be chosen has the deepest relation to the one who is choosing."[11] Simba has reached a moment of existential choice, requiring the sacrifice of his pleasure-based lifestyle. In this choice, he will choose which lion he will become: either the path of pleasurable aesthete abdicating responsibility, or the path of the ethical willing to take up the mantle of responsibility. Making such a choice is transformative: in making this kind of choice, "his inner being is purified and he himself is brought into an immediate relationship with the eternal power that omnipresently pervades all existence."[12] For Kierkegaard's theory, it is not about making the right or wrong choice; the process of making the choice forces the development of the personality. The Judge writes, "What, then, is it that I separate in my Either/Or? Is it good and evil? No, I only want to bring you to the point where the choice truly has meaning for you. It is on this that everything turns. As soon as a person can be brought to stand at the crossroads in such a way that there is no way out for him except to choose, he will choose the right thing."[13] Simba is brought to just such a point of *choosing*.

In one sense, Simba's previous choices all had some element of compulsion, making them lesser choices. He fell into exile through the influence and deception of Scar, and he went along with Timon and Pumbaa in part through the necessities of survival. Here, in this moment in the story, he is faced with a choice that he alone can make. In such a moment, faced with the choice, Simba must choose whether he will stay in the life of *hakuna matata*, or embrace the path to becoming the king he was born to be.

The Judge claims the role of awakening the Aesthete to the emptiness of his existence; in *The Lion King*, Rafiki takes Simba to the pool where he encounters Mufasa. There, Mufasa reminds Simba, "You are my son, and the one true king of Pride Rock." The Judge writes, "The point is not the reality of that which is chosen but the reality of choosing. This, however, is what is crucial, and it is to this that I shall strive to awaken you. Up to that point, one person can help another; when he has reached that point, the significance the one person can have for the other becomes more subordinate."[14] Rafiki and Mufasa can highlight Simba's need to choose. While another can elucidate the possibilities, the final choice is beyond aid. It is in the moment of individual choice, without help, without external voices, that the self becomes concretized and fused. For Simba, this happens as Mufasa's voice fades away, and he turns to banter with Rafiki. He then begins galloping to meet his chosen destiny.

Simba makes this choice, and in doing so he becomes most fully himself. He is physically powerful, the lion king in body, and now fully resolved in mind and spirit to fight for his land and establish just rule. If that requires payment for his part in Mufasa's death, so be it. He has left the aesthetic of the jungle for the ethical responsibility of being king.

The nature of the choice is shown to the audience visually: Simba must leave the jungle. He cannot wait until morning and bring his friends—he must leave immediately. "And yet the point here is a choice, indeed, an absolute choice, for only by choosing absolutely can one choose the ethical."[15] Simba has to choose, and he must execute the choice completely. His decision to leave functions as an implicit repentance for his previous life: the Judge writes that one can "choose himself ethically only by repenting himself, and only by repenting himself does he become concrete, and only as a concrete individual is he a free individual."[16] In his repentance and choice, Simba acquires a new kind of freedom. Making the choice results in an immediate change in Simba's character: "to choose gives a person's being a solemnity, a quiet dignity, that is never lost."[17] This dignity is why Simba's next scene shows him running in the desert—we see the mature lion's strength on display in the harshest conditions of the Sahara. No more the softness of jungle living; here is a dignified warrior *en route* to reconquer what has been taken from him. Gone is the troubled indifference to his family's suffering. Simba's single-mindedness, grounded in his absolute choice, gives him a *gravitas* lacking in his earlier character.

The Judge notes that the Aesthete, like many, fears that choosing based on the ethical will involve limiting himself in some way; rejecting the wrong and choosing the right forces him into some kind of mold, bearing an unavoidable opportunity cost. The Judge takes a different view:

> Here I now want to call to mind the definition of the ethical I gave before—that it is that whereby a person becomes what he becomes. It does not want to make the individual into someone else but into the individual himself; it does not want to destroy the aesthetic but to transfigure it. For a person to live ethically it is necessary that he becomes conscious of himself, so thoroughly that no accidental element escapes him. The ethical does not want to wipe out this concretion but sees in it its task, sees the material with which it is to build and that which it builds.[18]

Simba is not changed into some other, more perfect being. Instead, his choice to return to Pride Rock and take up rule causes him to become *himself* more fully than he could ever have been in the jungle. He was not really living the life of a lion; he was no famed "king of beasts" while living with a warthog and meerkat, eating insects. Becoming himself requires sacrificing through his choice, and yet, he also brings with him all of himself that is shaped by those years in the aesthetic jungle. In a sense, he is following the Apostle Paul's example: "When I was a child, I spoke like a child, I thought like a child, I reasoned like a child. When I became a man, I gave up childish ways."[19] Even so, the man is the child who used to play, but has since been transfigured into a state of authority and responsibility.

Simba returns, neither as the cub who left nor the playboy unworried by his mother's starvation. Instead, he returns committed to restoring what has been lost. "Yes, Timon. This is my home." In naming the Pride Lands his home, Simba takes up the mantle Mufasa describes at the beginning of the movie: "Look, Simba. Everything the light touches is our kingdom. A king's time as ruler rises and falls like the sun. One day, Simba, the sun will set on my time here, and will rise with you as the new king." It is his home, his kingdom, and as king he must rule with justice, completing the circle of life. He defeats Scar, and the wasteland flowers. Simba and Nala produce an heir, and the movie ends as Rafiki lifts up Kiara just as Simba was lifted.

Simba's journey to becoming a responsible king is a circuitous one; not for him the straightforward path. Such a journey resonates with a closing line from the Judge: "I am no ethical rigorist, enthusiastic about a formal, abstract freedom. If only the choice is posited, all the aesthetic returns, and you will see that only thereby does existence become beautiful, and that this is the only way a person can save his soul and win the whole world, can use the world without misusing it."[20] Through undertaking the ethical, through choosing to become the Lion King, Simba regained all the joys of community and happiness he gave up in the jungle, yet he regained them in such a way that his previous happiness seemed but a shadow, a stepping stone to the real.

Simba's journey is not complete; choosing the ethical never ends. It becomes a lifetime, as C. S. Lewis might put it, of going "further in and higher up."[21] Kierkegaard describes the one who chooses the ethical as "well aware that every human being develops in freedom, but he is also aware that a person does not create himself out of nothing, that he has himself in its concretion as his task; he will once again be reconciled with existence in perceiving that in a certain sense every person is an exception, and that it is equally true that every human being is the universally human and also an exception."[22] Choosing the ethical in a Kierkegaardian sense equips one with a sense of humility; right and wrong are less objective than in other ethical systems. Instead, choosing the ethical requires one to see in every human being an equal freedom to do the same, and to recognize that choosing existentially is the route of human formation. No one creates himself, but through choices we make the abstract concrete. Each person contains the universality of what it means to be human, while at the same time remaining the complete particular person formed by choices over a lifetime. Through his choices, Simba forms himself from an aesthetic cub into an ethical king.

Conclusion

The Lion King has been a classic since its initial release. While it is an excellent story, it also demonstrates the reality of self-formation and the necessity of making conscious choices. Simba transcends the typical Disney hero to become a model of ethical self-formation. In doing so, The Lion King illustrates

Kierkegaard's subjective personalist view of ethics formed through specific moments of choice.

Much of life lies beyond rational judgment or particular choice; no one can control the weather, the movements of disease, or the rise and fall of economic chance. Occasionally, there come moments where we do have choices. Simba reminds us that these moments matter. For him, the choice lies between an aesthetically pleasing, self-centered existence and an ethical, morally-responsible journey home. His life was once worry-free, with plenty of friends and even a one-night stand. But his easy existence was complicated when he learned of his homeland's suffering and his ability to exchange their pain for joy at the cost of his lifestyle. In choosing to give up the aesthetic for the ethical, Simba found that he became himself: a king in truth, bringing peace, justice, and prosperity to the Pride Lands.

In a sense, the awareness of this choice is the goal of education. It is far too easy to avoid the responsibility of choice. Yet, in doing so, we fail to become *ourselves* more fully. As Kierkegaard lamented,

> This is what is sad when one contemplates human life, that many live out their lives in quiet lostness; they outlive themselves, not in the sense that life's content successively unfolds and is now possessed in this unfolding, but they live, as it were, away from themselves and vanish like shadows. Their immortal souls are blown away, and they are not disquieted by the question of its immortality, because they are already disintegrated before they die. They do not live aesthetically, but neither has the ethical become manifest to them in its wholeness; nor have they actually rejected it, and therefore they are not sinning either, except insofar as it is a sin to be neither one thing nor the other.[23]

Each generation seeks to teach the next the importance of considering their choices carefully, and thereby developing themselves more fully into the complete picture of what it means to be human. Who will *you* become? The choice, as always, is yours. Simba exemplifies the choice to reject the allure of the aesthetic and embrace the call of the ethical. Because of his choice, he knows himself most fully, and the Pride Lands know justice restored.

Notes

[1]Soren Kierkegaard, *Either/Or Part II*, trans. and ed. Edna Hong and Howard Hong (Princeton: Princeton University Press, 1987), 176.

[2] Ibid., 206-207.

[3] Ibid., 223.

[4] Ibid., 225.

[5] Tim Rice and Elton John, "I Just Can't Wait to be King," in *The Lion King*, dir. Rob Allers and Rob Minkoff (Burbank, CA: Walt Disney Studios, 1994).

[6] Kierkegaard, 177.

[7] Ibid., 167.

[8] See, e.g., Jean Paul Sartre, *Existentialism is a Humanism* (New Haven: Yale University Press, 2007).

[9] Kierkegaard,163.

[10] Ibid., 179.

[11] Ibid., 163.

[12] Ibid., 167.

[13] Ibid., 168.

[14] Ibid., 176.

[15] Ibid., 177.

[16] Ibid., 247.

[17] Ibid., 176.

[18] Ibid., 253.

[19] 1 Cor. 13:11 (ESV).

[20] Kierkegaard, 178.

[21] C. S. Lewis, *The Last Battle* (New York: Macmillan Books, 1956), 154.

[22] Kierkegaard, 332.

[23] Ibid., 168-69.

16

Christian Hospitality in Disney's *Beauty and the Beast:* Two Perspectives

Zachary D. Schmoll and Neal Foster

Walt Disney's *Beauty and the Beast*[1] poignantly illustrates a tension in the Christian life. It encourages the viewer to consider how he or she must turn away from the curse of selfishness and toward the call to love, like the good Samaritan. This transition, however, often requires sacrifice. It can be unappreciated, undesirable, even painful, but it is the life to which the Christian is called. This chapter explores two perspectives[2] regarding Beast's development. As hospitality plays an important role in the Christian's transformation, Beast's tale serves as an apt metaphor for Christianity.

Be Our Guest

As the film begins, a young prince refuses to provide charity to an old woman knocking at his door. Few would consider him a good neighbor by Jesus's standard. Once transformed into a ferocious beast, the prince throws a lost man into the dungeon for trespassing. Beast is cruel and merciless. Even in allowing a trade for a loving daughter to take the place of her father, it is a far reach to see this as mercy and charity. Beast is anything but a sympathetic character for the first part of the film. He is a selfish abductor seemingly destined to life as a ferocious monster. It is hard to imagine anyone falling in love with him before his twenty-first birthday and breaking the curse. This seems just since all actions have consequences; he is reaping the consequences of his own actions.[3] Of course, that is not where the story ends. After being nursed back to health by Belle, a new side of Beast begins to emerge. When Belle's father collapses in the woods, Beast allows her to assist her father. Even at the end of the movie, Beast shows mercy on Gaston, who has come to Beast's castle intending to end Beast's life. Beast has an opportunity to kill Gaston but refrains. Exploiting this mercy, Gaston stabs Beast in the back before accidently falling to his death. The story culminates with Belle effectively breaking the curse on Beast and restoring his humanity by declaring her love for him. His metamorphosis, both physically and emotionally, is complete. Through showing love and mercy instead of selfishness and cruelty, Beast became lovable himself. He regained his humanity as soon as he became a neighbor to those around him.

The act of being a good neighbor and showing hospitality is an integral part of what Jesus Christ was talking about in the Parable of the good Samaritan.[4] When he saw a brutally beaten man lying on the road, the Samaritan did not pass on the other side, as the priest and Levite had; instead, he "took pity on him."[5] He gave him appropriate medical care and paid for his accommodations out of his own pocket until he recovered. Beast illustrates both possible reactions to the suffering man in the ditch. At the beginning of the story, he is much more reminiscent of the priest and the Levite. His selfishness leads to his disregard for the needs of those around him. By the end of the story, when he is attacked in his own home, he shows mercy and pity even on one who tries to kill him. This evolution can serve as a lens for the Christian to consider what it means to show hospitality in a world where "loving our neighbors" has somehow been translated into "loving our neighbors when it is convenient to do so."

Consider Beast's initial act of selfishness. He refuses to allow an old woman into his house. The same charge of selfishness and cruelty applies when he imprisons Maurice instead of helping an old man lost in the woods. Leah Libresco writes, "Hospitality is an unveiling, in which my guests show me their needs, and I show them something of what I am."[6] It is clear that there is an unmet need for one seeking shelter, and it is clear what type of person the young prince is at the beginning of the story. By imprisoning a lost traveler, he demonstrates his character at that point in time. Had that old woman never appeared on his doorstep, his selfishness might not have been revealed. The viewer might not fully comprehend the depravity of the Beast if Maurice did not come to his door looking for hospitality. His denial of hospitality shows the audience all they need to know about who he is and what he values. However, Libresco takes this concept a step further as she indicates that there is something unique about inviting someone into one's house. It is not just the question of charity at that point; it extends to a divine responsibility. She explains, "Hospitality is training to welcome others, to receive their welcome, and to anticipate the kingdom of God."[7]

Lee Roy Martin discusses the Old Testament tradition of hospitality through the story of Abraham entertaining angels in Genesis 18. He suggests that there are four ways that this tradition continues to influence Christian hospitality by recognizing, "(1) all humans bear the image of God, (2) all humans are relational Creatures, (3) all humans are dependent upon each other and (4) all humans are travelers hosted by God."[8] For the Christian, hospitality is not optional; it is preparation for our home with God in eternity. It begins as a motivation to meet someone else's need; however, it continues by recognizing our shared humanity and our divine responsibility to one another. The Beast fails to recognize that at the beginning of the story.

The Beast begins to change as the story progresses. As his love for Belle grows, he begins to show mercy. Even though she is his prisoner, he allows her to go and help her father who is collapsing in the woods. Beast begins to recognize the common good of helping his fellow man. The one who previously imprisoned Maurice without mercy is now willing to have pity on him, allowing his daughter to come to the rescue. Cathy Ross makes the provocative claim that "the best deterrent against crime is not burglar bars or an armed police force but a caring public, aware of the common good, able to be present and attentive to the other, to create space for the other, to live hospitably in both the public and the private realms."[9] Because Beast is becoming more familiar with the concept of love and care for another human being, through his relationship with Belle, it begins to impact how he acts in the public sphere. He begins to feel aspects of hospitality in his life, and the evidence begins to pour out into his life. Joel Green would offer his support to this claim by suggesting that, as followers of Jesus, actions ought to follow from the transformation of the heart. He explains, speaking about articles of faith like hospitality, "Such practices actually generate the realities they are thought to represent. They restructure relationships. They engender transformed patterns of human life."[10] Beast has not yet fully transformed, but he is beginning to act more like the Good Samaritan. He is at least showing care when before there was nothing but selfishness.

His final stage of evolution towards hospitality occurs in his fight with Gaston. The triumphant Beast holds Gaston by the throat and contemplates dropping him from the castle roof, but he chooses instead to show mercy. He leaves Gaston with his life, displaying signs of true honor. Even when this mercy is betrayed and Gaston stabs him in the back, Beast does not kill Gaston. While Beast is writhing in pain, Gaston loses his grip and falls to his death. Beast finally begins to act as a good neighbor. His mercy directly impacts his own well-being, and, because of his mercy, he is stabbed. The Samaritan incurs a financial cost through his willingness to pay for the injured man's room and board out of his own pocketbook. Neighbors are willing to do that, and Jesus clearly tells his audience to go and act like the Samaritan. Of course, this is different than the priest and the Levite. The actions of the Samaritan—the neighbor—are different than the others around him. Similarly, Beast is being hunted by Gaston. Beast responds with a different kind of action; he responds with mercy. Compare this to the sentiment expressed by Anthony Esolen, writing, "Those in the world who are weary of its broken promises will not listen to us if we speak the language of the world. They are longing for a different language entirely—the real language, which will restore to them the world's lost beauty and goodness and point them towards what is beyond the world. They do not want us to stretch ourselves out lazily among them. They want to join us on the way."[11] The expert of the law knows who he should want to be like. Jesus asks him who was the true neighbor, and he responds rightly. He knows what the answer should be because he knows that, to use Esolen's terminology, the Samaritan was speaking the right language. Through his actions and his mercy, the difference was self-evident. Beast shows that same revolutionary change.

That mercy even reaps rewards in a supernatural fashion. Belle is able to fall in love with him and break the curse. No longer is he trapped in the form of a hideous monster, but because of his metamorphosis, his humanity has been restored. The moral messages in this story are blatant. Renounce selfishness, show kindness and love towards those around you, and extend mercy to those who might not even deserve it. These dimensions make him more than just a living and breathing life form; they make him a human again. As Rod Dreher explains, "God created us to be social beings. Jesus said that the sum of the Law and the Prophets is that we should love the Lord our God with all our heart, soul, and mind and love our neighbors as ourselves. To love requires loving others and letting others love you."[12] Loving others requires both allowing others to love oneself as well as allowing for the potential that sometimes that love might be betrayed, as it was for Beast. Either way, hospitality is a part of the Christian's calling.

Beast progresses from a selfish monster to a merciful man. He demonstrates love to the unlovable and does so at his own personal expense. He reminds us of the question, who is my neighbor, and his tale offers a portrait of Jesus's answer. The answer is quite clear; it is the one who needs love and mercy—even one like Gaston. While we could all learn something from the Beast, his transformation from selfishness to mercy is a particularly strong metaphor for those who seek to imitate the selflessness of Jesus Christ.

The Knight of Infinite Resignation

Sacrificial hospitality is a key aspect of Christian transformation. As noted above, this is characterized by forsaking selfish actions to treat neighbors with love. Such hospitality becomes noticeably sacrificial when one's neighbor does not deserve kindness—or might even be considered an enemy. Beast's growth in hospitality raises a fascinating question concerning the nature and application of faith. When Søren Kierkegaard privileges the "knight of faith" over the "knight of infinite resignation," he appears to discount the value the latter can have in the Christian's spiritual growth. Beast's character development suggests, however, that Christians who fail to attain the status of a "knight of faith" can still act in genuine faith that transforms us and blesses those around us.

One of the major themes of the movie is, of course, love—specifically, how one gets it, and how one gives it. This is easily seen expressed in the value of hospitality, and the actions throughout the film which affirm or deny that value. Right at the beginning we see the root of the curse: the handsome young prince had all the things he could ever want, and (hence?) he was completely consumed with self-interest to the point of cruelty. This gives the viewer a clue that, in order to have a happy ending to this story, the prince may need to lose everything he desires, ending up with a void in his life that opens the way for love. Indeed, the spell will be broken only when he learns to love someone else, and "earn her love in return."

But how would that work? After all, love is a choice, not a payment earned. Perhaps, as a spoiled prince, the Beast had no clue about love, so the first step to becoming a decent person was to learn how to "earn" someone's love. On this point, the Beast and Gaston make an interesting contrast. Gaston's pursuit of Belle reveals even *him* to be a form of the pre-Beastly Prince, as his selfish perspective warps his perception of hospitality, thereby hindering his ability to understand love and warrant Belle's attention. Whereas Gaston envisions his beloved serving *him*, Beast begins to seek avenues for serving his beloved. At first, Beast does not yet know that true love needs no specific response. In time, he learns that the way to experience freedom from the curse is to make discrete practical choices to love regardless of the consequences. The story's conclusion reveals that love is earned—or at least returned—through hospitality, even when it leads to death.

After the Beast captures Maurice, Belle forces a choice on the Beast, surprising him with her hospitable sacrifice for her father (and foreshadowing the Beast's later decision), choosing the unknown curse of imprisonment, motivated by love.[13] The invasion of her other-centeredness has planted a seed in him,[14] which we find hints of later when he declares that his castle is her home, and all but the west wing is open to her wanderings. When her curiosity gets the best of her and leads her to the forbidden wing, the Beast short-temperedly and shortsightedly kicks her out, setting her free in a twisted way. In the wilderness outside the castle, Belle is attacked by wolves, but then the Beast's hospitable change of heart rescues her. He pays for his desire to atone for her earlier eviction, by suffering injuries at the hands of the wolves, which gives Belle a choice to run away or help him. She chooses hospitable generosity to him by tending to his wounds.

After this, step by step, love begins to grow between them. As they prepare for the crucial dinner and dance, the Beast shows a lack of faith in her potential as the beloved curse-breaker when he declares his doubt that Belle will ever be able to see him as something other than a monster. In the beautiful moments following the dance, the Beast faces the choice of his life when Belle looks through the magic mirror. The Beast has Belle in his home, he is wooing her, she is learning to appreciate him, but then they find out her father is in trouble. The Beast values Maurice's life because Belle does, and he is growing in love for her. But is it right to care for Maurice only because Belle does? And what if Belle is the curse-breaker? Sadly, despairingly, the Beast makes the only choice love allows him—to give Belle up. How does this choice lie at the intersection of hospitality, love, faith, and breaking the curse?

Kierkegaardian Absurdity and the Nature of Two Knights

Turning to Søren Kierkegaard may provide insight here. One of his most famous concepts, especially in regard to Christian faith, is what he calls the "absurd," used to good effect in *Fear and Trembling* when he contrasts between what he calls the "knight of infinite resignation" and the "knight of faith."[15] The knight of infinite resignation unconditionally gives up what he loves or desires for a greater cause or reason; in other words, he can logically justify the resigning of an otherwise good thing. The knight of faith performs the same outward action but makes an additional move to believe, "absurdly," that what he gave up will be returned to him.[16] Mere irrationality and absurdity must be distinguished here. Although Kierkegaard did think faith could not be logically justified, he goes further to describe the "knight of faith" as recognizing the impossibility of regaining what he has sacrificed, but "in the very same moment he believes the absurd," that somehow, some way, he ends up attaining his desire.[17] The distinction may be thought of this way: an irrational belief has little to no evidence for it; an absurd belief has all evidence *against* it.

Kierkegaard's example of the knight of faith is Abraham, willing to sacrifice his son in obedience to God but also, "by virtue of the absurd" belief "that for God all things are possible," trusting that God would fulfill his promise to make Abraham's descendants many.[18] This belief is absurd, at least in part because Abraham is actively (even literally) killing the only visible avenue by which God's promise can be fulfilled. A key point Kierkegaard makes is that the knight of infinite resignation, because he fails to embrace the absurd, has not yet attained faith.[19] So, even though at the moment of resignation there is no outward distinction between the actions of the two different knights, one acts in faith and the other in heroic tragedy. The knight of resignation may have an irrational hope that things may work out, but the knight of faith has faith to the degree he obeys God even by deliberately removing the avenue to God's promises in absurd trust that God can still, impossibly, fulfill those same promises.

At the moment of resigning Belle, it would seem that the Beast qualifies only as a knight of infinite resignation—not a knight of faith.[20] For in what would he have faith exactly—breaking the curse? Would it break the curse if he chooses to "love" so that the curse is broken (believing in faith that the curse would be removed as a result of that love)? That would not be love, because in love there is no *so that*—at least, not in a selfish sense. The paradox of the curse is that in order to be free, the Beast must truly love, which implies he must stop selfishly seeking his freedom by somehow "earning" the love of another. For the curse will not break until the Beast becomes the type of person who genuinely cares for others, even at his own expense. Truly, if he fails to do that, he is "doomed to remain a beast for all time," because his character will not change. As we see in the story, the expense he pays includes his own death, after which the curse is reversed, and he is resurrected and transformed (an obvious Christian allusion).

At this point an objection may be raised, especially when one considers the 2017 live action film. Does the Beast have any sort of hope when he gives up Belle? In other words, can his sacrifice be understood as a loving costly yet rational action in hope of breaking the curse? The live action film includes a song by the Beast whose lyrics, or at least their literal meaning, seem to point to the Beast acknowledging an absurd belief in Belle's possible return. He proclaims his desire to wait for her "forevermore" while also insisting that she will never leave him and declaring that he will continue to wait, by an open door, for her to walk back in.[21] Are these expressions of faith?

Actually, when examined in context, it seems that the song is an expression of deep emotion, even borderline despair, that he will never find love now. He sings of being tormented by her presence in his mind. His memory of her appears to have settled into an eternally unfulfilled potential, for he sings of how he will forevermore ponder all the things that could have transpired. Of course, he desires her and wants her physical presence and love, so he "rage[s] against the trials of love" and "curse[s] the fading of the light," her departure. In fact, he is finally tasting true love, the paradox of knowing he has to give up the beloved, which also means embracing the torment of being without her—which in his case is a literal curse wherein he will never again experience physical humanity, even as he psychologically and emotionally transforms out of beastliness.

Right before the song, he realizes his choice is sealed when he gives Belle the magic mirror, which has always been his window to the greater world. He seems to prepare unreservedly for a future without her, for his final words to her are, "Then you'll always have a way to look back on me." She leaves, and he exhales with the awareness of what he has done, what he has sacrificed. Therefore, the live action film shows that the Beast may have an irrational (or emotional and thus illogical) hope that Belle may someday return, but he does not have the absurd belief that the curse will be broken after he consciously chooses to release the only visible avenue (Belle) to break the curse.

When the end of the story comes, so does a disagreement with Kierkegaard, who would not expect this knight of infinite resignation to attain the promise. But the Beast does break the curse, despite his failure to make the last move of faith. In pushing back against Kierkegaard, this Disney tale would suggest that transformation out of our beastly flesh and into Christlike hospitality may not require an unshakeable Kierkegaardian confidence in a specific promise made by the God through whom all things are possible. Instead, even with a belief which to Kierkegaard might seem too infantile to call true "faith," if we make daily loving choices to show hospitality, we may find ourselves growing into Christlikeness, nevertheless. After all, the old woman looking for a place to stay in the storm, the old man pursued by wolves, the young woman giving up her life for her father, and even the homicidal enemy are all opportunities gifted to the Beast to begin the process of transformation through love.

This process is incomplete until the moment his kindness subverts normal hospitable behavior: after sparing Gaston's life, the Beast tells him to leave the castle. But Gaston the anti-Beast, of course, takes advantage of the Beast's mercy and deals him a mortal blow. So, the curse is not broken until after the Beast passes through his death caused by sacrificial hospitality; even in his final breaths, his heart is fixed on Belle. "Maybe it's better this way...at least I got to see you one last time."

On Faith and Love

The Beast shows hospitality greatest when he embraces — or ignores — "the curse." When he disregards the consequences of choosing love, he enables the supreme expression of his love for Belle. This is also a key contribution to her heart opening to love him in return. It seems, contrary to Kierkegaard's explanation, that experiencing transformational growth in Christlikeness does not require qualifying as a knight of faith. What's more, the character of the Beast reveals something that Kierkegaard may have missed.[22]

Perhaps there is a difference here between those, like Abraham, who were "credited" with righteousness (Rom. 4:22) according to a *faith-forward* (before Christ) and those who are now *declared* righteous by faith in the completed work of Christ in his flesh, and then *transformed* slowly within, according to the work of Christ within. Abraham believed in a future promise; early Christians believed it is finished. Or, perhaps the Knight of Infinite Resignation really represents a *faith-in* (the well-reasoned, faith of *justification*) while the Knight of Faith portrays more of a *faith-that* (the seemingly "absurd" trust that God works all things for the good of those that love him, and that he forms us into the likeness of Christ *through* the acts of service to which Christ has called us).

It certainly seems "absurd" at times to think possible—moreover expect—to *become* what is contrary to one's nature—whether it be the transformation from a heart of self-centeredness to one of self-sacrificial service, or the turning of a beast into a man; to *be* what one is not; to *become* what is antithetical to impulse; does this not require belief in the possibility of absurdity? That is to say, if Beast's growing encounter with love is so *transformative* that it would move him to serve and sacrifice for Belle, then arguably the curse was already unraveling as she rode away (for, recall that the condition of the curse only required that she love him in return; it did not actually specify a kiss, a romantic relationship, or even the physical presence of the one whose love had been earned).

In this sense, perhaps Beast profoundly represents *both* knights: it is absurd for him to let her go when he is so close to breaking the curse, and yet perhaps it is an existential confirmation—an awareness of a transformation already in progress—which gives him *reason* to believe that it is in love's greater interest to give up the object of his love. Perhaps the persistent, moment-by-moment unfolding of Beast's faith—in even the *possibility* of an inner transformation eventually working itself out in a glorification of his overall nature and form—qualifies as an "absurd" *leap of faith*, while he also deems it *reasonable* to *resign* his self-interest in service to another even if nothing is gained in return.

Regardless, the case can be made that Beast more accurately represents a Knight of Infinite Resignation rather than a Knight of Faith. Perhaps Beast as a knight of infinite resignation is symbolic of a unique aspect of the Christian life. Rather than trying to emulate Abraham in a Kierkegaardian way (that is, by staunchly clinging to an "absurdly" impossible promise of God), living the Christian life means making a series of choices to love practically, to show sacrificial hospitality, even when we are unable to see or reason out all the consequences. Still, since faith, hope, and love are entwined, we might also learn from Beast that the choice between a seemingly irrational hope and a seemingly absurd faith need not necessarily be dichotomous. Perhaps both paths can lead to growth in Christlikeness.

Love's Transformative Power

Hospitality ought to characterize the Christian life. If God is love and Christians should strive continually to be conformed to the image of Jesus Christ, then it follows that love should pour out of the lives of Christians into the world around them. Choosing to love and loving sacrificially can be a challenge, though. Unfortunately, ideals are often far more difficult to apply in one's daily living than they are to conceive in the understanding. In Disney's *Beauty and the Beast,* we see a man struggling with beastly impulses—a beast desperate to become a man. Hospitality is the key to Beast's transformation into "something there that wasn't there before,"[23] and so it is with the Christian's transformation into a new creation.[24]

Notes

[1] *Beauty and the Beast,* dir. Gary Trousdale and Kirk Wise (Burbank, CA: Walt Disney Studios, 1991).

[2] Schmoll contributes the first perspective, while Foster presents the second.

[3] Gal. 6:7.

[4] Luke 10:25-37.

[5] Luke 10:33 (NIV).

[6] Leah Libresco, *Building the Benedict Option: A Guide to Gathering Two or Three Together in His Name* (San Francisco: Ignatius Press, 2018), 114, Kindle.

[7] Ibid., 120.

[8] Lee Roy Martin, "Old Testament Foundations for Christian Hospitality," *Verbum et Ecclesia* 35, no. 1 (2014): 1.

[9] Cathy Ross, "'Often, Often, Often Goes the Christ in the Stranger's Guise': Hospitality as a Hallmark of Christian Ministry," *International Bulletin of Mission Research* 39, no. 4 (2015): 178.

[10] Joel B Green, "Embodying the Gospel: Two Exemplary Practices," *Journal of Spiritual Formation and Soul Care* 7, no. 1 (2014): 21.

[11] Anthony Esolen, *Out of the Ashes: Rebuilding American Culture* (Washington, DC: Regnery Publishing, 2017), 188, Kindle.

[12] Rod Dreher, *The Benedict Option: A Strategy for Christians in a Post-Christian Nation* (New York: Sentinel, 2017), 123, Kindle.

[13] There is a nice juxtaposition between her choosing, here, to be with Beast in order to free her father, and then refusing, later in the movie, to marry Gaston in order to free her father.

[14] Therefore, instead of an "adventure in the great wide somewhere," she finds adventure in the dark, small nowhere of the dwelling of a selfish Beast.

[15] A good summary is found in Ronald M. Green, "'Developing' *Fear and Trembling*," in *The Cambridge Companion to Kierkegaard*, ed. Alastair Hannay and Gordon D. Marino (Cambridge: Cambridge University Press, 1998), 260-262.

[16] Søren Kierkegaard, *Fear and Trembling. Repetition. Kierkegaard's Writings, VI*, trans. Howard V. Hong and Edna H. Hong (Princeton: Princeton University Press, 1983), 45-46.

[17] Ibid., 47-48.

[18] Ibid., 46.

[19] Ibid.

[20] If only he could see the ironic truth in Cogsworth's statement (before Cogsworth understands Belle is leaving the castle), "Everything is going swimmingly!" Going swimmingly in this case includes eventually passing through despair and death before obtaining the resigned object.

[21] Tim Rice and Alan Mencken, "Evermore," in *Beauty and the Beast*, dir. Bill Condon (Burbank, CA: Walt Disney Studios, 2017).

[22] Thank you to the editor for bringing this to my attention.

[23] Howard Ashman and Alan Menken, "Something There," in *Beauty and the Beast* (1991).

[24] 2 Cor. 5:17.

17

Faith, Hope, and the Human Condition in *Raya and the Last Dragon*

By Jeremy E. Scarbrough

aya and the Last Dragon offers a rich lens for inquiry into the nature of the human condition.[1] There is a close connection between our stories of possible worlds and our desire to understand the story of our own world. As professor of English and philosophy James Sire put it, in his study on worldview, "Folklore, myth and literature around the world from the ancient past to the present tell stories that put present human reality in the larger context of universal cosmic and human meaning. They act as orienting patterns.... stories by which societies interpret the universe and life around them."[2]

As many have observed,[3] both fictional narratives and worldviews (theological and a-theological) are built around a common (even if implicit) progression of motifs and questions (even if presented in a non-linear manner).[4] These include:

- Origins: the idea of an original state—the initial setting and nature of the characters—which provides a sense of meant-to-be-ness, what things were like before the plot thickened.

- Conflict: the driving force of the plot, a search for something (even meaning and identity), or for the setting right of a past wrong.

- Resolution: the setting right of all wrongs; restoration to the balance of justice (*just-as*-it-ought-to-be), or else, in some tales, a coming to terms with what has been lost, and finding an appreciation for the ways in which the journey has changed the protagonist for the better or cultivated within them a greater sense of strength, self-confidence, or even community, for facing tomorrow's anxieties.

This is the same progression of ideas central to any worldview—and this makes perfect sense if narratives and art are expressions of human beings wrestling with various questions of worldview (including questions of perspective). In the language of worldview, the questions are something like these:

- Who are we? Why are we here? Do we have a purpose? Is there a right-order, a way it was meant to be? Are human beings basically good or bad?

- Is the world as we find it (*thrown* here, as we find ourselves to be) right and good, or is it broken? If there is no way-it-ought-to-be, why does it often seem as though something is wrong with the world—that things are not quite as they ought to be? Is there such a thing as the good life? If so, how do we find it? To whom shall we look for answers? How should we live?

- Is the good life achievable? By human beings? Is true justice achievable? By human beings? Is there life after death; is there anything—some kind of ultimate goodness—beyond this journey, or is it the case that the only sense of meaning and significance achievable is to be found solely within the journey itself?

Fairytales in general, and Disney lore in particular, often emphasize kingdoms and ever-afters. Kingdoms represent order, while ever-afters are usually meant to evoke a sense of ideal goodness, happiness, and flourishing—even tales which draw out the reality of suffering and tragedy do not conclude with promises of evil-ever-after. Even when our tales are tragic, we hold onto the belief in an achievable sense of ever-after-happiness (heaven, or heaven-on-earth).

- Is there such a thing as a Kingdom-ever-after? If so, what sort of citizens would inhabit such a place? Would it be the sort of place just anyone could inhabit? (If injustice persists wherever humans exist, why think a kingdom-ever-after would be a good place, unless it were the sort of place only meant for—supposing it to be possible—human hearts purged of injustice?)

In theological language, this is none other than the creation-fall-redemption motif. In the words of Christian apologist Greg Koukl, every good story has four parts:

It has a beginning that sets the stage, telling you who the main characters are and how the story gets rolling. Then something goes wrong.... The main part of most stories tells how that conflict gets corrected, how the wrong gets fixed. That solution brings a final resolution... a satisfying ending ("They lived happily ever after").... The basic parts of a good story actually match the basic parts of a worldview: beginning (creation), conflict (fall), conflict resolution (redemption), and ending (restoration).[5]

Thus, any given narrative is already more closely connected to questions of theology than many realize. Different narratives press into or draw out different aspects of these worldview questions, but many press into both a conviction (even if unknowingly) of a created order (a way-it-should-be) and our desire to see restoration. Still, the most central part of many narratives is the in-between. The plot is what drives the narrative; we long to understand, to get the whole sense of the thing, to find resolution, restoration, or even redemption, precisely because this is the space amidst the grand narrative of humanity in which we find ourselves—whether thrown by absurd happenstance or purposefully created for exactly such a time as this. The motif of the human condition, then, is a powerful one.

The Fall: Exploring the Human Condition

Raya and the Last Dragon focuses on points two and three of this three-part motif—questions of the fall or the human condition, and restoration. One of the most powerful questions of the entire film (though there are many) is presented at the very beginning: How did this world get so broken? This question resonates deeply with all members of all worldview systems, and accordingly, this film could easily serve as a dialectical launchpad into the study of philosophy and theology. It is the right question to ask. Any satisfactory worldview must attempt to give an answer.

It is the question seated at the heart of the existential problem of evil—of pain and suffering. People have long understood that questions of suffering and the human condition are unavoidably tethered to the question of God. Expounding upon the philosophy of Karl Jaspers, Frederick Copleston once wrote, "To ask whether human existence and human history have any meaning and purpose *is* [emphasis added] to ask whether God exists,"[6] and John Bowker dedicated an entire work to examining the fact that the problem of suffering is the question fundamental to all religions throughout the world.[7] Their observations, almost five decades ago, are still ripe for dialogue. For all the talk about there being no universals, is it not true that there seems to be a universal conviction that things are not as they ought to be? For all of our zeal in advocacy and debate concerning justice and injustice, that is what justice *is*, is it not—a sense of things being as they ought to be? Why is our world so broken, what have we to do with its brokenness, and how is restoration to be achieved?

While brokenness may reveal a universal conviction, the nature of brokenness or injustice is a matter of dispute. In the biblical narrative, it is depicted more like a sickness—something which began within the human heart, slowly corrupting a good thing until it eventually became a curse upon humanity, as everyone continued to do whatever was right in their own eyes. And with the pride freely asserted from the self-seeking human heart, came increasing cases of injustice, oppression, abuse, and disregard for anything special about, or sacred between, human beings. So too, in this film, there is a plague which is derivative from a sickness within humanity—a proclivity to discord. This plague has become a problem of evil and suffering that has divided the united kingdom of humanity. It is particularly interesting that this sickness upon the world—the *Druun* or that-which-ought-not-to-be—turns the human hearts whence it came to stone, and severs human community and thereby increases enmity via fear.

In his work on *Narrative Apologetics,* Alister McGrath observes that "the Christian idea of sin is unpopular," and this is

> precisely because it articulates an unpopular truth: that human nature is deeply flawed... and that part of our problem is that we refuse to accept that there is a problem in the first place. Yet a truthful narrative has the power to release us from its destructive alternatives and offers us a way of seeing through the distortions of reality that are present in contemporary culture.[8]

He goes on to point out that some narratives are ripe for translating the Christian concept of sin because sin is personified; an abstract idea becomes a personal force. This film exemplifies McGrath's point well.

A Tale of Two Sacrifices

It is interesting that there are two tales of Sisu's sacrifice. First, there was a great sacrifice resulting in salvation for all of humanity... Yet it wasn't long before humans returned to their antipathy. Thus, this sacrifice was not good enough. It is ultimately human beings who must take the step (which does involve a sense of sacrifice) in order to actualize their own salvation. Herein lies a point with which some theists may take issue. Still, one thing that stands out about Sisu's first sacrifice is its resemblance to human history. The sacrifice of Jesus Christ was a game-changer in the course of history, to say the least. Yet, the appreciation for that sacrifice and its resulting passionate emphasis upon the goodness of Agape within community eventually took a backseat to the powerplays of rising human political institutions. Without going into all the contemporary debates over institutional injustices, it is striking that Raya presents us with a picture of exactly what we would expect to see: If there is a sickness within the human condition, a sacrifice might make it better for now, but why think it would make it better for good, *so long as* we remain as we are? Even though a remnant remains faithful to the meaning and power of Sisu's sacrifice, the sickness stemming from human nature creeps back in. And if this happens, why wouldn't we expect injustices within and between human institutions?

Sisu's second sacrifice involves her actual death, and this is later followed with a resurrection motif, but what is interesting about the second sacrifice is that it emphasizes the need for a step of faith—even when all hope seems lost—in light of one's encounter with the sacrifice of another. A primary motif in the film is faith, but while the emphasis is upon faith in one another, it is significant to note that the motivation for taking such a chance on one another grows out of a previously planted seed of trust and inspiration depicted in Sisu. So too, for the Christian, Jesus calls us to love one another, but our love and trust in one another is grounded in the love of Christ—a depiction of God's love for humanity and faith in the goodness of the human heart he created, and the goodness of the human community for which he made them. Both Sisu, in her death, and Raya, in *her* sacrifice, might be seen as mediators calling us to take the step of faith toward the hope that love can reign.

Encountering the Spiritual

The encounter with a dragon, not an embodiment of evil, but rather a mystical one, is presented as a spiritual encounter. There is a deep sense of reverence, appreciation, empowerment, and understanding within both Raya and Namaari when they gaze into the eyes of Sisu. Having encountered such a being, the power of such a being's sacrifice becomes the catalyst for growth in character and a newfound strength to enact change. C. S. Lewis similarly presses into the significance of encountering the great Aslan, in his Narnian tales. The encounter with a being-to-which-no-human-can-compare is one that either moves us to seek to imitate the goodness reflected from that being—a goodness which transcends the oppressive chains of our human condition—or else brings to light the moral deficit within us.

No Pixie Dust Here

"Faith" is presented well in this film—appropriately rendered as "trust." Some may take issue with the fact that it is faith in *us* and not explicitly faith in *God*, yet faith is a complex intersection of trust, hope, and love—and this film gets that. Raya has to learn to have faith in others, and she struggles with what exactly that means. Though an act of trust, faith is also presented as an act of love—a step of vulnerability because the potentially resulting community is in the best interest of others (as well as oneself). Yet, Raya understandably asks of others what my daughter once asked of God: how can I love and trust someone I do not know? Raya rightfully understands that she has no reason to trust blindly in people, given her experiences with people and with taking steps of trust. This is why Disney takes us on Raya's journey; it is the journey which gives us the perspective to consider why people might choose to act as they do. They may be just as desperate as we are to fix the world or secure themselves (or their communities) from the suffering that has become commonplace. With perspective comes understanding; with understanding comes reason; with reason we can find hope; and through hope we can find the justification for taking a step. Faith is still a step beyond what can be completely controlled by the exhaustion of knowledge. But it is not a leap into the dark. Raya's faith is a reasonable step based upon an understanding that we were meant for more than this, that we are all desperate to know restoration and escape our condition, but also that we need one another in order to endure the impact and withstand the destructive possibilities of our condition.

We all have faith in the reality defined by our narrative. Faith is not the sort of thing that only religious folk have. Our worldview shows up in our ethics, and Raya presses into this. Ought we to trust that there is hope for the world or that we must do what we need to in order to survive? Ought we to trust that others have our interest at heart, or that they are likely acting in their own self-interest? At every moment, there is a step toward an object or objective of faith. Raya is betrayed when she places her faith in the ideal that people are naturally good (even the presumption that infants are innocent), so she places her faith in the view that people are only out for themselves—and this shows up in her ethics, the ways in which she interacts with others.

In addition to Disney's correct portrayal of "faith" as "trust" and not wishful thinking, Disney rightly presses into the redemptive power of faith and its role in salvation and restoration. While Raya is blinded with rage and revenge, we see her friends—most of whom we first met as antagonists—working hard to do whatever they could to save those who were supposed to be the enemy. When Raya finally sees this, it pricks her heart with conviction, and she leaves the path of revenge to join her friends on a path toward the redemption and restoration of community.

Redemption & Restoration

This film is rich with redemption motifs. These include redemption for humanity, redemption for community and family, but the most moving motif is the redemption for the betrayer — and with it, upon the restoration and redeemed reputation for the other. While this aligns with many religious teachings and worldview sensitivities, it resonates profoundly with the Jewish and Christian scriptures.

The film presents no element of salvation as involving justice in light of human guilt (an element central to the Christian scriptures — though the biblical narrative tempers God's justice with an emphasis upon his lovingkindness). Still, there is an appropriate emphasis upon the setting right of a broken humanity, and its connection to a step of faith which empowers others to believe as well. There is a vulnerability in trust, to be sure, but also a deep and redeeming goodness to be experienced when an opportunity for trust is extended even in light of recurrent betrayal.

There is a deep longing in this film for the Kingdom-ever-after (a recurring motif in the Disney lore canon). In this film, the kingdom was united, but the sickness divided the kingdom before slowly devouring it. The Kingdom-ever-after is presented as *Kumandra*, a sort of heaven on earth wherein community is composed of faith, hope, and love. While the greatest of these may be love, this movie raises an appropriate question as to whether the greatest step in *seeking* the kingdom of love is not faith. There is also symbolism in the fact that the redemption which follows the final sacrifice — of hubris — involves a sort of spiritual baptism, as it is water which inevitably washes away the human sickness — allowing the "cursed" to be, so to speak, born again.

Charity Amidst Diversity

Not everyone agrees upon the nature of worldview narratives. Yet we share a conviction that something is not as it ought to be and a desire to see things get better. This is why *Raya and the Last Dragon* can speak deeply to anyone of any worldview — because the problems of the human condition, of suffering in the world, are problems with which all must deal. Unity amidst diversity is a beautiful *ideal*, but it is unlikely achievable while the world remains broken. It is naïve to think our problems simply come down to trusting one another. For one needs *reason* to trust, and what reason do we really have for believing others will play along and not stab us in the back when we are not looking? What obligates me to act in the interest of others when doing so is not in *my* interest, or when it conflicts with my conscience? Left to ourselves, without higher appeals to ground our ideals (or else when higher appeals clash), one group's "justice" becomes another's "injustice." As McGrath insightfully understood, "The history of the twentieth century—supposedly the most "enlightened" in human history—witnessed such violence, oppression, and destructiveness that awkward questions about a naive belief in human goodness simply cannot be overlooked." Expounding on a quote by John Gray, he writes, secular humanists may "delude themselves that they have a rational view of the world, "yet their core belief in moral progress is simply a 'superstition.'"[9] So, the film's ideal of unity—however appealing it may be in drawing out our yearning for a Kingdom-ever-after—seems too idealistic to be practical while we remain thrown into our human condition.

Still, there is something else here—something very practical—that we can take away from this film even if we disagree on worldview narratives. Progress—both in dialogue and in community—requires charity. (Of course, it also requires logic, and there is a humorous moment of logical wisdom in the film as well, when Sisu calls out Raya's fallacy of division. When Raya insists that all is well because she still possesses a piece of a now-shattered magical gem which represents the hope of *Kumandra*, Sisu insightfully asks whether a "big chunk" of a lost puppy is as useful as having the whole thing.) The Principle of Charity is an attitude and approach wherein one seeks to understand another's perspective in its strongest form, or best representation, before assuming a position of critique or rejection. When we can acknowledge the strengths or understandable reasons behind another's perspective, we build a foundation of credibility with one another—even amidst our differences and disagreements. Charity can show up in a number of ways, but it is all built around a position of trust—an effort of good faith in assuming that "others" are not trying to deceive or cause harm or hindrance.

When we paint the complexities of perspective and context in black and white terms, it becomes difficult to avoid seeing ourselves in terms of the us/them, the good/other. If, on the other hand ,we consider that we are all in this together, and the more we see the better we can see it, we might approach difference with dialogue and dialogue with charity—assuming the "other" might have a perspective that can help us, together, to get a bigger and better picture of our problem and a possible solution.

Some people try to apply this line of thought to morality, holding that there is no overarching moral narrative to which everyone has access now, but that morality at the end of all things will have amounted to a coming together of perspectives. This, however, provides an unsatisfactory grounding for morality, and it is not what is presented in *Raya*. This film speaks to our applied living even when we disagree—doing the best we can to get along together and seek one another's interests, even when trust is difficult or perspectival tensions are palpable. Even when it seems as though hope for a better world is unlikely; even if it seems as though we will never see eye-to-eye with those with whom we greatly disagree on moral and sociopolitical issues; we have to have enough faith in one another to take the first step of charity—in the way that we treat one another and in what we presume about one another. And dialogue is the first step; it allows us to explore one another's perspective and intent enough to begin laying the foundation for trust.

Should we judge people based upon where they are from, or what we think we know about them (as exemplified by Raya)? Or should we invite them to dinner—*as they are*, not once they appear more like ourselves—and feed them (as exemplified by Raya's father)? Both pride and fear can perpetuate discord. Extending charity is a liberation of perspective, as it allows us the freedom (from our own chains of desire and anxiety) to see that that all of us want a better world (even if we disagree on how that world should look). We have much in common: we want our condition to improve; we want an end to suffering; we want the community-ever-after. If charitable dialogue is the first step toward taking a chance on faith in one another, and if people really want to *be* the change they want to see in the world, who shall take the first step?

Notes

[1] This essay began as a blog for the Pop Culture and Theology website. It is reprinted with permission and expanded herein. Jeremy E. Scarbrough, "Reflections on *Raya and the Last Dragon* Part 1: How Did Our World Get So Broken?" *Pop Culture and*

Theology, April 28, 2021, https://popularcultureandtheology.com/2021/04/28/reflections-on-raya-and-the-last-dragon-part-1-how-did-our-world-get-so-broken/.

[2] James W. Sire, *Naming the Elephant: Worldview as Concept* (Downers Grove: InterVarsity Press, 2004), 100.

[3] See, e.g., Brian Godawa, *Hollywood Worldviews: Watching Films with Wisdom and Discernment* (Downers Grove: Intervarsity Press, 2009), 19-29; and Gregory Koukl, *The Story of Reality* (Grand Rapids: HarperCollins, 2017), 27. Godawa also identifies a spectrum of discernment between the extremes of cultural gluttons and cultural anorexics. This distinction is helpful in both navigating culture wars relating to media and in pondering the value of worldview questions embedded within films/narratives. Whereas gluttons unthinkingly and syncretistically *assume* the worldviews of art-objects they consume, the cultural anorexics reject all forms of pop culture as either pointless or corrupting, and thus miss the valuable food for thought and dialogue that pop-culture artifacts and narratives may offer.

[4] Some postmodern narratives avoid reading too much into the origins and/or leave the resolution out, as the character continues to search for such a thing; narratives like this focus upon the thrownness of existential anxiety.

[5] Koukl, 27.

[6] Frederick Copleston, *Contemporary Philosophy* (London: Search Press, 1979), 213.

[7] John Bowker, *Problems of Suffering in the Religions of the World* (London: Cambridge University Press, 1970).

[8] Alister E. McGrath, *Narrative Apologetics* (Grand Rapids, MI: BakerBooks, 2019), 66-67.

[9] Ibid., 66.

Epilogue

T he power of Disney stories in general, and Disney's animated musical features in particular, lies not within any one aspect of Disney's approach, nor within the stories themselves, but within the coming together of visual art with film, of animation with live action, of music with film in general—of synchronized and referentially symbolic animation in particular. Stories move us. The arts move us. Disney pioneered a unique coalescing of the arts and quickly established itself as an authoritative storyteller in the twentieth century. When it comes to the animated musical feature, especially, Disney has long served as an archetype by which other animated features are judged. The fact that Disney keeps retelling its celebrated take on classic tales—*Cinderella*, *Beauty and the Beast*, *The Lion King*, *Aladdin*, *Mulan*, *Pinocchio*, and others—and the fact that these remakes continue to do so well testifies to the aesthetic quality of Disney's animated cannon. (Although the remakes emphasize live-action, and in some cases, as with *Cinderella*, expand Disney's original narrative for the better, the aesthetic allure of these recast tales nevertheless trade on a nostalgia that originates with the animated features—and there are plenty of fans who will argue that the original, animated tales are aesthetically superior to the live-action remakes, even if the latter come close to reaching such an aesthetic standard.) Thus, Disney lore has clearly established an authoritative canon of animated narratives which now serve as a standard for successful Children's stories, and even as a measure for evaluating Disney's own future success.

For all that has been said, much remains unsaid. Disney lore is rich with theological symbolism and moral motifs, and replete with avenues for further apologetic exploration. The question of Disney's unique impact upon other animators and storytellers who have also played a powerful role in shaping our cultural imaginaries also warrants much investigation. Arguably, the most successful *non*-Disney animated features of the late twentieth century came from Disney-trained animators. Consider Don Bluth's *The Land*

Before Time or and Bill Kroyer's *Fern Gully*. To what extent did the emersion in Disney's method of animated storytelling play a direct role in the success of such animated features? (It is also worth noting that Kroyer's *Fern Gully* and Bluth's *All Dogs Go to Heaven, An American Tale, and Anastasia* were animated *musicals*—and music also played an important role in Bluth's *The Secret of NIMH*). We will leave it to readers and future writers to stake out and explore these possibilities.

This volume has covered a variety of ethical, aesthetic, and theological insights, and in so doing has also presented an implicit appeal to Disney's passion for defending a sense of moral objectivity. In closing a volume which considers the apologetic significance of stories, a reference to Narnian wisdom seems appropriate. The children of Lewis's tales must, eventually, say farewell to Narnia and learn to go find Aslan in their own world. Says Aslan, "This was the very reason why you were brought to Narnia, that by knowing me here for a little, you may know me better there."[1] I submit that this is how Disney stories work as well; by experiencing the truth of goodness therein, we return to our world of live-action woes, but we take with us a little hope and conviction—and we seek to find *there* the Good, as experienced in our nostalgic encounters with the aesthetic allure of Disney animation, the imaginative power of Disney's storytelling, and the magic of a Disney musical. The encounter beckons us to seek further the Good, both in application and in understanding. This is the power of the aesthetic to enrapture our passion for moral meaning, thereby entreating us to ponder more deeply the questions of theology.

---

[1] C. S. Lewis, *The Voyage of the Dawn Treader*, in *The Chronicles of Narnia* (New York: HarperEntertainment, 2008), 541.

Esmeralda offers Quasimodo a drink. "A Tear for a Drop of Water
[Book VI, Chapter IV]." An Illustration by Luc-Olivier Merson,
in the 1889 edition of Norte-Dame de Paris (The Hunchback of Notre Dame)
by Victor Hugo. Acquired via Paris Musées:
www.parismuseescollections.paris.fr/en/node/797775#infos-principales.

People flock to experience the kingdom-oriented
magic of Walt Disney World theme parks.
Photo credit: Magicguides.com, retrieved on 7/1/2022 from:
https://magicguides.com/free-disney-photos/magic-kingdom/#bwg2/344;
CC BY 3.0 US: https://creativecommons.org/licenses/by/3.0/us/.

Appendix

Film and Television References

Volume I: Disney As Doorway To Apologetic Dialogue

101 Dalmatians. Directed by Clyde Geronimi, Hamilton Luske, and Wolfgang Reitherman. Burbank, CA: Walt Disney Studios,1961.

Aladdin. Directed by Ron Clemens and John Musker. Burbank, CA: Walt Disney Studios, 1992.

Alice in Wonderland. Directed by Clyde Geronimi, Wilfred Jackson, and Hamilton Luske. Burbank, CA: Walt Disney Studios, 1951.

The Aristocats. Directed by Wolfgang Reitherman. Burbank, CA: Walt Disney Studios, 1970.

Bambi. Directed by James Algar, Samuel Armstrong, David Hand, Graham Heid, Bill Roberts, Paul Satterfield, Norman Wright, Arthur Davis, and Clyde Geronimi. Burbank, CA: Walt Disney Studios, 1942.

Beauty and the Beast. Directed by Bill Condon. Burbank, CA: Walt Disney Studios, 2017.

Beauty and the Beast. Directed by Gary Trousdale and Kirk Wise. Burbank, CA: Walt Disney Studios, 1991.

Bedknobs and Broomsticks. Directed by Robert Stevenson. Burbank, CA: Walt Disney Studios, 1971.

Black Cauldron. Directed by Ted Berman and Richard Rich. Burbank, CA: Walt Disney Studios, 1985.

Brave. Directed by Mark Andrews and Brenda Chapman. Burbank, CA: Walt Disney Studios, 2012.

Brother Bear. Directed by Aaron Blaise and Robert Walker. Burbank, CA: Walt Disney Studios, 2003.

Cinderella. Directed by Clyde Geronimi, Hamilton Luske, and Wilfred Jackson. Burbank, CA: Walt Disney Studios, 1950.

Cinderella. Directed by Kenneth Branaugh. Burbank, CA: Walt Disney Studios, 2015.

Coco. Directed by Lee Unkrich. Burbank, CA: Walt Disney Studios, 2017.

Descendants. Directed by Kenny Ortega. Burbank, CA: Disney Channel Original Productions, 2015.

Dug Days. Directed by Bob Peterson. Burbank, CA: Walt Disney Studios, 2021. Disney+.

Dumbo. Directed by Samuel Armstrong, Norman Ferguson, Wilfred Jackson, Jack Kinney, Bill Roberts, Ben Sharpsteen, and John Elliotte. Burbank, CA: Walt Disney Studios, 1941.

The Emperor's New Groove. Directed by Mark Dindal. Burbank, CA: Walt Disney Studios, 2000.

Encanto. Directed by Jared Bush and Byron Howard. Burbank, CA: Walt Disney Studios, 2021.

Enchanted. Directed by Kevin Lima. Burbank, CA: Walt Disney Studios, 2007.

Finding Dory. Directed by Andrew Stanton. Burbank, CA: Walt Disney Studios, 2016.

Finding Nemo. Directed by Andrew Stanton. Burbank, CA: Walt Disney Studios, 2003.

"Flowers and Trees," *Silly Symphonies*. Directed by Burt Gillett. Burbank, CA: Walt Disney Studios, 1932.

The Fox and the Hound. Directed by Ted Berman, Richard Rich, and Art Stevens. Burbank, CA: Walt Disney Studios, 1981.

Frozen. Directed by Chris Buck and Jennifer Lee. Burbank, CA: Walt Disney Studios, 2013.

Frozen II. Directed by Chris Buck and Jennifer Lee. Burbank, CA: Walt Disney Studios, 2019.

Fun and Fancy Free. Directed by Jack Kinney, Bill Roberts, Hamilton Luske, and William Morgan. Burbank, CA: Walt Disney Studios, 1947.

Hercules. Directed by Ron Clements and John Musker. Burbank, CA: Walt Disney Studios, 1997

The Hunchback of Notre Dame. Directed by Gary Trousdale and Kirk Trousdale. Burbank, CA: Walt Disney Studios, 1996.

The Incredibles. Directed by Brad Bird. Burbank, CA: Walt Disney Studios, 2004.

Incredibles 2. Directed by Brad Bird. Burbank, CA: Walt Disney Studios, 2018.

Inside Out. Directed by Peter Docter. Burbank, CA: Walt Disney Studios, 2015.

The Jungle Book. Directed by Jon Favreau. Burbank, CA: Walt Disney Studies, 2016.

The Jungle Book. Directed by Wolfgang Reitherman. Burbank, CA: Walt Disney Studies, 1967.

Lady and the Tramp. Directed by Clyde Geronimi, Wilfred Jackson, and Hamilton Luske. Burbank, CA: Walt Disney Studios, 1955.

Lilo & Stitch. Directed by Christ Sanders and Dean Deblois. Burbank, CA: Walt Disney Studies, 2002.

The Lion King. Directed by Rob Allers and Rob Minkoff. Burbank, CA: Walt Disney Studios, 1994.

The Lion King II: Simba's Pride. Directed by Darrell Rooney. Burbank, CA: Walt Disney Studios, 1998.

The Little Mermaid. Directed by Ron Clemens and John Musker. Burbank, CA: Walt Disney Studios, 1989.

Mary Poppins. Directed by Robert Stevenson. Burbank, CA: Walt Disney Studios, 1964.

Meet the Robinsons. Directed by Stephen Anderson. Burbank, CA: Walt Disney Studies, 2007.

Moana. Directed by Ron Clements and John Musker. Burbank, CA: Walt Disney Studios, 2016.

Mulan. Directed by Barry Cook and Tony Bancroft. Burbank, CA: Walt Disney Studios, 1998.

The Nightmare Before Christmas. Directed by Henry Selick. Burbank, CA: Walt Disney Studios, 1993.

Old Yeller. Directed by Robert Stevenson. Burbank, CA: Walt Disney Studios, 1957.

Oliver & Company. Directed by George Scribner. Burbank, CA: Walt Disney Studios, 1988.

Pete's Dragon. Directed by Don Chaffey. Burbank, CA: Walt Disney Studios, 1977.

Peter Pan. Directed by Clyde Geronimi, Wilfred Jackson, and Hamilton Luske. Burbank: Walt Disney Studios, 1953.

"Picture Perfect: The Making of Sleeping Beauty." Disc 2. *Sleeping Beauty*, platinum ed., DVD. Directed by Clyde Geronimi. Burbank, CA: Walt Disney Studios, 2008.

Pinocchio. Directed by Ben Sharpsteen and Hamilton Luske. Burbank, CA: Walt Disney Studios, 1940.

Pocahontas, Directed by Mike Gabriel and Eric Goldberg. Burbank, CA: Walt Disney Studios, 1995.

The Princess and the Frog. Directed by Ron Clements and John Musker. Burbank, CA: Walt Disney Studios, 2009.

Raya and the Last Dragon. Directed by Don Hall and Carlos López Estrada. Burbank, CA: Walt Disney Studios, 2021.

The Reluctant Dragon. Directed by Alfred Werker. Burbank, CA: Walt Disney Studios, 1941.

The Rescuers. Directed by Wolfgang Reitherman, John Lounsbery, and Art Stevens. Burbank, CA: Walt Disney Studios, 1977.

The Rescuers Down Under. Directed by Hendel Butoy and Mike Gabriel. Burbank, CA: Walt Disney Studios, 1990.

Robin Hood. Directed by Wolfgang Reitherman. Burbank, CA: Walt Disney Studios, 1973.

Sleeping Beauty. Directed by Clyde Geronimi, Eric Larson, Wolfgang Reitherman, and Les Clark. Burbank, CA: Walt Disney Studios, 1959.

The Small One. Directed by Don Bluth. Burbank, CA: Walt Disney Studios, 1978.

Snow White and the Seven Dwarfs. Directed by David Hand, William Cottrell, Wilfred Jackson, Larry Morey, Perce Pearce, and Ben Sharpsteen. Burbank, CA: Walt Disney Studios, 1937.

Song of the South. Directed by Harve Foster and Wilfred Jackson. Burbank, CA: Walt Disney Studios, 1947.

Soul. Directed by Pete Docter. Burbank, CA: Walt Disney Studios, 2020.

Steamboat Willie. Directed by Walt Disney and Ub Iwerks. Burbank, CA: Walt Disney Studios, 1928.

The Sword in the Stone. Directed by Wolfgang Reitherman. Burbank, CA: Walt Disney Studios, 1963.

Tangled. Directed by Nathan Greno and Byron Howard. Burbank, CA: Walt Disney Studios, 2010.

Tarzan. Directed by Kevin Lima and Chris Buck. Burbank, CA: Walt Disney Studios, 1999.

Tinkerbell and the Legend of the NeverBeast. Directed by Steve Loter. Burbank, CA: Walt Disney Studios, 2014.

Toy Story. Directed by John Lasseter. Burbank, CA: Walt Disney Studios, 1995.

Up. Directed by Peter Docter. Burbank, CA: Walt Disney Studios, 2009.

Wreck-It Ralph. Directed by Rich Moore. Burbank, CA: Walt Disney Studios, 2012.

Zootopia. Directed by Byron Howard and Rich Moore. Burbank, CA: Walt Disney Studios, 2016.

Volume II: Disney & The Moral Imagination

101 Dalmatians. Directed by Clyde Geronimi, Hamilton Luske, and Wolfgang Reitherman. Burbank, CA: Walt Disney Studios,1961.

Aladdin. Directed by Ron Clemens and John Musker. Burbank, CA: Walt Disney Studios, 1992.

The Aristocats. Directed by Wolfgang Reitherman. Burbank, CA: Walt Disney Studios, 1970.

Bambi. Directed by James Algar, Samuel Armstrong, David Hand, Graham Heid, Bill Roberts, Paul Satterfield, Norman Wright, Arthur Davis, and Clyde Geronimi. Burbank, CA: Walt Disney Studios, 1942.

Beauty and the Beast. Directed by Bill Condon. Burbank, CA: Walt Disney Studios, 2017.

Beauty and the Beast. Directed by Gary Trousdale and Kirk Wise. Burbank, CA: Walt Disney Studios, 1991.

Bedknobs and Broomsticks. Directed by Robert Stevenson. Burbank, CA: Walt Disney Studios, 1971.

Brave. Directed by Mark Andrews and Brenda Chapman. Burbank, CA: Walt Disney Studios, 2012.

Cars. Directed by John Lasseter. Burbank, CA: Walt Disney Studios, 2006.

Cinderella. Directed by Clyde Geronimi, Hamilton Luske, and Wilfred Jackson. Burbank, CA: Walt Disney Studios, 1950.

Cinderella. Directed by Kenneth Branaugh. Burbank, CA: Walt Disney Studios, 2015.

Dumbo. Directed by Samuel Armstrong, Norman Ferguson, Wilfred Jackson, Jack Kinney, Bill Roberts, Ben Sharpsteen, and John Elliotte. Burbank, CA: Walt Disney Studios, 1941.

Donald in Mathmagic Land. Directed by Hamilton, Luske, Wolfgang, Reitherman, Les Clark, and Joshua Meador. Burbank, CA: Walt Disney Studios, 1959.

Encanto. Directed by Jared Bush and Byron Howard. Burbank, CA: Walt Disney Studios, 2021.

Enchanted. Directed by Kevin Lima. Burbank, CA: Walt Disney Studios, 2007.

Fantasia. Directed by Samuel Armstrong, James Algar, Bill Roberts, Paul Satterfield, Ben Sharpsteen, David D. Hand, Hamilton Luske, Jim

Handley, Ford Beebe, T. Hee, Norman Ferguson, Wilfred Jackson. Burbank, CA: Walt Disney Studios, 1940.

Fantasia 2000. Directed by Don Hahn, Pixote Hunt, Hendel Butoy, Eric Goldberg, James Algar, Francis Glebas, Paul Brizzi, and Gaëtan Brizzi. Burbank, CA: Walt Disney Studios, 1999.

Frozen. Directed by Chris Buck and Jennifer Lee. Burbank, CA: Walt Disney Studios, 2013.

Frozen II. Directed by Chris Buck and Jennifer Lee. Burbank, CA: Walt Disney Studios, 2019.

Grand Canyon. Directed by James Algar. Burbank, CA: Walt Disney Studios, 1958.

Grand Canyonscope. Directed by C. August Nichols. Burbank, CA: Walt Disney Studios, 1954.

Hercules. Directed by Ron Clements and John Musker. Burbank, CA: Walt Disney Studios, 1997.

The Hunchback of Notre Dame. Directed by Gary Trousdale and Kirk Trousdale. Burbank, CA: Walt Disney Studios, 1996.

Into the Unknown: Making Frozen 2. Episode 1. "A Year to Premiere." Directed by Megan Harding. Aired on June 26, 2020. On Disney+.

The Jazz Singer. Directed by Alan Crosland. Burbank, CA: Warner Bros. Pictures, 1927.

The Jungle Book. Directed by Wolfgang Reitherman. Burbank, CA: Walt Disney Studies, 1967.

The Jungle Book (soundtrack), Walt Disney Records, 1997, CD.

The Lion King. Directed by Rob Allers and Rob Minkoff. Burbank, CA: Walt Disney Studios, 1994.

The Little Mermaid. Directed by Ron Clemens and John Musker. Burbank, CA: Walt Disney Studios, 1989.

Mary Poppins. Directed by Robert Stevenson. Burbank, CA: Walt Disney Studios, 1964.

Moana. Directed by Ron Clements and John Musker. Burbank, CA: Walt Disney Studios, 2016.

Mulan. Directed by Barry Cook and Tony Bancroft. Burbank, CA: Walt Disney Studios, 1998.

The Nightmare Before Christmas. Directed by Henry Selick. Burbank, CA: Walt Disney Studios, 1993.

"The Old Mill," *Silly Symphonies*. Directed by Wilfred Jackson. Burbank, CA: Walt Disney Studios, 1937.

Oliver & Company. Directed by George Scribner. Burbank, CA: Walt Disney Studios, 1988.

Pinocchio. Directed by Ben Sharpsteen and Hamilton Luske. Burbank, CA: Walt Disney Studios, 1940.

Pocahontas, Directed by Mike Gabriel and Eric Goldberg. Burbank, CA: Walt Disney Studios, 1995.

The Princess and the Frog. Directed by Ron Clements and John Musker. Burbank, CA: Walt Disney Studios, 2009.

Raya and the Last Dragon. Directed by Don Hall and Carlos López Estrada. Burbank, CA: Walt Disney Studios, 2021.

Robin Hood. Directed by Wolfgang Reitherman. Burbank, CA: Walt Disney Studios, 1973.

Saludos Amigos. Directed by Norman Ferguson, Wilfred Jackson, Jack Kinney, Hamilton Luske, and Bill Roberts. Burbank, CA: Walt Disney Studios, 1942.

Sleeping Beauty. Directed by Clyde Geronimi, Eric Larson, Wolfgang Reitherman, and Les Clark. Burbank, CA: Walt Disney Studios, 1959.

Snow White and the Seven Dwarfs. Directed by David Hand, William Cottrell, Wilfred Jackson, Larry Morey, Perce Pearce, and Ben Sharpsteen. Burbank, CA: Walt Disney Studios, 1937.

Song of the South. Directed by Harve Foster and Wilfred Jackson. Burbank, CA: Walt Disney Studios, 1947.

Steamboat Willie. Directed by Walt Disney and Ub Iwerks. Burbank, CA: Walt Disney Studios, 1928.

The Sword in the Stone. Directed by Wolfgang Reitherman. Burbank, CA: Walt Disney Studios, 1963.

Tangled. Directed by Nathan Greno and Byron Howard. Burbank, CA: Walt Disney Studios, 2010.

Tarzan. Directed by Kevin Lima and Chris Buck. Burbank, CA: Walt Disney Studios, 1999.

The Three Caballeros. Directed by Norman Ferguson, Clyde Geronimi, Jack Kinney, Bill Roberts, and Harold Young. Burbank, CA: Walt Disney Studios, 1944.

Toy Story. Directed by John Lasseter. Burbank, CA: Walt Disney Studios, 1995.

Toy Story 4. Directed by Josh Cooley. Burbank, CA: Walt Disney Studios, 2019.

Up. Directed by Pete Docter. Burbank, CA: Walt Disney Studios, 2009.

Acknowledgments

From Jeremy

I am thankful for my students at PHSC. Our in-class dialogue helped to sharpen my own thoughts, provoking new insights and inquiry. The idea for this project began in my Ethics classroom, wherein I used the arts—especially music and film—to make the course more accessible, to help students grasp complex content by showing them that they were already familiar with underpinning philosophical and theological questions and existential struggles. I found that Disney films were especially helpful for engaging questions of virtue/vice, good/evil, meaning, and identity. This prompted me to create a course module on the problem of evil and the moral imaginary, which pondered the meaning behind our convictions of injustice, and the moral power of storytelling through film, literary fiction, comic books, and music. Therein we considered how the arts are expressions and explorations of various philosophical ideas and worldviews. I decided to include a biographical study on the life of C. S. Lewis (one of the most recognizable defenders of moral truth in the 20th century), his struggle with the problem of evil, and, in particular, his eventual transition from analytic argument to narrative apologetics. I coupled this with a biographical sketch of Tolkien, and a brief overview of both his perspective on myth and his subtle approach to imbuing stories with appeals to moral convictions and a longing for the Good. I quickly realized that this connected with a majority of students from a wide array of backgrounds and perspectives. Many students were enthralled with the problem of evil and the power of the moral imaginary. These observations only fueled the fire of a passion already aflame—using pop-culture and the arts to explore and explain issues of philosophy and theology. While I had long been interested in Christian apologetics in general, and moral and aesthetic apologetics in particular, it was this series of events which prompted me to dig more deeply into narrative apologetics and to seek ways in my own apologetic methodology to integrate systematic philosophy, theology, and theistic apologetics with aesthetic inquiry, *and* to situate that interdisciplinary approach within pop-culture narratives (whether literary, film, or musical narratives). And so, I cannot overstate my thankfulness for the classroom dialogue, and every student who participated in it, from which this project has emerged. Thank you.

Thank you to those students who have continued to reach out over the years with questions concerning my own ideas on beauty and the intersection of aesthetics, ethics, and theology. Such ongoing conversations are always helpful in challenging me to evaluate my own consistency and clarity in thought and articulation.

Pat, thank you for all your help and hard work. Our volume is much better because you are a part of it. Thank you to the contributors of the second volume for your participation and enthusiasm, and for your patience amidst setbacks during the pandemic. This has been a long journey. I hope it blesses you all to see it all come to fruition. I thank the publisher for the forum. Thank you, Marybeth and David, for your support of these works, and for all you do at Moral Apologetics Press. Your vision for interdisciplinary dialogue, mediated between scholar and layperson, pop culture and the classroom, is a breath of fresh air.

I owe a special thank you to Holly Ordway for help, encouragement, and constructive criticisms along the way—especially for her assistance amidst a series of revisions involving the first chapter of the first volume. Thank you, Holly. It is much stronger in light of your feedback.

Thank you to my wife, Abby, and our cubs, Piper and Levi, for your love and support, your patience and encouragement, and for reminding me daily to demonstrate the character of which I write in several chapters. A special thanks is due my princess, Piper. It was her love for Disney songs, and our recurrent duets in the car, which prompted some of my initial insights for my chapter on music's referential power, and it was also a daddy-daughter date to see *Raya and the Last Dragon* in the theater which prompted my essay on the human condition. Levi, you were born the year this project began and endured many walks with the stroller, listening to me read these chapters aloud. These walks actually helped me to ponder and improve the overall flow of ideas more carefully—and also to catch a few errors. As you grew, you discovered your own love for the vintage Donald, Mickey, and Pluto animated shorts. Rewatching these old classics with you (a lot) also helped me to ponder more deeply Disney's use of comedy and the value of these animated shorts. While this was a different direction than the main concern of this volume, it nevertheless prompted me to consider Disney's impact further, and for that I am thankful.

To those who supported this project financially, donating funds to help with images costs and the purchase of royalty-free licenses, thank you. Thank you, reader, for your interest in the intersection of philosophical inquiry and theological dialogue. Thank you for supporting the work of the contributing authors and the vision of Moral Apologetics Press. Most importantly, I thank God for the vision, voice, and opportunity. For years I prayed for wisdom to understand the connection I sensed between apologetics, ethics, and the arts, especially music—long before "cultural apologetics" had become a more popular and easily identifiable subdiscipline of apologetics. I also prayed continually for an employment opportunity that would allow me to speak, and continue to grow, across these areas. Although there were times of confusion, frustration, and even disappointment, you have been so faithful in working circumstances I could not understand for my good and your glory, through opportunities I could not have foreseen. Thank you for your goodness, provision, and enduring love.

I have enjoyed editing this volume. It has been exciting to see everything come together in such an engaging and complimentary manner. I hope this work is both helpful for inquiring laypersons and useful to scholars interested in approaching the intersection of pop culture and apologetics from a lens of aesthetic appreciation (as this volume does not emphasize the approach of critical theories, common to cultural studies, which often focus on problematizing hegemonic aspects of pop culture). I also hope this volume may lend itself well to theological, moral, and aesthetic education. Many chapters could serve as source material for a series of modules on moral philosophy and the arts, theology and aesthetics, or cultural apologetic methodology. Regardless of one's worldview or interests, I believe the reader will find something herein that beckons further deliberation and dialogue.

From Pat

I would like to thank Jeremy for bringing me into this project. The project is clearly his labor of love and I feel privileged and extremely grateful to be a part of it. Getting to know Jeremy over these last several months has been a distinct honor. Jeremy, brother, my life has been notably enriched by our intersection. I look forward to a continued and deepening friendship as we head to the celestial city together. I would also like to thank everyone at Moral Apologetics Press. Your vision and efforts have brought this project to life. I am forever grateful. I would also like to thank my family – my dear wife, Wendy, and our awesome three kids, Hannah, Patrick, and Nicholas. You all mean the world to me. In keeping with our family's movie tradition of telling each other we love each other just before the movie starts, know that I love you more than life itself. I'm so proud you're my family. Finally, I'd like to thank the one true and living God. To Him be all glory, all honor, and all praise, forevermore.

Index

SUBJECT INDEX

abortion, 48, 144–45, 161 (n19), 218 (n20), 228
Abraham, 194, 401, 433, 437, 439
absurdity (vs irrationality), 437
abuse, 414
Adorno, Theodor, 127
aesthetic/aesthetic experience, 12, 19–27, 30, 34–36, 41, 56, 65–77, 109–10
aesthetic enculturation, 289
aesthetic sensibilities, 295, 300
aesthetic sensitivities, 289, 305

aesthetic tolerance of otherness, 291
affirmation, 95, 104, 112, 114, 115, 129, 132, 136, 154, 158, 178, 182, 183, 193
agape, 12, 58, 84, 93, 172, 447
alienation, 105, 172, 186, 190
Allah, 172
ambassadors of the kingdom, 6, 43, 55, 67, 81, 85, 92, 179, 180
American Anthropological Association, 125
analytic (in contrast to continental), 143–45
Andersen, Hans Christian, 353
angels, 421 (n26), 223

animation, 12, 31, 36, 65, 68, 75, 244, 245, 263, 264, 265, 274, 284, 285, 291
audience acceptance (n9), 293
computer, 338
live-action, 265, 270
anxiety, 11, 119, 144, 362, 364, 367
apologetics, 12, 14, 243
cultural, 5, 17, 36, 292
imaginative and aesthetic, 26, 30, 246, 247, 305
moral, 33, 36, 245
music and, 305
narrative, 25, 447
regarding "evidence" (n36), 231

Aquinas, 57, 279,
    314, 328, 402, 403
archetype, 48, 50,
    53, 54–57, 61, 67,
    75–77, 81, 84, 92,
    96, 202
    Jesus as
        Archetype,
        62, 82, 88
Arendt, Hannah, 22
Aristotle, 46–48, 49,
    56, 84, 86, 276,
    297, 349, 351,
    389, 390, 402
    on final cause, 46
art (as source of
    knowledge),
    345–46
Ashman, Howard,
    288
Augustine, 15, 84,
    92, 279, 326, 361–
    71, 402, 405
Ayer, A. J., 135
    (n8), 221

Bach, J. S., 285
Baggett, David, 170
Balthasar, Hans
    Urs von, 305
Basil the Great, 344
Beatific vision, the,
    327
Beatitudes, the, 368
beauty, 5, 6, 12, 18,
    23, 30, 33, 36, 49,
    50, 51, 54–57, 59,
    65, 67–79, 96,

102, 103, 198,
    275–80, 291, 295,
    302, 303, 304,
    305, 325–34, 344,
    346, 363, 366,
    400, 422, 434
    and education,
        325, 333–34
    and eternity, 366
    and excellence,
        276
    and holiness,
        328–29
    and order, 363
    and virtue, 56,
        325–34
    Aquinas on
        beauty, 57
    archetypes of,
        55, 56
    as moving, 326
    as spiritual, 327
    as transcenden-
        tal, 326
    criticisms of
        Disney
        regarding, 68–
        70, 71, 326,
        333
    emphasis on the
        eyes, 75
    objective vs
        subjective/rel-
        ative, 278, 326
    physical, 68–70
    pleasure in
        "ugly" things,
        277, 333

Beethoven, 285
Begbie, Jeremy
    (n1), 270
Benjamin, Walter,
    127
Bentham, Jeremy
    (n8), 221
Bettelheim, Bruno,
    338, 343
Birzer, Bradley, 398
blind men and the
    elephant, 152
Bluth, Don, 455
Boghossian, Peter,
    150
Bowker, John, 446
Butterfield,
    Elizabeth, 304

Campbell, Joseph,
    36, 55, 353, 403
Camus, Albert, 119
    (n7), 221
character, 48, 55,
    68, 78, 83, 91,
    102, 142, 174, 185
    formation, 41,
        394
    worth imitating,
        82, 313–22
charity, 48, 51, 58,
    84, 87, 92, 111,
    136, 172, 178,
    201, 290, 403,
    417, 432
    (n16), 217
    the principle of,
        451

Chesterton, G. K.,
254, 314, 388, 391
classicism (in
contrast to
romanticism),
20, 144
Clements, Ron,
352–54
Collins, Phil, 288
Collodi, Carlo, 381
colonialism, 133,
148
(n27), 226
community, 11, 12,
19, 21, 22, 33, 37,
60, 85, 88, 95,
103, 106, 115,
125, 148, 150,
153, 158, 172,
173, 174, 178,
179, 181, 184,
317, 416, 428,
447, 449, 450, 452
Cone, James, 191–
92, 197–98
conscience. See
moral conscience
consequentialism,
44, 46, 47, 81
continental (in
contrast to
analytic), 143–45
Cooper, Anthony
Ashley, 56
Copan, Paul, 166
(n16), 217
(n41), 231

Copleston,
Frederick, 446
cosmology, 397–
401
covenant, 193, 194,
377
Craig, William
Lane, 123, 159,
180
creation-fall-
redemption, 445
Crenshaw,
Kimberlé, 128
critical race theory,
111, 128
critical social justice
(CSJ), 105, 108,
109, 110–15, 131–
36, 157, 174, 178,
179, 181, 185,
190, 191, 198, 200
(n27), 226
critical social
theory, 66, 105,
111, 113, 128,
130, 150, 157
Critical Theory
(CT), 105, 108,
109, 111, 120,
127–28, 131, 157
culture wars, 243
curse, 58, 59, 60, 62,
78, 89, 93, 95, 96,
438, 440
and character,
435, 446

Darwinian system,
122, 164, 168
Declaration of
Independence,
163
deontology, 43–44,
164
(n27), 212
Descartes, René
(n8), 222
descriptive (vs
prescriptive),
108, 111, 113,
115, 135, 137,
139, 143, 146,
154, 157, 178, 200
(n40), 208
desire, 5, 6, 11, 19,
22, 23, 25, 27, 35,
49, 57, 63, 65, 87,
97, 102, 119, 138,
139, 153, 164,
165, 169, 174,
185, 188, 264,
295, 302
(n13), 207
/delight, 268
and music, 303
loss and longing,
303
to know order,
295, 297, 300,
304
devil, 52, 58, 59, 93,
118, 275, 304, See
also Satan

DiAngelo, Robin, 109, 111, 128, 131–35

Dies Irae, 298

Dippermouth Blues, 298

discrimination, 153, 173, 182 (n5, ch.9), 220

Disney
as corporation, 147, 243, 263
as storyteller, 12
controversy/criticism concerning, 68, 75, 147, 288 (n5), 250
Disney culture, 14, 36, 184, 244
parks, 31, 33, 36, 53, 55, 84, 203

Disney Channel, 287

Disney princesses, 70–77, 325–34

Disney Renaissance, 287

Disney, Elias, 118–19

Disney, Roy, 31, 118–19 (n6), 292

Disney, Walt, 30–36, 41, 75, 101, 118–19, 274, 275, 283, 284 (n6), 292
achievement and impact, 31, 244–45
and religion, 118 (n5), 221
as complementary to Lewis and Tolkien, 35
criticisms of, 34–35
moral vision, 58
nonsectarian approach, 33
on the influence of DeMolay, 31

double danger. See Kierkegaard

education, 12, 21, See also moral education
Disney films and, 31
subjectivist philosophies of, 23
the goal of, 423
the question of, 424
value education, 22
virtue, 54

Edwards, Jonathan, 279

egalitarian, 152, 161, 181, 182, 183 (n5), 220

egoism, 43–44, 45, 48, 50, 52, 53, 81, 88, 93, 368

Elfman, Danny, 288

Elgar, Edward, 350

emotion, 12, 19, 254, 257

emotivism, 24, 350

empathy, 289, 291, 301, 317

enchantment, 19, 23, 37, 56, 245, 249, 302
disenchantment, 19, 20, 22, 26

Engels, Friedrich, 120

enlightenment, 128, 131, 148, 165, 341

Enlightenment, the, 13, 19, 20, 164, 166, 296, 300 (n16), 217 (n8), 222

Epicurus/Epicureanism, 361–71, 424

equality, 82, 112, 125, 153, See also egalitarian (n16), 217

Erickson, Millard, 195

ethics
  complementarity
    , 82, 89
  normative, 43–44
  secular, 82
  sociobiological,
    122
eudaemonia, 403
euthanasia, 161
  (n20), 228
Euthyphro
  Dilemma, the,
    170–71
ever-after, 23, 43,
  53, 55, 62, 91,
  137, 188, 333, 444
  (n11), 210
  (n3, ch.8), 220
  community-
    ever-after, 452
  evil-ever-after,
    445
  happiness-ever-
    after, 37, 53,
    85, 91
  kingdom-ever-
    after, 6, 12, 26,
    43, 56, 57, 66,
    75, 79, 81, 83,
    87, 94, 96, 102,
    117, 119, 158,
    177, 180, 184,
    445, 451
  sorrow-never-
    after, 91
evil, 409–17
  argument from,
    412, 416

gratuitous, 410
  (n14), 419
  objectivity of,
    413
  the problem of,
    60, 142, 181,
    409, 446
existential, 19, 25,
  26, 49, 95, 136,
  142, 145, 162,
  181, 199, 246,
  303, 410, 440
  (n4), 453
  the significance
    of choice, 424,
    425
existentialism, 130,
  182
  (n15), 225
  (n8), 222

fact vs fiction, 249
fairy tale(s), 35, 143,
  254, 338, 392, 416
  the teaching
    power of, 343
faith, 12, 15, 19, 21,
  32, 33, 41, 51, 53,
  60, 61, 66, 75, 84,
  85, 88, 92, 117,
  119, 178, 410,
  413, 415, 448–49
  (n13), 207
  (n18), 207
  definition of, 17
  in vs that, 440
  knights of, 437

leap of, 119, 122,
  440
  step vs leap, 449
  vs works, 380
  wishful
    thinking, 449
Ferry, Luc, 166
  (n16), 217
Feuerbach,
  Ludwig, 120
  (n11), 222
  (n8), 222
forebearance, 409–
  17
Foucault, Michel,
  128
Frankfurt School,
  the, 121, 127
free will
  (libertarian), 95,
  412, *See also*
  Molinism
Freire, Paulo, 128,
  129
Freud, Sigmund
  (n8), 222
friendship, 362,
  366, 368, 369, 370
Fromm, Erich, 127

Gadamer, Hans-
  Georg, 350
Geisler, Norman,
  122, 264
gender, 48, 66, 105,
  110, 112, 151,
  168, 326
  (n8), 222

gender roles/norms, 289

gender studies, 128 (n1), 224

Gilkyson, Terry, 361

God and love, 5, 92, 166, 170, 171, 172, 173, 178, 179, 181, 183, 192, 197 (n35), 231

Godawa, Brian (n1), 205 (n3), 205

good life, the, 11, 21, 23, 33, 50, 53, 55, 56, 62, 78, 91, 92, 96, 117, 178, 183, 186, 188, 198, 243, 304, 362, 366, 388, 403, 422, 444

good Samaritan, 431

good vs evil, 12, 32, 36, 37, 41, 55, 58, 63, 82, 84, 89, 97, 101, 102, 137, 200
the cessation of evil, 83

good without God? (n14), 233

goodness
gradations (degrees) of, 363

goodness beyond justice, 27, 96, 102, 106, 177–85, 188

Gould, Paul, 5, 16, 142

grand narrative. See metanarrative

Greek mythology, 397–401
the Fates, 400

Grimm brothers, the, 34

Gu, Ming Dong, 303

Guroian, Vigen, 380

Gutiérrez, Gustavo, 194

Habermas, Jurgen, 127

habit/habituation, 22, 44, 49, 50, 69, 107, 185, 380, 393, 403

hamartiology. See sin

happiness, 362–70

Heaney, Maeve, 305

Hegel, G. W. F., 120, 129

hegemonic influence, 69, 74, 76, 104, 109, 121, 128, 146, 189

Heidegger, Martin, 13

Hell (as conscious choice), 394

Herodotus, 24

heroism (Aristotelian vs Homeric), 402

Hobbes, Thomas, 122, 123

Homer, 399, 402, 404

hope, 51, 383, 410, 413, 415–17, 449, 452
ambassadors of, 415
bearers of, 416
irrational, 437

Horace, 350

hospitality, 431–41

Hugo, Victor (n19), 215

human condition, 18, 22, 57, 60, 61, 63, 65, 94, 96, 125, 174, 244, 264, 292, 300, 301, 303, 313, 376, 384, 397, 423, 443, 448, 450
and guilt, 95, 192, 196, 450
sickness, 59, 174, 175, 446, 447
the world as broken, 446

human dignity,
104, 105, 158,
162, 166, 172,
181, 183, 190,
192, 200
human nature
(goodness), 366
human rights. *See*
rights
Hume, David, 313

identity/self-image
and affirmation,
321
imagination, 11, 14,
26, 27, 245, 253,
260, 265
and apologetics,
25
and incarnation,
258
and lived
experience,
302
and meaning,
256–57
and music, 286,
289, 290, 296,
298, 300, 305
as worldview,
13, 16
moral, 5, 14, 22,
68, 166, 244,
353
shaped by
culture, 22

social imaginary,
17, 19, 21, 22,
84
imago Dei, 25, 166
(n34), 308
inequality, 103, 122,
131, 161, 363
injustice, 23, 26, 36,
42, 44, 50, 51, 53,
57, 59, 61, 83, 87,
97, 102, 103, 104,
113, 114, 115,
136, 137, 138,
140, 145, 146,
147, 150, 153,
154, 168, 169,
174, 175, 177,
184, 189, 190,
197, 409, 414
(n9), 227
institutionalization,
113, 118, 132,
134, 135, 144,
180, 189, 198
interdisciplinary
studies, 246
intersectionality,
128, 133, 139, 151
(n6, ch.9), 220
intrinsic value, 46,
48, 87, 104, 105,
106, 122, 135,
140, 161, 168,
169, 192, 300, 364
(n16), 217
(n42), 232
Irwin, William, 18

James, William, 15
Jaspers, Karl, 446
Jefferson, Thomas,
163
Jesus, 6, 45, 56, 58,
82, 85, 151, 171,
179, 180, 183,
185, 188, 191,
192, 193, 195,
197, 198, 269,
370, 377, 383,
403, 410, 434, 435
(n14), 233
(n34), 236
and suffering,
412
(n14), 418
as foundation
for hope, 416
as moral
exemplar, 417
(n14), 418
the historical (vs
the popular),
411
the moral
theology of,
82
(n41), 231
Joel, Billy, 287
John, Elton, 288
Johnston, Ollie, 72,
273, 285
joy (as conditional),
392

Judeo-Christian, 43, 85, 89, 94, 97, 151, 188
Jung, Carl, 54
justice, 6, 23, 24, 25, 26, 36, 42, 44, 50, 53, 54, 57, 59, 82, 87, 97, 101, 104, 105, 108, 109, 112, 113, 114, 115, 117, 128, 133, 135, 146, 150, 152, 153, 154, 158–67, 167, 169, 181, 182, 183, 189, 190, 191, 193, 196, 197, 199, See also goodness
beyond justice (n16), 217
as distinguished from goodness, 180
as telos, 170, 171
final, 58, 413

Kant, Immanuel, 84, 164, 369
Kaufmann, Yehezkel, 401
Keane, Glen, 338
Kendi, Ibram X., 109
Kern, Jerome, 274
Kierkegaard, Soren, 421–29

double danger, 88
knight of faith vs infinite resignation, 435–41
kindness, 409–17, 434
King, Martin Luther Jr., 198 (n33), 236
kingdom. *See also* ever-after
heaven on earth, 269, 450
order/flourish-ing, 444
reconciliation of, 343
kingdom theology, 58, 60, 84
definition of, 6
Kipling, Rudyard, 361
Kodály, Zoltan (n27), 294
Koukl, Greg, 159, 167, 445
Kumandra, 27, 117, 125, 174, 177, 450, 451
Kuyper, Abaham, 78

leitmotif, 274, 275, 285, 298, 299
Levitin, Daniel, 287

Lewis, C. S., 92, 179, 197, 199, 266, 279, 296, 393, 428
argument from desire, 25
in reference to *Narnia*, 25, 26, 142, 448, 456
looking "at" vs looking "along", 258
on Disney, 34
on double seeing, 26
on moral objectivity, 24, 42, 413
on myth, 27 (n7), 210
on reason and imagination, 256
on Sehnsucht, 25, 27, 303
liberation, 106, 114, 121, 128, 131, 147, 151, 153, 158, 181, 182, 186, 190, 191, 192, 193, 194, 200
liberation theology, 191–99
Locke, John, 163, 167, 173
loss, 303, 366
love, 12, 18, 22, 23, 53, 58, 59, 62, 77,

83, 84, 86, 88, 91,
92–96, 118, 143,
166, 170, 171,
178, 184, 192,
196, 255, 327,
330, 337, 368,
369, 387, 404,
431, 434, 436,
438, 440, 448
(n41), 232
as transforma-
tive, 61, 118,
440
Platonic vs
Homeric, 404

MacDonald,
George, 11, 187
MacIntyre,
Alasdair, 13, 164,
165, 350, 351,
353, 357
magic, 33, 41, 47,
55, 59, 89, 95,
117, 120, 137,
142, 178, 185,
188, 243
(n19), 213
(n5), 221
and logic, 388
pixie dust, 448
Manning, Brennan,
180
Marcuse, Herbert,
127
marginalization, 70,
105, 109, 113,
115, 132, 135,

143, 146, 151,
158, 172, 182,
189, 199, 296,
411, 414
(n6, ch.9), 220
marriage, 48, 93,
169
Marx, Karl, 120,
141, 144, 158
(n8), 222
(n11), 222
dialectical
materialism,
120
on religion as
opiate, 121
Marxism, 120, 122,
127, 128
Neo-Marxism,
120, 121, 128
materialism, 104,
105, 110, 112,
115, 119, 120,
124, 125, 130,
134, 151, 157, 191
philosophical vs
economic, 121
May, Rollo, 13
McClellan, B.
Edward, 33, 66
McGrath, Alister,
14, 25, 54, 447
McGrew, Timothy
(n19), 207
mediator, 61, 94,
117, 185, 264,
267, 268, 448
myth as

(n7), 210
Menken, Alan, 288
mercy, 88, 143, 159,
368, 369, 412,
432, 434, 439
metanarrative, 13,
23, 25, 43, 53, 81,
91, 97, 106, 118,
120, 125, 128,
129, 135, 153,
164, 172, 181,
190, 196, 199, 257
(n17), 229
Mickey Mouse, 31
"Mickey Mouse",
253
"Mickey
Mousing",
273, 286
Miller, Roger, 287
Miravalle, John-
Mark, 328
misery, 364, 366
Molinism, 95
(n13), 219
monotheism, 162,
172, 173, 246
(n16), 217
moral
conscience/con-
viction, 6, 11,
15, 18, 23, 25,
26, 42, 47, 56,
58, 82, 94, 96,
160, 174, 182,
187, 199, 376,
384
deficit, 448

education, 30,
31, 33, 66, 202,
298
meaning, 21, 23,
104, 164
moral argument,
115, 159–62
objectivity, 24,
25, 37, 119,
122, 153, 161,
456
progress (ideals
of), 451
sense, 256, 257,
260
theology, 253,
255, 300, 334,
369
Mosaic law
(n41), 231
Mozart, 285
music, 6, 12, 34, 36,
65, 74, 118, 149,
198, 244, 245,
260, 273, 283
aesthetic
theories of,
297
(n34), 308
and empathy,
289
and moral
education, 301
and morality,
289, 290, 299–
305
art music, 285,
287

(n9), 293
art vs pop/folk,
285, 286, 288,
290
as connected to
transcendence
266
as organic
motion, 19,
288, 295
as passion for
order, 305,
308
emotional effect,
284, 293
enculturation,
289, 290, 291
(n26), 294
expressive
power, 264
familiarity and
accessibility,
287, 290
(n27), 294
folk, 287
incidental music,
284
jazz, 287
program music,
285
referential
power of,
295–305
referentialism,
285
simplicity and
complexity,
287, 290, 298

suggestive of
character, 273,
274
synchronized
sound, 31,
244, 273, 279,
286, 291
Walt's view on,
285
music education,
31, 286
philosophies of,
297
music theory
consonance/dis-
sonance, 275,
290, 302
steps vs leaps,
299
tritone, 304
musical reference
(n7), 306
extra-musical,
298
inter-musical,
298
intra-musical,
298
musical theatre, 264
animated, 265
Broadway, 286,
287, 288
(n22), 293
Oklahoma!, 288
song and dance,
264
Musker, John, 352–
54

Mussorgsky, Modest, 275
myth, 13, 27, 36, 42, 54, 70, 398
(n7), 210

narrative, 5, 11–18, 18, 19, 25, 26, 33, 36, 37, 41, 54, 65, 67, 77, 96, 103, 105, 113, 114, 125, 129, 134, 136, 137, 145, 147, 151, 154, 157, 158, 164, 174, 178, 187, 189, 199, 255, 259
(n40), 208
biblical, 59, 62, 179, 193
theistic, 161, 169, 200
natural law theory, 42, 159–67, 401–3, 405
(n30), 212
(n22), 230
Naugle, David, 13, 130
Nebuchadnezzar, 317
Newman, Randy, 288
Niebuhr, Richard, 15
(n1), 205
(n3), 205

Nietzsche, Friedrich, 13, 129, 130, 154, 366
nonsectarian, 6, 13, 30, 54, 82, 93, 106
nostalgia, 20, 56, 147, 296, 455
(n9), 222
as restorative longing, 304, 308

opera buffa, 286
operetta, 286
oppression, 104, 121, 128, 129, 133, 134, 135, 137, 146, 147, 151, 153, 154, 172, 178, 179, 182, 185, 190, 192, 195, 446, 451
(n17), 228
of conscience, 200
orphan, 53, 140, 148, 177, 178, 186, 196
ought-to-be, 23, 27, 30, 35, 67, 87, 125, 128, 149, 153, 160, 177, 184, 296, 444
outcast, 69, 137, 143, 158, 172, 178, 186, 187, 194, 195, 200

Pascal, Blaise, 15 (n13), 206
personhood, 105, 168, 186
perspective, 14, 16, 17, 21, 48, 52, 60, 105, 108, 113, 114, 115, 122, 125, 129, 130, 132, 133, 134, 135, 136, 137, 139, 143, 144, See also standpoint, See also worldview
and understanding, 449
liberation of, 452
Pinsky, Mark, 60, 62, 66, 118, 188, 243
(n2), 221
(n5), 221
Pixar, 288
Plato, 27, 56, 78, 84, 86, 279, 297, 327, 400, 402, 405
(n15), 216
pleasure, 92, 159, 179, 277, 291, 297, 304, 315, 362, 367, 369, 390, 391, 393, 422, 425
(n17), 229
(n31), 372
Pojman, Louis

(n14), 211
on
    egalitarianism
    161
on moral
    objectivity,
    169
on stories, 11
on theistic
    grounding for
    human value,
    166
pop culture, 17, 18,
    19, 21, 29, 36, 67,
    106, 109, 145
postmodernism,
    114, 119, 128, 130
power-play, 125,
    129, 133, 134,
    135, 151
prejudice, 51, 102,
    103, 104, 111,
    114, 132, 133,
    147, 186, 404
prescriptive. See
    descriptive (vs
    prescriptive)
pride/hubris (vs
    humility), 48, 58,
    60, 313–22, 365,
    450
proper order. See
    telos
property, 86, 103,
    104, 121, 141,
    163, 165, 168,
    169, 173, 182
    (n30), 212

(n8), 227
(n17), 229
(n42), 232

Rachels, James, 124
racism, 66, 110, 111,
    147
Rand, Ayn, 43
reality
    hyper-real
        world, 263–70
reconciliation, 59,
    118, 125, 172,
    174, 187, 217, 343
    (n16), 217
redemption, 53, 54,
    58, 63, 86, 88,
    187, 343, 375, 450
    (n3), 205
relativism, 24, 25,
    43, 112, 114, 125,
    130, 132
    (n26), 223
reorientation
    of conscience/
        heart, 50, 79,
        94, 95, 97, 200
    of habit, 87, 92,
        101
resurrection, 58, 60,
    448
revenge, 411, 414,
    449
Ricouer, Paul, 13
right-order, 23, 57,
    87, 96, 106, 162,
    167, 169, 179,
    184, 190, 198, 305

rights
    human, 46, 104,
        105, 125, 135,
        147, 154, 157,
        160, 167, 172,
        180, 181, 183,
        193
        (n16), 217
        (n8), 221
        (n17), 229
    natural, 162–67,
        168
Rogers, Fred
    (n27), 294
romanticism, 20,
    144
Rorty, Richard, 151
Russell, Bertrand,
    124

sacrifice, 259, 368,
    381, 402, 404,
    431, 447–48
Saint-Simon, Henri
    de, 120
salvation, 60, 379–
    83
    glorification,
        382–83
    justification, 93,
        380, 440
    sanctification,
        95, 382
Satan, 58
Schaeffer, Francis,
    21, 96, 119, 247,
    298

Schellekens,
    Elisabeth, 56, 68,
    300, 302
Schubert, Franz,
    275
Scruton, Roger, 288
secular humanism,
    134, 297, 451
self-interest/self-
    love, 43, 370, *See
    also* egoism
selfishness, 431
self-merit (faith vs
    works), 380
Sensoy, Özlem,
    128, 131–35
Sequeri,
    Pierangelo, 305
sex
    sexual
        dimorphism,
        73
    sexuality, 48, 66,
        73, 105, 110
        (n8), 222
    sexualization,
        68, 71–74, 76,
        243
sexism, 60, 66, 76,
    110
"male gaze", 71
Shakespeare,
    William, 257
shalom, 158, 184–85
Sherman, Richard
    and Robert, 287,
    361
sin, 378

Sire, James, 16, 443
Smith, James, 20–
    22, 25
Smith, R. Scott, 124,
    135
Sober, Elliot, 124
social goodness,
    158, 171, 173,
    182–85, 196, *See
    also* goodness
    beyond justice
social justice, 104,
    108–15, 131, 141,
    144, 151, 199
    (n16), 217
    (n34), 236
    (n5, ch.9), 220
Solzhenitsyn,
    Aleksandr, 174
soteriology. *See*
    salvation
spiritual warfare,
    58, 190, 200
St. George and the
    dragon, 254
standpoint/stand-
    point theory,
    130, 144
status quo, 113,
    121, 127, 152
Steiner, George
    (n45), 232
Steiner, Max, 286
Stokowski,
    Leopold, 285
stories. *See also*
    narrative

and
    embodiment,
    257
core elements
    (origin,
    conflict,
    resolution),
    443
the power of,
    11–23, 187,
    253
Stravinsky, Igor,
    350
subjectivism, 23,
    296
suffering, 409–17

Taylor, Charles, 13,
    14, 16, 17, 23, 25,
    84
Taylor, Richard,
    159
Tchaikovsky,
    Pyotr, 287
teleological
    justice/just-ness
    ("justice as
    telos"), 23, 27,
    174
teleology and the
    arts, 299–305
telos, 44, 45–48, 49,
    54, 84, 85–87,
    132, 162, 164,
    169–74, 178, 179,
    180, 182, 183,
    201, 297, 305, 403
    (n14), 211

(n15), 225
proper
  order/identity
  27, 162, 167,
  189, 190, 342,
  343
purpose/poten-
  tial, 48, 388
theodicy, 410
theological
  anthropology,
  337–38, 343, 375–
  84, *See also*
  human
  condition
theological
  symbolism, 57–
  63
Thielicke, Helmut
  (n7), 270
is vs ought, 266
Thomas, Frank, 72,
  273, 285
tolerance/intoler-
  ance, 114, 125,
  136, 154, 193
Tolkien, J. R. R., 33–
  36, 255, 398
  (n11), 210
Tolstoy, Leo, 166,
  393
torah
  (n41), 231

transcendence,
  263–70
Trinity, 376
  (n35), 231
trust (and
  vulnerability),
  448
Turek, Frank, 122

utilitarianism, 43–
  44, 45, 163, 164
  (n27), 212
  (n30), 212

value hierarchies,
  17, 33, 66, 109
virtue, 53, 92, 376,
  402
  Christian vs
  Aristotelian,
  84, 403
  Disney's virtue
  motif, 48–52,
  55, 77, 81–88
  virtue ethics, 43–
  44, 48, 101,
  184, 313–22,
  349–58, 366–
  68, *See also*
  complemen-
  tarity ethics

Wagner, Richard,
  285

Waititi, Taika, 352
Walls, Jerry, 170
Ward, Annalee, 59,
  66, 110, 243, 352
Ward, Michael, 24,
  256
way-it-should-be,
  6, 20, 36, 48, 54,
  82, 83, 89, 102,
  132, 148, 162,
  169, 174, 190,
  199, 305, 445
Westminster
  Shorter
  Catechism, 328
Wiesel, Elie, 417
Wilson, E. O., 122
Wolterstorff,
  Nicholas, 302
Wonderly,
  Monique, 65,
  301, 353
worldview, 5, 18,
  22, 33, 66, 146,
  158, 166, 175,
  183, 291, 397, 446
  and stories, 443
worry. *See* anxiety
Wright,
  Christopher, 193

YHWH, 172, 193

Zimmer, Hans, 288

DISNEY FILM/CHARACTER INDEX

101 Dalmatians, 186,
187, 258
  Cruella, 43, 52,
    75, 178, 254
Aladdin, 27, 44, 45,
50, 58, 86, 95,
102, 168, 186,
254, 287, 289,
291, 319–20, 321,
352
(n26), 212
  Genie, 86, 168
  Jafar, 58, 275
  Jasmine, 50, 70
Alice in Wonderland,
138, 302
Aristocats, The, 51,
159, 168, 186,
187, 254, 287
(n5), 250
Bambi, 75, 148, 186,
274, 275, 303
Beauty and the Beast,
27, 59, 94, 245,
287, 338, 431–41
  Beast, 48, 58, 63,
    86, 88, 94, 117,
    143, 177, 325
  Belle, 48, 94, 143
    (n1), 214
  Gaston, 48, 88,
    143, 187, 260,
    275

*Bedknobs and
Broomsticks*, 157,
186, 244, 263, 268
Black Cauldron, The,
51, 290, 304
(n19), 213
  Horned King,
    102
Brave, 59, 147, 349
  Elinor, 316–17
  Merida, 44, 58,
    73, 84, 140,
    316–17
  Mor'du, 107
Brother Bear, 140,
147
Cars, 259
Chicken Little
(n4), 346
Cinderella, 27, 51,
56, 60, 68, 69, 75,
85, 103, 117, 138,
142, 177, 186,
245, 389, 409–17,
455
Coco, 137
Descendants, 139,
178, 187, 244
  Mal, 139
  Donald Duck, 350
    in *Grand
    Canyonscope*,
    277

    in *Mathmagic
    Land*, 297
Dumbo, 51, 103, 148,
159, 168, 274, 290
(n20), 215
(n5), 250
*Emperor's New
Groove, The*, 52,
103, 140, 148,
249,
(n4), 346
Encanto, 59, 71, 149,
289
  Alma, 117
  Bruno, 138, 149,
    153
  Isabela, 71, 149
  Luisa, 297
  Mirabel, 27, 71,
    117, 138, 149,
    153
Enchanted, 91, 288
Fantasia, 249, 274,
285, 286, 298
Fantasia 2000, 350
Finding Dory, 139
Finding Nemo, 149,
254
*Fox and the Hound,
The*, 51, 304
Frozen/Frozen II, 53,
84, 93, 95, 149,
159, 177, 244,

254, 288, 289,
299, 339
Anna, 60, 63, 73,
82, 83, 93, 95,
96, 139
Elsa, 25, 27, 59,
63, 73, 82, 89,
93, 95, 96, 120,
295, 300
(n19), 213
Hans, 41, 53
Pabbie, 82, 93
Goofy Movie, A, 139
Hercules, 51, 87,
245, 397–405
Hades, 102, 275
Megara, 70, 71
High School Musical,
288
Home on the Range
(n4), 346
Hunchback of Notre
Dame, The, 52,
103, 158, 197,
289, 290, 298
Clopin
Trouillefou,
49
Esmeralda, 70,
72, 78, 88, 158,
167, 172, 175,
186, 192
Frollo, 52, 72,
103, 146, 154,
180, 192
Quasimodo, 52,
77, 78, 186,
198

Incredibles, The/
Incredibles 2, 138,
139, 258
Inside Out, 41, 149
Bing Bong, 172,
303
Jiminy Cricket, 315,
376, 378
(n3), 384
reaction to
Marixst
ideology, 122
Jungle Book, The,
187, 188, 245,
275, 287, 361–71
(n5), 250
Lady and the Tramp,
186
(n5), 250
Lilo & Stitch, 140
Lion King, The, 27,
49, 84, 189, 244,
245, 258, 274,
287, 288, 289,
298, 421–29
Lion King II, 139
Kovu, 139
Mufasa, 45, 49,
50, 59
(n1), 214
Scar, 45, 49, 59,
84, 103, 159,
190, 274
Simba, 49, 50, 59,
86, 88, 190,
304
(n1), 214

Little Mermaid, The,
147, 258, 274,
287, 289, 353
Ariel, 51, 59, 70,
77, 332–33
Flounder and
Sebastian, 51
Scuttle, 147
Triton, 51
Ursula, 51, 77,
78, 274, 332
Mary Poppins, 148,
244, 263, 264,
267, 298
Meet the Robinsons,
140
(n4), 346
Mickey Mouse, 31,
284
Mickey Mouse Club,
The, 31, 287
Moana, 27, 49, 59,
68, 71, 84, 85,
137, 149, 169,
245, 288, 289,
305, 339, 349–58
Chief Tui, 120,
137
Maui, 49
Tamatoa, 49
Te Fiti, 49, 120,
169, 177
Te Kā, 49, 85, 86
Mulan, 44, 45, 51,
71, 84, 89, 102,
179, 186, 289,
322, 327, 330–32
(n17), 215

(n20), 335

Newsies, The, 244

Nightmare Before Christmas, The, 26, 274, 287

   Jack Skellington, 26

   Oogie Boogie, 274

Old Yeller, 75, 141

Oliver & Company, 51, 186, 187, 287

Oswald the Lucky Rabbit, 31

Pete's Dragon, 186

Peter and the Wolf, 286

Peter Pan, 117, 254

   (n5), 250

Pinocchio, 47, 48, 82, 86, 245, 254, 258, 274, 275, 279, 280, 284, 315–16, 318, 321, 375–84, 387–94

   (n17), 215

   (n3), 384

Pirates of the Caribbean, 290

Pocahontas, 70, 103, 107, 148, 186, 249, 289, 290, 302, 317–18, 321, 349, 352

   Grandmother Willow, 26

Princess and the Frog, The, 147, 288, 298, 353

   Charlotte, 52

   Lawrence, 52

   Louis, 298

   Mama Odie, 330

   Naveen, 52, 58, 298

   Shadow Man, 52, 59

   (n19), 213

   Tiana, 52, 59, 71, 329–30

   (n1), 214

Raya and the Last Dragon, 27, 59, 88, 117, 125, 169, 174, 177, 245, 443–52

Reluctant Dragon, The, 148

Rescuers/Rescuers Down Under, 51, 75, 103, 177

   Cody, 87

   Medusa, 52

   Penny, 51, 87, 186

Robin Hood, 51, 87, 163, 186, 287, 291

   (n30), 212

Saludos Amigos, 289, 298

Silly Symphonies, 244, 285

   "Flowers and Trees", 31

"The Old Mill" (n11), 293

Sleeping Beauty, 27, 52, 62, 286, 287, 302

   Aurora, 52, 69, 70

   Maleficent, 52, 102

   (n9), 347

   Phillip, 52, 60

Small One, The, 37, 53, 148

Snow White, 31, 34, 41, 51, 60, 62, 70, 71, 253, 260, 273, 274, 275, 277, 338

   (n3), 384

   Evil Queen, 51, 78, 102

   (n9), 347

Song of the South, 158, 263, 266, 276

Soul, 85

Steamboat Willie, 31, 244, 284, 285, 286

Sword in the Stone, The, 51, 258, 287

   Merlin, 107, 249

   (n19), 213

   Mim, 154

   (n19), 213

   Wart, 107, 148

Tangled, 27, 52, 147, 152, 177, 245, 288, 298, 337–46

   (n22), 293

   (n4), 346

Flynn, 52, 58, 63

Gothel, 52, 78, 88
(n9), 347

Rapunzel, 52, 71

Tarzan, 140, 187,
288, 338

*Three Caballeros,
The*, 265, 298

Tinkerbell, 199

Toy Story, 51, 254

Toy Story 4, 259

Treasure Planet, 338

Up, 148, 303
Dug Days, 164
Mr. Fredricksen,
186, 187

Winnie the Pooh, 290

Wreck-It Ralph, 41
Glitch, 137
King Candy
(Turbo), 137,
189
Ralph, 137, 179,
187

Zootopia, 123, 147

SCRIPTURE INDEX

Old Testament

Genesis
1-12, 193
1:1–25 (n2), 376
1:26-28 (n17), 401
1:27 (n42), 25
2:15-17 (n4), 377
2:17 (n10), 378
2:18 (n34), 22
2:7 (n18), 401
3 (n17), 59
3:22-24 (n15), 379
3:6 (n41), 24
3:6 (n29), 86
5:5 (n11), 378
6:5 (n5), 377
12:3 (n19), 401
15:16 (n25), 196
16:13-14 (n11), 193
18, 433
35:18 (n9), 378

Exodus
1, 193
12:36 (n52), 370

Leviticus
19:15 (n28), 196
19:18 (n41), 232

25:35-38 (n27), 196

Numbers
14:18 (n25), 196
15 (n4), 179, 233

Deuteronomy
6:4 (n41), 232
10:17-18 (n26), 196
16:19 (n28), 196
27:19 (n26), 196
32:7 (n30), 355

Joshua
24:15 (n14), 95

1 Kings
19:12 (n3), 384

2 Chronicles
36:15-16 (n37), 172

Job
19:25-26 (n28), 382

Psalm
8:4 (n25), 61
8:4 (n11), 393

14:3 (n8), 378
16:11 (n6), 92
27:4 (n4), 326
34 (n22), 196
50:9-13 (n6), 82
51:14-17 (n21), 196
51:16-17 (n6), 82
53 (n8), 378
138:6 (n21), 196

Proverbs
6:25 (n25), 333
16:18 (n7), 58
21:3 (n6), 82
27:17 (n14), 150
31:30 (n24), 333

Ecclesiastes
12:7 (n9), 378

Isaiah
7:14 (n12), 193
9:6 (n13), 415
14:12-14 (n11), 58
57:15 (n21), 196
59:8-9, 14, 185
66:2 (n21), 196

Jeremiah
3:20 (n37), 172

7:22-23 (n6), 82
17:9 (n11), 94
29:7 (n12), 181
29:7 (n40), 198
31:31-32 (n37),
    172

Ezekiel
36:26 (n10), 83

Daniel
4 (n14), 317

Hosea
6:6 (n6), 82
11 (n37), 172

Micah
6:7-8 (n6), 82
6:8 (n19), 183
6:8 (n8), 414

Zechariah
7:12 (n37), 172

New Testament

Matthew
2 (n20), 401
4:17 (n24), 185
5:17-48 (n20), 196
5:21-22 (n15), 45
5:27-28 (n15), 45
5:29 (n2), 82
5:44 (n22), 85
5:44 (n16), 417

6 (n34), 198, 236
6:21 (n13), 58
7:12 (n32), 197
7:16, 94
7:21-23 (n25), 85
15:15-20 (n5), 82
16:24-26 (n3), 82
16:24-27 (n23),
    196
16:25-27 (n34),
    198, 236
17:1-8 (n14), 269
20:13-15 (n42),
    173
22:36-40 (n40),
    172
22:36-40 (n36),
    403
22:37-40 (n4), 82
23:12 (n7), 58
25:34-40 (n20),
    184

Mark
3:21 (n2), 412
9:2-8 (n14), 269
12:28-34 (n32),
    197
12:33 (n6), 82

Luke
6:45 (n33), 357
9:28-36 (n14), 269
10 (n38), 198
10:25-37 (n36),
    403
10:25-37 (n4), 432
10:27 (n33), 171

10:33 (n5), 432
14:27 (n23), 196
15:3-6 (n24), 60
15:3-7 (n26), 61
15:17-24 (n21),
    196
18:14 (n7), 58
24:36–43 (n30),
    383

John
1:1 (n2), 376
1:12 (n9), 83
3:3 (n14), 83
3:3–18 (n19), 380
4:24 (n5), 326
8:44 (n10), 58
8:44 (n2), 190
10:11 (n26), 61
14:6 (n17), 345
14:15, 23 (n11),
    83
15:13 (n22), 85
15:13 (n10), 94
15:13, 188, 370
15:18-21 (n36),
    198
15:19 (n38), 172
16:33 (n35), 198

Acts
2:5-9 (n16), 318
2:41-42 (16), 318
2:42-46 (n39), 172
2:42-47, 173
17, 5
28:24-28 (n37),
    172

Romans
1:18-25 (n37), 172
1:20 (n21), 401
2:14-15 (n22), 230
2:14–16 (n6), 377
2-3 (n7), 179
2:15 (n22), 401
3 (n8), 378
4:4–5 (n17), 380
4:22, 439
5:1–2 (n32), 383
5:12 (n12), 378
6 (n7), 414
6:14 (n12), 83
6:17-18 (n11), 83
6:22 (n15), 329
7 (n30), 87
7:14-24 (n15), 216
7:15-20 (n23), 185
7:18 (n23), 381
7:18-23 (n7), 58
7:19 (n5), 6
8 (n24), 85
8 (n15), 181
8:18-21 (n8), 43
8:19–20 (n13), 344
8:24–25 (n31), 383
8:28 (n37), 198
12 (n7), 58
12 (n15), 181
12:1–2 (n24), 381
12:21 (n8), 43
13:10–11 (n32), 383

1 Corinthians
3:1–4 (n21), 380
13 (n8), 92
13:11 (n19), 427
13:13 (n19), 330
15:12-19 (n29), 197
15:22 (n14), 379

2 Corinthians
3:18 (n23), 85
5:8 (n27), 382
5:17 (n14), 83
5:17 (n23), 85
5:17 (n16), 329
5:17 (n24), 441
5:20 (n21), 85
5:20 (n4), 92
7:1 (n14), 329
10:4-5 (n8), 58
11:14 (n9), 93
12:4 (n15), 269

Galatians
3 (n7), 179
3:23-25 (n12), 83
5:13 (n43), 200
5:16-17 (n7), 58
5:16-17 (n22), 381
5:17 (n5), 6
5:22-23 (n9), 180
5:22-23 (n22), 381
5:22-24 (n7), 58
6:7 (n3), 432

Ephesians
2:1 (n13), 379
2:5–10 (n32), 383

2:8–9 (n18), 380
6 (n28), 62
6:10-11 (n8), 58
6:12 (n9), 58
6:12 (n3), 190

Philippians
1:23 (n9), 378
2:3-7 (n20), 85
2:3-9 (n7), 58
3:7–11 (n32), 383
3:20–21 (n29), 383
4:8 (n18), 96
4:8-9 (n31), 87

Colossians
2:13 (n13), 379
3:1–4 (n33), 383
3:2 (n5), 92

1 Thessalonians
1:8–10 (n32), 383
4:3–8 (n20), 380
5:15 (n9), 414
5:18 (n28), 86
5:18 (n16), 181

Titus
2:11–12 (n7), 58
2:11–13 (n32), 383

Hebrews
10:1-22 (n6), 82
10:10-24 (n18), 181
11 (n18), 207

11:1-3 (n7), 92

James
   1:17, 344
   2:1-8 (n20), 85
   3:16 (n43), 174
   4:6 (n7), 58
   4:7 (n8), 58
   4:10 (n19), 321

1 Peter
   1:3-5 (n14), 83
   2:15 (n17), 181
   3:15 -16 (n20),
     322
   4:8 (n12), 58
   5:5 (n21), 196
   5:8 (n14), 59

1 John
   2:28 (n32), 383
   3:1–3 (n32), 383
   3:18 (n39), 198
   4:7-8 (n20), 85
   4:7-21 (n13), 181
   4:8 (n12), 58
   4:18 (n12), 95
   4:21 (n13), 83

2 John
   6 (n11), 83

Revelation
   7:9 (n7), 83
   19:16 (n8), 83
   21:1 (n8), 43
   22:3 (n18), 59

About the Authors

JEREMY E. SCARBROUGH holds a PhD in music (emphasis in philosophy, namely concerning the intersection of aesthetics, ethics, and education) from the University of Mississippi, an MA in Christian Apologetics, an MA in Theological Studies, an MME in Music Education, and a BA in Music (Vocal Performance). He has taught music and philosophy at the high school and college levels. Dr. Scarbrough resides in Ocala, FL, with his wife, children, and Golden Doodle. He currently serves as Associate Professor of Philosophy for Pasco-Hernando State College, just north of Tampa, FL. In his free time, he enjoys performing a variety of musical styles—from alt-rock and metal to vocal jazz and musical theatre. His research emphasizes interdisciplinary connections between philosophy, theology, music education, pop culture, and the arts. He has contributed a chapter on heavy metal in *Music, Theology, and Justice* (Lexington Books, 2017) and a chapter on Marvel Comics' Venom in *Theology and the Marvel Universe* (Lexington Books, 2019). His teleological philosophy of music (and its connection to our deep-seated convictions of justice) has been published (2022) in the *Journal of Interdisciplinary Studies*, an international journal of interdisciplinary and interfaith dialogue.

PAT SAWYER has an M.A. in communication studies and a Ph.D. in educational studies and cultural studies. He is a faculty member at the University of North Carolina at Greensboro and is a member of Heterodox Academy. Pat is on the editorial board of the peer-reviewed education journal, *Philosophy, Theory, and Foundations in Education*. His research interests are along three lines: cultural studies, media studies, and higher education. Pat is an active speaker in the academy and has presented his scholarship at a number of conferences and universities in the U.S., Canada, and the U.K. His work is published in academic journals and edited academic books as well as popular magazines and outlets including The American Conservative, The Gospel Coalition, and The Federalist, among others. He is co-author of the upcoming

book, *Critical Dilemma: The Rise of Critical Theories and Social Justice Ideology —
Implications for the Church and Society*. Pat is married with three children and
a long-time member of the Summit Church in Raleigh-Durham, North Carolina.

Contributing Authors

TIMOTHY E. G. BARTEL holds a PhD in Theology, Imagination, and the Arts
(University of St Andrews) and an MFA in Poetry (Seattle Pacific). His scholarship focuses on the influence of Early Christian Theology on American literature and culture. He has published essays on literary figures, like Dante
and Longfellow, as well as popular artists, like Rowling, Malick, and
Whedon. Dr. Bartel is author of several books of criticism and poetry, including, most recently, *The Heroines of Henry Longfellow: Domestic, Defiant, Divine*.
His poems and essays have appeared widely in periodicals including *Christianity and Literature*, *First Things*, *Notes and Queries*, and *Saint Katherine Review*. He currently lives with his family in Houston, TX, where he serves as
Provost and Professor of Great Texts and Writing at Saint Constantine College.

MIGUEL BENITEZ JR. is an Assistant Professor of Humanities at the State College of Florida. He holds a Ph.D. in Humanities from Faulkner University.
His academic interests include the philosophy of art and beauty and the
works of G.K. Chesterton. His wife Daniela, son Alexander, and daughter
Gabi consider themselves a Disney family as they all love visiting the Disney
parks and watching Disney movies on a regular basis.

RUSSELL CLAYTON is an Assistant Professor of Instruction at the University
of South Florida, teaching MBA courses on managerial communication. His
research has been published in the *Harvard Business Review* and has he been
mentioned in or written for such popular press outlets as *Psychology Today*, NBC News, Fox News, Inc. and *Fast Company*. In addition, his research
has appeared in several peer-reviewed academic journals such as *Human Resource Management* and he serves on the editorial board of *Management Teaching Review*. He was awarded the 2020 Mid-Career Distinguished Educator
Award by the Management & Organizational Behavior Teaching Society and
was voted 2021-2022 "Professor of the Year" by the Executive MBA students
in the Muma College of Business. Clayton earned a PhD in business

administration from the University of Mississippi, a master's degree in higher education administration from Middle Tennessee State University and a bachelor's degree in business administration from Auburn University.

D.J. CULP, JR. holds a PhD in Music from the University of Mississippi. He currently serves as Associate Professor of Music of Instrumental Music Education at Union University in Jackson, TN. He conducts the symphonic band and percussion ensembles, teaches percussion studio lessons, conducting, music theory, courses in music education, and observes student teacher interns. He has presented music research across Southern and Midwestern regions of the US. Dr. Culp also maintains an active performance agenda as a jazz and rock drummer and performs as a percussionist with the Jackson Symphony.

NEAL FOSTER holds an MDiv in missiology and a BS in science education. Hailing from Oklahoma, he previously served as missionary in Africa, and currently serves as staff member for Peace Catalyst International. He facilitates and supports Christians and Muslims in dialogue and community building, through practical application of Jesus's teachings. He enjoys exploring existential crisis and meaning through Kierkegaard, Camus, and heavy metal guitar solos.

SEAN C. HADLEY is a husband, father, lecturer, and author. He holds a PhD in Humanities from Faulkner University. His essays and book reviews have been published by a variety of outlets, including *Touchstone Magazine*, *An Unexpected Journal*, *The Imaginative Conservative*, and *The Hemingway Review*. Entering the classroom in 2009, Sean's teaching includes instruction in humane letters and service as Thesis Director at two different classical Christian schools. Sean has presented at conferences for the Association of Classical Christian Schools, the American Literature Association, and Faulkner University's Institute of Faith and the Academy. Since 2014, Sean has taught at Trinitas Christian School located in Pensacola, Florida.

JOSH HERRING holds a PhD in Humanities from Faulkner University. He currently serves as Professor of Classical Education at Thales College for Thales Academy. He works with teachers to deliver a classical education to the highest possible degree of excellence. He hosts The Optimistic Curmudgeon podcast, and writes frequently for the Acton Institute, Law and Liberty,

Public Discourse, and a variety of other outlets. Josh and his wife Jennifer live in North Carolina with their four cats, many trees, and infinite bookshelves.

MARK D. LINVILLE holds a PhD in philosophy from University of Wisconsin-Madison. He serves as Senior Research Fellow in Faulkner University's PhD program in the humanities. He is co-editor (with David Werther) of *Philosophy and the Christian Worldview* (Bloomsbury) and has written numerous articles on moral philosophy and philosophy of religion, including "The Moral Argument" in the *Blackwell Companion to Natural Theology.*

PAUL MILES holds a DMin in Bible and Theology from Tyndale Theological Seminary, an MA in Theological Studies, and a BA in Russian. He is the executive director of Grace Abroad Ministries, a ministry he began with his wife, Lena, in 2016 in order to serve the Church through translation, teaching, and outreach. The Miles family lives in Kyiv, Ukraine, and you can read their blog at www.TheMileses.com.

HOLLY ORDWAY is the Cardinal Francis George Professor of Faith and Culture at the Word on Fire Institute, and Visiting Professor of Apologetics at Houston Christian University. She holds a PhD in English from the University of Massachusetts Amherst, and is the author of *Tolkien's Faith: A Spiritual Biography* and the award-winning *Tolkien's Modern Reading: Middle-earth Beyond the Middle Ages.* Her other books include *Tales of Faith: A Guide to Sharing the Gospel through Literature* and *Apologetics and the Christian Imagination: An Integrated Approach to Defending the Faith.* She is also a Subject Editor for the *Journal of Inklings Studies.*

JOEL PAULUS holds a PhD in Theology/Philosophy of Religion from Southeastern Baptist Theological Seminary. He also holds an MA in Christian Apologetics and a BFA in Musical Theater. He has spoken on issues of worldview and religion both nationally and internationally. He has served in ministry roles, performed with regional dance companies and theater productions, and worked with the Metropolitan Opera. He has taught ballet classes in the greater Houston, Charlotte, and New York City areas. Currently, Dr. Paulus serves as Director of Library and Research Services for the Jamison Library at Southern Evangelical Seminary where he is an adjunct faculty member.

LORI PETERS is a doctoral candidate at Liberty University, completing a PhD in Theology and Apologetics. She serves as Director of Worldview Immersion at Concord Christian Academy in Concord, NH, where she teaches biblical studies, worldview studies, and bioethics. Lori formerly served with Ratio Christi as Regional Director for New England. Her research interests emphasize the problem of evil, bioethics, and exploring new ways to answer curious questions about Jesus. Lori resides in New Hampshire with her husband and college sweetheart, Kevin. They have nine children, including in-laws, and four grandchildren.

DOUG POWELL holds an MA in Christian Apologetics from Biola University. He is the author of more than a dozen books on apologetics, including the bestselling Holman QuickSource Guide to Christian Apologetics, and is a contributor to the Apologetics Study Bible, the Apologetics Study Bible for Students, and the Worldview Study Bible. He is also the author, designer, and developer of the iWitness family of apps. As a recording artist, Powell has released nine albums, and he has contributed, as songwriter and musician, to the Alan Parsons albums *The Secret* and *From the New World*. He has appeared on Late Night with Conan O'Brien, CNN, Cross Examined, and Stand to Reason. Most recently, he authored the Graham Eliot series of biblical archaeological thrillers, including, *The Well of the Soul*, *Among the Ashes*, and *The Place of Descent*.

ZACHARY SCHMOLL holds a PhD in Humanities from Faulkner University and an MA in Apologetics from Houston Christian University. He currently serves as an adjunct faculty member at Houston Christian University and Southeastern University. He is the author of *Disability and the Problem of Evil* (Public Philosophy Press, 2020) and was the Founding Editor of *An Unexpected Journal*.

JOHN L. WEITZEL is currently completing a PhD in Humanities (ABD) from Faulkner University. Additionally, he holds an MA in Theology, an MS in Counseling, and a BA in Psychology. He has taught at Marymount California University, Cypress College, and El Camino College. His research interests include pre-modern philosophy (especially Augustine) and philosophy/psychology of personhood. He resides in Harbor City, CA, with his wife and three sons.

SHAWN WHITE holds an MA in Christian Apologetics from Biola University and is currently completing a PhD in Humanities (ABD) at Faulkner University. His academic interests include G.K. Chesterton's life and writings on gratitude, wonder, and humility. His non-academic interests include his wife, their dog, playing all manner of board games, and playing music.

ERIC WILLIAMSON is Instructor of Religion and Philosophy at Blue Ridge Community College in Flat Rock, NC. He holds a PhD in Philosophy and Ethics from Southern Baptist Theological Seminary. His research interests are in virtue epistemology, aesthetics, philosophy of expertise, and philosophy of history. He has written on architecture and culture, pedagogical approaches in general education, and the epistemology of disagreement in religious diversity.